Margaret E. Forbes

PENGUIN HANDBOOKS

Fish Cookery

Jane Grigson was brought up in the north-east of England, where
there is a strong tradition of good eating, but it was not until many
years later, when she began to spend three months of each year
working in France, that she became really interested in food.
Charcuterie and French Pork Cookery (published as a Penguin
Handbook) was the result, exploring the wonderful range of cooked
meat products on sale in even the smallest market towns. Since 1968
she has been writing cookery articles for the *Observer Colour
Magazine*: *Good Things* (Penguin, 1973) is a collection from this
highly successful series.

After taking an English degree at Cambridge in 1949, Jane Grigson
worked in art galleries and publishers' offices, and then as a translator.
In 1966 she shared the John Florio prize (with Father Kenelm Foster)
for her translation of Beccaria's *Of Crime and Punishment*. In 1973
Fish Cookery was published by the Wine and Food Society. This was
followed by *English Food* (1974) and *The Mushroom Feast* (1975), a
collection of recipes for cultivated, woodland, field and dried
mushrooms. (Both these titles will be published in Penguins in 1978.)
She is married to the poet and critic, Geoffrey Grigson.

Jane Grigson

FISH COOKERY

Penguin Books

Penguin Books Ltd,
Harmondsworth, Middlesex, England
Penguin Books, 625 Madison Avenue,
New York, New York 10022, U.S.A.
Penguin Books Australia Ltd,
Ringwood, Victoria, Australia
Penguin Books Canada Ltd, 2801 John Street,
Markham, Ontario, Canada L3R 1B4
Penguin Books (N.Z.) Ltd,
182–190 Wairau Road, Auckland 10, New Zealand

First published by The International Wine & Food Publishing
Company 1973
Published in Penguin Books 1975
Reprinted 1977, 1979

Made and printed in Great Britain by
Hazell Watson & Viney Ltd,
Aylesbury, Bucks
Set in Monotype Plantin

For Geoffrey

a record of
Wednesdays in Montoire
Fridays in Oxford
and a journey to Nantes

Acknowledgements

Recipes:
MARGARET COSTA, *Four Seasons Cookery Book*, Nelson.
ELIZABETH DAVID, *Italian Food*, Nelson; *French Provincial Cooking*, Michael Joseph and Penguin; *Spices, Salt and Aromatics in the English Kitchen; Italian Food*, Penguin.
CLAUDIA RODEN, *A Book of Middle Eastern Food*, Nelson.
A. POTTER, *Pottery*, The International Wine and Food Society.
MARY LAMB, *New Orleans Cuisine*, Yoseloff.
F. MARIAN MCNEILL, *The Scots Kitchen*, Blackie and Son.
JAMES BEARD, *Delights and Prejudices*, Victor Gollancz.
From *The Gold Cookery Book*, by LOUIS P. DE GOUY, © 1947, 1948 by the author. Reprinted with the permission of the Publisher, Chilton Book Company, Philadelphia, Pennsylvania.

Special thanks are due to Anne Willan for advice on American flat fish.

Mrs Amy Dent of Lytham; Mrs Eberstadt of London; Mrs Bobby Freeman of Cardiff; Mrs Charlotte Sawyer of Woodsville, New Hampshire; Mr John Green, of J. B. Green Ltd., Crouch End, N.8; Mr R. F. Lyall of the White Fish Authority; Mr Jack Shiells of C. J. Newnes, Billingsgate; and the Whitstable Oyster Co. have all helped generously with information.

Contents

Introduction

The problem with a book on fish is how to stop writing it. To start with, there are 52 species of edible fish (including many different varieties) listed by the White Fish Authority. This does not include either shellfish or freshwater fish. It leaves out the extensive choice of cured fish, as well as fish imported from abroad to be sold to foreigners living and working here.

Think of this when you next visit your fishmonger. Count the choice of fish for sale. And count how many different kinds you have eaten in the last few months. You may then agree with me that fish is one of the great untapped areas of exploration, for curiosity, and for the delight of the cook and her family and friends.

Compare this abundance with the choice of meat. How often do you come across an animal you have never heard of before? At least, heard of in culinary terms. For me, the answer is 'once', and that was when I visited the strange shop of Monsieur Paul Corcellet in Paris not so long ago – he sells ready-prepared elephant's trunk, python, crocodile and monkey. Yet with fish one never seems to come to the end of perfectly reasonable possibilities.

To begin with, we eat too little of the best fish. We know about them, we may order them in restaurants on occasion, but we buy and cook them rarely. I am talking about sole, lobster, eel, scallops, oysters, clams, trout and salmon trout, monkfish (the *lotte* of the French) or squid. We think they are too expensive, and go off and buy steak instead, or a large joint. Partly, this is convention. I read a statement the other day which struck me as particularly foolish. The writer remarked that fish could not be served as a main course when men were present, as they needed steak or some other good red meat.

Why? The protein content of fish is as high as the protein content of meat. It is more easily digested, too – a point which concerns more men, I suspect, than women. And in the cooking of sole with its sauces, or of lobster, there is far more implied compliment to the guests than in grilling even the finest Scottish steak.

I suppose, too, that most of us grow up with the firm impression that fish means cod and plaice, overcooked and coated with greasy batter or coloured substances of unpleasant flavour. Certainly I was startled, when I first crossed the Channel, to find out that there were far more fish to eat than anyone had allowed me to believe. Later on, as we spent longish periods working in Europe, I discovered that many of the 'exotic' fish we had been enjoying swam in quantity and quality around the coasts of Great Britain, as well as in the Mediterranean and the Bay of Biscay, and off the Breton coast. Squid, for instance, and monkfish – two of the great delicacies of Italian and French cookery.

At the weekly stall in our local market at Montoire, forty-four miles north-west of Blois and 150 miles from the sea at Nantes, we can usually count between thirty and thirty-five different kinds of fish to buy. They are stiff-alive, as fishmongers say, with freshness. The owner's wife, Madame Soarès, took our education in hand, persuaded us into trying new fish, and told us how to cook them. With gestures and vivid phrases, she described the sauces, the flavours, the pleasure we would have at supper that night.

I wish I could take our fishmongers in England to that stall in Montoire, and keep them there for a few months! Some of them have increased their range of fish to sell to our new communities of Chinese and Italians and so on, but few of them can tell a doubtful English customer how to cook these new creatures, or what they taste like. One has the idea that they have never tried them themselves at home. They lack the warm enthusiasm of Madame Soarès – 'Here's some parsley for you. Have a lemon, too. And why not buy a handful of shrimps – they'll make a finish to the sauce! *Extrà!*'

The main fish authorities could be more help. They are anxious that we should eat more fish, it is true, but only more of the same few kinds. Their interest is in shifting the gluts of plaice and cod. They do not think of pointing out the special virtues of huss, let alone of the rarer John Dory. In the end it is up to the customers who enjoy good food to insist, and complain, and learn about fish, and complain again but more knowledgeably, so that things can be changed a little more rapidly.

Jane Grigson

Choosing, Cleaning and Cooking Fish

Choosing Fish

General advice – if you see a fish at the fishmonger's that is strange to you, buy it, but do not expect much advice on how to cook it. Ask the name and look it up in the index at the back of this book, when you get home.

More specifically – choose fresh fish, fish with a bright eye, red gills and no more than a seaweedy smell. Stale fish will look miserable; the eyes will be sunken or opaque, the skin gritty or dry or blobbed with yellow slime, it will smell, and you will be able to push the flesh in easily with your finger. This is a summary of the excellent advice given in *Which?* in May 1972. As you may have concluded already, the buyer of fish needs character for all this sniffing and prodding. *Which?* also remarks that getting good fish is easier once you find a fishmonger you can trust, but 'if he sells you poor fish, *go back and tell him so*'.

The naming of fish is a tricky business. One name may be used for quite different species. Local names abound. There are misleading inducements: certain fish which bear labels saying 'rock salmon' and 'rock turbot' have nothing in common with 'salmon' and 'turbot'. When you go on holiday, foreign names add to the confusion. Because of this intricately knotted muddle, the United Nations has produced the *Multilingual Dictionary of Fish and Fish Products*, an international compilation with names from 15 languages, which attempts to straighten matters out with an elegant system of indexing. Local names are there, as well as the Latin ones. A book to be recommended to anyone who enjoys eating fish. The index to this book is based upon it. (I can also recommend the *Atlas of the Living Resources of the Seas*, published by the Food and Agricultural Organization of the United Nations in 1972, again with an index but this time in three languages – English, French and Spanish; from Her Majesty's Stationery Office.)

Cleaning Fish

Although the fishmonger should do this for you, it is as well to know what to do. Cut off spiky fins and other extrusions first. Remove scales by pushing them up the wrong way with the blunt edge of a knife – spread newspaper round to catch the scales which fly about. Rinse quickly. Remove innards through the gills, or by slitting up the belly. Retain the livers and roes; they are often good to eat. Rub any stubborn traces of blood with a little salt. Cut off heads or not, as you please.

SKINNING AND BONING FLAT FISH. See page 92.

BONING WHOLE FISH, HERRING, ETC. Cut off head, slit the belly, and clean. Lay on a board, cut side down, and press along the backbone steadily. Turn the fish over and pick out the backbone and the other small bones, which will be sticking up.

Cooking Fish

COOKING IN FOIL. Large fish, see pages 15, 108, 219. Medium fish, see p. 232. Small fish and steaks, see p. 222. For the method of cooking fish in paper, *en papillote*, see p. 126, *Antoine's Pompano en papillote*.

BOILING. A method only suitable for soups, when every scrap of flavour is to be extracted from the fish for the benefit of the liquid.

POACHING. This is the correct way of cooking fish in water or other liquids, which should be kept just below boiling point. For timing and *court-bouillon* recipes, see p. 15.
    Even shell fish such as crabs and lobsters should not be boiled hard. See pp. 277, 297 and 298.

STEAMING. The fish is laid on a buttered plate, or piece of foil, and set over a pan of simmering water until cooked. For success, the fish must be fresh, really fresh, and well seasoned. It is a method much better exploited by Chinese than by European cooks: they add aromatics such as spring onion, ginger and soya sauce. In the West, steamed fish has the dull sound of sick-room cookery, which is unfair as it can be delicious.

FRYING. For finer fish, shallow-fry in clarified butter (p. 21) or olive oil. Unclarified butter mixed with oil is a second best expedient, but the flavour will not be so good. Unclarified butter on its own burns easily.

Keep deep-frying for fish in batter, for whitebait, and for *goujons* of sole (see page 102). The temperature should be 365°– 375° F.

GRILLING. Small plump fish, such as herring, mackerel, and mullet. Slash diagonally 2 or 3 times, brush with clarified butter or olive oil, and grill for 4–8 minutes a side.

Flatfish. Brush with clarified butter and seasoning. Allow 4–6 minutes a side, but timing depends on the thickness of the fish; chicken turbot will take longer than sole, for instance.

Steaks of fish. These need not be turned while grilling. Set them in a well-buttered grill pan, brush the tops with clarified butter, season, and cook for up to 15 minutes. They are done when the flesh turns opaque and the central bone can be moved easily.

Boned fish, and fillets. Always grill the fleshy, cut side first, brushing with butter and sprinkling with salt and pepper. When it is almost done, the fish can be turned over to give the skin a chance to become brown and crisp.

BRAISING, BAKING AND ROASTING. This includes all methods of cooking fish in the oven; sometimes on a bed of herbs and vegetables; sometimes with fish stock or wine, as well as butter and oil. Instructions are given with each recipe, as they can vary a great deal.

TO KNOW WHEN FISH IS COOKED. Pierce the thickest part with a larding needle or skewer (*not a fork*). The flesh should be opaque, and part easily from the bone. Never overcook fish. It is surprising how little time it takes compared with meat. Take into account the fact that it will continue to cook slightly while keeping warm in the oven, and while being dished up and brought to the table.

Court-Bouillons, Sauces and Butters

Court-Bouillons

Until recently whole fish, or large pieces, were always cooked in a flavoured liquid or *court-bouillon*. When the liquid was no more than salted water, the result was frequently a disaster, particularly if the fish had been allowed to boil rapidly. Few dishes are more disgusting than cod cooked in this way (the French call fish boiled in water *poisson à l'anglaise*). In religious households it cast additional gloom over Good Friday, and many other Fridays as well. I think that it has been the main reason for the general unpopularity of fish.

Now that kitchen foil has superseded the fish kettle things are better. Appropriate seasonings and aromatics are parcelled up with the fish, which cooks in its own juices plus a little butter or white wine. The flavour stays where it should, in the fish itself, and in the small amount of essence left in the foil as sauce. (See sauce Bercy, p. 47).

Sometimes though, a *court-bouillon* is essential for fish soup, for a sauce requiring a fair amount of the liquid in which the fish was cooked, for poaching turbot or skate, or for boiling live shellfish. Generally, vegetables and spices are simmered in the liquid for half an hour to extract their maximum flavour. When cool or just tepid the liquid is strained over the fish, which it should just cover. The pan, set over a moderate heat, comes slowly to the boil and is then allowed to do no more than simmer or shake slightly for the appropriate length of time. This is:

$1\frac{1}{2}$–2 lb. fish 7–10 minutes
4 lb.   „   15 minutes
6 lb.   „   20 minutes
8–10 lb.   „   30 minutes

If the fish is to be eaten cold, ignore these times. Instead, bring the pan slowly to the boil, give it time for a couple of strong bubblings, then remove from the heat and allow to cool. Because larger quantities of *bouillon* take longer to come to the boil and longer to cool down, this method is successful with large as well as small fish.

When cooking salmon, I combine the foil and *bouillon* methods. The fish is wrapped up in greased foil (use butter for hot salmon, oil for cold, to avoid congealed fat ruining the flavour and appearance), with a seasoning of salt and pepper. The parcel goes into enough cold water to cover it well. If you want it hot, follow the times given above: I use the second method for cold salmon. This is quicker than baking the salmon in the oven, yet it has the advantages of keeping all the flavour and moistness in the fish itself.

1. GENERAL PURPOSE COURT-BOUILLON. This makes an excellent start to fish soups.

1 pint water	16 lightly crushed black
1 pint dry white wine or dry	peppercorns
cider	1 heaped teaspoon pickling
1 tablespoon white wine vinegar	spices
2 carrots, sliced	*bouquet garni* of appropriate
2 leeks, sliced ⎫ or two mild	herbs
2 shallots, sliced ⎭ onions	

Simmer vegetables and spices in the liquid for half an hour. Allow it to cool and cook the fish according to instructions on p. 15. If you want to make a fish soup with the *bouillon* afterwards, tomatoes can be added, with a little sugar; cream and a couple of egg yolks make a final thickening. Fish cooked in the *bouillon* can be cut up or liquidized to give the soup body – or it can be left whole and served as the next course with bread and butter, or potatoes and butter, in the Breton style. Shellfish such as prawns or mussels can provide a final garnish. In other words a *court-bouillon* can be the start of many good meals, from the homely to the luxurious.

2. SIMPLE COURT-BOUILLON. For salmon, skate, salt cod.

2 pints water	1 onion, sliced
2 tablespoons white wine vinegar	12 lightly crushed black peppercorns
1 carrot, sliced	salt to taste

3. COURT-BOUILLON. For crab and lobster, prawns, shrimps etc.

sea water, plus salt, or plain salted water (an egg should be able to float in it)

4. WHITE COURT-BOUILLON. For turbot, brill, smoked haddock.

1 pint milk ⎱ or 2 pints milk 1 pint water ⎰ 1 thick slice lemon	salt and pepper (for smoked haddock, omit salt)

5. WHITE WINE COURT-BOUILLON. For marinated herring, mackerel, jellied trout, *écrevisses à la nage.*

1 bottle dry white wine	1 rounded teaspoon black
3 medium carrots, sliced	peppercorns
4 onions, sliced, or 6 shallots	salt
bouquet garni	*extra flavourings:* chili, aniseed, celery, tarragon

For whole fish, reduce by rapid boiling to half quantity and leave until tepid. Put in fish, bring to the boil, allow two bubblings, then remove pan from the heat and leave to cool. For *écrevisses* and other small shellfish put into boiling reduced *bouillon*, cook for 10 to 12 minutes and leave them to drain in a colander: for *à la nage* dishes, serve a little *bouillon* with the shellfish.

Fumet de Poisson

The delightful name of *fumet de poisson* means scent or bouquet of fish. In reality, it's no more than fish stock, with this advantage over meat stock that it's quick and cheap to make. Just as well, because there are no fish stock cubes to fall back on. Most fishmongers will give you the necessary trimmings; even if you have to pay for them, the amount will be small. Ask for turbot and sole bones, because they have a high proportion of gelatine, which improves the texture of the stock.

2–3 lb. fish trimmings, bones, skin, head etc. or 1½ lb. cheap fish such as whiting	*bouquet garni*
	10 peppercorns
	1 dessertspoon white wine vinegar
1 large onion, sliced	
1 medium carrot, sliced	¼–½ pint dry white wine
2 inch piece celery (optional)	water
white part of a leek (optional)	

Put the bones etc. into a large pan. Add the other ingredients with enough water to cover – about 3 pints. No salt, because the *fumet* will need to be reduced by boiling if it's to be used for a sauce and salt added now may prove too much later. Bring to the boil, skim well and simmer, covered, for half an hour. Strain through a muslin-lined sieve before reducing the fish stock, or the over-boiled bones will add an unpleasant flavour of glue.

Note. If you have no wine, remember the wily French trick of substituting a tablespoon or so of white wine vinegar, plus 2–3 lumps of sugar. This would be in addition to the dessertspoon of vinegar in the list of ingredients above.

ASPIC JELLY. Leave the strained fish *fumet* of the above recipe to cool. You will then be able to see how much extra gelatine it requires to achieve a firm set: this will depend on the bones used, the quantity of skin, etc. Clarify with the shell and white of an egg, (see ingredients).

To get the jelly to brushing consistency, stand the bowl of *fumet* in a bowl of warm water until it begins to melt. Brush it over the fish, which should be placed on a wire tray. When the first coat is dry, put decorations in place with a dab of jelly, then brush over again until the desired thickness is obtained. Left-over jelly can be chopped and placed round the fish.

If you don't wish to make a fish *fumet*, an ordinary aspic jelly will do instead. Put into a saucepan:

¾ pint water
3 oz. white wine vinegar
½ onion, chopped
½ carrot, chopped
½ stalk celery, chopped

rind and juice of ½ lemon
1 oz. gelatine
crushed shell and white of an
    egg

Bring all the ingredients slowly to the boil, whisking to dissolve the gelatine. A thick white foam will develop on top. Remove from heat when boiling, leave 10 minutes, then strain through a cloth. When the stock is tepid, add either 4 oz. dry white wine, or 3 oz. Madeira, Marsala or sweet sherry – these two amounts may be adjusted to taste: the flavour should be strong but not overpowering.

Note. For coating cold fish, many people prefer the flavour of jellied mayonnaise, p. 53.

Two Batters

Egg White Batter

4 oz. plain flour
pinch salt
tablespoon olive oil

generous ¼ pint lukewarm
    water or beer
white of 1 large egg

Mix the flour and salt with the oil and the water or beer, beating well together. Cover and leave in the kitchen, *not the refrigerator or cold larder*, until required. This gives the flour a chance to ferment slightly, which improves the texture of the batter. Just before the batter is required, beat the egg white stiff and fold it in carefully.

Whole Egg Batter

This is a *tempura* batter from Japan, which is quick and simple to make, and very light; particularly good for large prawns.

Break an egg into a measuring jug. Add four times its volume of water, then five times its volume of flour. Whisk well until smooth.

Savoury and other Butters

The underlying principle of northern fish cookery is butter. So long as you have butter and the usual seasonings, you can do without many other things. Butter comes before wine, cream or eggs.

A fresh trout fried in clarified butter is food for the most demanding. So is Dover sole, brushed with melted butter, then grilled and served with *maître d'hôtel* butter as sauce and seasoning. A cod, salmon or halibut steak baked in well-buttered foil is a delicious thing to eat. And what about the sauces – how many of them begin and end with butter? Can you imagine eating whitebait or smoked salmon without brown bread and butter? What about shrimps potted in mace-flavoured butter? And all the traditional English pastes made from smoked haddock and smoked salmon, bloaters and kippers, pounded up with butter? Think, too, of the things we serve with fish – well-buttered spinach, new potatoes in parsley butter, sorrel or gooseberries melted to a purée in butter, and slices of mushroom stewed in butter. Have you ever tried mussels or oysters baked in snail butter?

Butter is the flavour one misses most if margarine or some kind of innominate dripping has been used instead, or one of the tasteless oils of modern cookery. The only alternative for frying and grilling is olive oil and occasionally lard or bacon fat. But for all sauces except mayonnaise, vinaigrette and tomato sauce, which do need olive oil, butter is essential.

The best butter to choose is unsalted, preferably from Normandy. Lightly salted butters such as the Danish Lurpak do almost as well, but Normandy butter is best. And the finest comes from Isigny, a small port on the Cherbourg peninsula. This is easy to buy in Britain nowadays; use plenty, and avoid meanness. It's better to buy a cheaper fish than to economize on butter. Our own butters are made from sweet cream (most European butter is prepared from ripened cream), and have a fair amount of salt added to them: for these two reasons they are not as good for savoury butters.

Clarified Butter

Remember that butter burns at a lower temperature than other fats. If you are frying or grilling fish, it pays to clarify it first, so that the salty particles which catch the heat and blacken are strained out before cooking starts. Some people use a mixture of unclarified butter and oil for frying: this works quite well from the non-burning point of view, but the buttery flavour is sadly diluted.

As clarified butter will keep well in the refrigerator it's worth dealing with half a pound at one time. Cut it into pieces and put in a pan. Bring to the boil, bubble for a moment or two, and then pour into a jar through a sieve lined with damp muslin. If you only want to clarify enough for one dish, the butter may be strained straight into the frying pan.

Beurre Manié

This is kneaded butter – a useful substance for thickening sauces, soups and stews at the end of the cooking time. A tablespoon of butter is mashed together with a tablespoon of flour to form a paste. This is divided into knobs, which are stirred one by one into the *almost boiling* liquid until it reaches the desired thickness. Allow 5 minutes over a moderate or slow heat. If the sauce begins to boil it will taste floury.

This sounds odd – one simmers a *béchamel* or *velouté* sauce for at least 20 minutes to lose the flavour of flour in the *roux*. But with *beurre manié* one keeps the sauce below simmering point and cooks it for no longer than 5 minutes with exactly the same purpose.

Beurre Noir. See p. 181.

Savoury Butters

BEURRE MAÎTRE D'HÔTEL. As far as fish is concerned, this is the most useful of the savoury butters, particularly with grilled sole, salmon, turbot, cod, and almost any other fish.

As with all these recipes, an electric beater is a great help. Warm the bowl and beater slightly first, just enough to soften the butter without melting it. As *beurre maître d'hôtel* has so many uses (grilled meat, potatoes and many green vegetables, sandwiches), it's a good idea to start with as much as half a pound of unsalted butter, cut into small pieces. As the beater creams it, add 4 good table-spoons of finely chopped parsley, and lemon juice to taste. Form into a roll, wrap in greaseproof paper or foil and store in the refrigerator. Neat round slices can be cut off as required.

BEURRE COLBERT. Add two teaspoons of finely chopped tarragon to the *maître d'hôtel* recipe above, plus two or three tablespoons of meat glaze or rich meat jelly from underneath beef dripping. Served with *sole Colbert*, p. 101.

LIME BUTTER. Lime butter is even nicer with fish than *maître d'hôtel*. Here is a recipe for it given by Skeffington Ardron in the *Guardian*. To 2 oz. butter, add 2 teaspoons lime juice, 2 teaspoons of grated peel, 1 teaspoon of chopped chives, a pinch of powdered thyme, and a very small pinch of grated ginger.

ORANGE BUTTER. Although this butter can be made with sweet oranges quite successfully, it is best made with Seville oranges. To 2 oz. of butter, add 2 teaspoons orange juice, 2 teaspoons grated peel, 1 teaspoon tomato concentrate.

TARRAGON BUTTER. Scald 2 oz. fresh tarragon in boiling water for a few seconds. Drain, dry and chop. Mix with 4 oz. butter. Sharpen with a few drops of tarragon vinegar.

ANCHOVY BUTTER. Add 6–8 anchovy fillets, well mashed, to 4 oz. butter.

SHRIMP AND PRAWN BUTTER. *Either* pound shrimp or prawn meat with an equal weight of butter.

Or crush the shells in a blender and melt with an equal weight of butter. When the mixture boils, pour through a muslin-lined sieve.

LOBSTER OR CRAWFISH BUTTER. *Either* pound the coral and creamy parts of the lobster with an equal amount of butter.
Or dry some lobster shells in the oven, then pound them as finely as possible. Put into a pan with an equal weight of butter. Bring to the boil then strain through a muslin-lined sieve.

SMOKED SALMON BUTTER. Pound 4 oz. smoked salmon trimmings with 4 oz. unsalted butter.

ANISE BUTTER. Mix 1 tablespoon Pernod or Pastis Ricard with 4 oz. butter.

MUSTARD BUTTER. Cream 4 oz. butter. Add 1 tablespoon French mustard (or to taste). Season with salt and pepper. Use with herring and mackerel.

SNAIL BUTTER. Cream 8 oz. butter. Add 2–3 crushed cloves garlic, a little salt, 2 oz. finely chopped shallot or onion, at least 4 tablespoons of finely chopped parsley, and salt and pepper to taste. Very useful for mussels and shellfish baked in scallop shells or small pots.

MONTPELLIER BUTTER. Assemble 4 oz. of herbs, in approximately equal quantities, including as many of the following as possible – parsley, chervil, chives, tarragon, spinach and watercress. Put them, with a heaped teaspoon of chopped shallot, into boiling water for 1 minute. Drain well and dry. Put into a liquidizer or moulinette (or mortar), with 4–5 anchovy fillets, 1 tablespoon capers, 1 tablespoon pickled gherkin or cucumber, 3 hard-boiled egg yolks and 1 raw egg yolk. Blend to a smooth paste. Transfer to a bowl, and beat in, drop by drop, 2 oz. of olive oil. Season finally with a little lemon juice.

This softish butter is usually spread over cold salmon and trout but it's delicious with many other fish as well. Using a moulinette or liquidizer makes Montpellier butter quite easy to produce at home.

Hot Sauces

Eliza Acton's Rich Melted Butter

A useful basic sauce for fish, to which many flavourings can be added – hard-boiled egg, lobster, oyster, crab, anchovy essence, some pounded anchovy fillets with mace and cayenne, or shrimps as in the recipe following.

1 dessertspoon flour	½ pint cold water
½ saltspoonful of salt	4–6 oz. butter

'Mix to a very smooth batter a dessertspoonful of flour, a half-saltspoonful of salt, and half a pint of cold water: put these into a delicately clean saucepan, with from four to six ounces of well-flavoured butter, cut into small bits, and shake the sauce strongly round, almost without cessation, until the ingredients are perfectly blended, and it is on the point of boiling; let it simmer for two or three minutes, and it will be ready for use. The best French cooks recommend its not being allowed to *boil*, as they say it tastes less of flour if served when it is just at the point of simmering.'

(*Modern Cookery*, Eliza Acton)

English Shrimp Sauce

'Half-quantity melted butter sauce [see preceding recipe] plus boiled fresh shrimps, ground mace, cayenne pepper.

'Shell a half-pint of freshly boiled shrimps. Stir them into the prepared melted butter sauce, heat them through, add the seasonings.

'English shrimp sauce is traditional with poached turbot. An alternative way of making it is to boil the shrimp shells and debris in water to cover, and to use this stock, strained and cooked, to make the initial melted butter sauce. When freshly boiled shrimps (not to be confused with what the Americans call shrimp, which are prawns) are unobtainable, use the contents of a two-ounce carton of potted shrimps, from which the protective covering of butter should be removed. When potted shrimps are used, no additional spices will be necessary, but a good squeeze of lemon juice improves the sauce; a spoonful of chopped fresh fennel or parsley will also be an improvement.'

(*Spices, Salt and Aromatics in the English Kitchen*,
Elizabeth David, Penguin)

Sauce Béchamel

The invention of *sauce béchamel*, one of the basic sauces of cookery, is attributed to the Marquis Louis de Béchameil, Louis XIV's Lord Steward. Certainly it bears his name. But a white sauce, based on a flour and butter roux moistened with veal stock and finished with cream, was known before his time. The interesting thing is that this *grasse* version of *béchamel*, which seemed to predominate up to the mid 19th century, has now become in simplified form our *sauce velouté*; while the *béchamel maigre*, made with milk and served with fish and Lenten dishes generally, has taken over the name.

Whatever the exact date of origin may be, both versions go back to the 17th century, that wonderful period when French chefs set to work to develop Italian Renaissance cookery, adapting it to the rather different resources of northern France. Marie de'Medici, arriving from Florence in 1600 to marry Henri IV of France, brought chefs with her, as had Catherine de'Medici in the previous century. This second injection of Italian civilization stimulated French cookery, which already had a high reputation, to reach its perfection.

2 oz. butter	*optional:*
3 tablespoons flour	slice of onion
1 pint milk	piece of carrot
salt	bay leaf
freshly ground white pepper	2 sprigs parsley
	grated nutmeg

If the *béchamel* is to be served as it is, without additional flavourings apart from cream, put the milk into a pan with the optional ingredients, and heat very slowly to just under boiling point. Melt the butter in another pan, stir in the flour and cook for 2 minutes. Remove this pan from the heat and pour in a little of the flavoured milk through a strainer. Beat until smooth, and continue to add the milk – this time over the heat – until you have a thin smooth sauce. Simmer gently for at least 20 minutes; if you don't wish to stand over the sauce put the pan into another pan of water and give an occasional stir. The sauce should reduce to a generous half pint of creamy thickness.

For a richer *béchamel*, substitute single cream for half the quantity of milk.

SAUCE MORNAY. To the *béchamel* add a ½ cup of mixed Gruyère and Parmesan cheese, grated, and reduce by one third. Invented by one of the chefs, Joseph Voiron, at the Restaurant Durand, which opened in 1830 in La Place de la Madeleine, in Paris.

CREAM SAUCE. A name sometimes given to straightforward *béchamel*. It's less disappointing to guests or family if cream sauces are made with cream. The simplest thing to do is to add ¼ pint of double cream to the finished *béchamel* sauce, made with half single cream and half milk. If you want to achieve a most superior ivory coloured sauce, boil down ½ pint of double cream by half, then add it to the single cream/milk *béchamel*. Reduce further by simmering and sharpen with lemon juice.

MUSSEL SAUCE. Open 2 dozen mussels and add the strained liquor to a cream sauce. Reduce until thick but not pasty. At the last moment add the mussels, cut into three or four pieces according to size, and a little chopped parsley. Delicious with sole.

ENGLISH LOBSTER SAUCE. Season the *béchamel* with about ½ teaspoon anchovy essence and some cayenne pepper. Stir in 2–3 tablespoons of chopped lobster meat (including coral and tomalley).

SAUCE CARDINAL. A most superior lobster sauce, which should I suppose come close to the red of a cardinal's hat. To the *béchamel* add ½ pint fish *fumet* (p. 18), and reduce to about ¾ pint. Finish with 3–5 tablespoons of lobster butter, p. 23, some chopped truffle and 3–5 tablespoons of double cream. This method can be used to make sauce from other shellfish. Serve with lobster and fine white fish.

Without truffles, the cardinal disowns this sauce – or he should do; in fact many restaurants call an un-truffled lobster sauce 'Cardinal' just the same.

SAUCE NANTUA. A fine sauce made with freshwater crayfish – *not with lobster*. Any dish with the word Nantua attached to it means 'garnished with freshwater crayfish and served with *sauce nantua*',

Once after a brief holiday at Lake Annecy, we stopped at this small town in the mountains with its own calm blue lake, I went to buy picnic food, and remember being disappointed that the streets were not paved with *écrevisses*. There weren't any in the shops either. Perhaps I was just unlucky. Perhaps it was the wrong day. Perhaps the entire haul of those miniature lobsters from the many streams around the town is taken by the two best hotels. Certainly their menus proclaimed *quenelles de brochet Nantua, gratin d'écrevisses Nantua, croustade de queues d'écrevisses*.

In our part of western France the lack of crayfish is lamented. Detergents are blamed, so are chemical fertilisers and weed killers washed by rain from the soil into small streams. If you are lucky and live in the Cotswolds, or some other part of England where crayfish are to be found, plan to make this delicious sauce. Then go out and find pike or whiting for the *quenelles* on p. 248–9: or else invest in a boiling fowl, as this is good with *sauce Nantua*: or serve the sauce with poached sole or salmon.

Once you have achieved the crayfish, your troubles are over. To the *béchamel* sauce above, add ½ pint of single cream and reduce to about ¾ pint – a nice creamy consistency. Finish with 3 tablespoons double cream, 3–5 tablespoons of crayfish butter, and a generous tablespoon of shelled crayfish tails. Some truffles and truffle juice may be added, but for most people this is even further beyond expectation than crayfish. A few mushrooms stewed in butter can be used as a garnish, and their cooking juice added to the sauce instead.

CAPER SAUCE. Add 2 tablespoons of capers and 1 tablespoon of chopped parsley to *béchamel* sauce, just before serving. Serve with skate (though I admit to preferring *beurre noir*, p. 181, with capers added) and members of the cod family which have been poached in court-bouillon, or halibut or turbot.

PARSLEY SAUCE. To the *béchamel* sauce, add up to ¼ pint thick cream, and reduce slightly. Finish with about 2 oz. of chopped fresh parsley, a few drops of lemon juice and a tablespoon of butter. A good sauce, if rich and made with plenty of parsley.

CURRY SAUCE. When making the *béchamel*, cook a medium-sized chopped onion slowly in the butter, and add 2 teaspoons of curry powder with the flour. Finish in the usual way. It's much improved by the addition of ¼ pint cream, beaten with an egg yolk, particularly if it's being served with scallops. Remember not to let the sauce boil once the cream and egg yolk have been added. This is a true French sauce, with the curry powder being used as a spicing ingredient; it has no real relationship to Indian cooking.

ANISE SAUCES. The flavour of star anise goes beautifully with fish. Either a flower-like head of star anise can be used to flavour the milk for the *béchamel* (don't strain it out until the sauce has enough flavour) or else you can use a small amount, starting with less than ¼ teaspoon, of the Chinese 5-spice blend, in which anise predominates, obtainable from oriental stores and some delicatessens. Or, best of all, your can stir in Pernod, Anisette, or Pastis Ricard, all anise-flavoured, until the taste is delicate but noticeable. Serve immediately.

MUSTARD SAUCE. Just before serving, stir in 1 teaspoon or more of French mustard (tarragon mustard, if you like) to taste. Don't boil again as mustard loses its strength when it's cooked. For herrings, mackerel, coley, bream and porgies.

SAUCE SOUBISE. If you ever go to Paris, and wander round the Marais district, take a good long look at the courtyard of the Soubise palace. The recollection of the colonnade and statues, in pale-honey stone, will help you through a lifetime of onion-tears. The sauce was invented by Marin, chef to Charles de Rohan, Marquis de Soubise, at the beginning of the 18th century – he also wrote a cookery book as attractive as its name, *Les Dons de Comus*, which was published in 1739. A good sauce with fish, if it is lightly made.

Chop 1 lb. onions roughly and blanch them for 5 minutes in hard-boiling water. Drain. Simmer until cooked, with 1 oz. butter, a glass of dry white wine, and a little fish stock, if you have it, or water – just enough liquid to keep the onions from catching. When your *béchamel* sauce is ready, stir in 4 tablespoons of thick cream and then, little by little, the cooked onions, which have first been sieved. Keep tasting, and stop adding this purée before the sauce tastes too robust.

MUSHROOM SAUCE. Either cook 6 oz. mushrooms in 2 oz butter and add them to a *béchamel* sauce; or else cook the mushrooms in the butter for the sauce, with a tiny chopped clove of garlic. Add flour, then the hot milk in the usual way. Flavour with plenty of black pepper and a little lemon juice. Cream does not come amiss.

ANCHOVY AND MUSHROOM SAUCE. Sliced mushrooms, both culti- vated and wild, fried in butter, go well with many fish. I'm not so sure about mushroom sauce. The *béchamel* seems to dull the savour. One day, though, I found a Swedish recipe in which anchovies were used to season mushrooms, and I took the hint. A surprising combination, but it works well. The flavour of each ingredient, clear and piquant, raises *béchamel* sauce to the most interesting deliciousness.

6 oz. mushrooms, chopped	¼ pint double cream
½ clove garlic, crushed	salt and black pepper
3 tablespoons butter	¾ pint *béchamel* sauce, p. 25
½ tin (4–5 fillets) anchovies	chopped dill weed or parsley

As the *béchamel* sauce simmers, fry mushrooms and garlic gently in the butter. After about 10 minutes, add the roughly chopped anchovy fillets. Stir well, and add the cream, which should bubble down to make a thickish sauce. Tip the mushroom mixture into the *béchamel*, and leave to simmer together for 10 minutes or so until you're ready to serve the fish. Add the chopped herbs at the last minute.

Excellent with all the firm white fish, and with mullet, huss, snapper, redfish and so on.

ANCHOVY SAUCE. Pound 6 anchovy fillets with 3 tablespoons unsalted butter. Stir into the *béchamel* sauce just before serving. With a liquidizer, the anchovies, butter and a little sauce can be blended to smoothness very quickly. Reheat this mixture with the rest of the sauce before serving.

Note. I much prefer a simpler anchovy sauce for fish – it also goes with veal, or escalopes cut from pork tenderloin – particularly for white fish of the cod type which can do with a little assistance. Melt 4 oz. of unsalted butter and put into it a finely chopped clove of garlic. Simmer slowly for 5 minutes. Meanwhile crush 6 or 8 fillets of anchovy. Stir them into the melted butter, keeping on a low heat until the anchovies have disintegrated into the sauce. Correct the seasoning. Excellent. See recipe for *crostini alla provatura* on p. 376.

SAUCE CHIVRY. I like herb sauces. They mean summer, when so many fish are at their best – and look their best, served with a pale green sauce. I like walking down the garden – the genius of man having placed the herb patch as far away from the kitchen as possible, on the principle, I suppose, that exercise is good for cooks – past catalpa and hibiscus, to find chives, tarragon, and parsley, which flourish at the foot of a most entangling rose.

Recipes for herb sauces and butters usually glide over the main pitfall. They state 1 tablespoon, or 3 sprigs, with authority. What this apparently firm direction means is 'a handful, more or less, as opposed to a sackful'. Reflect on this: last year we split a bushy tarragon plant in two, half for Wiltshire, half for our tiny garden in the Bas-Vendômois. In France eight or ten leaves will permeate a chicken: here I use three times as many and still don't quite achieve the same result. There's a veil between us and the sun in England, a lack of clarity of light. To be fair, I should remark that a Vendômois friend grows basil in a successful quantity, but it hasn't the flavour of Ligurian or Provençal basil – again the sun. So be guided by the season, and by your own taste and climate. Be prepared to use far more than I – or anyone else – suggest.

1 glass dry white wine	2 oz butter
3 oz. spinach (a handful)	¼ pint cream
tarragon, chives, chervil, parsley, watercress	¾ pint *béchamel* sauce, p. 25

Chop equal quantities of the first four herbs, with half the amount of watercress (which has a strong flavour, so must not be allowed to be too dominant). Put half into a small pan with the wine, and boil down until there's about a tablespoon or two of liquid left. Add to the *béchamel* sauce with the cream, and leave to simmer. Cook the spinach with the remaining herbs. Press out all liquid, and mash this greenery with the butter (a liquidizer saves time). When you're ready to serve the sauce, stir in the spinach butter gradually until the flavour seems right to you: don't let the sauce boil while you do this, or the flavour of the butter will be spoilt.

A good sauce with poached salmon or bass, or with any really fresh fish of a non-oily kind.

Note. Keep this sauce for summer. Don't be tempted to try it with dried herbs.

SAUCE AURORE. Sadly the *sauce aurore* served in many restaurants falls far short of its name, being a floury *béchamel* dyed pink with tomato concentrate. Some cookery books recommend this method. But when tomatoes are the main point of a sauce, they should be present in bulk (try making *sauce américaine*, p. 44, with tomatoes, then with concentrate – you'll see the difference), not just as a squirt from a tube. If you want to improve the flavour, because the tomatoes in your part of the world are of the watery, greenhouse kind, then certainly add some concentrate as a seasoning, or a little sugar and vinegar. But you need tomatoes to transform the texture of the sauce.

béchamel sauce, p. 25
¾ lb. ripe tomatoes, peeled and coarsely chopped
1 heaped tablespoon chopped onion
1 small clove garlic, crushed
3 tablespoons butter
salt and pepper
chopped parsley, tarragon, or chives (optional)

While the *béchamel* simmers down to a thick-cream consistency, make the tomato purée. Melt onion and garlic in 2 tablespoons of butter, in a frying pan. When they're yellowish and softening, tip in the tomatoes. Raise the heat to evaporate the juice and cook until you have a coherent mass in the pan. The purée should not be too dry: neither should it be watery. Season with salt, plenty of freshly ground black pepper, and any other seasonings that may seem necessary (see above). Gradually stir the purée into the *béchamel* sauce, stopping when flavour and colour are to your liking; any left over can be used up in many ways. Correct the seasoning. When the meal is ready, stir the last tablespoon of butter into the hot sauce, with some green herbs if you have them (don't use dried ones). Serve with turbot baked in milk, sole, a tailpiece of fresh cod or monkfish – any firm white fish of quality.

MADAME SOARÈS'S SHRIMP SAUCE. Shrimp sauce with turbot is

appreciated in France as in England (see p. 109). This recipe was given me by Madame Soarès who runs the fish stall in our market town of Montoire, in the Bas-Vendômois. Her other recipe for fillets of turbot (with mushrooms) is found on p. 110. She has a power of energizing description which makes our mouths water and our purses open. *Extrà!* she says, as she hands over our purchases. *Extrà* her fish certainly is, coming fresh from that morning's early market at Nantes, 150 miles away.

¼ lb. cooked shrimps (or prawns)	tomato ketchup
dry white wine	4 oz. whipping cream
béchamel sauce, p. 25	lemon juice, salt, and pepper
	chopped parsley

Shell the shrimps and put the shells into a pan. Cover with white wine, simmer for 10 minutes so that all possible flavour is extracted from the shells. Strain into the *béchamel*, then add the cream and just enough tomato ketchup to turn the sauce a delicate pink colour and to give it a light sharpening of flavour. (Tomato ketchup is the present status symbol in French kitchens, and it can be useful for sauces. I'm not so sure about its arrival on French tables.)

Season the sauce with salt, pepper and lemon. Just before serving, stir in the shelled shrimps (or prawns) and some chopped parsley.

Note. You can be more generous with the shrimps – up to ½ lb.

CRAB AND PRAWN SAUCE. For a rich sauce flavoured with crab and prawn, and the white wine in which the fish was poached, see the recipe for *pompano en papillote*, p. 126. It is suitable for turbot, brill, John Dory, sole, monkfish.

Velouté Sauce

Made in the same way as *sauce béchamel*, in this sauce fish stock is substituted for half or all of the liquid, and mushrooms for the vegetables and aromatics. Obviously the sauce to choose when the fish has been poached in a court-bouillon, or when a little stock can be made from the skin and trimmings of a filleted sole or other flatfish. The juices of foil-baked fish can also be used and give an excellently concentrated flavour. The favourite enrichment for *velouté* and its derivatives is egg yolk, with or without cream. Many of the seasonings used with *béchamel* sauce such as lobster butter, mustard, shellfish, etc., can be used to vary *velouté* too. I like sauces closely linked with the food they accompany, which is why I prefer the *veloutés* to the *béchamels*. But they do take a little more time and attention.

2 oz. butter
3 tablespoons flour

either { ½ pint fish stock, *fumet* etc. ½ pint milk or single (light) cream

or 1 pint fish stock
2–3 oz. mushroom stalks, trimmings etc.
salt, pepper

Melt the butter, stir in the flour and cook for 2 minutes. Add the heated stock, then gradually add the heated milk or cream to make a smooth thin sauce. Add the mushrooms. Simmer down to a creamy consistency. Correct the seasoning.

Note. A fish *velouté* can also be made by reducing a pint of fish stock by half, thickening it with *beurre manié* (p. 21), and enriching it with cream.

SAUCE ALLEMANDE. Make the *velouté* sauce. Beat up 2 egg yolks with 2 oz. of thin and 2 oz. of thick cream. Pour in a little of the sauce, return to the pan and stir steadily over a low heat (*don't boil*) until the sauce is very rich. Use with the finest white fish, poached or baked in white wine or fish stock; the stock is used in making the basic *velouté* sauce.

SAUCE ANDALOUSE. Make the *velouté*. Peel and chop 2 very large tomatoes. Cook them in a little olive oil, with a clove of garlic, crushed. When they are reduced to a purée, add to the sauce, plus 2 tinned peppers, chopped small. (Fresh peppers can be used but they must first be de-seeded, then boiled, peeled and chopped.) Last of all stir in some chopped parsley. A good sauce for mullet of all kinds, and any firm fish such as tunny.

SAUCE NORMANDE. The full recipe for *sole à la normande* is given on p. 102. Here is a summary of the sauce, which is served with many other fish, e.g. poached turbot, brill, bass, or John Dory. Garnish with mushrooms and oysters or mussels; their trimmings and juice will be used to flavour the sauce.

velouté sauce, p. 33, made with all fish stock	6 oz. thick cream
	lemon juice
2–4 oz. oyster or mussel juice	4 oz. unsalted Normandy butter
3 egg yolks	salt, pepper

The *velouté* sauce should be warm, and the consistency creamy without being very thick. Beat the yolks, 4 oz. of the cream and a little lemon juice, with the shellfish liquor. Stir into the *velouté*. Heat without boiling, and add 2 oz. of butter, in little bits. The sauce should thicken and reduce slightly. Just before serving, stir in the rest of the cream and butter. Season with salt, pepper and more lemon, if needed.

SAUCE NORMANDE (simpler version). Use when a creamy sauce is needed for a *gratin*, or to go with a fish pie, or with some poached fish of a firm texture.

2 oz. butter	½ pint thick cream or thin and and thick mixed
3 tablespoons flour	
¼ pint fish stock or liquor from shellfish or light meat stock	salt, pepper, dash wine vinegar

Make the sauce in the usual way, adding the vinegar just before serving, when the pan is off the heat. Sherry or Madeira can be used instead; or dry white wine or vermouth, in which the fish has been cooked. Reduce it to a few tablespoons after removing the fish.

SHRIMP SAUCE. To the *velouté* sauce, add at the last moment a 4 oz. carton of potted shrimps. The spiced butter gives an excellent flavour to the sauce. (Potted shrimps can be added to a *béchamel* sauce in the same way.)

MUSTARD SAUCE. To the *velouté* sauce, made with half milk and half fish stock, add a teaspoonful of French mustard or more, according to taste, just before serving. A more piquant sauce than the *béchamel* version on p. 28.

POULETTE SAUCE. Make the *velouté* sauce with a few more mushrooms than usual – about 4 oz. in all. Beat up 2 egg yolks with 2 tablespoons thick cream, and incorporate this with the hot sauce, which should not be allowed to boil. Season with lemon juice and chopped parsley. An excellent sauce for mussels or eel. The liquid from cooking the fish is used to make the *velouté* sauce.

Sauce au Cidre

A Normandy sauce, like the white wine sauce which follows.

5 oz. butter	about 1 pint cider
1 onion, chopped, or 2 shallots	3 tablespoons flour
trimmings of the fish, plus its bones	2 egg yolks
	2 oz. thick cream
bouquet garni	lemon juice
salt, pepper	

Fry the onion or shallot, and the trimmings of the fish, very gently, in 1 oz. of butter. When the onion begins to soften, pour in the cider, plus ¼ pint water. Add the fish bones, *bouquet* and a seasoning of salt and pepper. Simmer steadily for half an hour, with the lid off the pan; there should then be between ¾ and 1 pint of stock.

Make a *roux* with 2 oz. of butter and the flour, add the strained stock, and complete the sauce as if it were a *velouté*, thickening it with the egg yolks beaten into the cream. Just before serving, whisk in the last 2 oz. of butter and season with salt, pepper and lemon juice.

Sauce au Vin Blanc

One of many similar recipes (see also *sauce Bercy*, p. 47).

½ pint white wine	2 oz. butter
1½ pints water	3 tablespoons flour
2 lb. fish bones	4 oz. double cream ⎫ or 8 oz.
bouquet garni	4 oz. single cream ⎬ double cream
1 carrot, sliced	salt, pepper
1 onion, sliced	

Put the first six ingredients into a large pan and boil steadily for half an hour. Strain off and measure the liquid. If necessary boil down again to ¾ pint. Use this stock, and the cream, to make a *velouté* sauce in the usual way. Let it mature and thicken by slow simmering. This makes a good general sauce for many fish.

Prawn Sauce

A beautiful sauce which goes with a variety of white fish – cod, sole, turbot, brill, halibut, hake, angler fish, John Dory, bream and porgies – and enhances the pleasure of lobster, scallops and octopus.

¼ lb. prawns in their shell	dessertspoon wine vinegar
2 oz. butter	1 lump sugar
1 heaped tablespoon flour	3 oz. heavy cream
¾ pint water	¼ pint Marsala
up to 1 tablespoon tomato	salt, pepper
concentrate	walnut-sized lump of butter

Put the shells only of the prawns into a pan, and cover with the water. Simmer for about 20 minutes, then liquidize in the blender or put through the fine plate of a *mouli-légumes*. Pour the resulting gritty mixture through a fine sieve, and keep warm.

Melt the butter in a clean pan, stir in the flour and cook for 2 or 3 minutes. Stir in the sieved shell liquid gradually, until the sauce is smooth. After 10 minutes simmering, or a little more, flavour with tomato concentrate. Add vinegar and sugar. Cook for another five minutes before stirring in the cream, then the Marsala, little by little, to taste. Correct the seasoning before putting in the prawns to heat through. Remove from the heat, stir in the butter and serve immediately.

To serve, pour some of the sauce over the poached, or lightly-fried fish, and hand round the rest in a sauceboat. Pieces of lobster can be mixed with this sauce; divide between little pots, and brown quickly under a hot grill. Any sauce left over can be mixed with a spoonful or so of mayonnaise, and used as a dressing for cold fish.

Cream sauces made with cream and butter

Sometimes I come across people, invariably people in cosy circumstances, who complain in my direction that they haven't time to make sauces, that sauces take too much trouble. I then suggest the following recipe, remarking that an average 10 year old boy or girl could make it successfully in 5 minutes. Their eyes glaze over with puritanical horror – 'What! Just cream and butter?' These two substances of neolithic respectability are made to sound like a sexual perversion.

I can't think that such people make good cooks (or, I suspect, good anything else). They're mean-spirited. First they're mean with time and intelligence, then they're mean with money too. They might get away with one meanness, indeed most of us are obliged to whatever our inclinations, but they expect to get away with both.

Reflect, though. Cooks are lucky. Money alone can produce delicious food – wouldn't you enjoy a meal of smoked salmon, grilled steak, and peaches sliced into a glass of champagne? – but a sculptor buying an exquisite hunk of Carrara marble can still produce a bad statue: a dressmaker has no guarantee of success even if she uses cloth of gold. So I reckon cooks should pay up gracefully one way or the other. And thank the Lares and Penates, or whatever gods inhabit our household shrine.

Simple Cream Sauce

4 oz. unsalted butter
¼ pint thick cream
salt, pepper, lemon juice

chopped parsley, or *fines herbes*

When everything else is ready for the meal, melt the butter in a frying pan about 8 to 10 inches across. Stir it, and when it has dissolved, pour in the cream. Continue to stir until the sauce bubbles into a thick homogeneous consistency – about 5 minutes at the most, depending on the amount of heat used. Don't burn the butter: this means keeping the heat low at first, then raising it to moderately hot when the cream is added.

Season with salt, pepper and lemon juice. Finish with 2 tablespoons of chopped herbs. If you have a good supply of fresh tarragon, it flavours the sauce well for sea fish. With trout, grayling and so on, stick to parsley and perhaps some chives.

Avranches Sauce for Salmon (and other Fish)

Coming back to England at the end of summer, we stop in Avranches, our first town in Normandy. We love Avranches. The sea-wind scours its stone houses, turning the dullness of granite to sparkle. There's the collection of illuminated manuscripts to look at and from the Botanic Gardens the view of Mont Saint Michel:

> '. . . Cheops of our West, pyramid
> of the seas, by itself on its bitter tides.'
> (From *Near Avranches*, by Victor Hugo, translated by
> Geoffrey Grigson)

We visit an antique shop full of Oceanic and African objects of startling beauty. We picnic by the stone where Henry II knelt in penance for the murder of Thomas à Becket. And we buy Normandy cream to take home:

½ pint double cream	salt, pepper, lemon juice
2 or 3 tablespoons chopped	1 tablespoon capers
fines herbes	1 oz. butter
tomato concentrate	

Heat the cream to just below boiling point. Add the herbs and a discreet flavouring of tomato concentrate. Season with salt, pepper and lemon juice. Finally stir in the capers and butter. Pour into a hot sauceboat to serve.

Sauce Verte de Chausey

The Îles Chausey, several miles out from Granville in Normandy, once provided granite for the quays and cathedrals and monasteries of that coast, including Mont St Michel. The green sauce named in their honour, and perhaps made on the island when quarrymen still lived there, goes well with gurnard, or garfish, flying fish, herring or mackerel. It would be too strong for delicate fish like trout and whiting. It is a great improver of the cod family. I found the recipe in *Gastronomie Normande*, by Simone Morand (Flammarion, 1970), and make it often.

3 chopped shallots	3 oz. thick cream
2 chopped cloves garlic	parsley and tarragon, enough
3 oz. unsalted butter	to turn the sauce green
1 tablespoon French mustard	salt, pepper
dash of wine vinegar	

Melt shallots, garlic and 2 tablespoons of chopped parsley in the butter, and cook until the shallots soften to a golden colour. Stir in the mustard and vinegar. Add the cream and about a tablespoon of chopped tarragon. When the sauce is thick, season it well. Add more herbs, and more wine, vinegar and mustard if you like.

Herb and Cream Sauce

See *salmon in pastry with herb sauce*, p. 223.

Egg and butter sauces

Sauce Hollandaise (with Sauces Maltaise and Mousseline)

I can never decide which gives me greater pleasure – making this sauce, which is in effect a hot mayonnaise, or eating it. But its origins elude me, which shades the pleasure. One thing only is certain: it's not Dutch at all, but French. Sometimes it's called *sauce Isigny*, a genuflection to the hometown of France's best butter.

Hollandaise has its problem, the problem of all egg sauces – it can turn. Here's Carême, known as the King of Chefs and the Chef of Kings, writing from his great Directoire kitchens, where the criss-cross and curses of sweaty cooks, and the uncontained heat of stoves and roasting fires, raised the temperature to stifling cruelty. 'Almost all cooks make *sauce hollandaise* with egg yolks, butter, vinegar, salt and pepper: but the great Laguipiere, by adding a little *velouté* and *glacé*, has made it perfect and succulent. The *velouté* adds enough body to the sauce to bind it so that the eggs cook to just the right point, while the ordinary *hollandaise* is likely to turn as it stands around.'

So – if you're nervous, you can do the same with the blessing of authority. But you'll have to make the *velouté* first. (*Béchamel* is too floury and thick in texture.) In our kitchens nowadays, with simpler meals to prepare, there's no reason why *hollandaise* should ever separate to oil.

3 tablespoons white wine vinegar	3 large egg yolks
2 tablespoons water	6 oz. unsalted butter, cut into 12 pieces
10 white peppercorns	salt and lemon juice to taste

CLASSICAL METHOD. Put vinegar, water and peppercorns into a small pan and boil down to about 1 tablespoon of liquid. Pour into a pudding basin and leave to cool. Beat the egg yolks into the reduced vinegar mixture, then set the basin over a pan of barely simmering water on low heat – *the water must never boil*, or the sauce will get too hot and curdle. Add the butter, knob by knob, stirring all the time. Remember you're making a hot mayonnaise, and don't add more butter until the previous piece is absorbed; should the sauce turn, the remedy is the same as for mayonnaise – first a tablespoon of very hot water, then, if that doesn't work, a fresh egg yolk in a clean basin and start again, pouring in the curdled sauce gradually.

The sauce is finished and ready for its final seasoning when it coats the back of the spoon and looks thick. Remove the saucepan from the heat, while you dish up the food; if it has to wait around, leave the pan on heat turned down to the absolute minimum (with gas, use an asbestos mat).

QUICK METHOD. As above, but instead of adding the butter bit by bit, melt it, and when it is tepid, add it in a slow stream to the egg yolks, beating all the time with a wooden spoon, as if you were making mayonnaise.

MALTESE SAUCE. Stir in the grated rind of a blood orange, and use the orange juice instead of lemon for the final seasoning. A Seville orange makes an even better flavour. Delicious with firm white fish.

MOUSSELINE SAUCE. Whip up 4 oz. thick cream. Fold into the sauce just before serving, and readjust the seasoning. Good with a solid fish like salmon.

CAVIARE SAUCE. Fold 3–4 tablespoons of pressed caviare into the finished *sauce mousseline*. Adjust the seasoning. For the finest fish – sole, turbot, trout, really fresh bass, John Dory.

SAUCE TRIANON. Use lemon juice (1 tablespoon) and sherry medium-dry (2 tablespoons) instead of vinegar.

CUCUMBER HOLLANDAISE. See p. 127, Grilled Pompano with cucumber *hollandaise*.

Sauce Béarnaise

This is a 19th century sauce, invented by a chef at the Pavillon Henri IV at St German-en-Laye, and named for that great French King, who came from Béarn, close to the Basque country, on the Spanish border. This chef had the idea of spicing the egg and butter innocence of *hollandaise* with a reduction of wine, tarragon, shallot and wine vinegar, seasoned with plenty of coarsely ground black pepper, a simple addition, perhaps, but it quite changes the character of the sauce. Serve with grilled fish of fine flavour and substance – salmon, sunfish, tunny, pompano, large mackerel.

The Pavillon was part of Henri IV's château, a pretty building of stone and warm brick, overlooking what was once a magnificent view, now spoilt by industrial incrustations and smoke. It became a hotel in the 19th century. Dumas stayed there while writing *The Three Musketeers* and *The Count of Monte Cristo*. In his *Grand Dictionnaire de Cuisine* (1873) he gives a recipe for this sauce using oil – olive oil of course, the fat of southern French cookery – rather than butter. It seems, though, that this is a retrospective attempt to give the sauce a Béarn ancestry.

1 heaped tablespoon of shallot, chopped	pinch of salt
2 tablespoons chopped tarragon and chervil	pinch of Cayenne pepper
4 tablespoons tarragon vinegar	1 tablespoon chopped tarragon and chervil for finishing
4 tablespoons white wine	egg yolks and butter, as for *sauce hollandaise*, p. 40
good grating of black pepper	

Put the shallot, tarragon and chervil, vinegar, wine and black pepper into a small pan. Boil down until about 2 tablespoons of liquid is left. Put into a large pudding basin, and when cool add the egg yolks. Continue as for *hollandaise* sauce. Strain, and whisk in about a tablespoon of chopped tarragon and chervil. Add salt and cayenne. Serve in a warmed sauceboat.

SAUCE CHORON. When the *béarnaise* sauce is completed, beat in 3 or 4 tablespoons of tomato purée or tomato concentrate. Sometimes a little cream is added as well. Choron, a famous chef born at Caen in Normandy, invented this sauce, or rather this variation of *sauce béarnaise*.

Beurre Blanc

The château of La Goulaine, south of Nantes, has a reputation for muscadet, the wine of the district. It also has a reputation for being the birthplace of *beurre blanc*, one of the best of fish sauces. The first reputation is well-bestowed; I am not quite so sure about the second. A love of good food is often garnished with undeclared fairy tales. But this one has plausibility.

One day towards the turn of the century, so the story goes, the Marquis of Goulaine's cook, Clémence, was preparing a dinner party. She asked a helper to get on with the *béarnaise*, while she attended to other things. When everything was dished up, Clémence glanced at the *béarnaise* and realized that the egg yolks had been forgotten. No time to make a fresh sauce; the mistake – which tasted surprisingly good – was sent up. After dinner Clémence was summoned to the dining-room. She arrived red-faced and ashamed, expecting trouble. Instead, the 'new sauce' was praised. She was asked to repeat the mistake many times, and when she left the château to open a restaurant at la Chébuette, a mile or two away on the banks of the Loire, her *beurre blanc* soon became a speciality of the region, from Nantes to Angers and Tours.

As you'd expect, *beurre blanc* is served with shad, brochet and salmon from the Loire. Try it, too, with saltwater fish such as turbot, sole, John Dory, brill and whiting. The fish should be poached in a half-wine, half-water *court bouillon*, baked in foil, or braised. *Not* a sauce for fried fish.

3 shallots, chopped to a mash	½–1 lb. unsalted butter
3 tablespoons white wine vinegar	(recipes differ as to the amount)
3 tablespoons white wine or court bouillon	salt, pepper

Cut the butter into 8 or 10 pieces and put them in the refrigerator, or in a cool place.

Put the shallots into a small, heavy pan, with the vinegar and wine or bouillon (taken from the fish kettle, or foil, in the case of baked fish). Cook steadily until the liquid is reduced by three-quarters and the shallots are tender. Remove from the heat and cool.

These two operations can be completed before the fish is cooked. The final stage must be carried out when the fish is ready to serve, and lying on its warm plate.

Put a large bowl of iced water near the stove. Heat the onion mixture until it's tepid. Whisk in the pieces of butter, very quickly, with a fork. Keep raising the pan from the heat so that it never becomes really hot. You should find that the butter turns to a whitish cream of mayonnaise consistency. It shouldn't become oily or transparent; if this looks like happening, plunge the base of the saucepan into the iced water, until the sauce thickens to a cream, then continue to add butter until it looks and tastes right to you.

If you have a total collapse, don't despair. Beat a couple of egg yolks in a basin over a pan of simmering water, and add the butter/shallot mixture gradually until you have the thicker and yellower sauce more usually known as *hollandaise*.

Sauce à l'Américaine

This sauce comes, in spite of its name, from southern France. So it's important to use olive oil and garlic, and to liven the tomatoes up with sugar and black pepper, should you happen to be cooking in a less sunny climate. Apart from other grape brandies, there is, alas, no substitute for cognac. If you haven't any, turn to a different tomato sauce (*Marinara*, p. 45, or *Aurore*, p. 31).

In its classic version, this sauce is cooked with the dish in the style of a stew. (See pp. 130, 280.) But if you can only buy ready-boiled lobster, or if you serve the sauce with a fish that can't stand the fierce reduction, for instance huss or hake or *quenelles* of whiting, here's a recipe allowing for this:

1½ lb. tomatoes, peeled and roughly chopped	1 large clove garlic, crushed
¼ pint olive oil	½ gill cognac
1 lb. cheap white fish	½ pint dry white wine
seasoned flour	¼ pint strong beef stock
shell of lobster, crab or prawn	salt, pepper, cayenne pepper, sugar
4 oz. chopped shallot or mild onion	tarragon, and chervil or parsley
4 oz. chopped carrot	1 good tablespoon butter

Cook the tomatoes to a thick purée in half the olive oil. Cut the white fish into large cubes, turn them in seasoned flour and fry in the rest of the olive oil with the shallot, carrot and garlic. When the fish is lightly browned, add the warmed cognac and set it alight. Turn the mixture, so that the flames last as long as possible. Add lobster, crab or prawn shell, the wine, stock and tomatoes. Season with plenty of black pepper, and ½ teaspoon of salt. Cook vigorously for half an hour, or until the sauce looks thick rather than watery. Remove as much shell as possible, then put through the very coarse plate of the *mouli-légumes*. Correct the seasoning, add herbs, and reheat. Stir in the tablespoon of butter, pour over the cooked fish and serve.

If you are using ready-boiled lobster, reheat it in the sauce before adding the butter.

Note. As with *sauce aurore*, the important thing is to use real tomatoes. By all means help the flavour with a little tomato concentrate, if it seems necessary, but never make tomato concentrate a substitute for tomatoes.

Sauce Orientale

> ingredients for *sauce américaine*   *plus* 1 tablespoon curry
>   above   powder
>   ¼ pint double cream

When making the tomato sauce, add the curry powder to the frying fish and vegetables when the cognac flames have died down. Measure out ¾ pint of the finished sauce and reheat with the heavy cream. Correct the seasoning, stir in the butter.

A rich sauce for a large piece of fish, or a sizeable whole fish, which has been poached in a *court-bouillon* or baked in the oven.

Marinara or Italian Tomato Sauce

This is the basis for fish stews and soups, and for pasta sauces. One of the girls in our family works in Rome. The first time she came home on holiday, she pushed me affably from the stove. 'I'm going to show you how to make a proper tomato sauce,' she announced. 'First, you must put in some chopped carrot – and second, you mustn't keep stirring it once it comes to the boil.'

> 1 generous tablespoon olive   2 lb. tomatoes, peeled
>   oil   and chopped, or a 2 lb. 3 oz.
> 1 medium onion, chopped   can Italian tomatoes
> 1 medium carrot, chopped   salt, pepper
> 1 clove garlic, crushed

Brown the onion and carrot lightly in the oil. Add the remaining ingredients and bring to the boil, stirring. Leave to simmer, uncovered, until the sauce reduces to a fairly thick stew – at least 30 minutes. Sieve or not, as you please.

A glass of red wine may be added to the ingredients above. And the sauce may be finished by the addition of a nice lump of butter and some Cayenne or chili flakes, but be careful not to overdo them.

This is one of the most useful of all fish sauces. Small fish, squid, shrimps or prawns, clams and mussels can all be added to it, or cooked in it, to make the most satisfactory fish stews. Dilute with fish stock, add some shellfish, and you have a delicious soup.

Sauce à la Créole

Tomato sauce made sweeter, and a little hotter, by the addition of peppers and a discreet seasoning of chilis.

2 oz. butter
½ lb. chopped onion
2 large stalks celery, chopped
3 fresh red peppers, deseeded and chopped, or 4 canned peppers

2 lb. 3 oz. can of tomatoes
1 small green chili, or ⅓ teaspoon crushed hot chili flakes
salt, pepper, thyme, basil

Fry the onion, celery, peppers and chili in the butter, gently at first until they begin to soften, then a little more strongly until they brown lightly. Pour in the contents of the can of tomatoes, add a sprig or two of thyme, plenty of freshly ground black pepper and only a little salt (because the sauce is to be reduced). Leave the lid off the pan so that the liquid has a chance to evaporate, and cook until the sauce becomes a stew.

Remove the sprigs of thyme, check the seasoning and add more salt or chili flakes if required. Add a final chopping of fresh basil.

Like the *marinara* sauce in the last recipe, *sauce créole* makes an excellent basis for fish stews. When the flavour is to your liking, add some lightly-browned fish such as turbot, brill, hake, shark, anglerfish, or squid, and cook for another 5 or 10 minutes. (See *sunfish à la créole* on p. 215). If using mussels or clams, open them in a large saucepan and remove the shells, before adding them to the sauce – stir in the strained shellfish liquor too.

Sauce à la Bourguignonne, or Sauce Matelote

A red wine sauce, the basis of freshwater fish stews such as *meurette*, which can also be served separately with baked fish. For recipe, see p. 73–4.

Sauce Bercy

This intense concentration of onions, wine and meat essence usually accompanies plainly-cooked food such as grilled steak or liver. But if the juices from a foil-baked fish are substituted for meat essence, it goes equally well with bass, bream or salmon.

1 heaped tablespoon chopped shallot or onion	¼ pint white wine
1 level tablespoon butter	salt, pepper, lemon juice
	chopped parsley

About 25 minutes before the fish is cooked (see pp. 219, 222 and 232 for foil-baking), put the shallot or onion and the butter into a small heavy pan. Cook gently until golden and transparent. Add the wine and boil hard until there's about a couple of tablespoons of liquid left. Remove from the heat. Transfer the cooked fish to a warm serving plate. Pour the juices from the foil of ½ pint of fish *fumet* into the onion and wine mixture. Reheat, and correct the seasoning with salt, pepper and lemon juice to taste. The amount required is bound to vary according to the type and quantity of seasoning put into the foil package with the fish. Add some chopped parsley and serve very hot in a separate sauceboat.

Remember that this is intended to be a concentrated sauce, to be eaten in small quantities. If the juices in the foil were too abundant and watery – though this is unlikely – the sauce must be reduced a second time before the final seasoning.

Note. A more copious amount of sauce can be provided by adding up to ¼ pint of thick cream. Thicken with *beurre manié*: a tablespoon butter and a tablespoon flour, forked together, and added to the sauce in little knobs at the end. Stir until the sauce is smooth and very hot without boiling. For another *sauce au vin blanc*, see p. 35.

Two Sorrel Sauces

In France people still seem to be leaving the countryside – I mean leaving it in large numbers, without being able to sell their houses to weekenders as they can here. Walking along a lane, you see a farm compound over the hedge. There are no barks to greet your arrival, no flutter and squawk of fowls on the dung heap. You see nothing hanging from the nails by the kitchen door. It's ghostly. Passing the house, you come to the kitchen garden, overgrown perhaps but undeniably there. Pushing the gate open, freeing it from the overhanging rose, you stumble over a lusty patch of sorrel, placed where it was easy to grab a handful to flavour the evening's soup, or to make a sauce for the fish brought home from market. How grateful that clear flavour is in the spring, sharp as lemon juice to one's tired winter taste.

1 large handful sorrel leaves (approx. 4 oz.)	1 oz. butter
4 oz. each single and double cream (8 oz. in all)	stock or juice from cooking the fish
	salt, pepper

Remove toughest stems from the sorrel. Wash and melt it to a purée in the butter. This takes no more than three or four minutes. In a saucepan, bring the cream to the boil, stir in the sorrel and 3 or 4 tablespoons of stock from cooking the fish. If the fish has been fried or grilled, add some water to the pan juices, boil up well and use them instead of stock. Season to taste. Serve with mackerel, salmon, white fish, shad, pike. This recipe is from *French Provincial Cooking* (Penguin), by Elizabeth David.

about 30 leaves of sorrel, a large handful	4 egg yolks
1 oz. butter	2 tablespoons water
1 lb. unsalted butter	salt, lemon juice

Make a sorrel purée as above. Put the unsalted butter into a saucepan, cut in chunks, and bring to the boil over a gentle heat. Meanwhile beat the egg yolks and water in a large pudding basin. Set the basin over a pan of barely simmering water. Keep stirring the yolks, and as the butter comes to a frothing boil, pour a little of it on to the yolks. Go on beating – a wooden spoon is best for this – and add the butter slowly: the mayonnaise process. As the sauce thickens the butter may be added more rapidly. Watch the water underneath – it should not boil.

When the sauce coats the spoon, take the basin from the pan and stir in the sorrel purée to taste. Add salt and lemon juice if required.

This recipe comes from Mrs Stevenson of the *Horn of Plenty* near Tavistock in Devonshire. She serves it with the delicious Tamar salmon. Of course there is no reason why the sorrel purée shouldn't be added to the conventionally made *hollandaise* sauce on p. 40. This method, though, is quicker.

Three Gooseberry Sauces

Strange to put gooseberry sauces after sorrel ones? Not really, because they have a remarkably similar taste, as Elizabeth David remarks in *French Provincial Cooking*. The two acidities are interchangeable. I must confess, though, to never having eaten gooseberry sauce with salmon, because when the fruit is at its small, acid-green best, salmon is unpleasantly expensive. Mackerel, at their finest, arrive with the first gooseberries; nobody can complain at the price of either, though Parson Woodforde, the greediest of Norfolk parsons in the 18th century, did complain, in his diary, when the spring was late and he had to eat the first mackerel of the season without gooseberry sauce.

In spite of this, it's the French and not the English who christened this hardy fruit *groseille à maquereau* – which is odd, at first sight, because the gooseberry grows super-abundantly in the British Isles (and indeed as far north as the Arctic Circle), and gooseberry sauces are more common in our old cookery books than in French ones. Perhaps the reason is that we use gooseberries in so many ways, for pies or tarts, for boiled puddings and for jam, whereas in France it's largely a question of gooseberries with mackerel.

The first sauce is made by substituting half a pound of gooseberries for the sorrel leaves, in recipe one for sorrel sauce. (See previous recipe.) Strain the purée through a sieve and add the boiled cream and the fish stock or juice.

The second sauce requires:

1 lb. gooseberries	1 teaspoon sugar
1 oz. butter	ground ginger or freshly
either 1 egg or 3 tablespoons	grated nutmeg
béchamel sauce, p. 25	

Top and tail the gooseberries (it's easiest to use scissors for this). Cook over a low heat with the butter, until soft enough to put through a sieve or *mouli-légumes*. Beat in either the egg or the sauce. Reheat without boiling, and season with the sugar, and the ginger or nutmeg, to taste.

The third sauce includes fennel:

1 lb. gooseberries	heaped dessertspoon fennel
1 oz. butter	leaves, chopped
1 oz. flour	nutmeg, salt, pepper, lemon
¾ pint milk	juice, sugar

Top and tail the gooseberries. Put them in a pan, cover with water and bring gently to the boil. Boil until a gooseberry taken from the pan will give between the fingers without collapsing completely. Drain, and set aside while you make a white sauce in the usual way with the butter, flour and milk. Let the sauce reduce, simmering, to the consistency of thick cream. Mix in the gooseberries and the chopped fennel, and add the seasonings to taste: the sugar should not be added unless the gooseberries are very young and tart. Reheat gently.

The gooseberries may be sieved into the sauce, instead of being left whole.

Cold Sauces

Mayonnaise

Sometimes one hears people talking about the making of mayonnaise as if it were one of the major kitchen skills, and I suppose this accounts for the huge sales of non-mayonnaise 'Mayonnaise', with less than 50% oil – home-made has about 75% – and a starch thickener. In fact a child can master it; if two things are understood, there's no need ever to have a failure. First, all ingredients – and equipment – need to be at warm room temperature; second, there must be no hurry to add oil at the beginning. Be patient, mix it in drop by drop.

As to warmth, in winter I make mayonnaise on the enamelled side of a solid fuel stove. A damp tea towel twisted round the base of the bowl or mortar stops it walking over the edge to perdition.

In summer, the eggs are taken from the refrigerator either the previous evening or several hours before the sauce is made. The oil is poured into a measuring jug which has been rinsed in very hot water, then dried.

As to patience, it's not so necessary as it used to be. With an electric beater, the whole job can be completed in 5 minutes. On the other hand, making mayonnaise with mortar and wooden spoon is a soothing business (why should the cook always be rushed?). And I have the conviction that mayonnaise made in this old, slow way tastes better.

My own feeling is that the best mayonnaise, in particular if it is to go with cold fish, should be made with olive oil. A light-flavoured oil – mayonnaise emphasises the fruity flavour – but an oil tasting of olives. When strong flavourings such as curry powder are to be added, corn or ground nut oils may be substituted. It's interesting to see how variations on mayonnaise increase the further north you go, with some of the liveliest ones to be found in Scandinavia, ingenuity compensating for an oliveless existence.

Never spoil mayonnaise with malt vinegar. Red and white wine vinegar, tarragon wine vinegar or lemon juice are the sharpeners to use.

2 large or 3 small egg yolks	1–2 tablespoons vinegar or
½ pint olive oil	lemon juice
	salt, pepper

Beat yolks, with a teaspoon of vinegar or lemon juice, until they thicken slightly. Add the oil drop by drop, beating all the time, until the mixture turns creamy and heavy. The oil can now be added more rapidly. Correct the seasoning with more vinegar or lemon juice, salt and pepper. Store in a covered jar in a cool place, or in the least cold part of the refrigerator. To prevent a skin forming on top, add 2 tablespoons of boiling water at the end.

Should the mayonnaise curdle, beat a tablespoon of boiling water into the mixture. If this doesn't work, put another egg yolk into a clean bowl and start again, pouring in the curdled mixture drop by drop, then the remaining oil. No eggs left? Then put a tablespoon of French mustard into a hot, clean bowl, and beat in the curdled mayonnaise drop by drop; the flavour will be altered of course, but it will be delicious in a stronger way.

I reflect that it's less trouble in the long run to go slowly at first.

MALTESE MAYONNAISE. Grate the rind of an orange, preferably a blood orange, into the bowl, before putting in the egg yolks with 1 tablespoon of lemon juice. Flavour at the end with the juice from the orange, and a little more lemon juice instead of vinegar, if extra sharpness is required. Good with cold white fish.

MUSTARD AND DILL MAYONNAISE. The proportions for this superb Scandinavian sauce come from *The Great Scandinavian Cook Book*[1]; they can be varied to suit your taste. The egg yolk may be omitted, in which case the sauce is a variant of vinaigrette. Serve with pickled salmon, trout or herring, or with boiled crab or lobster.

2 tablespoons French or German mustard	¼ pint corn or ground nut oil
1 tablespoon white sugar	2 tablespoons wine vinegar
1 large egg yolk	generous teaspoon dill weed
	salt, white pepper

Beat the first three ingredients together, and finish the mayonnaise in the usual way.

CURRY MAYONNAISE. In Danish museums one sometimes sees the most unusual platters for serving cold food. They consist of a large round or oval pottery dish with a stemmed bowl fixed in the centre – the whole thing fired together. The raised bowl was to hold the sauce, usually a mayonnaise, above an abundance of cold meat and cured fish. Nowadays, in hotels, metal ice cream cups are placed on large serving dishes to give the same effect. They usually contain a curry mayonnaise, which goes well with the strong flavours of the various cold foods like pickled herring, meat, and salad vegetables, arranged so beautifully below.

This sauce is simple to make. Add 1 teaspoon of finely grated onion, and 1 teaspoon of curry powder or paste, to the 2 egg yolks of the basic mayonnaise ingredients, and finish in the usual way. Corn or olive oil may be used.

TUNNY MAYONNAISE. Makes a good salad when combined with rice, hard-boiled eggs and shellfish.

[1] Allen & Unwin Ltd., ed. Ellison.

3 oz. tunny canned in oil
3 anchovy fillets, chopped
1 large egg yolk

¼ pint olive oil
lemon juice

Pound tunny and anchovies to a paste. Beat in the egg and finish in the usual way. This mayonnaise is often spread over a dish of cold veal (*vitello tonnato*), in which case it is thinned slightly with veal stock.

ANCHOIADE. For anchovy mayonnaise, see p. 374.

CHILEAN MAYONNAISE. In *The Tenth Muse* – the muse of eating intelligently – Sir Harry Luke describes a sauce served, in a club at Santiago, the capital of Chile, with cold langoustes, '... brought to the mainland from Robinson Crusoe's island of Juan Fernandez, 360 miles out in the Pacific'. It had the consistency of mayonnaise, but the colour was brownish-pink, and the flavour subtle and intriguing. 'Persistent enquiry ... finally elicited that it is compounded of ordinary mayonnaise with a little Pan Yan pickle worked into it. It is as simple as that – and very good.'

Sieve the pickle first, about a tablespoon to the mayonnaise quantities given above, and beat it up with the egg yolks before making the mayonnaise in the usual way.

Serve with lobsters and other cold shellfish – or, in more homely circumstances, with tinned tunny in a mixed rice salad.

JELLIED MAYONNAISE FOR CHAUDFROID. Instead of coating a cold, poached fish with aspic jelly (p. 18), jellied mayonnaise may be used instead. The mayonnaise is made in the usual way, using ½ pint of oil and 2–3 egg yolks. Fold in gently ¼ pint of firm aspic jelly, or ¼ pint water in which ¼ oz. of gelatine has been dissolved, while the gelatine is on the point of setting but still liquid. *Use at once.*

AVOCADO MAYONNAISE. Excellent with shellfish, on account of its beautiful colour, as well as its flavour. (See *croûte aux fruits de mer*, p. 330). I do not find it very harmonious with other fish; it seems to need the sweetness of shellfish for complete success. Here are two recipes, the first quick and simple, the second a little more work but much better in flavour and so worth the trouble.

Avocado pear, peeled and stoned (pitted)	juice of ½ lemon
1 egg	½ teaspoon salt
4 tablespoons salad oil	½ teaspoon mustard

Cut avocado into rough cubes. Mix in blender with other ingredients, at top speed, for 10 seconds, until creamy. Adjust seasoning to taste. A hint of sugar may be needed.

Basic mayonnaise made with salad oil, p. 51	pinch Cayenne pepper
1 tablespoon tomato ketchup	1 avocado pear, peeled and stoned (pitted)
1 teaspoon tabasco sauce	1 measure vodka (optional)

Season the basic mayonnaise with the next three ingredients. Mash or sieve avocado to a fine purée. Fold it into the mayonnaise and add vodka if used. Adjust seasoning to taste.

PERNOD REMOULADE. A piquant sauce good with many of the round fish – grilled grey mullet, sea-bass, John Dory, sea-bream – and with mackerel.

Basic mayonnaise made with salad oil, p. 51	Dessertspoon each chopped parsley and tarragon
Dessertspoon chopped sweet-sour cucumber	about 1 tablespoon Pernod

Fold the other ingredients into the basic mayonnaise, using the above measurements as a guide only.

GREEN MAYONNAISE. Every cookery book gives *sauce rémoulade*, *sauce tartare*, *sauce ravigote* – all versions of mayonnaise. These sauces use herbs and sharp pickles, such as gherkins, anchovies or capers, with the occasional spice of some raw, chopped onion or shallot; the kind of sauce that each cook can alter to her own taste.

Here's a less commonly encountered herb mayonnaise, a green sauce of distinction. As a rule it's served with salmon, salmon trout and shellfish, but it goes with cold white fish too, turbot or John Dory, for instance.

According to the resources of your garden or neighbourhood, assemble one or other of these herb mixtures:

either	or
½ oz. each parsley, chervil, tarragon, chives, sorrel, salad burnet	1 oz. each parsley, tarragon, chervil or chives
1 oz. spinach and watercress leaves	1½ oz. each spinach and water-cress leaves

Make your basic mayonnaise (p. 51). Blanch the herbs for 2 minutes in boiling water. Pour out into a sieve and run under the cold tap. Leave to drain. Press the last moisture out, and pound to a paste either with pestle and mortar, or in a liquidizer with a little of the mayonnaise. Mix into the mayonnaise just before serving.

Green Herb Sauce from Frankfurt am Main

This recipe, a version of *sauce rémoulade*, was sent me by Mrs Eberstadt, from Frankfurt, who now lives in London. She remarked that when it was necessary to leave their native town, in the years before the last war, many people regretted only one thing left behind – not the house where Goethe was born and so on, but *grüne sosse*. (A sentiment Goethe would probably have shared, as *grüne sosse* is said to have been one of his favourites too.) It's eaten with hard-boiled eggs, as a sandwich filling, with boiled beef and other cold meats; and best of all, with fried or poached fish, and with cold fish such as cod, salmon, sole, John Dory.

1 egg yolk
¼ pint corn oil
1 tablespoon German or French mustard
1 tablespoon lemon juice
2 hard-boiled eggs, chopped
1 small gherkin, sweet-sour with dill, chopped
1 small onion or shallot, chopped
½ clove garlic, chopped

3–4 oz. chopped herbs, chosen from parsley, chives, tarragon, chervil, sorrel, watercress, salad burnet, and borage
salt, pepper, grated lemon rind, extra lemon juice
2 tablespoons yoghourt or sour cream } (optional)
1 raw egg yolk

Make a mayonnaise with the first four ingredients. Add all the chopped ingredients and correct the seasoning with salt, pepper, lemon rind and extra juice. If tarragon is not among the herbs, substitute tarragon vinegar for lemon juice throughout.

If you use yoghourt and sour cream, add them gradually, stopping before the firm consistency of the sauce is lost. Sometimes a raw egg yolk is mixed in at the end. Mrs Eberstadt remarks that borage, with its strong cucumber-like flavour, should be used sparingly: so should watercress. All the herbs should be young and fresh.

Note. If you prefer to serve herb butter with hot fish, use ¼ lb. softened unsalted butter: beat in 4 or 5 tablespoons of oil, then the first raw egg yolk and mustard, and finally the rest of the ingredients.

In Germany you can buy a collection of seeds – *Küchenkrauter für die Frankfurter grüne sosse* – required for producing the correct herbs for Frankfurt green sauce – borage, sorrel, parsley, chives, tarragon, salad burnet, chervil and a garden cress which resembles our mustard-and-cress. This is the recipe given on the packet. As you'll see from these two recipes, Frankfurt green sauce can be varied to suit the cook's taste and circumstances:

| equal amounts of borage, salad burnet, parsley and sorrel | rather more chives and garden cress a little tarragon and chervil |

Chop finely. Mix with vinegar and oil as for a salad dressing. Stir in half a pint of sour cream, a little salt and some finely chopped shallot or onion. Mix well. Add two hard-boiled eggs, mashed to crumbs.

Ailloli and Aillade

Ailloli, the garlic mayonnaise from Provence, gives its name to the great spread of cold food for which that part of France is so famous. Salt cod and other fish provide the centrepiece (see p. 335). The sauce can quite well accompany the salt fish in simpler combinations or even alone; though I think a modifying salad of some kind is a good idea.

up to 8 cloves garlic	½ pint Provençal olive oil
salt	pepper
2 egg yolks	lemon juice

Crush the garlic with a little salt in a mortar. (The first time you make the recipe start with four cloves of garlic; when everyone's got used to the idea, work up gradually to eight.) Add the egg yolks and finish the mayonnaise with the rest of the ingredients.

The unexpected ingredients of *aillade*, another garlic mayonnaise, are hazelnuts and walnuts. To me, this is the ideal sauce for a simpler arrangement of cold fish:

8 large shelled hazelnuts	2 egg yolks
8 shelled walnuts	½ pint Provençal olive oil
3–6 cloves garlic	pepper
salt	lemon juice

Grill the hazelnuts lightly, until the skins can easily be rubbed off; pour boiling water over the walnuts, and remove their skins. Crush the nuts with the garlic and a little salt in a mortar, and continue with the mayonnaise in the usual way.

Rouille

A fiery sauce of Mediterranean origin, which is served with *bouillabaisse*, fish soups and stews, or with fish in a large mixture such as *ailloli garni*. Here are two recipes:

1. Pound in a mortar 2 cloves of garlic and the flesh of 2 small red chili peppers. Add the liver of bream or red mullet, if they are appearing in the final dish.

Squeeze out a thick, crustless slice of white bread in a little fish stock. Add to the garlic and pepper. Stir in gradually, as if you were making a mayonnaise, 3 tablespoons of olive oil and a little fish stock, or the juices from cooking the fish in foil.

2. If a richer sauce is required, pound 3 cloves of garlic with the two red peppers. Beat in 2 egg yolks, then gradually add 8 oz. olive oil, and season with French mustard, salt, and pepper. This is excellent with salt cod or cod fritters.

Skorthalia

This is the Greek version of *ailloli*, the pungent mayonnaise given solidity by the addition of breadcrumbs or potatoes. Delicious with boiled salt cod (beetroot, tomato, and pepper salads provide the vegetable element) and with salt cod fritters. An improver of white fish in general, served hot or cold.

I first made it with the enormous quantities given by Joyce M. Stubbs in the *Home Book of Greek Cookery* (Faber), and found it overwhelming. Now I use the recipe given by Elizabeth David in *A Book of Mediterranean Food* (Penguin):

2 egg yolks	2 oz. fresh white breadcrumbs
6 cloves garlic	2 oz. ground almonds
¼ pint olive oil	lemon juice, parsley

Pound the garlic, add the yolks, then the oil, drop by drop. Stir in the breadcrumbs and almonds carefully. Season with lemon juice and parsley.

Mrs Stubbs' recipe omits egg yolks and almonds, altogether a heartier affair. (It has a tendency to separate.) Here are half quantities – plenty for 6 people:

3 or 4 cloves garlic	½ pint olive oil
2½ medium potatoes, boiled in their jackets, then peeled	wine vinegar, lemon juice
or 1 slice stale bread, 2 ins thick	½ small coffee cup water
	salt

Put garlic, and potatoes or bread, through a mincer (or *moulinette*). Pound until smooth, then add the oil slowly. Season with lemon juice and stir in the water.

Horseradish Sauce with Fresh Walnuts

One November at the turn of the century, the great chef Escoffier was invited to a shooting weekend in the Haute-Savoie. Saturday lunch began with a dish of *ombles-chevalier* (a speciality of the lac du Bourget, in nearby Savoie) which had been cooked, and left to cool, in white wine from his host's own vineyard. The surprising thing was the sauce which accompanied the fish; it was made from horseradish, and the juicy fresh walnuts which are so delicious an item of French meals at that time of year.

Now *omble-chevalier*, or arctic char, isn't likely to come our way very often, but there's no reason why the exquisite sauce shouldn't be served with trout of various kinds (including salmon trout), other char, and grayling, which have been poached in a white wine *court-bouillon*.

5 oz. shelled walnuts	1 dessertspoon lemon juice
1 dessertspoon caster sugar	or wine vinegar
2 tablespoons white	pinch salt
breadcrumbs	5 oz. grated horseradish
½ pint double cream	

If you've been able to buy fresh walnuts, you will find that the pale skin is easily removed; older walnuts need to have boiling water poured over them before the darkened skins can be rubbed off. This sounds a fiddly business, but it's worth doing because the sauce will taste much more delicate without the slight bitterness one can get from walnuts. Chop them finely, and mix with the sugar, breadcrumbs, cream, salt and part of the lemon juice or wine vinegar. Now add the horseradish slowly, to taste (if you have no fresh horseradish, use one of the prepared brands – again to taste), and the rest of the lemon juice or vinegar, as necessary. For ways of using horseradish with hot fish, see the recipes for *Poached Turbot with Horseradish*, p. 113, *Charles Cotton's Boiled Trout*, p. 234, and *Carpe au bleu with Horseradish Sauce*, p. 257.

Tarator Sauce from the Middle East

I usually make this recipe – from Claudia Roden's *A Book of Middle Eastern Food* (Penguin) – with walnuts, in the Turkish style. This is because we bring them home by the kilo, every autumn, from our neighbour's tree in France. After the hard work of the vintage is over, he finds walnut picking a pleasant job. The tree grows at the foot of a steep slope, and one suddenly sees his head, and the heads of nephews, cousins, and friends, popping out

of the leaves like Jacks in the Green. Down below wife and children
bash at the branches with sticks, and the nuts come raining to the
ground. We munch steadily for days, walnuts with the new wine,
walnuts with new bread, walnuts fried with apples to go with
boudins noirs. And when I get back to England and electricity, we
drink walnut soup and enjoy this sauce with fish; with the bass,
bream or John Dory, with mussels, or with cod steaks to liven them
up.

If your abundance happens to be hazelnuts, almonds or pine
kernels, they can be used instead of walnuts.

2 slices white bread, crusts removed	3–4 tablespoons wine vinegar
¼ lb. nuts	1–2 cloves garlic, crushed
¼ pint olive oil	salt, pepper

Dip the bread in water and squeeze it dry. Crumble roughly and
add to the nuts, which should have been finely ground. Mix in the
olive oil gradually, beating all the time, then the vinegar and
garlic. Season with salt and pepper.

The simplest way is to put all the ingredients, except salt and
pepper, into the liquidizer, and whirl at top speed until you have
a smooth sauce. Finally season to taste.

Tahina Cream Salads

In cooking, as in much else, one homes continually on the Middle
East as the central knot of our world. So in Claudia Roden's book,
one finds the ancestors of Escoffier's walnut and horseradish sauce
(p. 59) in the tarator sauce above, or in these sesame meal salads.
I give her proportions.

1–3 cloves garlic	6 tablespoons chopped
salt, about ½ teaspoon	parsley, or 2 only, to
¼ pint lemon juice, or the juice of at least 2½ lemons	garnish
¼ pint tahina (sesame seed) paste	sliced hard-boiled eggs, to garnish
½ teaspoon ground cumin (optional)	

Mix first five ingredients in electric blender or with a beater. Parsley in quantity can be mixed into the salad, or else the smaller amount can be used as a garnish with the egg.

Serve with baked fish or cold fish. Or serve on its own as an hors d'oeuvre, mixed with a tin of chopped, well-drained anchovies.

1 clove garlic	¼ pint tahina paste
salt, about ½ teaspoon	5 tablespoons ground almonds
¼ pint lemon juice, or the	a little water if necessary
juice of at least 2½ lemons	5 blanched almonds to garnish

Mix first five ingredients in blender or beater, using water to soften the mixture, if necessary for creaminess. Turn into a bowl, and decorate with a daisy of whole almonds.

Serve with cold fish: John Dory, turbot, sole, cod.

¼ lb. walnuts	juice of 2 lemons
2 cloves garlic	a little water if necessary
salt, about ½ teaspoon	4 tablespoons chopped parsley
3–4 tablespoons tahina paste	

Mix as above, folding parsley in at the end.

Serve with fried mussels, baked fish or cold fish.

Sauce Vinaigrette

Frequently used for dressing salads, this sauce is made with 1 tablespoon of vinegar to 5 tablespoons of olive oil, seasoned with salt and pepper.

Fish Stews and Soups

Soupe de Poisson

This simple soup, a glorified *fumet de poisson*, can be varied by adding different ingredients at the end.

6 servings:

head of 1 cod, conger eel, or salmon	*bouquet garni*
	3–4 pints water
2 lb. fish bones, preferably sole	¼ pint dry white wine
1 medium carrot, quartered	dash white wine vinegar
1 large onion, quartered	salt, pepper
1 large clove garlic, chopped	good pinch saffron
3 tablespoons of olive oil	3 oz. vermicelli

Put first six ingredients into a large pan. Cover and stew gently for 5 minutes. Add *bouquet*, water, wine and vinegar. Bring to the boil and simmer for 30–40 minutes. Pour through a strainer into a clean pan, pushing through as much of the soft debris as you feel inclined. Bring back to the boil, add saffron and vermicelli. Season to taste. When vermicelli is cooked, correct the seasoning if necessary, and serve.

Additions. Just before serving, add the chopped flesh of a large peeled tomato. It should not cook in the soup, or its fresh flavour will be lost.

Or when the soup is ready, stir a ladleful of the hot broth into 4 tablespoons of *ailloli*, the garlic mayonnaise of Provence (p. 56). Stir it back into pan of soup, and pour the whole into a soup tureen.

Avgolemono Soupa

6 servings:

The Greek name means egg and lemon soup; egg and lemon being
the two important finishing ingredients. We're used to *avgolemono*
soup made with a basis of chicken stock; many Greek restaurants
serve it this way. But I think it's even more delicious when made
with fish *fumet*. Follow instructions for *soupe de poisson* stock in the
last recipe, omitting white wine. After straining, reduce the stock
to about 2½ pints.

Add 3 oz. rice to the reduced stock and simmer until it's cooked.
Have ready in a large pudding basin 3 eggs beaten up with the
juice of 1 lemon and a little of the grated rind. Pour in a ladleful of
soup, whisking all the time. Return to the pan, and, *without boiling*,
cook until the soup is slightly thickened – keep whisking all the
time. Add more lemon if necessary; the soup should be both sharply
refreshing and bland. Serve at once; this is not a soup to be kept
waiting around.

Velouté de Poisson

Fish soup made on the principle of *sauce velouté*, but with finer,
richer ingredients.

6 servings:

3 lb. fish – redfish, conger,
gurnard, wrasse
1 lb. shellfish – lobster,
mussel, prawn, scampi
2 carrots, chopped
2 leeks or onions, chopped
3 large tomatoes, peeled and
chopped
bouquet garni
3 cloves garlic, chopped
1 tablespoon white wine
vinegar
1 pint dry white wine, or dry
cider
2–3 pints water

2 cloves
salt, pepper, Cayenne, nutmeg
To finish:
2 oz. butter
2 shallots, chopped
2 heaped tablespoons flour
1 glass brandy (optional)
4–6 oz. cream
2 large egg yolks
lemon juice
chopped parsley, tarragon,
chives
croûtons of bread fried in
butter

Put 3 lb. of fish into a pan, with vegetables, *bouquet*, garlic, spices, vinegar, wine and water. Bring to the boil. Add live lobster if used — otherwise add *shells only* of cooked prawns, lobster, or scampi; with mussels, open them and add their liquor. Set aside the meat of these shellfish. When the lobster is cooked remove it, take out the meat, set it aside, and return shell to the pan. After 10 more minutes, sieve the contents of the pan and season well.

Melt the shallots gently, without browning, in butter. Stir in the flour, then the sieved fish stock. When smooth, add brandy and seasoning, and simmer for 20 minutes. Mix the cream and egg yolks and use to thicken the soup. Sharpen with lemon juice and taste for seasoning. Stir in shellfish and chopped herbs, and serve with croûtons.

Smoked Haddock Soup

A starred soup, providing it's made with good smoked haddock, and not those bright yellow 'fillets'. Look for kipper-shaped Finnan haddock, which have the most beautiful, low-keyed tawny colour and a flavour to match.

6 servings:

½ lb. Finnan haddock	about 1 pint milk
¾ lb. cod	3–4 oz. single cream
1 oz. butter	lemon juice, salt, pepper
1 large onion, chopped	chopped parsley
1 generously rounded tablespoon flour	

Pour enough boiling water over the haddock to cover it by half an inch and leave for 10 minutes. Meanwhile cook the onion slowly in the butter, lid on the pan, for about 8 minutes, without browning it. Stir in the flour, then the water from the haddock and about ¾ pint milk. Remove about a tablespoon of haddock flakes and put aside, add the rest, with the cod, and including skin and bones, to the pan. Simmer for 15 minutes. Strain through a sieve or *mouli-légumes* into a clean pan, pushing through as much onion and haddock as possible. Pour in the cream, and correct the seasoning with salt and pepper and just enough lemon juice to bring out the flavour. More milk can be added, or water, or both. Stir in the reserved haddock flakes, and some chopped parsley, and bring to simmering point. This soup should have the consistency of thin cream; thickness counteracts the delicacy of the haddock.

Note : there is another haddock soup on p. 257.

Matelote Normande

As you would expect in a *matelote* from Normandy, dry cider is substituted for red wine, and Calvados (their famous apple brandy) for eau de vie. Whisky is a possible alternative to Calvados. The fish, too, are typical of the area; the same fish that we can buy in Britain.

6 servings:

2 lb. fish (including ½ lb. conger eel, and a mixture of plaice, dabs, whiting and gurnard)
3 oz. butter
3–4 tablespoons Calvados
½ pint dry cider
liquor from mussels
¼ pint fish or light meat stock
4 oz. thick cream

beurre manié, p. 21, of 1 tablespoon each butter and flour
chervil, salt, pepper
garnish:
½ lb. mushrooms, lightly fried
2 pints mussels, opened
croûtons of bread fried in butter

Clean and cut up the fish. Cook in butter until the pieces are very lightly coloured. Pour over the warmed Calvados, set it alight, and stir the fish about in the flames. Add cider, mussel liquor and stock. Season with salt and pepper, and add some chopped chervil. Simmer until the fish is just cooked. Add the *beurre manié* in small knobs to thicken the cooking liquor. Pour in the cream. The sauce should not boil, but should thicken gradually over a moderate heat. (Two egg yolks can be used instead of the *beurre manié*, if you prefer: they should be beaten up with the cream.)

Transfer to a serving dish, and arrange mushrooms, mussels and croûtons round the fish. (In Normandy, you might get oysters and crawfish as well as mussels, if you were lucky.)

Oyster Soup I

The most delicate of fish soups, and the easiest of all to make. Until oysters become cheap again, you might prefer to substitute mussels, clams or cockles. (This is not a bad joke: with modern methods of fish farming, oysters will be large, plentiful and less expensive before many years have passed.)

6 servings:

2 dozen oysters, or 2 lb. shellfish	¾ teaspoon anchovy essence
	nutmeg, cayenne pepper
2 oz. butter	¼ pint double cream
2 tablespoons flour	salt, pepper
1 pint hot milk or veal stock	lemon juice, parsley

Clean and open the oysters or other shellfish in the usual way (see pp. 308 and 321). Discard the shells, but keep the liquor carefully.

Melt the butter in a large pan, stir in the flour and cook gently for 2 or 3 minutes. Add the milk or stock gradually so that the mixture remains smooth. Season with the anchovy essence and a little nutmeg and cayenne pepper. Put in the cream. Simmer for 15–30 minutes. Just before serving, add the oysters and their liquor to the pan to heat through. (Don't overcook shellfish, they become tough; oysters are ready when they *start* to curl at the edges.) Correct the seasoning with salt, pepper, and more nutmeg and cayenne if you like. If the flavour is not quite sharp enough, lemon juice will bring it out. Pour the soup into a hot bowl, scatter a little parsley on top and don't wait for the dilatory guest to appear because the shellfish will go on cooking in the heat of the soup.

Oyster Soup II

An excellent recipe from the *Restaurant de la baie des anges* at Aber-Wrach, in Finistère, the extreme north-west corner of France.

6–8 servings:

stock:
bones, skin and heads of 2
  soles
1 carrot, sliced
1 medium onion, sliced
1 small leek, sliced
1 stick celery
bouquet garni
6 oz. dry white wine
1¾ pints water

salt, freshly ground black
  pepper
soup:
½ lb. leeks white part only,
  chopped
2 oz. butter
4 oz. peeled and diced potato
4 dozen oysters, opened
8 oz. single cream
heaped tablespoon chopped
  parsley

Simmer the stock ingredients together for 25 minutes. Meanwhile, melt the leeks in butter gently for 10 minutes, add the potato, and pour on the strained stock. When the vegetables are cooked, liquidize, or put through the *Mouli*: the result should be very smooth. Put the oysters and their liquor into a pan and cook gently for a moment or two over a moderate heat, until the edges curl. Strain the liquor into the soup and pour the cream onto the oysters. Bring oysters and cream to just below the boil, being careful not to overcook the oysters, and put into a large soup tureen. Add the rest of the soup gradually, sprinkle with parsley and serve.

Lightly salted butter and rye bread go well with this soup.

Note. Mussels may be substituted for oysters. Open them in the usual way, add their liquor to the soup and cut the mussels into four if they are large, in half if they are small, before reheating with the cream.

Bisque de Homard

I can think of no better soup than *bisque de homard*, when it is made at home with the correct ingredients. It is not difficult to make, a little prolonged perhaps, and certainly expensive, but not difficult. For the best result, buy a live lobster. But a ready-boiled one is better than no *bisque de homard* at all.

6 servings:

1 small lobster	*bouquet garni*
2 carrots, diced	2 pints fish stock
1 medium onion, diced	4 oz. double cream
1 stalk celery, diced	3 tablespoons rice
4 oz. butter	salt, pepper, Cayenne pepper
2 oz. brandy	bunch of parsley
8 oz. dry white wine	

Cut the lobster in pieces (see p. 278). Remove the coral from the meat and set aside. Cook the vegetables gently in 2 tablespoons of butter until they soften. Add the lobster. When the pieces redden, pour on the brandy and set it alight. Turn the lobster over in the flames. Pour in the white wine, and boil hard until reduced by half. Put in enough fish stock to cover the lobster and simmer for another 5 minutes until the lobster is cooked. Remove the pieces. Add the rest of the stock and the *bouquet*, with the rice. Meanwhile remove lobster meat from the shells, restoring a few large bits of shell to the pan of soup. Dice the meat and set aside. When the rice is cooked, take the shell out of the pan and liquidize the rest, or sieve it, with the cream and most of the lobster meat. Season. Mix the coral with the remaining butter and add to the reheated but not boiling soup, together with the last few bits of lobster meat that were not liquidized. Sprinkle with plenty of chopped parsley and serve.

If you have a ready-boiled lobster, shell the meat and add the shell to the vegetables which have been softened in the butter. Flame with brandy, add wine and continue with the recipe above. This method is a good way of using up the shells from a lobster – it is surprising how much flavour they contain, and if you have the forethought to put aside a piece or two of lobster meat from the meal before, the *bisque* will be quite good. Sometimes a spoonful of tomato concentrate or chopped tomato improves this kind of economical recipe.

Crab or Shrimp Soup

Crabs, shrimps, prawns and freshwater crayfish can all be used to make a *bisque*, even the tiny crabs you pick up on holiday.

Use the *bisque de homard* recipe above, as a guide. You will need
2–3 lb. of crab or shrimps. Substitute water for fish stock and add
a pound or more of good tomatoes. With tiny shellfish there is
obviously no point in attempting to separate meat from shell, but
it is important to break them up in a rough and ready fashion,
about halfway through the main cooking time, so that none of their
flavour is wasted.

For a more southern flavour, substitute olive oil for butter,
include garlic and saffron in the herbs, and cook some fine pasta
(forget the rice) in the soup after it has been sieved.

This recipe shows that no fish, however tiny, are useless to the
cook, so long as the quantity is there.

Partan Bree

Partan is the Gaelic for crab, and bree the mode of pronouncing the
Gaelic *brigh*, meaning juice. The recipe comes originally from *The
Cookery Book of Lady Clark of Tillypronie* (Constable, 1909). The
important thing is to have as fresh a boiled crab as possible, for the
best flavour. This very often means boiling it yourself (see p. 295).

6 servings:

1 large crab (10–12 oz. crab meat)	¾–1 pint light fish, chicken or veal stock
2 oz. rice	salt, white pepper, anchovy essence
1 pint milk	¼ pint cream

Pick the meat from the crab. Slice the claw meat and set it aside
for the final garnish. Simmer the rice in the milk until soft, and
then liquidize with the crab meat (not the claw meat). Dilute with
stock to the consistency required. Season to taste with salt, white
pepper, and anchovy essence a teaspoonful at a time. Bring to just
below the boil, add claw meat, then the cream, and serve immediately.

Scallop and Artichoke Soup

Some of our favourite soups I owe to Margaret Costa. Here's one of them, a winter evening's pleasure, from her *Four Seasons Cookery Book* (Nelson, 1970).

6 servings:

1½ Spanish onions	salt, pepper
good 2 oz. butter	4 large or six small scallops
1½ lb. Jerusalem artichokes	½ pint milk
2 medium potatoes	2 egg yolks
1¾ pints well-seasoned chicken stock	6 tablespoons cream
	chopped parsley

'Chop the onions and cook them in butter until soft and transparent. Add the peeled and sliced Jerusalem artichokes, and the potatoes, peeled and chopped. Stir till they are all buttery. Cook gently for about 15 minutes. Add 1¾ pints of strong, well-seasoned chicken stock. Cover and simmer for about 20 minutes longer – then put through a liquidizer, a vegetable mill or a sieve. Return to the pan and season well with salt and freshly ground pepper.

'Cut the white part of 4 large or 6 small scallops, lightly poached in the milk, into dice. Add the scallops, and the milk in which they were cooked, to the artichoke soup and heat through. Stir in the egg yolks beaten up with the cream, and let the soup thicken without boiling. Just before serving add the uncooked scallop corals cut into 2 or 3 pieces and scatter really lavishly with chopped parsley.

'Crisp oatcakes make a very pleasant accompaniment to this soup.'

Note. For another good combination of shellfish and artichokes, see the prawn salad on p. 293.

Hamburg Eel Soup

I have read some most superior remarks about this famous dish, which make me think that the writers have never actually tried it.

The ingredients may seem to promise a hefty, even muddled collection of flavours, too medieval for pleasure, but don't be put off. This is a delicate and delicious soup.

6 servings:

¾–1 lb. eel, skinned	strip lemon peel
1 onion, quartered	2½ pints beef stock
dash wine vinegar	sage, tarragon, thyme
1 bay leaf	½ small cauliflower
¾ lb. pears, peeled, cored, sliced	½ 14 oz. can French petits pois
	1 large egg yolk
¼ pint dry white wine	salt, pepper

Cut the eel into 2 inch pieces. Sprinkle with salt, and leave for 2 hours.

Meanwhile simmer the pears in wine with the lemon peel. Cook the cauliflower, divided into sprigs, in the stock with a seasoning of sage, tarragon and thyme. Dry the eel; put into a pan with enough water to cover, plus the onion, vinegar and bay leaf, bring to the boil. After 15–20 minutes, you should be able to remove and discard the bones. Put the eel fillets into a soup tureen to keep warm and strain their cooking liquor into the beef stock. Put the pears into the soup tureen too, and add to the beef stock the white wine in which they've cooked.

Simmer for 10 minutes. Pour a little hot liquid onto the egg yolk, beat together and return to the pan with the drained peas. Stir without boiling over a low heat, to thicken slightly. Correct seasoning, pour over the eel and pears and serve.

Dutch Eel Soup

The idea of eating fish in Lent has never struck me as much of a penance, particularly in the past when monks and the rich often kept large fish ponds, and the poor were fobbed off with oysters. Neither am I impressed by the penitential characteristics of this excellent eel soup, said to be much eaten in Lent by the Dutch. It's mild and delicate and rich, an excellent way of introducing eel to someone who dislikes the prospect. It's also easy to make.

6 servings:

2¼ pints water	2 rounded tablespoons flour
10 peppercorns	2 small egg yolks
2 teaspoons salt	2 tablespoons cream
½ bay leaf	chopped parsley
1 eel, skinned and cut into 1½ inch pieces	lemon juice
2 generous tablespoons butter	extra salt and pepper

Simmer eel, peppercorns and bayleaf in the water, with the salt, for 20–30 minutes, until the eel is ready to part company with its bone. Don't overcook it. Meanwhile make a roux with the butter and flour in another pan and, when the eel is done, strain the cooking liquor into the roux, stirring all the time to avoid lumps. Cook gently for about quarter of an hour, then add the eel pieces to reheat. Whisk the egg yolks lightly with the cream, and a ladleful of soup. Add to the pan and stir over a low heat for the soup to thicken a little more, but don't let it boil or the egg will curdle. Stir in the parsley and season to taste with lemon juice and more salt, and some freshly ground pepper if necessary.

(Based on a recipe in *The Art of Dutch Cooking*, by Countess C. van Limburg Stirum, André Deutsch.)

For other eel soups see pp. 259 and 265.

Water-Souchy

Water-souchy, or waterzöi, comes from the Dutch waterzootje – a stew of freshwater fish, originally perch but now a mixture of eel, perch, carp and so on, boiled in water. Obviously this rather unaided formula will only be successful if the fish are perfectly fresh – in other words, it's a recipe for anglers only.

Allow 5 lb. of fish for 6 people. Clean, and cut them into chunks. Butter a large saucepan lavishly and place the fish in it, plus a couple of leeks, a stalk or two of celery, a *bouquet garni* with plenty of parsley, and seasoning. Just cover the whole thing with water. Bring to the boil and simmer for 20–30 minutes; the fish must not be allowed to disintegrate. Serve with croûtons of bread fried in butter.

Once the fish is past its first freshness, you will have to assist the sauce with a thickening of egg yolks and cream. But then you will not be making water-souchy, and will have to think of another name.

Meurette à la Bourguignonne

Meurette is the famous Burgundian stew of river fish cooked in red wine. *Pochouse* or *pauchouse* is a similar concoction made with white wine, Meursault preferably, and garnished with small caramelized onions as well as triangles of bread. They are both a form of *matelote*, see p. 270. Incidentally, *meurette* shows that red wine goes as well with fish as white; one more 'rule' tumbling to the ground. (You can think of sole with Chambertin as well as the rich-fleshed salmon.)

This is a fisherman's recipe; when a bag of mixed fish is presented to you, it is an excellent way of dealing with them. Divide them into thick, medium and thin piles, so that none gets overcooked.

6 servings:

3–4 lb. river fish, pike, tench, eel, bream etc.	1 bottle red wine (from Burgundy for preference)
3 large carrots, sliced	liqueur glass of marc[1] or brandy
2 large onions, sliced	
4 cloves garlic	4 oz. butter
thyme, bay leaf, bunch of parsley	1 tablespoon flour
	3 or 4 slices bread
salt, freshly ground black pepper	

Clean the fish. Cut off the heads and tails (and put them into a piece of muslin if they are numerous and muddled). Chop the fish into roughly equal pieces and season them.

Butter a sauté pan with a butter paper. Line it with rings of carrot and onion, 3 of the 4 cloves of garlic crushed, the thyme, bay leaf and parsley stalks. Put in the bottle of wine and bring to the boil. Tie the muslin bag of fish heads to the pan handle, and let it sink well into the bubbling liquid. Simmer for 20 minutes.

Meanwhile cut the bread into triangles and rub them with the

[1] Marc is a crude brandy distilled from the fruit debris left after making wine or cider.

fourth clove of garlic. Fry them in an ounce of the butter, on both sides, and keep warm. Mash up another ounce of butter with the flour and divide the resulting paste into little pieces; leave to one side until later on.

Put the thickest pieces of fish into the sauté pan. After five minutes cooking, add the medium ones. After five minutes again, the thinnest ones. In another 5 minutes or less everything should be cooked. Discard the fishes' heads, in or out of the muslin. Pour off the liquor into a saucepan. Warm the marc, set it alight and tip it over the fish and vegetables, stirring them about in the flames. Keep warm, while you finish the sauce.

Add the little pieces of flour and butter to the liquor in the saucepan, keeping it just below boiling point. Stir until the sauce thickens nicely. Beat in the remaining 2 oz. of butter, and the chopped parsley leaves. Pour over the fish and vegetables. Tuck in the triangles of bread and serve straightaway (with some more red wine to drink).

Note. Sauce à la bourguignonne, or *sauce matelote,* is made by following the basic bones of the recipe above. Use the fish trimmings only (no fish): omit croûtons and brandy. Suitable liquor from cooking the main fish can of course be incorporated with the sauce.

Chowder, chaédrue and cotriade

These are the fish and potato stews of the Atlantic coasts of France and America, seamen's food that can be prepared in a boat; a rough food that can be softened on land with the resources of gardens and store cupboards. I had thought that chowder sounded a thoroughly American word, even a Red Indian word; in fact it's an anglicization of *chaudière,* the large iron cauldron in which Breton fishermen off Newfoundland and Iceland made their soup. (It was also used on whaling ships for boiling down the blubber . . .) *Chaudrée* means 'cooked in a *chaudière*'. The meaning of *cotriade,* the origin of the word, I've not been able to find.[2] The odd thing is that it always contains potato, and the recipes are closer to the

---

[2] A *cotriade* should be cooked over a wood fire. *Cotret* means a faggot. Perhaps this is the origin of the word. Editor's note.

American chowder recipes than the *chaudrées* of the French Charentes, which only contain potato in some districts.

They are the sort of recipes I like because the result tastes different every time. They're an invitation to experiment, to try adding something from the garden or larder that wasn't available last week. Such recipes are a stated principle, not a detailed plan of construction. Each person will have an individual view of the most important ingredients. For me it's the bay leaf, which, with the milk of a chowder, produces the most deliciously fresh-tasting background for cod or shellfish.

If you love chowders and fish soups, I can recommend *Long Island Seafood Cook Book*, by J. George Frederick.[3] He gives 56 recipes; here is one of them:

Oyster (or Clam or Mussel) and Okra Chowder

Okra or ladies' fingers are those delicately shaped pods that one sometimes sees in the best greengrocer's shops. They can also be bought tinned. Their virtue is to add a smooth jellied consistency to soups and stews, which contrasts with the slightly rough texture of the actual pod.

6 servings:

1 large onion, chopped	2 sweet peppers, chopped
2 oz. salt pork, or unsmoked streaky bacon	2¾ pints light stock
	⅛ teaspoon curry powder
3 large tomatoes, peeled and chopped	1 teaspoon arrowroot
	2 dozen oysters, mussels, or
4 okra pods	clams

Cook the salt pork in its own fat, adding the onion as it begins to melt. When lightly browned, add tomatoes, okra and peppers, then the stock and curry powder. Simmer for 15 minutes. Add the arrowroot, dissolved in a little cold water. Cook 5 minutes longer. Correct the seasoning. Just before serving, heat the oysters or clams in their own liquor for 3 or 4 minutes and add to the soup; mussels should be opened in the usual way, quartered if very large, and then added with their strained liquor to the chowder.

[3] Reprinted in 1971 by Dover Publications, Inc., New York.

Cod and Shellfish Chowder

A most satisfying dish when everyone's tired at the end of the day. Don't despise the frozen packs of cod or haddock on sale in the grocery, they do nicely for chowders; so do frozen scallops or prawns if clams and fresh mussels aren't available.

6 servings:

1 tablespoon lard or butter
4 oz. salt belly of pork, or streaky bacon diced
6–8 oz. chopped onion
heaped tablespoon (1) flour
¾ pint water or fish stock, p. 17
¾ pint milk
bouquet garni, including a bay leaf

1½ lb. cod, or other firm white fish
6 medium potatoes, diced
salt, freshly ground pepper, mace, cayenne
at least ¼ lb. shelled mussels, clams, scallops etc.
¼ pint cream
parsley and chives for garnish

Brown pork (or bacon) and onion lightly in the fat. Stir in the flour and cook for a couple of minutes. Add the water or fish stock gradually, then the milk, *bouquet*, and potatoes. Season well with salt, mace and peppers.

When the potatoes are almost cooked, put in the cod, cut into rough 1-inch pieces. After 5 minutes, stir in the cream and shellfish (and any liquor from opening mussels etc). When the soup returns to the boil remove from the heat. Remember that the cod continues to cook in the heat of the chowder as it comes to table, and should not be overcooked – neither should the shellfish. Correct the seasoning and sprinkle with parsley and chives. Hot buttered toast or hot crackers usually accompany a chowder: ship's biscuits if you can get them.

Note. Curry powder can be added with the flour. Final garnishes can include sweet red pepper or sweet corn. Every town on the East Coast has its own small variations.

Clam Chowder

Being English, and of a tranquil disposition, I hesitate to offer comments on one of America's sacred institutions. Even to suggest a recipe verges on impiety. But now that we have our own clam-producing beds, I can't duck the issue, or any missiles that may come my way in consequence. It's strange how the monotheistic spirit has entered the kitchen. Each clam-chowder missionary expects everyone to bow down before his one true recipe (it's the same with *bouillabaisse* in France). Tomatoes or no tomatoes? Milk or water? Onions – how many? Fanny Farmer instructs readers to take a pint of hard clams or a dozen large clams and one thinly sliced onion . . . In response Louis P. de Gouy thunders, 'A dozen clams forsooth! . . . Men and women of Rhode Island and Massachusetts Bay never sat down to less than a peck of clams apiece.' A peck, if I may remind the new metricians, is quarter of a bushel – think of a bushel basket for picking apples – in other words two gallons. They were gods in their appetite, the men and women of those days, cast in a gigantic mould. Here's one of them, Ishmael in *Moby Dick*, describing his first encounter with chowder at the Try Pots Inn run by Mrs Hosea Hussey in Nantucket: 'Oh! sweet friends, hearken to me. It was made of small juicy clams, scarcely bigger than hazel nuts, mixed with pounded ship biscuits, and salted pork cut up into little flakes; the whole enriched with butter . . .'

Walt Whitman, too, would have found Fanny Farmer and her Boston School a little on the meagre, ladylike side:

'The boatman and clam-diggers arose early and stopt for me,
I tuck'd my trowser-ends in my boots and went and had a good
    time;
You should have been with us that day round the chowder-kettle.'[4]

Here, therefore, is Louis de Gouy's recipe from *The Gold Cookery Book* (Greenberg, 1948):

'Take 4 or 5 dozen good soft clams, if your family is a small one . . . Then take 6 large onions and ½ pound of the finest salt pork. Cut

[4] *Song of Myself*. 10.

the pork in half-inch dice and brown them slowly in an iron skillet,[5] then add the onion slices to the pork fat and let them turn to golden-brown rings. Meanwhile wash the live clams, using a brush to get rid of all sand, and heat them slowly in a pan till the shells open. Save the juice, cut off the long necks and remove the coarse membrane, then chop half of the clams, not too finely, and keep the rest whole. Put pork, onions, clam juice, and 1 quart of boiling water in a kettle,[5] add 3 large peeled tomatoes, 1 bunch of leeks cut finely, 2 stalks of celery, finely minced, 2 young carrots, diced, 1 tablespoon of parsley chopped, ½ teaspoon of thyme leaves, 2 large bay leaves, 1 teaspoon of salt, ½ generous teaspoon of freshly ground black pepper, a slight grating of nutmeg, and let the mixture boil up smartly. Then reduce to the simmering point, and put in 3 large potatoes, peeled and cut in neat small dice. Prepare a roux by browning 2 rounded tablespoons of flour in 2 rounded tablespoons of butter, and make it smooth and creamy by stirring in broth from the kettle. Put all the clams into the kettle before the potatoes begin to soften, and simmer slowly until the potatoes are just tender, then stir in the roux and 2 large pilot biscuits coarsely crumbled, and add 1 tablespoon of Worcestershire sauce and a dash of Tabasco sauce. Serve sizzling hot.

'If preferred, omit the tomatoes and add instead 1 cup of scalded cream.'

Three Cotriades

The fish soup of Brittany; or, if you like, the fish supper, because the liquid is drunk first, as soup, with the fish and potatoes as a main course to follow. The cooking method for the first two recipes is close to that of American chowder. All three come from Simone Morand's *Gastronomie Bretonne* (Flammarion, 1965). The point of variation between the three, and between so many other fish soups, lies in the different resources of the places where they're made. For this reason, mackerel is included – an unusual creature in most fish soups.

Cotriades are excellent food for large parties of people. One

[5] Skillet and kettle mean frying pan and saucepan. An American quart equals 32 liquid ounces, as opposed to the Imperial quart of 40 ounces. Pilot biscuits are ship's biscuits – cream crackers will have to do instead.

cooking pot to watch (and wash up), the simplest of preparations which means that everyone can help, and a lavish result after a short cooking time. The only possible mistake is to overcook the fish. Provide a great deal of butter to eat with the fish and potatoes. (Breton butter is often salted, unlike Normandy butter which is too softly creamy for this kind of food.) Failing butter, *vinaigrette* will do instead. Provide plenty of bread, too, and toast some of it lightly for the soup. Another essential item is a bottle of full-bodied red wine.

Simone Morand so feelingly implores her readers not to cut off the heads of the fish, that I'm reminded of a Chinese cookery writer who declared that Westerners missed something through feeling unable to look at a fish with its head on, 'they miss experiencing the delicate taste of fish head'. True.

COTRIADE DES BORDS DE LA RANCE

6 servings:

vegetables etc.:
2 onions chopped
spoonful of lard
3 cloves garlic, chopped
2 lb. potatoes, quartered
chervil, parsley, chives in
   quantity

fish:
2 medium mackerel, 3 gurnard,
   piece of conger eel sliced,
   2 whiting, 1 bream
liquid:
water
plus:
salt and pepper

COTRIADE FROM CORNOUAILLE (Brittany)

6 servings:

vegetables etc.:
1 onion chopped
good handful of sorrel
lump of lard or butter
bouquet garni
2 lb. potatoes, sliced

fish:
1 gurnard, 1 red mullet, 1
   garfish, cod etc.
liquid:
water
plus:
salt and pepper

Cook the onion in the fat until it is lightly browned. Add vegetables, herbs and seasoning, and about 3 pints of water. Cover the pan, and simmer until the potatoes are almost cooked, then add the fish, cut into chunks. Add more water if necessary to cover all the

ingredients. Bring back to the boil, and simmer for a further 10
minutes until the fish is cooked, but not overcooked.

COTRIADE FROM BELLE-ÎLE (Quiberon; the extreme N.W. of
France)

6 servings:

vegetables etc.:
2 lb. potatoes, sliced
4 onions, sliced
6 large tomatoes, peeled,
  pipped (seeded) and
  chopped
1 stalk of celery, chopped
the white part of two or three
  leeks, chopped
parsley, chervil, thyme, bay
  leaf
tumbler of olive oil or melted
  butter

pinch of saffron, salt, pepper
firm fish:
conger, mackerel, pollack,
  saithe
soft fish:
sardines, skate, cod, ballan
  wrasse etc.
shellfish:
crawfish, lobster, crabs of
  various kinds, mussels,
  shrimps

The method is slightly different for this feast. First season and cut
up the various fish. Put the firm-fleshed ones on a plate with crawfish, lobster and crab. Put the soft-fleshed ones on another plate
with mussels and shrimps or prawns. Pour the oil or butter over
both piles. Leave while the vegetables cook in plenty of water, with
seasoning, herbs and saffron. When the potatoes are nearly done,
add the firm-fleshed fish etc. Boil hard for 5 minutes exactly. Add
the soft-fleshed fish etc., and boil hard for another 5 minutes. Not
a moment longer. Serve separately in the usual way, after correcting
the seasoning of the soup.

La Chaudrée

Here is another 'chowder', this time from La Rochelle, but without
the seaman's flavouring of salt pork. The liquid should be white
wine (ideally from the Île d'Oléron or the Île de Ré, islands off the
S.W. coast of France); and the *chaudron*, or cauldron in which the
soup is made, should be buried in a fire of prunings from the island
vines, which are fertilized with seaweed. Even if you haven't the

possibility of such an aromatic smoke as flavouring, or the right wine, *chaudrée* is an excellent dish. This recipe comes from *Recettes des Provinces de France*, chosen by Curnonsky.

6 servings:

4 lb. assorted fish, small sole, plaice, eel	salt, peppercorns
12 onions, quartered	3 cloves
1 clove garlic	1 litre white wine or half wine/ half water
large *bouquet garni*	whole potatoes (optional)
4 oz. butter	

In a large pot arrange the onions, garlic and *bouquet*. Season, with not too much salt; add about 8 peppercorns and the cloves; dot with butter. Next, if you like, put in the potatoes, well-scrubbed but not peeled – one per person, or more if they're small; they turn the soup into a meal, a filling one, on American chowder lines. Arrange the cleaned fish on top – eel should be cut into chunks. Cover with wine, or wine and water; bring to the boil and simmer for half an hour or more. Remove the fish to a warm plate as it's cooked, do the same with the potatoes. Reduce the liquid to half by boiling down, and correct the seasoning. Restore fish and potatoes to the pot and serve immediately.

La Migourée de Matata

A finer soup of more elaborate preparation than the *chaudrée*; although the ingredients are much the same, the extra details make quite a difference.

Migourée is a local word from *mijoter*, to simmer – an appropriate name for the soup, as you'll see from the recipe. And *mijoter* – this is the nice part – originally meant to bring fruit to ripeness in a storing place or *mijot*. I can't think of a better definition of the purpose of simmering – to bring the food to ripeness, to wait patiently and let it ripen in its own time, having provided the right circumstances.

Like the last recipe, this comes from *Recettess de Provinces de France*, chosen by Curnonsky.

6 servings:

1 litre white wine	salt, pepper
1 litre water	spices
2 onions, chopped	2 oz. olive oil
4 shallots, chopped	6 oz. butter
2 cloves garlic, chopped	3 lb. fish: cod, angler, skate,
bouquet garni of parsley,	squid, conger, grey mullet,
plenty of thyme, tarragon	gurnard etc.
and a large bay leaf	1 heaped tablespoon flour

Put wine, water, onion, shallots, garlic, herbs and seasonings into a wide pan. Simmer for 3 hours until the quantity has reduced by half, more or less. Meanwhile, cut up the fish, and brown it lightly in the oil and half the butter (as Curnonsky says, the greater the variety, the better the *migourée*). Mash the flour with the remaining butter and gradually stir the mixture, *beurre manié*, into the wine *bouillon*, to thicken it. Add the browned fish and simmer for 10–20 minutes to complete the cooking. Be careful not to overcook the fish. Correct the seasoning and serve very hot with croûtons of fried bread.

Breton Conger Eel Soup

A good homely soup, to which extra vegetables can be added to taste; for instance soaked haricot beans, a small amount of turnip, or onion.

6 servings:

1½ lb. conger eel	*bouquet garni*
2 large leeks	salt, pepper
14 oz. tin tomatoes	oil
1½ lb. potatoes, peeled	

Cut the conger eel into thick slices; then cook gently with the leeks in a large saucepan, with just enough oil to cover the base of the pan in a thin layer. Don't let them brown, but turn them about for 5 minutes. Add 3 pints of water. When it boils, add the tomatoes, the potatoes cut into dice, and the *bouquet garni*. Simmer for 45 minutes, skimming off the murky looking foam which rises. Remove the conger eel, discard the skin and bones and return the pieces to the soup. Discard, too, the *bouquet*. Correct the seasoning and serve.

Bouillabaisse, Bourride and Cacciucco

These Mediterranean stews have an air of romantic gastronomy about them. Their reality is in fact as simple as Atlantic *chaudrées* and chowders. The cook assembles whatever freshly caught fish he can, stews them in water with vegetables, embellishes them with such grace notes as the district can offer, and serves the whole thing up with bread. Of course if the local fish include lobster, John Dory and squid, the local vegetables huge sweet tomatoes and onions, and the grace notes olive oil, saffron and garlic, the stew is likely to be a winner.

At the opposite end of existence, it can be perfectly disgusting. A friend told me recently that his grandmother once went into a dark cottage in the Highlands of Scotland. There she saw a woman, apparently alone except for a cow, stirring a pot over the fire. In a few moments she poured the contents of the pot on to a pile of heather in front of the hearth. And from a shadowy hole in the wall darted two filthy children, who grabbed as many potatoes and raggy herrings as they could, and darted back again to eat them in obscurity. The liquor drained away through the heather stalks to be soaked up by the mud floor. That woman's resources were poor, her skills undeveloped, in such circumstances of life; but the method of cooking the stew was the same as the one used by any Marseillais fisherman to make his *bouillabaisse*. The result could have been perfectly edible, if the fish hadn't been overcooked, and if there had been plenty of butter to eat with it.

In other words, it's the clemency of nature plus the skill of the cook which makes everyone seek out *bouillabaisse*, *bourride* or *cacciucco* rather than tatties an' herrin'. Another sad truth about such dishes is that they cannot be reproduced elsewhere, not satisfactorily. Even if by some magic, you could acquire a spiny and beautiful *rascasse* (scorpionfish), always claimed to be the key fish of *bouillabaisse*, along with the other proper ingredients, the results in Manchester or Milwaukee can never come up to the real thing in Marseilles. Cooking – thank heavens – still knows this particular disillusionment, in spite of the universal sameness of frozen food. In the autumn I always bring back tomatoes from France, olive oil, sea salt, fresh basil, yet the tomato salad I make in Wiltshire never tastes the same as it did when I used the same ingredients in France two days earlier. If you do not believe me, reflect on the unsuccessful efforts made to produce Scotch whisky outside Scotland.

Of course there is no reason why you shouldn't use the recipes for your own entertainment. But to avoid disillusion, remember the uniqueness of local food when you visit an inland restaurant far from France, which has *bouillabaisse* on the menu, at a reverential price.

Bourride and *cacciucco* are less sacrosanct. They, after all, were not 'discovered' by Prosper Merimée, the French writer who was a friend of Napoleon III. *Bouillabaisse* comes into his *Colomba* (1840). Cookery writers have since tried to give it a pedigree, and have traced it, with a considerable number of gaps, back to a recipe given by the Roman gastronome Apicius for scorpionfish. For a longer discussion of *bouillabaisse*, turn to *The French at Table* by Raymond Oliver, or to Elizabeth David's *French Provincial Cooking* (Penguin). She gives two excellent recipes; here is a third, from a Marseilles restaurant, the *Brasserie des Catalans*:

Bouillabaisse

The interesting thing about *bouillabaisse* and *bourride* is that the fish is removed from the soup, but served with it; and the enrichment is provided by large bowls of *ailloli* (p. 56) and *rouille* (p. 57). The bread is toasted, then fried in olive oil, and finally rubbed with garlic before being put into a basket for the table. As the soup itself doesn't take long to cook, prepare all the accompanying dishes first.

6–8 servings:

Use the following kinds of fish: *rascasse* or scorpionfish (*Scorpaena scrofa*); monk or angler-fish; conger eel; John Dory; weaver; *galinette* or gurnard; crawfish or spiny lobster; Dublin bay prawns or scampi; mussels (if prawns are not available).

6¼ lb. fresh fish
4 oz. olive oil
2 large onions, chopped
white part of 2 leeks, chopped
4–6 cloves garlic
2 huge tomatoes, peeled and
  chopped
parsley, fennel
small chili
good pinch saffron filaments

cayenne pepper, salt
4 potatoes, sliced
5 pints water, warm
garnish:
12 slices French bread, toasted
  lightly in the oven, fried in
  olive oil and rubbed with
  garlic
bowl of *rouille*, p. 57
bowl of *ailloli*, p. 56

Sort out the fish and clean them. Put oil, vegetables (except potatoes), herbs, and seasonings into a large pot. Add the thickest fish (conger, monk or angler) on top of the vegetables, and top with slices of potato. Pour on the water, bring to the boil and boil hard (this enables the water and oil to thicken together). After 5 minutes add the crawfish. After another 5 minutes add the Dublin Bay prawns, and John Dory. After another 5 minutes add the rest of the fish, and the mussels if you are not using Dublin Bay prawns. Boil 4–5 minutes.

Remove fish and potatoes to a hot serving dish, split the crawfish head in two and slice the tail. Prawns and mussels are left in their shells. Taste the soup and correct the seasoning. Boil hard for a few moments, then pour through a strainer into a soup tureen. Serve immediately with the fish and potatoes, the bread and sauces.

The correct wine is a *rosé de Provence*, well chilled. Other *rosé* wines can be substituted.

Note. A friend told me the other day that the water by Marseilles is becoming so polluted that the fisherman's *bouillabaisse*, caught and cooked on the spot, is becoming impossible to contemplate with serenity . . .

_____

Bourride

Any firm white fish can be used; one alone, or a mixture. The ideal fish is monkfish, turbot or John Dory, but squid make an excellent *bourride* as well. Saffron is occasionally used to scent and colour the soup, but the most usual flavouring is orange peel, one or two good strips of it, preferably from a Seville orange. The *ailloli* is used to thicken the soup. Croûtons rubbed with garlic are served with it, as with *bouillabaisse*. Potatoes can be cooked and presented separately, or included in the soup.

6 servings:

3–4 lb. firm white fish, or squid	1 lb. potatoes sliced (see above)
2 large onions, chopped	salt, pepper
1 leek, chopped	*ailloli*
4 cloves garlic	*garnish:*
strips of orange peel	12 slices French bread, toasted
bouquet of herbs: thyme, fennel, parsley, bay	lightly in the oven, fried in olive oil, and rubbed with
2 tomatoes (optional)	garlic

Clean the fish and cut into good-sized slices. Put onions, leek, garlic, tomatoes, and potatoes (if included), into a large pot. Lay the fish on top, with the herbs, orange peel, and seasoning. Add 2 pints of water, or enough to cover the fish; stock made from head and bones of fish can be used instead for a finer result; in some places sea water is used. Cook *gently* for 10 minutes at simmering point. Remove fish, and potatoes, to a warm serving plate. Boil the liquor hard to less than a pint Correct the seasoning. Then strain slowly on to the *ailloli*, in a large bowl, mixing the two together carefully. Return to a clean pan and stir over a low heat until the mixture thickens slightly. Pour over the fish, sprinkle with extra parsley, and serve with bread as above, and with potatoes if not included in the soup-making.

Cacciucco Alla Livornese

Cacciucco is the fish stew of Leghorn and the coast thereabouts – the north of Italy's west coast. It's black, black as Chinese ink; and the first time I encountered it, only a well-drilled upbringing prevented me from asking for something else – and from missing one of the best experiences in European food. A family friend, an Italian, and his wife descended on Florence where I was a student. They took me to Viareggio for the day. At a small restaurant at lunchtime this strange dish appeared. Being poor, I was excessively hungry, which no doubt helped my manners, and I dipped my spoon in carefully. *Cacciucco* turned out to be the best thing I had ever eaten. Afterwards we sat on a fallen pine tree on the beach to digest our food. We looked towards the thunderous Carrara mountains, white against purple-grey, as Mario talked about the Etruscans and their strange, hidden gaiety. And about this soup.

The recipe comes from Ada Boni's *Italian Regional Cooking* (Nelson). It produces a good dish even if you are not in Italy; more successful, I think, than an effort to recreate *bouillabaisse*. Use squid, small octopus, cuttlefish; *plus* eel, shrimps, prawns, gurnard, whiting, hake, red mullet, John Dory, crawfish or spiny lobster.

6–8 servings:

4–5 lb. fish	1 sprig thyme
1 large onion, finely chopped	2 lb. tomatoes, peeled and
1 medium carrot, finely chopped	chopped, or a can
2 stalks celery, finely chopped	salt, pepper
2 sprigs parsley, finely chopped	olive oil
2 cloves garlic, crushed	½ pint red wine
2 small hot chili peppers	12–18 slices toasted or fried
2 bay leaves	bread

Clean the fish, cut off their heads and put them aside. Cut the larger fish, including the squid, eel, cuttlefish and octopus, into pieces. Put them into a shallow dish and leave for 30 minutes sprinkled with salt, pepper and olive oil.

Meanwhile, heat 6–8 tablespoons olive oil in a large pan. Add the vegetables, parsley, garlic, chilies, bay leaves, thyme and finally the fish heads. Brown the heads well, moisten with wine, and continue cooking until this has reduced. Add tomatoes and about 2½ pints water. Season and continue cooking for 30 minutes. Rub the soup through a fine sieve.

In another large pan, preferably an earthenware one, heat another 6–8 tablespoons olive oil. Add the squid, cuttlefish and octopus, and cook these for 15 minutes. Add the crawfish and shrimps or prawns, and 5 minutes later the remaining fish. Add salt if necessary, and plenty of pepper, and cook for another 10 minutes.

Fry in oil or toast in the oven the slices of bread. Put these in the bottom of a large soup tureen or into large individual soup bowls. Add the fish and pour the soup over the top.

Note: crush the squid ink sacs (see p. 196) with a little water, and cook with the fish heads etc.

The Flat-fish

Sole, Turbot & other Flatfish

For the scientist the two main groups of flat-fish are the *Pleuronectidae*, the side-swimmers (halibut, turbot, plaice, flounders, dabs), and the *Soleidae* (which include Dover sole or common sole, lascar sole, and thickback sole).

For the practical cook, flat-fish fall into two different groups, small (plaice, sole, dabs), and enormous (halibut and turbot). Recipes are divided in this way in most cookery books, including this one. First there are recipes suitable for all the small flat-fish, then slightly different ones for steaks and fillets from the huge fish.

For the lover of good things, though, these groups are immaterial. There are only two flat-fish – the sole and the turbot. They shine out among all the fish of the seas. They are in the top class, along with trout and salmon caught from stream and river, with eel, lobster, and crayfish. All the other flat-fish are ghostly reflections of these two. Plaice can be cooked in the manner of sole, brill in the manner of turbot: but they won't taste the same, nowhere near the same. Which is not to say that they won't be enjoyable and worth cooking at a more median level. A very fresh, grilled lemon sole can be delicious.

The flat-fish sold in America is rather different. Turbot, brill and plaice are unknown in American waters and so is the true European sole. Plenty of flat-fish are labelled sole but they invariably belong to the flounder family. Small quantities of imported European sole and turbot can be found in fish markets in large cities.

The Sole (Sole)

It must be confessed that the life history of the sole is not entertaining, delicious though it may taste. Mostly it lies supine on the bed of the sea, dark side up, attracting as little attention as possible. Its name means 'flat', like the sole of the foot. The most dramatic episode of its life – to the outside observer – is when the left eye of the perfectly normal, fish-shaped larva moves up and over the head to the right side, as the sole flattens into its characteristic shape. But then, this happens to the humblest of the flat-fish, one way or the other (sometimes the right eye moves to the left side, as with the turbot). The sole also shares the chameleon quality of other flat-fish, though not with such enthusiasm as the plaice, whose rust-coloured spots change to white when it lies on a pebbly patch of the sea-bed.

But why should we expect the sole to astonish or entertain us, to provide us with the pleasures of intellectual excitement? Such expectations seem tawdry by comparison with its gift of exquisite flavour and firm but dissolving texture. The sole is the darling of the sea, of all the things we eat the greatest stimulus to chefly lyricism. It's cherished in cream and good wine, set off by muscat grapes, truffles, mushrooms and shellfish, yet is arguably at its most beautiful when unadorned by amorous attentions, when served à la meunière or plainly grilled, with no more fuss than a few pieces of lemon.

The secret of the sole's flavour is, it appears, no more than an accident of chemistry. 'The palatability of a fish,' explains J. R. Norman in A History of Fishes, 'is due to the presence of some peculiar chemical substance in the muscles which gives it its characteristic flavour . . . In the Plaice, as in most other fishes, the chemical substance is present in the flesh when the fish is alive, but unless it is eaten soon after capture this soon fades away and the flesh becomes comparatively tasteless. In the Sole, on the other hand, the characteristic flavour is only developed two or three days after death in consequence of the formation of a chemical substance by the process of decomposition; thus it forms a tasty dish even when brought long distances.'

What a shame that this accident should not have happened to the superabundant plaice. In Europe every year between 100 and 120 thousand tons of plaice are landed, over four times the weight of sole, and more than all the other flat-fish put together.

Here are some of those other flat-fish which may be cooked in the style of sole (but need more culinary attentions):

TORBAY SOLE OR WITCH. A beautiful pinkish-purple marble-skinned creature, not unlike the sole in its blunted shape. You can be caught out both by the name and appearance of this fish, if you're not too familiar with the true sole, the one and only *Solea solea*. The French name is *plie grise*.

LEMON SOLE. Has the delightful Latin name of *Microstomus kitt*, and a decidedly yellowish-brown appearance. Again not a true sole. Other names are merry or Mary Sole, and sweet fluke. French name *sole-limande*, which is thoroughly confusing because –

THE DAB. Is called a *limande* in French, and has more right to the name, seeing that it's *Limanda limanda* in scientific terminology (from the latin *lima*, a file, on account of its rough skin).

MEGRIM, WHIFF, SAIL-FLUKE, OR WEST COAST SOLE. Has a thinner, translucent appearance, and the name of *Lepidorhombus whiff-iagonis* – there's invention for you. *Cardine* in French.

THE FLOUNDER OR FLUKE. Has a poor reputation, and is not particularly good to eat, though it hardly deserves one description which compares it to wet flannel. I suppose one must here specify European flounder (Fr. *Flet*) because in America 'flounder' in-cludes a number of flat-fish that can be good eating when they are freshly caught. The names vary in different parts of the US, but the most common varieties are black back (winter) flounder, summer flounder (fluke), dab (yellowtail), gray sole and lemon sole.

The average weight of a sole is about 12 oz. Some are larger, some can be tiny. In France we buy very cheaply minute creatures, 3–4 inches long, called *séteaux*. They are a true sole and quite good eating for this reason, in spite of their small size. They are not, as we at first thought, infant Dover soles, but a species on their own, first recognized I believe by Jonathan Couch, the great naturalist of Polperro in Cornwall, in the last century.

At present prices, a 12–14 oz. sole has to do for two people. For a meal which may have several courses, this is not unreasonable. Better to eat a small amount of something delicious (and fill the corners up with some good bread) than a lot of something mediocre. Ask the fishmonger to skin it for you, and grab the skin before he throws it into the waste bucket; this will give you the opportunity of asking him for the bones and skin of other flat-fish which he has filletted already, so that you have the all-important basic material for fish stock for the sauce. If you have to skin the fish yourself, make a cut across, just above the tail. Ease the skin a little with a pointed knife, and pull it off. Do the same thing with the other side.

I have a preference for cooking fish whole, on the bone, complete with head, but there are times when they must be filleted. This is easy with flat-fish. Run a small, sharp knife along the central division of one side. Then scrape gently from the head end of the centre towards the side, keeping the knife close to the bone, until the whole fillet is raised. Repeat on the other side of the central division. Turn the fish over, and remove the last two fillets in the same way.

Grilled Sole

Choose fish of about 8–10 oz., and allow one for each person (reflect that you will be saving money on sauce and garnishing). They need to be skinned both sides, the heads left on.

Brush with butter – clarified butter gives the best results in colour and flavour – and cook for about 5 minutes a side. Time depends, obviously, on the thickness rather than the weight of the fish. Do not salt before grilling, but serve with two or three pats of savoury butter arranged down the centre of each sole (see p. 22). The usual one is *maître d'hôtel* (parsley and lemon), but you might like to try something different for a change. The butter, melting in the heat of the fish, forms a small amount of concentrated sauce which gives all the seasoning required.

Sometimes grilled sole is served with a sauce, a proper sauce, but it is usually one of pronounced flavour, as in this recipe:

Fillets of Sole Saint-Germain

A delicious recipe for summertime, when fresh tarragon is available
for the *sauce béarnaise*.

6 servings:

12 fillets of sole	salt, pepper
1 lb. new potatoes, scraped and diced	seasoned flour
	breadcrumbs
6 oz. butter	*sauce béarnaise*, p. 41

First clarify the butter (see p. 21), and strain it into a frying pan
which is off the heat. Dip the sole fillets in flour and shake off all
surplus. Pour off a little of the clarified butter into a bowl, and with
a brush spread it over the sole fillets, then press them gently but
firmly in breadcrumbs. Put the frying pan on to the heat and cook
the potato dice, stirring them about so that they brown evenly.
Keep the heat moderate. Season the potatoes when done.

Meanwhile grill the sole under a low to moderate heat to avoid
burning the breadcrumbs. Allow about 10 minutes, turning them
over at half time.

Arrange the grilled sole on a serving dish, surround with the
potatoes, and serve with *sauce béarnaise* (which the prudent cook
will have made in advance of cooking the fish and potatoes, leaving
it to keep warm over a pan of hot water. Hot, not boiling or even
simmering water).

Note. Grilled sole and potatoes fried in clarified butter can also
be served with *sauce Choron*, p. 42, which is a *béarnaise* flavoured
with tomato purée. Sprinkle the potatoes with a little chopped
parsley before arranging them on the serving dish.

Sole sur le Plat

One of the simplest ways of cooking a sole is to bake it in the oven,
preferably with wine. There are many variations possible with this
excellent method.

The recipes which follow are all for 2 people; they require a sole from 14–16 oz.

2 servings:

1 sole skinned	½ glass dry white wine
salt, pepper	½ glass water or fish *fumet*
lump of butter	juice of ½ lemon

Season the sole. Put it into an ovenproof dish, which has been well-buttered. Pour over it the wine, water or *fumet*, and lemon juice. Bake for 15 minutes, at moderate heat mark 4, 350°F. basting from time to time. Put for 2 minutes under a very hot grill, before serving, to glaze the fish.

Variations

BONNE FEMME. (2 servings.) Cook 1 chopped shallot and 3 oz. of chopped mushrooms in 2 oz. of butter. Add a tablespoon of parsley and spread out on an oval ovenproof dish. Put the seasoned sole on top; add white wine, water or *fumet* and lemon juice as above. When the sole is cooked, transfer to a serving dish and thicken the sauce with *beurre manié* (see p. 21). Pour over the sole, glaze, and serve.

SOLE SUR LE PLAT AUX MOULES. (2 servings.) Open one pint of mussels in the usual way; remove from their shells. Use the strained mussel liquor to replace the water in the *sole sur le plat* recipe, and add a shallot chopped almost to pulp. When the sole is cooked, place the mussels round it and sprinkle the sole with a mixture of parsley and white breadcrumbs. Cook a moment or two longer under the grill and serve.

SOLE MÉNAGÈRE. (2 servings.) Substitute all red wine for the white wine and water in the *sole sur le plat* recipe. Omit lemon juice. Add a sliced onion and a *bouquet garni*. Thicken with *beurre manié* (see p. 21). Stir in a piece of butter. Glaze in the usual way.

If a well-known red wine is used, the dish adopts its name and becomes, for instance, *sole au Chambertin*, or *sole au Clos-Vougeot*. Garnish with strips of sole fillet, floured, and crisply fried in butter.

SOLE MORNAY. (2 servings.) Sole baked in fish *fumet*, in the usual well-buttered dish. Strain liquor into 6–8 tablespoons béchamel sauce, and cook together, until moderately thick. Put half this sauce on a serving dish, then the sole, then the rest of the sauce. Sprinkle with grated Gruyère and Parmesan, mixed, and glaze under a hot grill.

As an alternative, the fish may be baked in white wine.

SOLE DUGLÉRÉ. (2 servings.) This dish was invented by the famous Adolphe Dugléré, chef at the Café Anglais, in Paris, in the middle of the last century (*sole Mornay* was another popular dish there). It can easily be adapted to round fish, such as bass, they are cut across into sections before being arranged in order in the cooking platter. The quantities of onion, tomato and wine need to be increased according to the size of the fish. Here is the recipe for sole, which should be skinned and no more.

Butter an ovenproof dish. Put the sole into it with 1½ oz. chopped onion, 8 oz. peeled and chopped tomato, a good tablespoon of parsley and 4 oz. of dry white wine. Season. Bake in the usual way. When the sole is cooked, transfer it to a heated serving dish and reduce the cooking liquor by about a quarter. Thicken with *beurre manié* (see p. 21), and add a final knob of butter when the sauce is removed from the heat. Correct the seasoning, and sharpen with a little lemon juice. Pour over the sole and serve.

SOLE FLORENTINE. (2 servings.) Bake the sole in fish *fumet*, in a buttered dish. Spread a layer of cooked, well drained, and buttered spinach on a serving dish. Lay the sole on top. Cover with Mornay sauce (p. 26), then sprinkle on some grated cheese – Gruyère and Parmesan are best – and glaze under a hot grill.

Paupiettes de Soles Sophie

The simple method of baking sole in the oven (or poaching it), can be elaborated into the favourite restaurant dish of *paupiettes de soles*. Fillets, spread with some delicious mixture, are rolled into a neat shape and cooked in white wine, or wine and stock: the cooking liquor is finally used in the making of a creamy sauce. Although such dishes look pretty and often taste agreeable, I do confess to a preference for sole on the bone; it keeps more of its natural flavour when cooked that way. But I make an exception for this recipe from *Les Recettes Secrètes des Meilleurs Restaurants de France* (Albin Michel, 1972). At first the title and ingredients were irresistible; then I found that the smoked salmon adds a most delicious flavour to the sauce, an unexpected piquancy.

Here you have the basic recipe for all *paupiettes* of fish; it can be adapted to humble herring fillets or varied to make many dishes of sole, lemon sole and turbot. The fish bones can be used to make a little stock to go with the white wine when a larger amount of sauce is required.

8 servings:

16 fillets of sole	*mushroom duxelles:*
8 oz. dry white wine: Chablis or Sancerre	1 lb. mushrooms, chopped
2 oz. butter	2 oz. butter
salt and pepper	lemon juice, salt, pepper
	2 generous tablespoons thick cream
salmon butter:	
4–6 oz. smoked salmon	*sauce:*
2 oz. butter softened	2 large egg yolks
lemon juice, pepper, salt	3 generous tablespoons cream

First make the salmon butter. Reduce the smoked salmon to a purée in a liquidizer or moulinette, with the butter. Season to taste with salt, pepper and lemon juice.

Season the cut side of each sole fillet; spread with salmon butter and roll up – use cocktail sticks to keep the fillets in shape. Butter an oval ovenproof dish and place the rolled fillets in it, packed closely together, side by side. Pour the white wine over them. Bring the liquid to the boil, cover with aluminium foil, and either place in a moderate oven for up to 10 minutes (mark 4, 350°F.) or leave to simmer gently on top of the stove for 5–7 minutes, turning the *paupiettes* once. Whichever method you use, do not overcook the fish.

Meanwhile cook the mushrooms quickly in the butter. Season with salt, pepper and lemon juice. Remove from the heat, stir in the cream and put onto a warm serving dish.

Pour cooking liquid off the sole into a measuring jug; then into a saucepan, and reduce it by half. Beat the egg yolks and cream together, stir a tablespoon or two of the reduced liquid into this mixture; return to the saucepan and cook slowly without boiling until thick. Place *paupiettes* on the mushrooms, coat them with the sauce and serve. At the Domaine de la Tortinière at Montbazon, where this dish is on the menu, 16 small fish shapes are cut out of a piece of smoked salmon and used to garnish the *paupiettes*.

Filets de Sole Véronique

'Monsieur Malley, *saucier* at the Paris Ritz and later *chef des cuisines* at the London Ritz, was my professional ideal . . .' writes Louis Diat, the inventor of *crème Vichyssoise glacée*. 'Malley had a fertile mind, and many of the fish sauces served in good restaurants today were originated by him. *Filets de sole Véronique*, for instance, was a Malley invention. A special party was planned, and Malley decided to add tiny white grapes to the white-wine sauce for the fish course. He gave instructions to a trusted under-chef, and went out, as usual, for the afternoon. When he returned, he found the young man so excited that he could hardly work. Monsieur Malley discovered that the young man's wife had just presented him with a baby girl, their first child. Monsieur Malley asked what they would name the child. '*Véronique*,' was the reply. '*Alors*,' said the *chef des cuisines*, 'we'll call the new dish *filets de sole Véronique*.' And so it is called to this day.'

4 servings:

8 fine fillets of sole	¼ pint béchamel sauce, p. 25
2 oz. butter	1 egg yolk
2 shallots, or ½ small onion, finely chopped	4 tablespoons double cream
¼ pint dry white wine	½–¾ lb. seedless white grapes or muscatels
¼ pint water	salt, pepper

Grease a shallow pan with 1 tablespoon of butter, and put in the chopped shallot or onion. Roll up the fillets of sole, salting and peppering them first, and secure with a cocktail stick. Arrange them on top of the onion. Pour in wine and water, cover with foil, and either simmer on top of the stove for about 10 minutes, or else bake in a hot oven (mark 7, 425°F.) for 15 minutes. (The first way is best.) When the fillets are just cooked, transfer them to a heatproof serving dish and keep them warm.

Strain the cooking liquid into a clean pan and boil it down to half a pint. Stir in the béchamel sauce, which should be on the firm side, and 2 tablespoons of cream, beaten up with the egg yolk. Cook without boiling until the sauce thickens nicely, stirring all the time. Place the pan over another pan of simmering water, so that it keeps warm, without further cooking, while you finish the recipe.

Whisk the remaining 2 tablespoons of cream until they're light and stiff. Heat the grapes through in just-boiling water, then arrange them round the fish. Stir the last 2 tablespoons of butter into the sauce to give a good gloss and flavour. Lastly fold in the whipped cream and pour the sauce over fish and grapes. Brown lightly under a hot grill and serve immediately.

Note. Small seedless grapes do not have a long season, neither do the muscatel grapes recommended by Elizabeth David as the right ones for this fine and delicate dish.

If the only white grapes on sale are the coarser Almerian, which will need skinning and de-pipping, buy a cheaper fish and follow the recipe on p. 147 for *bass or bream à la vendangeuse*. (I wonder if this country dish was the original inspiration for M. Malley's *sole Véronique?*)

Sole à la Meunière

The miller has rarely enjoyed the respectful admiration of his fellow citizens. (Old remarks such as: 'Hair grows in the palm of an honest miller', were brought up to date not so long ago by an actress who described her ex-boss, owner of many flour mills and cinemas, as having 'the sack in one hand and corn in the other'.) But the miller's wife, *la meunière*, is another matter. In cooking at least her reputation is high. What could be more delicious than a fresh trout or sole, dipped in flour and fried golden brown in butter?

A simple dish perhaps, but there is a snag. Butter burns at a low temperature. If you don't want your beautiful fish to come to table with a covering of black flecks, you must clarify the butter first. This is easy; bring it to the boil in a small pan, and after a few bubblings let it stand for a moment or two, then pour it into the frying pan through a damp muslin-lined sieve. All the salty white particles which catch the heat will be left behind.

4 servings:

4 whole sole, skinned, or 8 large fillets seasoned flour	8 oz. butter lemon quarters sprigs of parsley

Clarify 4 oz. of the butter. Turn the fillets or skinned sole in seasoned flour and shake off the surplus. Fry until golden brown in the clarified butter, turning once. Remove to a hot serving dish and garnish with the parsley sprigs and lemon quarters. Wipe the pan out with kitchen paper. Put the remaining butter into the pan and rapidly bring it to a golden brown foam. Pour this over the fish and rush to table. Not a dish to be kept hanging around.

Variations of Sole à la Meunière

Sole meunière is a beautiful dish. It really doesn't need decoration. But then, at certain times of the year when the fishmonger's repertoire is poor, when we're working hard and need light food, I seem to be cooking it a lot and I want to disguise the fact. And with the lesser breeds of flat-fish *à la meunière*, something extra is needed to take people's minds off the fact that they are not eating sole.

Two observations – always prepare the garnish in advance so that the sole has to wait as little time as possible once it's been cooked; and do not be too lavish or too ingenious. (I was once sent a leaflet urging me to pour a tin of Californian fruit cocktail over fillets of sole.)

a) *aux amandes*. Cook 3–4 oz. flaked almonds, in the final four four ounces of butter, until they are golden brown.

b) *aux champignons*. 8 oz. sliced mushrooms lightly fried in the final four ounces of butter. If *ceps* are available, or *morels*, so much the better.

c) Peel and dice half a cucumber. Sprinkle with salt and leave to drain in a colander for at least an hour. Rinse and squeeze dry. Cook in final four ounces butter, with a sprinkling of sugar to caramelize the cucumber slightly.

d) Skin and pip ¾ lb. large grapes. Heat them in the final four ounces of butter.

e) Put a line of trimmed orange slices down each sole. Serve with small pats of orange butter (p. 22), and omit the final four ounces of butter in the recipe.

f) As above, but substitute lime slices for orange and use lime butter.

g) *à la marocaine*. Cook 1½ lb. peeled, chopped tomatoes in the last four ounces of butter, for 20 minutes. Season well. Stir in 1½ tablespoons *Grand Marnier cordon rouge* and pour over sole immediately.

h) Serve on a bed of well-buttered, well-drained spinach, surrounded by small new potatoes which have been boiled, and finally turned in parsley butter.

Soles aux Crêpes

This recipe may not sound exciting, but we enjoyed it very much one cold rainy night in Bayeux, at the Hôtel du Lion d'Or. We were tired after a protracted visit to the Bayeux Tapestry. We needed just this kind of dish, appetisingly buttery but light. I do recommend it.

4 servings:

Ingredients for *soles meunière*, p. 99	2 tablespoons oil or melted butter
pancake batter:	good pinch salt
2 oz. flour	about ¼ pint milk and water
1 large egg	mixed

Sieve the flour into a basin. Make a well in the middle and pour in the oil or butter, the egg, and a little milk and water. Mix together, adding more liquid to produce the usual pancake consistency. Grease a frying pan or griddle with a butter paper and cook the pancakes (about 3 or 4; it doesn't matter). Roll each one up and cut into thin slices; this will give you a pile of pancake ribbons.

Prepare the *soles meunière*. Transfer the fish to a warm serving plate and clean out the pan. In the last four ounces of butter, *sauté* the pancake ribbons until they are buttery and hot. Stir in plenty of chopped parsley and arrange on top of the sole. Put the lemon quarters round, and serve immediately.

Sole Colbert

When buying sole for this dish, be sure you know the width of your frying basket. If they are too large for it, the whole appearance will be spoiled.

6 servings:

6 sole, skinned	white breadcrumbs
milk	*beurre Colbert*, p. 22
seasoned flour	parsley to garnish
beaten egg	

Make a cut down the centre of one side of each sole. Slide the knife in so that the flesh is eased away from the bone, without the fillet being removed. Snip the backbone at each end and in the centre (this is to make it easily removable when the fish is cooked). Roll back the cut edges a little to make an opening in the fish.

Dip the sole in milk, then in flour, then in egg and finally in breadcrumbs, making sure they have a good coating. Deep-fry one at 360°, until golden-brown and cooked. Remove the pieces of backbone; leave to drain on kitchen paper in the oven until cooking is completed. Fill the openings with pats of *beurre Colbert*, and garnish with sprigs of parsley.

Sogliole Alla Parmigiana

Sole baked with parmesan cheese is piquant, and appetizing, a favourite Italian dish. But the only recipe I have ever found for it comes from Elizabeth David's *Italian Food* (Penguin):

'Have medium sized soles, one for each person, skinned on both sides. Lay them in a buttered flame-proof dish, well seasoned with salt and pepper, and with more butter on the top. Let them brown gently, and turn them over so that they brown on the other side. Spread a thin layer of grated Parmesan over the top of each and add 1 tablespoonful of chicken or fish broth for each sole. Cover the pan and simmer slowly for 5 minutes, until the soles are cooked through and the cheese melted. Serve in the dish in which they have cooked, with halves of lemon and a green salad. The cooking can be done in the oven instead of on top of the stove.'

Goujons de Sole

Goujons de sole means that the fillets of the fish have been cut into narrow strips more or less of the size of freshwater gudgeon. Other flat-fish can also be used, but they lack the close firmness of sole: a better economy is to buy a half quantity of sole and add about the same amount of potatoes, also cut into strips.

6–8 servings:

6–8 large fillets of sole or 3–4 fillets, plus 3–4 potatoes	4 oz. clarified butter, p. 21 lemon quarters and parsley to garnish

Cut sole, or sole and potatoes, into strips. Fry them in clarified butter until golden brown (start the potatoes first, then add the fish when they're almost ready). Remove to a hot serving plate and garnish with lemon quarters and parsley.

Serve, if you like, with brown bread and unsalted butter, and a mayonnaise type of sauce such as *ailloli* (p. 56).

A most excellent dish as long as you keep people waiting for it: not the dish waiting for people. It should go straight from pan to table.

Filets de Sole à la Normande

If a dish requires extra time and attention, a cookery writer is supposed to be apologetic. I fail to see why. People spend hours in a dark room, or watching birds. Why shouldn't a cook be allowed to enjoy an hour or two with an interesting occupation? *Sole normande* is certainly that. Purists may complain that it can only taste as it should in Normandy (on account of the butter and cream there, which differ from ours in texture and flavour). In fact the dish was probably invented in Paris by Carême – not by a fisherman stirring his iron pot over a driftwood fire in a smoky cabin, not even by the plump wife of some Rouen ship owner (her recipe would be similar to *sole normande à la bourgeoise*, which follows). Of course nowadays the dish in one form or another is on the menu of most self-respecting Normandy restaurants – a tribute to modern communications and cross-fertilization rather than to authenticity.

Serves 6:

12 fillets of sole	1 chopped onion
trimmings and bones of the sole	*bouquet garni*
	salt, pepper
1 bottle of dry cider or dry white wine	8 oz. unsalted Normandy butter
6 oz. prawns in their shells	3 tablespoons flour
6 oz. mushrooms	5 oz. thick cream
2 dozen oysters, or 2 pints mussels	3 yolks of eggs
	lemon juice

Butter an ovenproof dish with 1 oz. of butter. Lay the sole fillets in it. Pour a quarter of a pint of cider over them, plus a little water if it's needed; enough liquid just to cover the sole. Season well and leave to marinate.

Trim the stalks from the mushrooms, shell the prawns. Put stalks and shells into a large pan with the fish bones and trimmings, the onion, *bouquet* and the rest of the bottle of cider. Simmer for half to three quarters of an hour. You should end up with something between ½ and ¾ pint of stock.

Meanwhile cook the halved mushroom caps in 2 oz. butter, so that they stew and exude juice. When they're just tender, strain off the liquid into a basin. Put the mushrooms in a bowl and leave for the moment. Open the oysters and simmer them for a few seconds in their own juice until the edges *just begin* to curl. Drain the juice into the mushroom juice. With mussels, put them into a large pan over a good heat Set the lid on the pan and shake until the mussels start to open. Then strain the mussel juice into the mushroom juice; remove the shells and discard them. Set the shellfish to one side, oysters or mussels and prawns all together.

Make a roux with 2 oz. of butter and the flour, stir in the mushroom and shellfish juice, then the strained fish and cider stock. Simmer gently to mature to a thick consistency. (Now's the time to put the fillets of sole into the fairly hot oven – mark 5, 375°F. – for 15 minutes.) Beat the egg yolks with 3 oz. of cream. Pour in a little of the sauce, then return the mixture to the pan, and stir in the reduced cider from the cooked fillets of sole. Keep stirring over a low heat, without allowing the sauce to boil, and so curdle. As a final enrichment, stir in the remaining 3 oz. of butter and 2 oz. of cream. Correct the seasoning with salt, pepper and lemon juice.

Arrange the fillets of sole on a hot serving dish. Surround with mushrooms, prawns, and oysters or mussels. Pour some of the very hot sauce over the whole thing and put under a hot grill to glaze for a few seconds. The remaining sauce should be poured into a warm sauce boat.

Note. Up to the time of putting the sole into the oven, the recipe can be prepared in advance. The final enrichment and thickening must be done at the last moment.

Sole Normande à la Bourgeoise

A simpler, domestic, version of the grand recipe above.

6 servings:

3 large sole, skinned, or 2¼ lb. sole fillets	¼ pint white wine
	½ pint béchamel sauce, p. 25
2 oz. butter	2 egg yolks
6 oz. mushrooms	3 tablespoons cream
2 dozen large mussels	salt, pepper

Butter an ovenproof dish generously, and lay the sole in it. Season well. Pour over the wine. Open the mussels in the usual way (see last recipe) and strain their liquor over the fish. If the mushrooms are large, slice them and place them round the fish. If they're small to medium, cut them in half. Either bake in a fairly hot oven (mark 5, 375°F.), or simmer over a low heat until the fish is half cooked and the liquid somewhat reduced.

Meanwhile heat the béchamel sauce, which should be about the consistency of double cream – not too thin. Beat the egg yolks and cream together, and use them to thicken the béchamel even further. Pour this sauce over the partially cooked fish and complete the cooking. Keep an eye on the oven, to make sure the sauce doesn't boil and curdle; the wine and mussel liquor will thin the sauce down. Just before serving, put the mussels round the dish and put it under a hot grill for a few seconds.

If the first part of the cooking was carried out on top of the stove, it may be convenient to finish it under the grill, after the addition of the sauce, rather than in the oven.

Sole à la Dieppoise

The classic version of this dish much resembles *sole normande*, the garnish being mussels and shrimps with a *sauce normande*. Here is a simplified version which gives another method of preparing sole in a cream sauce.

6 servings:

3 fine sole, or 6 large fillets	8 oz. thick cream
skins and trimmings of sole	*beurre manié* made from 1
3–4 lb. mussels	tablespoon of butter forked
¼ lb. shelled shrimps or	up with 1 tablespoon of
prawns	flour
2 oz. butter	salt, pepper, parsley

Cover the skins and trimmings, plus the shrimp or prawn shells if you have them, with a pint of water. Season very lightly, and add a couple of sprigs of parsley. Simmer down steadily with the lid off the pan, until you have a ¼ pint of fish stock more or less. Open the mussels in a large pan in the usual way and strain their liquor into the fish stock.

Butter an ovenproof dish and put in the sole. Pour the stock and mussel liquor over the fish and poach it either on top of the stove or in the oven, whichever is most convenient. When the sole is cooked, pour off the liquor into a small pan; arrange mussels and shrimps round the sole and put into the oven to keep warm. Reduce the cooking liquor, by rapid boiling, to a good strong flavour; add the cream, and then the *beurre manié* bit by bit to thicken the sauce – keep it just below boiling point. Pour enough sauce over the sole and garnish to coat them lightly, and glaze by putting the whole thing under the grill for a few seconds. The rest of the sauce should be served in a separate warmed sauce boat.

Sole à la Deauvillaise

Deauville on the coast of Normandy, and its twin town of Trou-ville, were much painted in the time of the Empress Eugenie by Boudin. Dufy has recorded its gaiety in more recent times. I hope the two painters sometimes sustained themselves with this unusual combination of sole with onion.

6 servings:

6 oz. chopped onion	salt, pepper, nutmeg
6 oz. butter	puff pastry diamonds, or
8 oz. thick cream	bread diamonds fried in
4 oz. thin cream	butter, to decorate
3 fine sole, or 6 large fillets	

Melt the onions to a golden purée in 2 oz. of butter. They must not brown. Add the cream, seasoning and a good tablespoon of the remaining butter. Cook the sole in this sauce, either on top of the stove or in the oven (moderate heat, 350–375°F., mark 4–5). Transfer the fish to a serving plate and keep warm. Sieve the sauce into a pan, bring to the boil, remove from the heat, and beat in the last of the butter. Pour over the fish. Decorate with the puff pastry diamonds, or the bread croûtons, and serve straightaway.

Sole Walewska

Coming at last to dinner in a Warwickshire hotel after a long drive, we saw *sole Walewska* on the menu. I remembered that the elegant owner of Arnold Bennett's Imperial Palace Hotel had ordered *sole*

Walewska after a quite extraordinarily trying day. I remembered,
too, that Arnold Bennett knew about fish. (The recipe for omelette
Arnold Bennett is on p. 365.) Anything that soothed his exhausted
hero would certainly soothe us. A long wait. The dish arrived. We
dug into the rather large acreage of sauce, which turned out to be
insipid. When I say sole, I mean *Solea solea*, the Dover, common or
English sole. So did Escoffier, whose beautifully simple recipe is
below. (So, I'm sure, did Marie, Countess Walewska, Napoleon's
Polish mistress.) That Warwickshire chef meant Lemon or Torbay
sole, which in honesty is no more than a jumped-up flounder. He
also thought that two ½-inch cubes of lobster represented a decent
portion of crawfish, and three black specks, truffles. *Moral*: this
recipe tests the generosity, rather than the skill, of the cook. It's
for a celebration.

6 servings:

12 good fillets of sole	2½ oz. butter
fish *fumet*, p. 17, made from sole bones	1 small tin truffles
	sauce Mornay, p. 26
3 crawfish tails, or 1 small lobster	

Make the béchamel part of the Mornay sauce. Poach the crawfish or
lobster in the *fumet*, if they're alive. Shell them, and slice the meat.
(If you like to get the most from the shellfish, use the shells and
2 tablespoons butter to make crawfish butter, p. 23). The recipe up
to this point can be prepared in advance. Just before serving, poach
the sole fillets in the *fumet*. Drain them, and arrange on a hot serving
dish. Reheat crawfish or lobster pieces in 2 tablespoons butter, and
put them round the sole, with the sliced truffles. Add the cheese to
the simmering sauce, pour it over the sole etc. (don't swamp the
dish – any left over can be served in a sauce boat, or kept for another
occasion) and put under the grill for a few moments to glaze and
colour slightly.

Sole à l'Antillaise. See p. 143

Sole with Orange Sauce. See pp. 121 or 124

Tourte Béarnaise with Sole. See p. 132

Turbot, Chicken Turbot, Brill and Topknot
(Turbot, turbotin, barbue and targeur)

One thing I do resent – having to be in France, 150 miles from the sea, before I can buy turbot regularly. No doubt if I lived in London, things would be different, but like most of the population of these islands, I don't. And yet turbot has been vaunted – until recently at any rate – as a national delicacy. Dover sole class, right at the top of life's gastronomic experiences.

Nowadays, visiting grand houses and coming at last to the kitchens, we stand and stare at the diamond-shaped copper turbot-kettles artistically nailed to the wall. Many people in the party (sometimes including the guide) have no idea of the use to which such enormous pans were put. How could they, rarely having seen a lusty, knobble-skinned turbot on the fishmonger's counter?

Turbot is not always of such an aristocratic size. There are small ones, weighing 2–3 lb., which will fit – just – into a particularly large frying pan. Appropriately they're known as chicken turbot, and they make an excellent meal for four to six people on a special occasion. It's wise to cut the fish along the backbone (on the dark, bossed skin side), so that it keeps flat when cooking.

What would you do, though, if you were suddenly faced with a good-sized turbot? Brillat-Savarin once had to solve this problem unexpectedly. He had been invited to dinner in the country, with the promise of turbot. He arrived to find that the turbot was so unexpectedly large that no one had been able to cook it. I suppose a *turbotière* is not usually to be found in small country houses, but Brillat-Savarin knew there would be a basket big enough to hold 50 bottles of wine.

He cut away the sides to make a flat wicker tray, and covered it with chopped onions. The turbot was reverentially laid on top and smothered with more onions. The whole thing was then put on top of the house water-boiler, which still forms part of many French stoves even now. A large semicircular pan was inverted over the top. The turbot was perfectly cooked.

Nowadays the solution lies with foil. And we should, I think, be thankful. The whole fish, wrapped up with seasonings, can then be cooked over a large barbecue grill. Or it can be cut in half, each piece wrapped in foil and baked in a moderate oven (mark 4, 350°F.,) for 40–50 minutes, the two halves to be reunited on the serving dish.

There are not the same problems with brill, which is a smaller fish and not so squarely shaped. In the great days of turbot, in the 19th century, brill was regarded as a poor man's fish. You would not think so from the price today. But it's true that it falls far short of turbot, lacking that tender firmness. Topknot comes even lower on the list. (Sometimes it's called bastard brill.) It is not commonly seen, being on the small side for commercial favour.

Sole recipes can be adapted easily to these three fish, and vice versa. Here are some special turbot recipes, followed by an extravaganza of brill from Madame Prunier, and a simpler way of cooking it as well.

Turbot with Shrimp Sauce

6 servings:

1 chicken turbot
milk, or milk and water
slice of lemon
salt, pepper
1 heaped tablespoon shelled
  shrimps

chopped parsley
either the English or French
  shrimp sauce on pp. 24 and
  31

Put the turbot into a large frying pan or roasting tin (making use of a low rack if possible), light side uppermost. Cover with milk, or with half milk and half water. Add the lemon and a seasoning of salt and pepper.

Bring slowly to the boil and simmer until the fish loses its transparency, coming easily away from the bone in well defined shape like a sole. This takes about 15 minutes.

Have the shrimp sauce ready by the time the turbot is cooked. Slide the fish from the pan, having poured off as much milk as possible, on to a serving dish. (A large old-fashioned meat dish with a pierced strainer is ideal.)

Mix the peeled shrimps with the chopped parsley and scatter them over the turbot (it can look rather pallid, if there's no garnish at all). Serve very hot, with the shrimp sauce in a separate sauce boat.

Note. Fillets can be poached in the same way, but they will require much less time – 8 minutes should be quite enough. Don't leave the turbot bones behind at the fishmongers – if they are boiled with the cooking milk, or milk and water, they make a good gelatinous stock for fish soup.

Turbot Fried in Butter with Mushroom Sauce

We were standing dejectedly, one Wednesday afternoon, by the fish stall at Montoire market, comparing the size of the turbot in front of us with the size of my largest frying pan. Madame Soarès clumped up to us briskly in her Wellington boots. 'Don't worry. I'll cut you a beautiful fillet. *And* I'll give you a recipe. *Extrà!*' In Madame Soarès' hands we are as spineless as squid; she treats us like gentle barbarians who need to be shown the light, and to be pushed a little for their own good. We watched her remove a large section from the majestic creature, then shape two pieces from it of exactly the right size. 'Now,' she said, leaning forward earnestly, 'this is what you do ...'

6 servings:

2–2½ lb. turbot fillets	½ large clove garlic
seasoned flour	3 oz. double cream
6 oz. butter	salt, pepper, lemon juice
¾ lb. mushrooms, sliced	chopped parsley

Ask the fishmonger for six pieces of turbot fillet. Dip them in seasoned flour. Bring 4 oz. of the butter to the boil in a small pan, then pour it into a large frying pan through a cloth-lined strainer. (This is clarified butter – it won't turn black and murky as the

turbot cooks). Heat up the frying pan, and put in the turbot fillets;
turn them over when they're golden brown, and don't let them fry
too fast – particularly if the fillets are very thick ones.

At the same time, put the mushrooms and garlic to simmer in
the remaining 2 oz. of butter in a separate, covered frying pan.
They will produce a fair amount of liquid, if the heat isn't too high.
After 7 or 8 minutes, remove the lid and stir in the cream to
make a sauce with the mushroom juices. Season well with salt,
freshly ground black pepper and lemon juice; turn up the heat to
reduce the sauce if it is too runny – it should be creamy and fairly
thick.

Arrange the cooked turbot fillets on a hot serving dish, pour over
the mushroom sauce and sprinkle with chopped parsley.

Turbot au Poivre

Although *steak au poivre* has now become a national dish, in
England at least, we have not yet followed the French in cooking
fish by the same method. It also works extremely well for firm
steaks of halibut, tunny or monkfish. Surprisingly the strong
pepperiness does not overwhelm the delicate flavour of fish.

6 servings:

6 one-inch thick turbot steaks	4 oz. unsalted butter
salt	2 oz. brandy
2 heaped tablespoons peppercorns	2 oz. port
	¼ pint light beef or veal stock
1 rounded tablespoon flour	¼ pint double cream
1 tablespoon oil	

Salt the fish steaks. Crush the peppercorns coarsely, and mix with
the flour (more pepper can be used, if you like). Coat the fish with
this mixture. Brown it lightly in oil plus 2 oz. of the butter, then
lower the heat until the fish is almost cooked and just beginning to
part from the bone. Flame with brandy, deglaze with port. Pour
in the stock. Remove the fish to a hot serving plate when it is *just*
cooked. Boil the pan juices down slightly, stir in the cream and
continue to boil until the sauce is rich and thick. Correct the

seasoning, stir in remaining butter and pour round the fish. Serve very hot with boiled potatoes.

One of the best fish recipes.

Turbot à la Crème

Occasionally one reads disapproving sentences about wasteful housewives who buy too much, more than is necessary exactly to feed their family. Now the best and most frugal cook I've ever known, widow of a director of Cooks Wagons-Lits in Paris, went out of her way to create remains, buying or making more than she needed quite deliberately. This extra amount was always put aside before the meal was served, never coming to table unless it was absolutely unavoidable. 'There's the beginnings of supper,' she'd say to me as she tucked little pots of this and that into the larder – or 'Now we can make that hors d'oeuvre I was telling you about.' And sure enough 'les restes' would appear on the table – unrecognizable to anyone who hadn't her agility of mind in culinary matters, or who hadn't been let into the secret.

Turbot is such a firm-fleshed and excellent fish that its remains can provide the basis of second dishes which are quite as delicious as the first ones. Buy ½–¾ lb. more than you need, and next day mix it with some very hot béchamel sauce, top it with buttered breadcrumbs and brown under the grill or in a hot oven. Or, more luxuriously, serve Mrs Beeton's *turbot à la crème* in one large or several small *vol-au-vent* cases as the first course at a dinner party. (She also observes that the remains of cold salmon can be dressed in the same way.)

¾ lb. cold turbot	¼ pint double cream
4 oz. butter	salt, cayenne pepper, mace

Remove the skin and bones from the turbot while it's hot (assuming a whole turbot has been cooked; with fillets this is obviously not necessary), and divide it into small even-sized pieces.

Using a frying-pan, melt the butter and then stir in the cream and seasoning. Once these ingredients are amalgamated – it takes a few seconds only – put in the fish pieces and simmer them in the sauce as briefly as possible to heat them through.

Pour into very hot *vol au vent* cases, or on to a hot serving dish bordered by triangular croûtons of bread.

Poached Turbot with Horseradish

At Krogs Restaurant in Copenhagen, they serve the freshest and finest turbot you are ever likely to eat. It is first seasoned and left for a while to absorb the flavour, then it is poached in a well-flavoured *court-bouillon* (p. 16). If you suspect that your fish – turbot is the ideal, but other firm white fish will do very well – is not as fresh as it should be, bake it in buttered foil (inch-thick steaks will take 20 minutes at mark 5, 375°F.).

While the fish is cooking, grate a bowl of fresh horseradish from the outside of the root (the central core is the hot part), and melt 8 oz. of butter in another bowl.

When the fish is served, everyone helps themselves to the horseradish, sprinkling it over the fish. The melted butter is poured over the top. This is really excellent, the horseradish is sweetly piquant, and the butter adds the richness that poached fish requires. A few boiled new potatoes go well with the turbot, too.

Turbot Salad

Divide cooked fish into pieces and arrange them in a dish. Make a vinaigrette sauce (p. 61), flavoured with chopped herbs (parsley, tarragon, chives etc.), a few capers, 3 or 4 anchovy fillets and some hard-boiled egg. Pour over the fish and keep in a cool place for at least 4 hours. Serve chilled, as part of an hors d'oeuvre, or as a course on its own.

Turbot or Brill with Orange Sauce. See pp. 121, 124

Tourte Béarnaise with Turbot. See p. 132.

Kulebiaka. See p. 224.

Filets de Barbue de Prince

This dish, from *Madame Prunier's Fish Cook Book*, was created at her Paris restaurant for the eightieth birthday dinner of Curnonsky, 'the prince of gastronomes'.

6 servings:

6 fillets of brill about 4 oz. each	3 shallots
1¼ lb. fresh salmon	1 lb. 2 oz. tomatoes, peeled and chopped
2 large glasses dry white wine	¼ pint thick cream
thyme, salt, pepper	5 oz. mushrooms, lightly fried
1 egg yolk	4 oz. peeled, cooked shrimps
1 large tablespoon thick cream	crescents of puff pastry, cooked
6 oz. butter	

Slice each fillet of brill across, to make two *escalopes*. Cut from the salmon six *escalopes* of about 2 oz. each. Pour 1 glass of wine over them, season with thyme, salt and pepper, and leave for an hour. With the salmon trimmings make a mousse. Crush, then sieve the salmon, and mix it, on ice, with egg yolk and a tablespoon of cream (use a liquidizer, if possible). Season and spread on the brill *escalopes*.

Drain the salmon *escalopes*, and sandwich each between two *escalopes* of brill, the mousse towards the salmon. Grease an oven-proof dish with 2 oz. butter. Put in shallots and tomato, then the fish 'sandwiches' and pour over them the wine and the remaining salmon marinade. Cook in a fairly hot oven (mark 6; 400°F.), for about 10 minutes or until the fish is done. Transfer to a serving dish and keep warm. Sieve the cooking juices into a wide pan; reduce by three-quarters. Add cream; then, off the heat, the rest of the butter in small pieces. Pour over the fish. Arrange the shrimps, and the mushrooms cut into strips, beside the fish. Glaze in the oven, or under a hot grill for a few seconds, and garnish with reheated puff pastry crescents.

Note. A real restaurant dish, but fun to do if you have some time to spare.

Brill with Vermouth

Dry white vermouth is an excellent wine for cooking fish. When the amount of liquid being used is small, its pronounced flavour gives a better result than dry white wine. Use extra dry Martini, or a French vermouth like Chambéry.

6 servings:

6 large fillets of brill	3 shallots, finely chopped
salt, pepper	1 heaped tablespoon chopped
2 oz. melted butter	parsley
3 oz. butter	10 tablespoons vermouth
8 heaped tablespoons soft	
white breadcrumbs	

Season the fish, using salt and freshly ground white pepper. Brush it with a little of the melted butter, and press it into the breadcrumbs until coated. Grease an ovenproof dish with a butter paper. Place the fillets in it, on top of the shallots and parsley. Pour the vermouth round the sides of the fish. Sprinkle any remaining breadcrumbs on top, and pour the rest of the melted butter over them. Bake in a very hot oven (mark 8; 450°F.) for about 10 minutes. Put the cooked brill onto a warm dish. Pour the cooking juices into a small pan and whisk in the 3 oz. butter in little knobs. Pour over the fish and serve immediately.

Halibut and Chicken Halibut (Flétan)

Halibut is one of the largest fish you will see at the fishmonger's and by far the largest of the flat-fish. It can measure 6 feet in length, and in proportion it doesn't look particularly flat either. Sometimes you may find chicken halibut, weighing a couple of pounds or so, and looking much like the other small flat-fish. They are good eating, though not so good as sole or turbot. Usually halibut is sold in steaks. It's a pleasant fish, but it has a tendency to dryness, which you must take into account when cooking it.

Our halibut comes mainly from the great sandy sea bed between Norway and Scotland. There is also an immense fishery off the Pacific coast of Canada where a related species is caught. Nowadays it is organized in a starkly efficient manner. In the last century, though, the Red Indians would go out by the hundred in their canoes, 12 miles offshore, and catch these immense creatures with hooks of Douglas pine or yew, and lines of dried seaweed and deer sinew. When the fish bit on the trailing lines, they would pull them in and spear them, and drag them into the canoes. In a high sea, inflated seal skins, turned inside out and painted, were fixed to each side of the canoes to keep them buoyant with their heavy loads.

Grilled Halibut

On account of the fish's dryness, it is advisable to wrap the steaks completely in buttered foil. Season them first, and give them eight minutes a side under a hot grill. Serve garnished with parsley, with pats of one of the savoury butters on p. 22. The fruit-flavoured butters are particularly good with halibut.

Chicken halibut is grilled like a sole. Skin, brush with clarified butter and leave under a hot grill for 5–7 minutes a side (or until cooked – the time depends on the thickness of the fish). No foil is necessary. Obviously, any sole recipe will do for this miniature halibut.

Flétan au Fromage

Halibut is good when baked with a moist topping like this one.

6 servings:

6 halibut steaks	1 tablespoon French mustard
2 oz. butter	3 tablespoons cream
8 oz. grated cheese, preferably Gruyère	

Use the butter to grease a baking dish. Place the steaks in it. Mix the rest of the ingredients to a paste, and spread this over the upper surfaces of the steaks. Bake in a moderate to fairly hot oven (mark 4–5; 350–375°F.), until the fish is done; about 20 minutes. If the cheese mixture becomes too brown, protect it with butter papers. New potatoes go well with this dish.

Note. This is a good way of cooking cod steaks.

Flétan de Jonghe Marc

This recipe comes from *Gourmet Magazine* (March, 1972) and it is an excellent method of cooking halibut to counteract its dryness. I use a little more vermouth than recommended:

6 servings:

2½ lb. halibut fillet	8 good tablespoons dry
8 oz. breadcrumbs	vermouth
8 oz. butter	4 cloves of garlic, crushed
	salt, pepper

Cut the halibut into 1-inch cubes. Mix the breadcrumbs in a bowl with half the butter, melted, the vermouth and the garlic. This produces a moist paste. Spread half of it on a dish which has been greased with a butter paper, arrange the seasoned cubes of fish on top fairly close together, and cover them with the rest of the paste. Melt the rest of the butter and pour it over the top as evenly as possible. Bake in a moderate oven (mark 4; 350°F.) for 25 minutes, or a little less if you find that the fish is cooked. Brown under the grill.

The garlic can be reduced, but combined with the vermouth it gives the dish a really excellent flavour. A dish for midday, good with young broad beans as a vegetable. Or serve a green salad afterwards.

Halibut au Poivre. See p. 111.

More Fish from the Sea

Whiting (Merlan)

Some people do not care for whiting. They remember small grey fish coming to table, curled round so that the tail was stuck through the eye sockets – a perverted fancy sometimes known as *merlans en colère*. They may also remember how wholesome this object was supposed to be (wholesome was once the English excuse for serving tasteless and watery food to children). They shudder at such recollections.

It is not worth arguing against prejudice of this kind. Just buy filleted whiting, and present them under their old name of marling or merling. Make sure, of course, that they taste delicious. (I suggest the whiting with orange sauce on p. 121.) When filleted, whiting lack their blunted heads and have an attractive kipper-shape because the bone is removed from the back and not from the belly.

What are the advantages of whiting? For a start it is one of the more rewarding members of the cod family. Not, you may think, a relationship to raise the cook's blood pressure. But it does mean that the flesh is firm, with sweet flakes, and that it is abundant – in other words cheap. It is well up in the landing tables, right behind plaice: in 1971 this meant over 774,000 hundredweight, most of which was landed in Scotland (see Scottish dried whiting, p. 333). In my experience, whiting comes to the fishmonger's counter in far better shape than most cod, and of such quality that it can be used for sole dishes without inviting sour comments: rather as mussels can be used for oyster recipes.

The French, who know a good fish when they see one, recognize this. They serve whiting with beautiful sauces like the two following; they turn them into *jeux d'esprit* like *quenelles* (p. 248) and dish them up with white wine, mushroom or shrimp sauce; they may simply dip them in egg and breadcrumbs, and fry them (fried aubergines go well with whiting cooked this way); or they turn them into delicate stuffings for other fish (see p. 261) and use the larger ones for soup.

There is a proviso. Never be fobbed off with tired whiting. After all the fresh is easy enough to spot. It has a bright look, a look of pearly crispness. Faded whiting blurs to a flop as truthfully as any rose.

Merlans à la Dieppoise

Whiting with mussels and mushrooms, in a white wine sauce.

6 servings:

6 filleted whiting	juice of half a lemon
2 lb. mussels	½ pint dry white wine
8–10 oz. mushrooms	1 tablespoon flour
3 oz. butter	salt, pepper

Season the whiting and place them in a single layer in a flame-proof pan. The fillets can be doubled back to their original shape, if you have problems of size.

Clean and open the mussels. Discard the shells, and strain the liquor into a basin. Cook the mushrooms, sprinkled with the lemon juice, in 2 oz. of the butter. Pour off their juice into the mussel liquor.

Pour wine and mussel/mushroom juices over the fish. Bring to simmering point, and cook for about 5 minutes. When done, remove the whiting to a serving dish, and surround them with the mussels and mushrooms. Keep warm, either in the oven, or under a gently heated grill. Quickly reduce the cooking liquor. Mash remaining butter with the flour and use it to thicken the sauce in the usual way (*beurre manié*, p. 21). Make it very hot, without boiling, and pour over the fish, mussels and mushrooms. Glaze under the grill for a few seconds and serve.

Les Filets de Merlan Vallée d'Auge

The vallée d'Auge in Normandy is famous for cider and cream (and cheese, though Gruyère is used in this recipe).

6 servings:

6 boned whiting	½ pint dry cider
5 tablespoons oil	2 oz. grated Gruyère cheese
10 oz. chopped onion	salt, pepper

Cook the onions gently in the oil until soft and golden. Season and put into a large gratin dish. Lay the whiting on top and season well, and pour the cider over them. Sprinkle the cheese on top and cook in a moderate to fairly hot oven (mark 4–5; 350–375°F.) for about 20 minutes, or until the whiting are done.

Merlans aux Olives et au Vin Blanc. See p. 135.

Merlans Farcis à la Fécampoise. See p. 154.

Merlans à la Verdurette

This recipe, quoted by Madame Prunier, is for the wise people who go collecting their own woodland mushrooms, or for the lucky people who can buy them.

6 servings:

6 filleted whiting	3 oz. butter
beaten egg	2 chopped shallots
breadcrumbs	1 teaspoon each parsley,
4 oz. clarified butter	chervil, chives, all chopped
1–2 lb. *chantrelles* or *ceps*	4 leaves tarragon, chopped
(woodland mushrooms)	juice of a lemon (optional)
cooking oil	

Dip the fish into egg and breadcrumbs, then fry in the clarified butter. Meanwhile wash and chop the mushrooms, discarding any blemished parts. Fry them in a little oil until almost cooked and lightly browned. Drain off the liquid in the pan. Add the butter, the shallots and herbs and cook gently for a few moments. Season and pour foaming over the fish. Squeeze lemon juice over the whole thing, if you like.

Note. Cultivated mushrooms can obviously be used instead, but the flavour will not be so exquisite as anyone who has ever eaten *chanterelles* or *ceps* will understand.

Whiting with Orange Sauce

As I was looking one day at Hannah Glasse's *Art of Cookery*, which was published in 1747, I came across a recipe for scallops stewed in white wine (p. 305), and seasoned with Seville orange juice.

It sounded delicious, the orange juice would add just the right sweet and sour note. So off I went in search of scallops – not easy to find in north Wiltshire where I live – and came home disappointed. Extra disappointment that evening, when I came across a similar modern recipe, a French one, for whiting. I'd seen and spurned hundreds of whiting in my scallop-hunt. Next day I set off again, brought whiting home and discovered that this is the best way of all to prepare them.

Seville oranges are one of the most neglected of seasonings. It's understandable, because they're only to be bought during January and February, and these days we tend not to use things unless we can use them the whole year round. A sad mistake. One of the great pleasures of existence is to observe the changing seasons and celebrate them in one's diet. But if this doesn't convince you, never mind; Seville oranges can be deep-frozen, whole, for year-round consumption.

6 servings:

6 filleted whiting	salt, black pepper, cayenne
3 Seville oranges or 2 sweet oranges and 1 lemon	pepper
	seasoned flour
3 large egg yolks	5 oz. butter
4–5 oz. dry white wine	chopped parsley
4 tablespoons double cream	

Sprinkle the fish with the juice of half an orange (or half the lemon), and leave in a cool place while the sauce is made. Beat together in a large pudding basin the cream, egg yolks, wine, and the juice of 1½ Seville oranges (cut the last orange down into wedges for the garnish). With sweet oranges, use the juice of one orange and of the second half lemon, and cut the second orange into wedges.

Set the basin over a pan of simmering water, or cook the sauce in a pan directly over the heat, if you are used to making egg-thickened sauces. Stir until the sauce thickens to a pouring cream consistency or a little thicker. Season with salt and the two peppers. Beat in 2 ounces of butter. Lower the heat so that the sauce keeps warm without more cooking.

Dip the whiting in the flour and fry to golden brown in the last 2 oz. butter. Arrange on a serving dish with the orange wedges tucked in between, and a little parsley scattered on top. Serve the sauce separately in a warm sauceboat.

Note. A good recipe for many firm white fish – turbot, brill, sole, fresh cod, flounder, John Dory, monkfish and so on.

John Dory (Saint-Pierre, zées or dorées)

One of the most desirable of the creatures of the sea, to be compared with sole and turbot for quality. As a Mediterranean fish it is outstanding, a star which Venetian cooks hide under the depressing title of *pesce bolito con maionnese* – boiled fish with mayonnaise, see below. Lucky the visitor who manages to penetrate that particular language barrier before his fortnight is up. Couldn't the city of painters, architects, poets and Eastern merchants do better than that? It's certainly a reminder that if the Venetians built St Mark's, they also invented double-entry book-keeping.

Once you have eaten John Dory, you will not be surprised to know that it has divine connections. It was sacred to Zeus – its scientific name is *Zeus Faber*. When that deity lost his lustre, it came under the hand of St Peter the Apostle – literally, as you can see from the dark 'fingermarks', which have been there ever since the saint, at Christ's bidding, caught the fish in the sea of Galilee, and picked it up to remove a piece of money from its mouth to pay off some rapacious tax collectors.

Spaniards, Italians, French, Swedes, Norwegians, Icelanders – all remember this story when they call the fish, in their various languages, St Peter's fish. The English name seems first to have been dory by itself, from the French *dorée*, describing the golden sheen of the scales. John was added in the 17th century. Perhaps it was an affectionate response to its frankly ugly but amiable face. Perhaps it was the same impulse as the one which gave names like Jenny Wren, Jack-run-by-the-hedge, and Robin Redbreast to things we have liked and felt at home with.

Not, I'm afraid, that you are likely to feel familiar with John Dory these days. Hoteliers and restaurateurs snap it up. Try ordering it specially from your fishmonger, and persist if you aren't lucky the first time. Look out for it on holiday in Europe – or in the Canaries. A friend who was there the other day had one, fried in a crisp batter; he was told that if the catch had been better, he wouldn't have been eating it, because the big fish merchants buy them all for export immediately they are landed. That particular day there had been too few for them to bother with.

As to other ways of cooking John Dory, recipes for sole and turbot are suitable, particularly those with creamy sauces, or egg sauces. Usually the easiest thing is to ask the fishmonger to fillet the fish, as it's a plump flattish creature. But you will do best with a whole one for this first recipe:

Pesce Bolito Con Maionnese

Choose a John Dory of 3–4 lb. or two smaller fish. Remember that the firm flesh is substantial, and so is mayonnaise, so you will not need a large quantity.

6 servings:

3–4 lb. fish
court-bouillon, no. 1, p. 16
mayonnaise, p. 50, made with
 2–3 egg yolks and ½ pint
 olive oil

1 heaped teaspoon gelatine
3 tablespoons hot water

Put fish into cold *court-bouillon*. Bring to boiling point over moderate heat. Let it shudder for a moment or two, then remove from the stove and leave to cool in the larder. Now drain and skin the fish. Divide the fillets into portions and place them on a wire rack, over a baking tray. Make the mayonnaise and put half into a serving bowl. Melt the gelatine in the hot water, and as it cools to an egg-white consistency fold it into the remaining mayonnaise. Cover the fish with this mixture and put a chaste decoration or two in place – a sprig of tarragon; some capers. When the jellied mayonnaise has set, put the pieces of fish on to a serving plate, on leaves of crisp lettuce. Serve chilled, accompanied by the remaining half of the mayonnaise.

Saint-Pierre à l'Orange

Orange with fish is becoming as popular again as it was in the 18th century. Bitter oranges were used then, as a rich but still sharp substitute for lemon. Nowadays, unless you keep a supply of Sevilles in the deep-freeze, you will have to use sweet oranges sharpened with lemon juice.

6 servings:

6 fillets John Dory	1 tablespoon flour
2 oranges	½ pint double cream
1 small lemon	salt, pepper, cayenne
3 oz. butter	¼ pint Madeira or brown
1 chopped shallot	sherry
water	2 egg yolks

Season the fish. Peel the oranges and lemon thinly and squeeze out their juice. Cut the peel into matchstick strips, blanch for 2 minutes in boiling water, and drain.

In a large frying-pan, melt the butter, put in the shallot and fish, and add a little water to come about ¼ inch up the pan. Pour in the citrus juices, and lay the strips of peel on the fish. Cover and simmer until the fish is cooked.

Meanwhile make a sauce with the remaining butter, the flour and the cream.

Arrange the cooked fish on a plate and keep warm. Boil down the cooking juices by about half and add to the cream sauce, together with the wine and seasoning. Thicken with egg yolks in the usual way. Pour over the fish slowly so as not to displace the peel completely.

Note. This recipe was given for pompano (*filet of pompano Florida*) in the *Gourmet Cook Book* of 1957. As an alternative, use the Hannah Glasse orange recipe on p. 121.

Saint-Pierre à la Vendangeuse. See p. 147.

Pompano (Pompano)

The pompano is one of America's most famous delicacies. It is caught in the Mediterranean, too, but the place to eat it is undeniably at New Orleans in Antoine's restaurant. One of the best known recipes for this fish, *pompano en papillote*, was devised there by the son of the Marseillais founder, Antoine Alciatore, at the beginning of this century. The occasion was, I believe, the visit to that city of the great Brazilian balloonist, Alberto Santos-Dumont. Like the Alciatores, he was French by origin, and no doubt appreciated the fine contents of the *papillotes*, which had puffed up in the oven to the shape of one of his own dirigibles.

The early 1900's were the era of paper-bag cookery. The *en papillote* method had long been known, but was generally unsatisfactory because the taste of paper clung to the food inside. This problem was overcome by the development of special paper which did not have this disadvantage. In England, Spicers created the famous Soyer bag, at the instigation of Nicholas Soyer, grandson of the great chef, whose *Paper-bag Cookery* was published in 1911. Nowadays we use foil, which is completely neutral, and has the extra advantage over paper of being more efficiently twisted into a seal. Soyer demonstrated that almost anything could be cooked

by this method, from cakes to 15 lb. joints of beef, but I think it
is most successful of all with fish.

Antoine's Pompano en Papillote

If you cannot buy pompano, do not despair. Use fillets of any good
firm fish instead – John Dory, turbot or brill, salmon trout, rainbow trout, or bass. The rich crab sauce is excellent with this type
of fish.

6 servings:

6 fillets pompano	½ lb. shelled prawns
skin, bones and head for stock	salt, pepper
1¼ pints water	½ clove garlic, chopped
1 shallot, chopped, or 1	½ lb. onion, chopped
heaped tablespoon onion,	sprig of thyme
chopped	bay leaf
3 oz. butter	1 heaped tablespoon flour
1 pint dry white wine	2 egg yolks
½ lb. crab meat	

Season the fish. Simmer skin, bones etc., in the water for 30
minutes, strain into a measuring jug (there should be about ¾ pint
of stock). Cook shallot in 1 oz. butter until it begins to soften; add
fillets. When they are lightly coloured on both sides, pour in the
wine and simmer until the fish is just cooked and no more. Strain
off the wine and set it aside. Leave the fish to cool.

Meanwhile, lightly fry crab, prawns or shrimps, and half the
crushed garlic in another ounce of butter. Add the onions and the
remaining garlic. Cook gently for 10 minutes, covered. Add herbs
and ½ pint of the fish stock. Make a thick sauce in the usual way
with the remaining butter, the flour and the stock. Incorporate the
white wine in which the fish was cooked, and the crab and onion
mixture. Thicken further with the egg yolks. Correct seasoning.
Remove the thyme stalks and bay leaf.

If you want to present the pompano properly, cut 6 paper or
foil hearts large enough to contain the fillets. (Otherwise cut six
oblongs, about 9 × 12 ins.) Brush them lightly with oil. Put a layer
of sauce on one half of each heart, then the fish and more sauce.

Fold over the other side and twist the edges tightly together to make a close seal. Put these parcels on a baking sheet; place them in a very hot oven (mark 8; 450°F.) for about 10 minutes.

Note. This is said, by Marion Brown in *The Southern Cook Book*, to be the genuine recipe from Antoine's. I have seen variations elsewhere in which crab meat alone was used, with no prawns, and ¼ lb. of sliced mushrooms added to the onions.

There is no reason why such a delicious sauce should not be served with pompano, and other fish, which have been poached in white wine, without the *en papillote* finish.

Grilled Pompano with Cucumber Hollandaise

Split and bone pompano. Brush with melted butter, season, and grill with the cut side up. When the fish is almost cooked, turn it over and grill the other side if you like, but this is not necessary – the fish can be cooked completely without being turned over.

Serve with this sauce:

Sauce:
1 large cucumber
salt

hollandaise sauce, p. 39
Tabasco sauce

Slice the cucumber thinly. Put it into a colander, sprinkle with salt, and leave to drain for at least an hour. Rinse if the slices are too salty, squeeze dry in a clean tea towel, and then chop roughly. Make the *hollandaise* sauce, incorporating a dash of Tabasco with the seasonings at the beginning. Fold in the cucumber just before serving, and adjust the seasoning.

Grilled Pompano with Shellfish Stew

Serve the pompano with 1 pint of shelled mussels, clams, or oysters, poached and then drained and roughly chopped. Mix the liquor with ¼ pint thick cream, and bind the sauce with 3 egg yolks. Flavour finally with sherry or Madeira, and fold in the chopped shellfish to reheat.

Baked Pompano with Prawn or Shrimp Stuffing

6 servings:

1 pompano	1 small onion, chopped
butter	1 tablespoon butter
white wine or cream	1 heaped tablespoon parsley
stuffing:	6–8 oz. shelled prawns or
2 oz. breadcrumbs	shrimps
milk	salt, black pepper

Clean and season the fish. Make the stuffing; melt the onion in the butter until soft. Squeeze out the breadcrumbs in a little milk. Add to the onions and stir in the parsley off the heat. Chop the prawns or shrimps roughly and mix them in, too. Season to taste, and stuff the fish.

Butter an ovenproof baking dish and lay the pompano in it. Pour a little white wine over it – about a glassful – or some cream. Bake in a moderate to fairly hot oven (mark 4–5; 350–375°F.) for three quarters of an hour.

Monkfish, or Angler (Lotte de mer, baudroie)

The great fish apart – by which I mean sole, lobster, turbot, eel – my own favourite both to cook and eat is monkfish. Its beautiful sweet flavour and succulent firmness of flesh have led some writers to compare it with lobster – not really fair, I think, to either, but it gives a hint of the monkfish's virtues.

Although a fair weight is landed in Britain each year, and although it is a common enough fish round our coasts, monkfish is not always easy to buy. It's only to be found where there's already a demand for it; a situation most aggravating to people who live elsewhere and would like to cook the fish they have probably eaten on holiday in France (or in Italy, where it appears on the menu as *Coda di rospo*). We come across it frequently in Normandy, Brittany and

Touraine; from books on Provençal cooking, I know it must be common in the south as well. Look out for *bourride de lotte*, *gigot de mer*, and dishes of monkfish with mayonnaise. Recently we have eaten *lotte sauce Choron*, the fish poached in a *court-bouillon* and served with *sauce Choron* (p. 42), and *lotte normande*, poached and served with a Normandy sauce and mussels.

If you are camping or renting a house in France, or if you live in one of the right areas in England, do look out for monkfish in markets and fishmongers'. It's always sold without its head, and can easily be passed over. The general shape is that of a slightly squashed cone, anything from one foot long upwards. The flesh looks milky and smoothly solid rather than flaked, like cod or haddock. In the centre you will observe a single cartilaginous spine. As it is an expensive fish in France, it is usually sold in steaks cut across the body, but if you can afford it, a tailpiece of 2–3 lb. makes an excellent dish (see p. 131). In my experience the larger fish have the best flavour. I once bought some small tail-pieces, thinking they would be even more delicate. They weren't, they were rather tasteless. I should have taken warning from the lower price; fishmongers in France know what they are selling. The small bits and pieces sold as *joues de lotte* – what we should call monkfish 'knobs' by analogy with skate 'knobs' – are quite pleasant, but again they cannot be compared in flavour with the large steaks.

The reason for the monkfish's invariably headless state is that this appendage is thought to be too horrifying for the customer's sensibilities. In fact it is both curious and interesting, because the first dorsal fin emerges right over the snout, and is prolonged into a supple rod with a tiny 'flag' at the end. The fish snozzles its way into the sandy or muddy bed of the sea – the French name *baudroie* is said to have the same origin as the word *boue*, meaning mud – invisible on account of its matching colour. It gently waves this plumed rod in front of its capacious jaws, waiting to lure fish into Jonah-like oblivion. It doesn't stop at fish either. This greedy and well-named angler has been known to trap quite sizeable sea birds, at low water.

Monkfish is beloved of French chefs and housewives because, like sole, it can be partnered by many beautiful sauces, each enhancing the other. Cream or *hollandaise* or tomato sauces in their variety can turn a pound or two of monkfish into a feast. And cold, with mayonnaise, it is one of the best summer dishes I know.

Lotte à l'Américaine

This is one of the best ways of serving monkfish, which, like lobster, has a firm enough flesh to marry well with the strong flavours of the sauce.

6 servings:

3 lb. monkfish
seasoned flour
4 oz. olive oil
2 shallots, chopped
3 onions, chopped
1 large clove garlic, chopped
3 oz. brandy
generous ¾ pint dry white wine
¾–1 lb. large ripe tomatoes, peeled, chopped

bouquet garni
1 tablespoon tomato concentrate
1 teaspoon sugar
salt, pepper, cayenne pepper
chopped parsley and tarragon to garnish
croûtons of bread fried in olive oil to garnish

Cut the fish in pieces and turn in seasoned flour. Meanwhile fry the shallot, onion and garlic in the oil until they begin to colour. Add the fish; when it is lightly browned, warm half of the cognac, set it alight and pour it into the pan, stirring the contents about in the flames. When these die down, remove the fish to warm plate. Pour the wine into the pan, add tomatoes, *bouquet*, tomato concentrate, sugar and seasonings. Boil hard to reduce to a well-flavoured sauce – it must not be watery. Allow 20–30 minutes for this. Return the fish to the sauce and simmer gently until cooked, about 10–15 minutes, adding the rest of the brandy at the same time. Arrange on a hot serving dish, sprinkle with parsley and tarragon, and tuck the *croûtons* of bread round the edge. One of the finest fish recipes.

Lotte en Brochette

Monkfish cut into chunks makes an excellent fish for grilling on skewers. Here are two suggestions:

Put on the skewers 1-inch cubes of monkfish with 1 large mussel,

a square of unsmoked bacon, and a piece of bay leaf between them.
Brush with olive oil. When grilled, serve on a bed of rice, with
tomato sauce in which the juices of the grill pan have been incorporated.

1-inch cubes of monkfish left to soak for an hour in olive oil
flavoured with rosemary and origano, along with pieces of tomato
and sweet pepper and onion which has been blanched for 5 minutes
in boiling water. Cook on skewers. Serve with butter and plenty
of pepper, or with a very simplified form of *beurre blanc*: soften,
but do not melt, 4 oz. unsalted butter over warm water; off the
heat, add the juice of a lemon, drop by drop, beating all the time as
if you were making a mayonnaise. Flavour with salt and Cayenne
pepper.

Allow 10–15 minutes cooking time and turn the skewers occasionally. Two and a half pounds of fish should be just enough for 6
people, but three pounds would be better.

Lotte au Poivre. See p. 111.

Lotte en Gigot

A tailpiece of monkfish does have a similar shape to a leg of lamb –
hence the *gigot*. Here, and in the next recipe, are two variations of
this popular French recipe, which can also be used for other firm fish:

6 servings:

2½–3 lb. tailpiece of monkfish	1 lb. mushrooms, washed and
6 tablespoons olive oil	quartered
4 oz. warm water	4 oz. olive oil
salt, pepper	2 cloves garlic, chopped
sauce:	1 tablespoon parsley, chopped
2 lb. tomatoes, peeled and	salt, pepper
chopped	4–6 oz. thick cream
	lemon juice, extra parsley

Put the fish into a presentable, ovenproof dish, pour oil over it, and
season. Place in a hot oven (mark 7; 425°F.) for 15 minutes, then
turn the heat down to moderate (mark 4; 350°F.). Add the water
and leave for another 30 minutes, basting from time to time.

Meanwhile make the sauce: cook tomatoes in half the oil until they are reduced to a thick purée; add garlic and parsley. At the same time, in another pan, cook the mushrooms in the rest of the oil. Season.

When the fish is just done, pour tomatoes, mushrooms and cream over it. Stir well, add seasoning, and lemon juice if required, and return to a hot oven, for 5 minutes (mark 7; 425°F.). Serve in the cooking dish.

Gigot de Mer à la Palavasienne

This recipe is from Languedoc, on the south coast of France. *Pique* the monkfish with 4 cloves of garlic, cut into slivers, and season it. Make a *ratatouille*: cook 3 chopped onions and 3 chopped cloves of garlic in some olive oil. As they soften, add 3 sweet peppers cut in strips. As they soften in turn, add half a pound each of sliced aubergines and courgettes, and, after 10 minutes, 1 lb. peeled, chopped tomatoes. Simmer steadily for 45 minutes, uncovered. When you have a well-flavoured, unwatery stew, put it into an oven-proof dish, lay the fish on top and bake in a moderate to fairly hot oven (mark 4–5; 350–375°F.) for 30–45 minutes. Turn the fish over from time to time.

Tourte Béarnaise à la Lotte

This is the kind of fish recipe which we do not often use in this country. I think it's a pity, because it sets off a fine monkfish, sole, turbot, or lobster with style, and is not difficult to make. The other advantage is that both pastry case and sauce can be made in advance, which makes it an ideal dish for a dinner party.

6 servings:

shortcrust pastry:	1 lb. monkfish, sliced, and
8 oz. flour	weighed after boning
4 oz. butter	salt, pepper
1 egg yolk	3 oz. butter
cold water	¾–1 lb. mushrooms, chopped
pinch salt	chopped tarragon
sauce béarnaise (see p. 41)	

Make the pastry in the usual way. Line an 8 to 10 inch tart tin and bake blind (i.e. without filling). Make the sauce and keep it warm over a pan of tepid water.

Season the fish and fry it in half the butter. Use the rest to cook the mushrooms. Season them.

To assemble the tart, put the mushrooms in first, lay in the fish slices next, and pour the sauce over the top. Sprinkle with chopped tarragon and put into a hot oven (mark 7; 425°F.) for 5 minutes or so to glaze the sauce. Serve immediately.

Note. Sauce Choron can be used instead of *béarnaise*; or else *sauce Trianon*, which is *sauce hollandaise* made with lemon juice plus a tablespoon of medium-dry sherry.

Grey Mullet (Mulets, muges)

There are about 100 species of mullet spread about the warm and temperate seas of the world, a fact which may surprise you in view of their comparative scarcity at the fishmongers'. In the eastern Mediterranean, though, and in the Black and Caspian Seas, they are abundant enough to provide roes for *taramasalata* and that piquant substance known as *botargo*, once prized by Rabelais and Pepys as a stimulus to thirst, but now difficult to find in northern Europe (see p. 385). Our grey mullet is likely to come from the sea off Cornwall and the west of England during the summer and autumn months. The fish move in shoals, sometimes coming right into estuaries and ports where the brackish polluted water may give them a muddy taste. I have never experienced this with grey mullet, but if you have reason to think they have been caught in such places, wash them in several changes of salted, vinegared water.

Grey mullet looks like sea bass, silvery in colour, pointed with dark grey. A svelte creature. The flesh is firm and delicate, the price reasonable. The other mullet one sometimes sees, the exquisitely striped rainbow mullet, which can come from as far away as Hong Kong, is in my opinion for looking at only, not for eating.

By the time they have been removed from their individual plastic bags and allowed to thaw out, there is little flavour left, and the lovely iridescence vanishes in the pan.

The best way to cook grey mullet? You could try the Green Fisherman's recipe from *Pinocchio*. He floured it and flung it into a huge frying pan full of olive oil, which smelt like newly snuffed candles. It was part of a *fritto misto*, a mixed fry-up, which included red mullet, hake, sole, anchovies and spider crabs, all freshly caught, straight from the sea. It must have been good; absolutely delicious.

Another way is to grill grey mullet. Larger ones can be chopped up and strung on skewers with pieces of fat bacon and bay leaves, to be cooked *en brochette*. Small ones should be grilled whole, after being scaled, cleaned and lightly slashed three times on each side. Brush them, in the usual way, with clarified butter, and serve them with a tomato sauce, or *hollandaise* and its derivatives or with sauce *andalouse* (p. 33), also delicious with red mullet.

Do not discard the roe by accident, when cleaning the fish: it's a delicacy and can be mixed up with breadcrumbs, herbs, and onion stewed in butter, to make a stuffing for the fish.

Mulets en Papillote

6 servings:

6 mullet, about ¾ lb. each, cleaned and scaled	2 oz. butter
stuffing:	*for baking:*
mullet roes	12 tablespoons pastis
6 tablespoons breadcrumbs	good ½ pint olive oil
6 teaspoons each thyme and fennel seed	3 teaspoons each thyme and fennel seed
3 shallots or 1 onion, chopped	salt, pepper

Crush mullet roes, mix with breadcrumbs and herbs. Melt shallot or onion in the butter until soft and golden and add to the mixture. Season and use to stuff the fish.

Lay each mullet on a large piece of foil. Mix the remaining ingredients together, having first crushed the thyme and fennel seed in a mortar. Spoon it over the six fish on their six pieces of foil, and fasten up the packages, pressing the edges firmly together to make a proper seal. The packages should be on the baggy side.

Bake in a fairly hot oven (mark 5; 375°F.) for about 30 minutes, until cooked. Serve in the foil.

Grey Mullet with Bacon and Sage

Grey mullet may not be the most distinguished of fish, but its good points can be brought out by baking in a hot oven with savoury additions. Then it makes good eating. Choose mullet weighing about 1 lb. each.

6 servings:

3 mullet	3 oz. butter
6 good rashers of smoked	4–5 oz. dry vermouth
back bacon	salt, pepper
12 sage leaves	4 oz. thick cream (optional)
2 oz. breadcrumbs	

Scale and clean the mullet and slash in 4 or 5 places on each side. Chop the bacon and sage leaves finely together; use a moulinette if possible. Put a little of the resulting paste into the cuts on the mullet. Mix the rest with the breadcrumbs and season well; stuff this into the cavities of the mullet. Butter a baking dish lavishly and arrange the mullet side by side. Bake in a fairly hot oven (mark 6; 400°F.) for 15 minutes. Pour over the vermouth and put back for another 10–15 minutes until done. If the mullet are to be eaten as a first course, the dish will be lighter if you omit the cream. If they're providing the main dish, pour the cream over them and give another 2 minutes in the oven.

Bring the dish to the table sizzling hot. The fish should be lightly browned, and the buttery juices crusted with brown where they meet the dish.

Mulet aux Olives et au Vin Blanc

'A very simple and effective recipe which can be applied to many sorts of fish, including red mullet, sea-bream, sea-bass, whiting and mackerel; I have chosen grey mullet as an example because for some reason it is sold in this country at prices far below its true value, and represents something of a bargain.'

4 servings:

2 mullet, 1 lb. each	slices of orange or lemon
2 oz. olive oil	a sprig of fennel if possible,
3 tablespoons white wine	otherwise thyme or a bay
12 stoned black olives	leaf

'Put cleaned fish into a shallow oval fireproof dish, pour the oil over them, add your herbs, a sprinkling of salt and pepper, and the white wine. Bake, uncovered, for 15 to 20 minutes in a medium oven, Gas No. 4, 350°F.

'Now add the stoned black olives and cook another 5 minutes. The mullet can be served in the dish in which they have cooked, or be transferred to a flat serving dish, in either case with their own juice and slices of orange or lemon arranged along each fish. May be served hot or cold.'

(Elizabeth David, *French Provincial Cooking*, Penguin)

Mulet à la Vendangeuse. See p. 147.

Mulets Farcis à la Fécampoise. See p. 154.

Red Mullet (Rouget de roche, rouget barbet, surmulet)

Red mullet is one of the finest fish in the sea; it can also be one of the most confusing. First of all your eye may be deceived by the similar but paler rose-coral of the gurnard (and, in France, by the similar name of *rouget*, see p. 153). Secondly your ear can be deceived so that you buy other cheaper mullet, grey or rainbow for instance, thinking they are going to taste the same: they do not, and belong to quite another family, the *Mugilidae* or true mullets. The red mullet is a goatfish of the *Mullidae* family, and far superior in flavour.

Sometimes it is called Sea Woodcock, because of its liver which must on no account be discarded with the other innards. This delectable item was much prized by the Romans, who had a passion for red mullet. Martial exhorted his readers not to sully their gold platters with red mullet weighing less than 2 lb. (the Romans had a vulgar weakness for size). Personally I am grateful for any red mullet I see, and have never noticed any difference in flavour between an 8 oz. and 16 oz. fish.

It's a commonplace of cookery that the best fish need the simplest cooking. One or two flavourings, though, have become part of the red mullet tradition, fennel for instance, and tomatoes. Certainly such things are a help, not because the mullet needs them but because it is too expensive a fish to buy in lavish quantities. I sometimes meditate ruefully on the subject, and recall that one night in August, 1819, 5000 red mullet were taken in Weymouth Bay. Now if Constable had been there then, instead of three years earlier in 1816, the pink glow of that vast catch might have been reflected in his paintings of the bay. These days the red mullet are snapped up by restaurateurs, and eschewed by provincial fish-mongers who think their clients won't pay the price. Go on asking your fishmonger, be persistent, and one day he may listen to you.

Red Mullet with Mushrooms

6 servings:

3 large mullet, about 1 lb. each, or 6 small ones	2 oz. butter
1 large onion, chopped	chopped parsley
¾ lb. mushrooms, chopped	salt, pepper
2 oz. breadcrumbs	lemon quarters

Scale and clean the mullet, without removing the liver. Grease an ovenproof dish with a butter paper. Cook the onion gently in the butter until golden and soft. Mix with mushrooms, breadcrumbs, plenty of chopped parsley and season well. Make a bed of the stuffing in the dish and lay the mullet on it. Bake in a moderate to fairly hot oven (mark 4–5; 350°–375°F.) for 20–30 minutes until the fish is cooked. Put the lemon quarters between the fish before serving. If you are using large mullet, it is a good idea to divide them in two, discarding the backbone, before bringing them to table – place each half, skin side up, on the stuffing.

Red Mullet à l'Orientale

A beautiful cold dish – the important thing is to have the sauce concentrated and well spiced, not watery. The best mullet to use are small ones, but large ones can always be split in two when they're cooked (discard the backbone) and the halves arranged skin side up.

6 servings:

6 mullet	small bay leaf, chopped parsley
2 lb. tomatoes	a few grains of coriander
¼ pint dry white wine	1 clove garlic, chopped finely
¼ pint olive oil	seasoned flour
pinch of saffron threads	salt, pepper, sugar
thyme, chopped fennel leaves	1 lemon

Peel and roughly chop the tomatoes. Put into a frying pan to cook with about ⅔ of the oil and the garlic. When they begin to reduce to a purée add the white wine, the saffron and the herbs and coriander. Cook for 20 minutes, steadily, so that you end up with a stew or a substantial sauce. Season with salt and pepper, sugar if necessary, and more herbs if you like.

Meanwhile clean the mullet, leaving the livers in place. Dip them in flour and fry in the rest of the oil for 5 minutes on each side. Put them into a lightly oiled baking dish, and pour the boiling tomato mixture over them. Cook in a hot oven (mark 7; 425°F.) for a further 5 to 8 minutes. Leave to cool. Serve well chilled, and decorated with slices of lemon.

Surmulets à la Niçoise

6 servings:

3 large red mullet, about 1 lb. each
¼ pint dry white wine
¼ pint fish stock or light veal or chicken stock
2 large onions, finely chopped
1 bay leaf

scant teaspoon fennel seeds
marinara tomato sauce, p. 45
¼ lb. small black olives
olive oil, salt, pepper
slices of lemon and chopped parsley, to garnish

Brush an ovenproof dish with some olive oil. Put in the onion and bay leaf and half the fennel seeds, which should be lightly crushed. Lay the cleaned and scaled fish on top. Pour in the wine and stock; bake for 20–30 minutes, until cooked, in a hot oven (mark 7; 425°F.).

Meanwhile re-heat the *marinara* sauce and sieve it coarsely (don't liquidize it to smoothness). Put on to a hot serving dish. Arrange the cooked and drained mullet on top, with the olives and slices of lemon round them. Sprinkle with parsley.

Note. Keep the liquid in which the mullet was cooked for a shell-fish risotto, a soup, or a sauce.

Red Mullet Baked with Fennel

Red mullet are often grilled on a bed of fennel branches, from the feathery *Foeniculum vulgare* which grows in gardens, and wild at the seaside. They are also good with Florentine fennel, the flattish bulbs of celery texture with the agreeable flavour of aniseed. Blanch 3 heads, sliced, in boiling water for 10 minutes. Sweat them with a large chopped onion in butter, and lay the seasoned mullet on top. Bake in a moderate to fairly hot oven (mark 4–5; 350–375°F.) for 20–30 minutes, until the mullet are cooked.

Rougets Barbets à la Bourguignonne

In southern France, red mullet are sometimes wrapped in vine leaves before being grilled. In this recipe from Burgundy, they are wrapped in vine leaves, stuffed with grapes, and baked in foil. The sauce is a variation of *sauce Bercy*, using a reduction of white wine and shallots as a base. If you don't have access to a vine, it's sometimes possible to buy canned, unstuffed leaves: they won't need the preliminary blanching given in the recipe.

6 servings:

12 small or 6 large mullet	2 generous tablespoons thick
12 vine leaves	cream
1 lb. white grapes	4 oz. unsalted butter
2 shallots, finely chopped	salt, pepper
8 oz. dry white wine, ideally Chablis	

Peel and pip the grapes, saving any juice that may emerge. Clean the mullet and scale them. Stuff them with some of the grape halves and wrap them in the vine leaves – which have been put into boiling water for 1 minute, then drained and cooled under the cold tap. (The large mullet will need two vine leaves each.) Enclose the fish in individual packages of aluminium foil. Put into a hot oven (mark 7; 425°F.) for 15 minutes, or 20–25 minutes for large mullet.

Meanwhile put the shallots and wine into a small pan and boil hard until there is no more than a couple of tablespoons of liquid left. Stir in the cream, then the butter. Heat until the sauce is just below the boil. Add the rest of the grapes and any juice, and keep hot, without boiling, on a low heat, or over a pan of simmering water, while you dish up the mullet. Arrange them on a hot serving dish, still wrapped in their vine jackets; pour a little sauce over them and serve the rest in a warmed sauceboat. For another recipe with grapes, see p. 147, *Bass à la Vendangeuse*.

Red Mullet Sauce Andalouse. p. 134.

Sea Bream, Pandora and Porgies (Brème de mer, daurade or dorade, pageau, pagre)

Like sea bass, the name of 'sea bream' encloses, rather baggily, a number of fish, mainly of the *Sparidae* family. One of them, the pandora (French, *pageau*), is now imported from the Aegean and sold under the Greek name of *lithrini*; which is confusing if you try to look it up in a cookery book. Like most of the breams it tastes best when baked or grilled. Porgy is the North American name for sea bream:

> 'My father was the keeper of the Eddystone Light,
> Who slept with a mermaid one fine night,
> And of that union there came three –
> A porpoise, a porgy and the other was me . . .'[1]

You may recall that the porgy ended up in a chafing dish, presumably being fried, which is the best fate for this kind of fish when it comes in small sizes.

As I say, the name sea bream covers a multitude of fish, but one it should not include is the so-called 'bream' displayed on many of our fish counters. The confident ticket is stuck usually, into large foot-long fillets displaying a skin of pink and silver light, something like the skirt of Velasquez' Infanta in tone. But do not be deluded. This is a most ordinary fish correctly named redfish, Norway haddock or ocean perch; in general it should be treated as an inferior type of cod, and it is most usefully employed in soup-making, as a background fish flavour.

I discovered this some years ago, the hard way; we had just been taken to a new Japanese restaurant in London, the excellent Hiroko, and had particularly enjoyed the raw fish *sashimi*. We were told that a favourite fish for it was sea bream.[2] And the following week, I saw some fillets labelled 'bream' at the fishmongers. Were they fresh, very fresh? I asked. The answer was yes (fresh is one of those words which advertising has reduced to no meaning at all).

---

[1] From a popular ballad.
[2] The Japanese fish is the red sea bream, *Chrysophrys major*, one of the *Sparidae*, only found in that part of the world.

And I bought some. My *sashimi* was not a success; in fact it was repulsive because the texture was wrong – the 'bream' was really redfish – and the fresh flavour non-existent.

This is not to say that true sea bream are one of the world's great gastronomic delights. They are not, but some varieties like the gilt-head bream (the true *daurade*, named for its golden colour) are very good. And even the more ordinary ones do not deserve to be confused with redfish. I once saw a bream on our market stall in France which stood out because of its colour. The consistent deep rose was astonishing, as brilliant almost as a Zéphyrine Drouhin in full bloom. We couldn't resist buying it, but I have to confess that the flavour, though pleasant, was not outstanding.

Small bream, or porgies, are delicious when treated in the American style – i.e. rolled in corn meal, fried crisply in oil or bacon fat, and served with lemon and parsley. Larger bream weighing about 1½ lb. are good when grilled in this unusual Japanese style:

Seabream Grilled with Salt (Tai Shio-Yaki)

I make no apologies for including this Japanese recipe in a book on European fish cookery. It is one of the most successful ways of cooking a bream, and very simple. The result is not noticeably oriental, which means that the dish can be included in the usual kind of western meal. (Incidentally this is an excellent method of cooking many other small whole fish weighing up to 1 or 1½ lb.) Obviously the seabream, or *tai*, of Japanese waters is superior in flavour to our species, because it's regarded as one of the most delicious – and luckiest – of fish, to be eaten on ceremonial occasions. Even the least critical of cooks in the west would not give ours quite such high honour.

6 servings:

3 seabream, washed and scaled   unadulterated salt, preferably
sea-salt

Make a small cut below the pectoral fin and take out the entrails; wash the cavity of each fish. Weigh them, then calculate 2 per cent of the weight in salt. Put the fish on a plate and pour the salt over them. Leave for at least 30 minutes. Wipe the fish dry just before grilling.

The Japanese now shape the fish carefully with thin oiled skewers, pushing one below the eye (keep the head to the left) so that it comes out by the tail, curving it up slightly. The second skewer goes in underneath the first and should emerge underneath the tail. You can omit this if you like, but it certainly improves the final appearance of the bream.

Rub the fish again with salt, particularly in the tail area: this is to give a whitish, powdery finish. Grill over charcoal if possible – 4 minutes each side should be enough – cooking the 'front', i.e. head-to-the-left side, first. Put on a serving plate, remove skewers, and decorate with lemon quarters, or young, tender stems of ginger.

(From: *Japanese Cooking*, by Peter and Joan Martin, André Deutsch.)

Filets de Dorade à l'Antillaise

I was surprised to read this recipe in a local French newspaper, as rum in the kitchen is usually kept for sweet things, chocolate desserts in particular. But I tried it and everyone liked it very much. The things is not to overdo the rum. (I'm not sure how genuinely West Indian the recipe is, or whether the title is a genuflection by a French cook to the source of the most powerful ingredient.) Sea-bream is not always available: any firm white fish will do instead, from sole to shark (p. 208).

6 servings:

6 fillets of sea-bream	8 oz. thick cream or half
2 oz. rum	thick/half thin
3 oz. butter	2 egg yolks
salt, black pepper, cayenne	crescents of puff pastry to
pepper	garnish

Arrange the bream in a baking dish into which it fits closely in a single layer. Pour the rum over it, and leave for at least an hour. Season well with salt and black pepper, dot with the butter and bake in a fairly hot to hot oven (mark 6–7; 400–425°F.). It should be cooked in about 20 minutes. Bake or reheat the puff pastry at the same time.

Meanwhile beat the cream and egg yolks in a small pan with a good pinch of cayenne pepper (or a few flakes of crushed chilies). Heat slowly, stirring all the time, until the cream thickens without boiling. When the fish is done, pour the cream sauce over it and tuck the crescents into the dish in a decorative manner. Serve straightaway.

Sea Bass, Sea Perch and Groupers (Bar, serran, loup de mer, mérou)

To walk into the fishmonger's and see a tray of sea bass is a beautiful sight. Their scales, arranged in exact gradation of colour, shine with silver and dark grey markings. Their shape is slim and elegant. I find that the white flesh can be a little on the soft side, and for this reason prefer them baked or cooked in a crisp style, rather than poached in white wine or *court-bouillon*. The bass, or *spigola*, is a great speciality of Naples. When very fresh, it is simply stuffed with garlic and a chopping of herbs, brushed with olive oil, sprinkled with crumbs, and baked in the oven. Olive oil and lemon juice are used for basting. For a bass which is not so newly arrived from the water, an interesting stuffing should be added to the simple formula. Alice B. Toklas's recipe for carp with chestnuts, on p. 256, can be adapted to it most successfully, but be sure to leave the chestnuts in a crumbly state. If reduced to a purée they make the mixture too heavy.

Many fish recipes – recipes for sole (Florentine or *meunière* for the smaller fish), recipes for salmon, bream, John Dory, and so on can be used for bass, though, as I've observed, a little vigour is preferable to a bland mildness.

The bass we normally see is only one of a huge family of fish, the *Serranidae* or sea perches. It includes the groupers, which unfortunately have a marked preference for the warm seas of the Caribbean and Mediterranean. In his *Mediterranean Seafood* (Penguin), Alan Davidson comments on the superiority in firmness and flavour of the dusky sea perch or grouper (*mérou*) over the generality of the *Serranidae*. It is apparently imported from time to time, so look out for it. The Latin name *Epinephelus gigas* gives you a clue to its appearance, as Mr. Davidson observes; the first word means 'with clouds upon it', which is a good description of the dark patches blurring the yellow or reddish brown of the skin. Groupers have chameleon-like qualities, with the Nassau grouper apparently capable of eight different colourings.

These firmer fish can be treated like turbot and John Dory. Mr Davidson gives one particularly unusual and piquant recipe, a Spanish one, for grilled or fried steaks of grouper with orange sauce, really a *sauce bigarade*. He also recommends this recipe:

Mérou au Bresse Bleu

6 servings:

6 slices grouper (or turbot, halibut, monkfish etc.) from 5–7 oz. each	clarified butter
	1 baby Bresse Bleu cheese
	2 pints fish *velouté*, p. 32
seasoned flour	3 egg yolks

The slices should be even and well trimmed. Flour and cook them *à la meunière* in the clarified butter. Grate the cheese and work it over a low heat in a small pan until it turns to a paste. In another pan heat the *velouté* sauce, thicken it with the egg yolks and add the cheese paste. Season if necessary. Put the fish slices into a buttered ovenproof dish, in a single layer, and cover with the sauce. Glaze in a hot oven for a moment or two.

The recipe came originally from Monsieur Max Maupuy of the Restaurant Max in Paris. He also suggests serving *mérou*, poached in a *court-bouillon* and left to cool, with a choice of two sauces. The first is *Rougaille*, which is simply the drained chopped flesh of 2 lb. of tomatoes, chilled and mixed with a tablespoon of strong Bornibus or French mustard, and seasoned. The second consists of half a baby Bresse Bleu cheese mixed with a generous ¾ pint of double or thick cream, and passed through a fine sieve; the seasoning is a pinch of cayenne pepper. Serve the sauce cold but not chilled.

Porov Troug

A recipe from *The Armenian Cookbook* by Rachel Hogrogian. Originally for bass, it works well with seabream, grey mullet, and any large fish of about 3–4 lb. which does not possess too delicate a flavour. It is a combination of the Palermo sardine recipe on p. 176, and the red mullet *orientale* recipe on p. 138, with one or two variations. An excellent summer dish. Apart from the bass, you will need:

6–8 servings:

stuffing:
1 lb. onions
6 tablespoons olive oil
4 oz. currants
4 oz. pine nuts
¼ teaspoon each cinnamon and
    allspice
1½ teaspoons salt
¼ teaspoon pepper

4 tablespoons chopped
    parsley
2 tablespoons lemon juice
sauce:
¼ pint *marinara* tomato sauce,
    p. 45
2 oz. dry white wine
1 lemon, sliced thin

Slice onions lengthwise. Cook until transparent in olive oil, without browning. Add currants, pine nuts, seasoning, and stir over heat for a few minutes more. Stir in parsley and lemon juice. Taste and correct seasonings.

Scale the fish diligently. Bone it in the usual way (p. 12). Grease a baking dish with a butter paper, and lay the fish inside. Put stuffing in the middle.

Mix the sauce and the wine and pour round the fish. Arrange the lemon slices evenly along it. Bake in a fairly hot oven (Mark 5; 375°F.) for 45 minutes. Serve chilled.

Sea Bass Anisette

4 servings:

2 lb. sea bass fillets	¼ teaspoon ground mace
3 heads fennel	8 peppercorns, slightly
4 oz. butter	crushed
salt	6 tablespoons olive oil
marinade:	*sauce:*
¼ teaspoon coriander leaves,	Pernod-flavoured mayonnaise,
chopped	p. 54

Leave the fish in the marinade for 3 hours before cooking it. Make the mayonnaise. Slice up the fennel, putting one-third aside. The rest can either be served as a salad with vinaigrette dressing, or it can be blanched in boiling salted water for 10 minutes, then cooked gently in 2 or 3 oz. of butter until soft – I think the second way is best, if the fish is being eaten hot.

Butter a grill pan, lay the reserved fennel on it, then the fish fillets (dispense with the grill rack) which should be cooked under a medium-hot grill for 7 or 8 minutes a side. Sprinkle with salt.

Serve the fish immediately with the cooked fennel and the sauce; with new potatoes as well if you like. Or leave it to cool, and serve it with the fennel salad and the sauce.

Bass or Bream à la Vendangeuse

The name of this dish – bass in grape-picker's style – isn't the fancy of some Parisian chef. It reflects the reality of a land where, in many districts, the ordinary person's food is still genuinely local. Main items such as meat and fish are cooked with what's to hand. So in September and October, after a day in the vines, pickers will go home with a basketful of grapes. Grape-picking is an affair of sweat and ribaldry. No autumn melancholy in the air, but the shrieks of women pickers trying to bring some young man to his knees, as they pile more and more grapes into his huge shoulder basket. He escapes at last, leaves and fruit in his ears, and staggers to the press.

4–6 servings:

2–3 lb. bass or sea bream (or John Dory or grey or red mullet)	*bouquet garni*
	½ pint dry white wine
	½–¾ lb. large white grapes
4 oz. butter	1 oz. flour
large mild onion, chopped	juice of half a lemon
2 cloves garlic, chopped	chopped parsley, salt, pepper

Ask the fishmonger to clean and scale the fish, but to leave the head on. Using 2 oz. of butter, grease an oval dish large enough to hold the fish. Make a layer of onion and garlic, put the *bouquet* in the middle, and the fish on top. Season well. Pour over the wine. Bake in a hot oven (mark 7; 425°F.) for 20 to 25 minutes, until the fish is cooked. Meanwhile peel and pip the grapes, and mash the flour into a paste with 1 oz of butter.

Transfer the cooked fish to a serving plate, and the juices to a saucepan (remove the *bouquet*). Bring to simmering point, and add the flour and butter paste in small knobs, stirring them into the sauce to thicken it. Season with lemon juice, and more salt and pepper if necessary. Keeping the sauce below the boil, beat in the last ounce of butter (this gives the sauce a delicious flavour, and a beautifully glossy appearance). Add the grapes, still keeping the sauce below boiling point, and leave for 1 minute, then pour round the fish. Scatter chopped parsley on top. Make sure that the plates are very hot, and whatever you do, *don't overcook the fish.*

Note. This is a homely recipe for fish with grapes. Turn to p. 97 for the more elegant sole with grapes, *sole Véronique.* I'm not implying a preference – each dish has its place and occasion. Or to p. 140 for *Rougets Barbets à la bourguignonne* with the vine leaves and grapes.

Samak Tarator (Fish with Tarator Sauce)

'This is a great gala dish, particularly popular in Egypt, Syria and the Lebanon. It is usually served lavishly decorated in a variety of brilliant colours and traditional designs according to local taste. Today it is sometimes replaced on special occasions by the French *poisson à la mayonnaise,* or decorated in a more European manner.

'Choose a large fish such as sea bass, bream or John Dory. Clean and wash it. Leave the head on but remove the eyes. Rub all over with salt, pepper and olive oil, and bake in an oiled baking dish (45 mins for a 2–3 lb. fish, at mark 3 (warm); 325°F.) or wrapped in foil (an hour at mark 4 (moderate); 350°F.).

'Serve the fish on a large dish on a bed of parsley or lettuce. Decorate it with lemon slices, sliced green pickles, black olives, radishes, fried pine nuts or almonds, and pieces of pimento. Make an oriental design, for example a criss-cross pattern. Serve cold, accompanied by bowls of *tarator* sauce. [See p. 59.]

'A delightful version of this dish is boned fish *tarator*. Prepare the fish and bake it in foil. Allow to cool. Cut off the head and tail neatly and set aside.

'Skin the body of the fish and bone the flesh. Season to taste with salt and pepper. Place the boned fish on a large serving dish, patting it back into its original shape. Place the head and tail at each end and mask the whole body of the fish with *tarator* sauce.

'Serve decorated with whole pine nuts or almonds, lightly fried, pickles, olives, and whatever else you like.

'This method of boning and reassembling the fish is particularly useful if dealing with a very large fish that does not fit into the oven. It can be cut into manageable pieces instead, and then baked in foil as usual.'

(*A Book of Middle Eastern Food*, Claudia Roden, Penguin)

Croakers and Drums

There are many kinds of croakers and drums spread all over the world. Like the gurnard, they owe their names to the pronounced noises they make by vibrating a muscle attached to the air-bladder, which then acts as a resonator (see p. 154). The drums include the *corvina* of Peru, the fish traditionally used to make *ceviche* (below); the weakfish and kingfish of North America; the *kabeljou* of South Africa; and the mulloway of Australia; and also the meagre, which I first came across in France. It lay on the fish-stall, plump and silvery-grey, looking like a sea-bass. This was not surprising as these fish are related to the sea-perches, or groupers, of which the bass is one: the recipes for bass and bream are all suitable for the meagre. Large drums and croakers can be cooked according to recipes for cod steaks and fillets; really small fish can be grilled, or else dipped in beaten egg and breadcrumbs and deep-fried (in America corn meal would be used instead of breadcrumbs).

Our fish was ¾ lb. in weight. Madame Soarès, who sold it to us, suggested we should bake it in the oven. Then remembering we had no oven, she suggested we fry it *meunière*, in clarified butter (p. 21). This was most successful, because the skin turned to a golden crispness which made an excellent contrast to the sweet flavour and soft texture of the bass-like flesh. Some lemon juice and a few potatoes were all the addition it needed.

Ceviche

One of my favourite ways of pickling fish. It is simple to do, and tastes deliciously fresh and unusual. This method of 'cooking' fish by submerging it for several hours in citrus juice comes originally from Peru. There cooks use *corvina* (*Sciaena gilberti*). Sea bass would be the nearest equivalent, but any good white fish with a minimum of bones can be used – sole is the obvious choice; freshness is the quality to look for.

The main principle is to cover small pieces of the filleted fish with lime or lemon juice, or a mixture of both, and leave them to marinade for three hours at least. I have left it for three days and it still tasted excellent. The surprising thing is how quickly the juice turns the transparent flesh opaque, just as if it had been cooked by heat. Apart from the unusual freshness of flavour, I do not think anybody would suspect that the fish had not been cooked in a conventional manner.

The juice should be slightly salted and well peppered. In Peru a small amount of one of the native hot peppers gives the pickle a fiery flavour. Some crushed chili could be used instead. A clove of garlic, and onion rings, are essential (1 sizeable onion to 1 lb. fish). As in the *escabeche* on p. 353, the liquid jellies slightly.

Although this is a pre-refrigeration method, designed to help fish keep in a hot climate, *ceviche* benefits by being served well chilled. The drained fish should be placed in crisp lettuce leaves, on individual plates or on one large dish, with a few of the onion rings on top. A variety of soft and sweet vegetables are added, to mollify the sharpness of the citrus flavour and the hot pepperiness of Peruvian aji or chili; sweet potatoes boiled and cut in pieces, sweet corn, boiled on the cob and cut across into slices, tomatoes, sweet peppers and quarters of hard-boiled egg, all go to make the dish a most attractive and original hors d'oeuvre, particularly for a summer meal.

Garfish and Saury (Orhie and balaou)

Garfish may not be an epicure's delight, but they have some enchanting characteristics, more than enough to enhance the good but unexciting flavour. Although they're plentiful enough in our waters, we saw them first in France at our weekly market. The blueish-green glow of their long narrow bodies stood out amongst the herring and mussels; so did the protracted beaks armoured with a row of tiny vicious teeth (garfish – the name goes back to the Middle Ages – means spearfish or javelinfish, from the shape of this beaky snout). The label said *orphies*. Name and appearance were worthy of a fairy tale, or one of the lighter stories of mythology. In her quick way, Madame Soarès the fishmonger saw we were hooked, and came over to explain that the glowing sheen of the skin was repeated in the bones. 'I'll cut one up to show you . . . See?' Sure enough they were an exquisite greenish-blue, like Persian plates in a museum. The colour doesn't disappear in the heat of of cooking either, so you have an elegant articulation of peacock glory against the white flesh on your plate. (It's caused by a harmless phosphate of iron, discovered in 1823 by J. G. Vivian and named vivianite.)

Another amiable characteristic is the way garfish leap out of the water to escape prowling tunny fish, or to snap at the tiny herrings and sprats they live on. It's not the real flight of a bird, a flight which changes direction and soars and dips, but more of a 'skittering' over the sea propelled by strong tail movements.

Garfish arrive on the west coast of England in early summer, swimming into shallow water just ahead of the mackerel – in some parts they are called Mackerel Guide – to spawn in the seaweed.

Apparently housewives in the East End of London like to buy them. The rest of England doesn't get much of a chance. No demand. (I always wonder how we are expected to 'demand' fish we have never had the opportunity of seeing or hearing about.) Madame Soarès doesn't suffer from that kind of fishmonger's laziness and stupidity. She delights in the unusual. The moment your eye flickers towards something new, she's there. Like a Colette of the marketplace, she pours out information with feeling and drama, from a treasure of hoarded experience. Usually there's a recitative on the history, capture and character traits of the fish, rising to an aria of recipes and sauces. In this case the recitative was the thing, because the garfish doesn't offer much scope for culinary enterprise.

The best way to cook it is to cut it into 2 inch pieces, dip them in seasoned flour and fry them in clarified butter. A few lemon quarters, some bread and butter, a glass of white wine, and there you are – simple gustatory pleasure, but plenty of conversation. Or the pieces can be skewered with bits of fat bacon in between them, and grilled – being slightly oily, garfish stands up well to this method, and benefits from the lightly scorched flavour of the crisp edges of bacon.

The saury (*Scomberesox saurus*) is related to the garfish, and looks very like it. The beak is similarly protracted – for which reason Americans call it Needlenose. It leaps from the water, too, though rather more vigorously, and is sometimes called the Skipper. Two things distinguish it from its cousin the garfish (*Belone belone*) – externally, two rows of small tuftlike fins between the dorsal fins and tail; internally, bones of no colour at all, no peacock glory there. It's caught down the east coast of America and in the Caribbean, as well as in Europe and North Africa. Other related species are found in the Pacific; they can be bought occasionally in cans.

Flying Fish (Poissons volants, exocets)

Several varieties are caught in the tropical and sub-tropical seas of the world. Their flight is more apparent than the garfish's or saury's, lasting for quite a few seconds with the help of the huge pectoral fins which sustain the leaping movements of the tail. Their head is a conventional fish-shape, with no protracted beak. When you spread out the spiny fins, they give an almost bird-like impression of flight.

Flying fish come to this country as frozen, grey-black creatures, about 8–10 inches long, fins plastered to their body by ice. I do not really think that the flavour justifies the journey. When grilled, the flesh is firm, almost white, pinkish-brownish, in nice flakes. It has a slightly cured taste, with a hint of buckling about it. It's not as oily as mackerel, but richer than garfish. As we ate it, I reflected that fish from warm seas do not have the flavour of northern fish. Many people have said this and I don't think that the observation is a matter of cold-climate chauvinism.

But they are worth buying a time or two, for the experience of their beauty.

The following gurnard recipes would also be suitable for flying fish; so would some of the baked herring and mackerel recipes on pp. 164–7 and 170–71.

Gurnard (Grondin)

Three species of gurnard are commonly caught in the Atlantic and Mediterranean: the grey gurnard (*grondin gris*), the yellow (*grondin perlon*) and the red (*grondin rouge*). They are easily distinguished from all other fish by their strange, mail-cheeked heads, with boney plates which give them a prehistoric, almost fossil-like appearance. The body attenuates from the large head in a cone, which lacks the elegant curves of more conventionally-shaped fish such as sea-bream or herring. The flesh is firm and white, good for baking, stews and soups. It's not a fish of the first water, but it's useful and cheap, well worth buying.

One snag. The lovely colour of the red gurnard, in my experience the most commonly seen of the three in this country, means that it can be confused with the red mullet. Take a good, long look at the head and general body shape, or you may be disappointed in your expectations. Not even the gurnard's most devoted admirer could say the flavours were comparable. On hotel menus in northern France, we have also been confused by the word *rouget* on the menu. Expecting *rouget-barbet* or red mullet, we learned the hard, unforgettable way that gurnard are sometimes caled *rougets-grondins*.

The names of this fish reveal an interesting thing: the gurnard's ability to make short, sharp noises. Both *grondin* and gurnard come from French words for growling (*gronder*) and for grunting (*grogner*). These strange sounds are made by a special muscle in the air-bladder wall, which can vibrate many times a second: the air-bladder acts as a resonating chamber. There are other fish with the same ability, which has led to all kinds of speculation about the origin of the Sirens' song. A shoal, say of meagre or drums (p. 149), many feet below the surface of the sea, can be heard quite clearly on board a fishing boat. Like the noises made by whales and dolphins, they have not been interpreted so far.

A practical point – the size of gurnard can vary enormously. Judge the amount you require by eye, allowing for the size of the head, rather than by weight. The recipes following are based on gurnard weighing about 8 oz. each.

Moulines Farcies à la Fécampoise

I found this very pleasant appetizing recipe in Simone Morand's *Gastronomie Normande*. It makes the best of a most obligingly cheap fish ('mouline' is the local name for gurnard).

6 servings:

6 gurnards	*stuffing*:
2 glasses of dry cider	10 oz. mushrooms, chopped
2 onions, or 2 large shallots, sliced	2 large tablespoons good sausage meat
1 tomato, sliced	1 chopped shallot
2 tablespoons thick cream	1 ½-inch slice bread
chopped parsley	milk
butter	chopped parsley
bouquet garni	sprig of thyme
	lemon juice, salt, pepper
	3 oz. butter

Make the stuffing first. Melt the butter and fry the mushrooms and onion and sausage meat gently. Squeeze the bread in a little milk, just to moisten it, and add to the pan. Season with parsley and thyme, lemon juice, salt and pepper. Divide this mixture between the 6 gurnard.

Butter an ovenproof dish which will hold the stuffed gurnard cosily. Tuck the onion slices and the *bouquet* into the gaps. Pour in the cider and dispose the tomato slices in a decorative manner on top. Bake in a moderate to fairly hot oven (mark 4–5; 350°–375°F.) until the fish are cooked – about half an hour. If the dish seems dry, add a couple of spoonfuls of water during the cooking. About 5 minutes before the end, pour the cream over the whole thing. Sprinkle with chopped parsley and serve.

Note. Also a good recipe for mullet and whiting.

Gurnard with Cheese and Wine Sauce

The firm texture of gurnard makes it a successful fish for a *gratin*. The main preparation can be done several hours before the meal, with a last minute reheating in the oven or under the grill.

6 servings:

3 lb. gurnards, filleted	½ pint hot milk
court-bouillon, or light chicken	2 oz. Parmesan cheese, grated
or veal stock plus a dash of	2 oz. Gruyère cheese, grated
wine vinegar	2 oz. breadcrumbs
4 oz. butter	salt, black pepper, nutmeg
3 tablespoons flour	3 or 4 tablespoons thick
scant ¼ pint white wine	cream (optional)

Put the cleaned and filleted gurnard into *court-bouillon*, or stock and vinegar; there should be enough to cover it comfortably. Bring slowly to simmering point, and remove the fish the moment it is cooked. Put head, skin and bone back into the cooking stock, and continue to boil gently. Leave the fillets to drain while the sauce is made.

Melt half the butter in a small pan, stir in the flour. Cook for 2 minutes, then pour in the wine and cook for a further 2 or 3 minutes. Now pour in a good ladleful of the boiling fish liquor (through a strainer) – about ¼ pint or a little more – then the hot milk. Simmer to a thick but not gluey consistency. Stir in the cream if used, then half the grated cheese. Season well with salt, pepper and nutmeg. Put a layer of the sauce into a *gratin* dish, then the gurnard fillets.

Cover with the rest of the sauce. Mix the remaining cheese with the bread-crumbs and scatter evenly on top. Dot with the last 2 oz. of butter, and reheat in a very hot oven or under the grill until brown and bubbling.

See also *Fish Stews and Soups*, pp. 63, 65, 79, 81, 84, 85.

Greater and Lesser Weever (La grande et la petite vive)

First acquaintance with weevers can, quite literally, be agonizing. Walking barefoot on a sandy beach in Cornwall (or in many other places of the kind in Europe), you may suddenly feel the most excruciating, stabbing pain. One friend says that it vanishes suddenly and completely after 15 minutes: other accounts are not so cheerful, and add inflammation and itching as well. These spiky fish like to bury themselves in sand, right up to the eyes (which are positioned at the top of the head), with just the spines of the first dorsal fin sticking up, almost invisibly, through the sand. They are really waiting for shrimps, though you may not appreciate this at the time, and are even more of a nuisance to the shrimpers of Lancashire than they are to holiday-makers. Even the strongest and most knowledgeable of these fishermen are sometimes caught as they walk through the shallow waters of that coast, and can be laid up for a fortnight.

Along these spines, and along another strong spine attached to the gill-cover, are grooves that conduct the poison from the fish's poison glands to the victim. Not surprisingly, both French and English names derive from the Old French *wivre*, meaning viper. If you come across these fish at the fishmonger's do not spurn them, because they have an excellent flavour and firm flesh. Follow recipes for gurnard, or this one from Hannah Glasse's *Art of Cookery* (1747):

To Broil Weavers

'Gut them and wash them clean, dry them in a clean Cloth, flour them, then broil them, and have melted Butter in a Cup. They are fine Fish, and cut as firm as a Soal; but you must take Care not to hurt yourself with the two sharp Bones in the Head.'

Dolphinfish or Dorado (Dorade tropicale, coryphène)

One of the fish now being imported from the Caribbean is the dolphinfish or dorado. It is also fairly common in the Mediterranean where it usually appears under the name of *lampuga*.

This strange grey and gilded creature, with a blunt, cat-like head and unbroken fins down its long body, has a delicious flavour. It should be better known. Do not be put off by the name – this fish has nothing to do with true dolphins which are mammals.

Dolphinfish is a suitable candidate for the *américaine* treatment, (p. 130). In general it should be treated in a southern style – for instance, steaks baked in the oven with some kind of chopped and moistened mixture on top. The pine-kernel stuffing on p. 176 is good, or a chop-up of onions, butter, herbs and a few breadcrumbs, with grated lemon peel (what the Italians call a *battuto*).

If steaks are to be grilled, it is wise to marinate them first (oil, lemon, garlic); or if there is not time for this, wrap them in foil before grilling (buttered foil, plus lemon, finely chopped onion and so on). The parcels can always be opened for the last part of the cooking in order to brown the tops.

Red Snapper (Vivaneau)

Red snappers are easily recognized. They look as if a designer had improved the conventional fish shape by emphasizing the curve of the head and back, flattening the belly and pointing the nose; an elegant adjustment. The scales blush from silver-pink to a deep rose red; though much of this colour has to be removed before the fish is cooked, something remains of its beauty. The flesh is firm and pleasant. I suspect that a freshly-caught red snapper on the Atlantic sea coast of America is good eating: in Britain, unfortunately we have to buy from small frozen shoals, which need chiselling apart. As they are not too expensive, they are worth eating from time to time, with a well-flavoured sauce of the following kind – my own feeling is that the Worcester sauce makes all the difference:

Red Snapper Créole

6 servings:

6 red snappers (about 3½ lb.), cleaned	2 oz. chopped parsley
seasoned flour	½ teaspoon each rosemary and thyme
1 lemon	1 bay leaf
sauce:	2 cloves garlic, finely chopped
12 oz. chopped onion	2 14-oz. tins tomatoes
3 stalks celery, chopped	1 tablespoon Worcester sauce
1 chopped green pepper (6 oz.)	Tabasco
2 oz. butter	salt, freshly ground black
2 cloves	pepper, sugar
grated rind of the lemon	

Make the sauce first, taking trouble to get the reduction and seasonings to your taste before baking the fish. It's an elaborated version of the *sauce créole* on p. 46.

Put onion, celery and pepper into a frying pan with the butter. Cook gently until soft. Add cloves, lemon rind and herbs, including garlic. Quickly drain the tomatoes and add them (keep the juice for another recipe). Leave this mixture to boil down busily for about 20 minutes, or until it has lost its wateriness and become a liquid purée. Stir in the Worcester sauce, then add the rest of the seasonings to taste.

Sprinkle the fish with seasoned flour and place them in an oven-proof baking dish. Arrange slices of lemon on top, two to each fish, and pour the sauce round and between them.

Bake in a moderate oven (mark 4; 350°F.) for about 20 minutes until the fish is done. Baste occasionally.

Note. One large red snapper can be used instead of six little ones; it will take longer to cook: 35–45 minutes.

Some recipes suggest making the sauce above in half-quantity, and adding enough breadcrumbs and egg to bind it to a stuffing. Chopped shrimps and prawns are sometimes mixed in as well. Filled with this mixture, the fish are then baked in the juice from the tomatoes, plus a little water and lemon juice, or simply in a well-buttered dish.

Bluefish (Tassergal)

The gracefully shaped bluefish, long, with a blue-green shine on its grey body, comes in to the Atlantic coast of America by the million every summer. It is a most ferocious animal – 'an animated chopping machine' – of carnivorous and wasteful habits. Its progress through the sea is marked by the bloody remains of other fish which have had the misfortune to cross its path.

It is quite a good eating fish, not very firm but fairly oily. This means that it grills well, and needs rather positive flavours to go with it.

Grilled Bluefish

Clean the fish, and bone it from the back, so that it opens out like a kipper. Brush with melted butter (or with the piquant barbecue sauce on p. 210) and put under the grill cut side up. When it is nearly done, turn it over and grill the other side.

Serve with melted butter sharpened with capers or lemon juice, or with pats of *maître d'hôtel* butter (p. 22). Mussel or oyster sauce can go with it, or a *béarnaise* (p. 41).

Baked Bluefish with Cucumber

Turn to the recipe for *Herring baked with cucumber* on p. 165, and follow that. Bluefish being larger than herring, do not roll them up or bone them, but stuff in the usual way.

Bluefish Bustanoby

Many herring and mackerel recipes are suitable for bluefish. It is rich enough to take the sharpness of gooseberries, or the contrasting smoked flavour of bacon. In this recipe from the *Long Island Seafood Cook Book*, by J. George Frederick, smoked ox tongue is used.

6 servings:

1 3-lb. bluefish	pinch salt, pepper
3 tablespoons mushroom juice	3 tablespoons tomato sauce
½ glass Chablis, or other dry white wine	1 tablespoon cooked smoked beef tongue, finely minced

Clean and score the bluefish. Dry it and place in a buttered oven-proof dish. Add mushroom juice (obtained by stewing mushrooms *gently* in butter so that they exude their moisture), the wine and seasoning. Cover with buttered paper and put into a fairly hot oven (mark 5; 375°F.) for half an hour. Pour off the juices into a pan, add the remaining ingredients to them, and boil for 2 minutes. Pour over the fish and serve.

Bluefish à la Créole

Follow the recipe for *red snapper Créole* on p. 158.

Herring (Hareng)

The herring is a versatile fish, and a cheap one, on account of its abundance. Unlike most cheap food, it can be cooked in high style or very simply, and still be a pleasure to eat. The fatness of its flesh makes it suitable for endless refinements of curing: roll mops, soused and marinated herring, kippers, buckling, *maatjes* fillets, sweet-sour fillets in the Danish style, bloaters, red herrings, *gaffelbiter*, *bouffis* and the lovely *harengs saurs* of France. Do you know that mysterious nonsense poem by Charles Cros:

> Il était un grand mur blanc – nu, nu, nu,
> Contre le mur une échelle – haute, haute, haute,
> Et, par terre, un hareng saur – sec, sec, sec[3]

– someone comes along, climbs up the ladder and with his hammer (*qui tombe, qui tombe, qui tombe*) knocks in a nail and hangs the *hareng saur* up by a string.

> Et depuis, le hareng saur – sec, sec, sec,
> Au bout de cette ficelle – longue, longue, longue,
> Très lentement se balance – toujours, toujours, toujours.[4]

I am not surprised about the poem. But what does surprise me is that the herring trade has never had a Pierre Loti, or a Giovanni Verga, let alone a Herman Melville. Perhaps one cannot compare the hazards with those of the Iceland fishermen from Brittany, or the whalers; but a whole complete world has grown around it, with its own customs, and movement, and vocabulary. Do you know the meaning of klondyking, farlanes, gipping, crans, lasts, redding? Did you know that the herring's scales are described as deciduous because they fall as easily as leaves from autumn trees? Did you know that the word herring means 'army' – because of the vast shoals they travel in? One shoal, measured in 1877, was 18 fathoms deep (118 feet): it covered an area which would have reached from Marble Arch to the London docks beyond the Tower, and from the House of Commons to Euston station.

This explains why the herring was rather beyond the capacity of early fishermen; why it didn't really come up until the Middle Ages, when Europe began to settle down and organize its existence into states and towns where a population could prosper. People had to be fed, and in Christian Europe they had to be fed at least once a week, sometimes twice or more, on fish. The herring with its curable nature was the answer. Towns like Amsterdam, Yarmouth and

[3] There was a large white wall – bare, bare, bare,
Against the wall a ladder – high, high, high.
And, on the ground, an *hareng saur* – dry, dry, dry.
[4] And ever since, the *hareng saur* – dry, dry, dry,
At the end of that string – long, long, long,
Very gently swings – always, always, always.

Lowestoft were built on herrings. They caused battles and international incidents as East Anglian and Dutch fishermen raced for the first huge catches in the spring. The way of life of millions of people has been shaped by the herring. Not bad for a small fish weighing on average 5 oz.

Herrings may have no *Pêcheurs d'Islande*, or *Moby Dick*, or *I Malavoglia*, but there is one splendidly readable book by W. C. Hodgson, called rather prosaically *The Herring and Its Fishery*,[5] which has all the information one could wish for. I sometimes think, when reading it, that W. C. Hodgson is the herring novelist *manqué*. He writes so tenderly of this extraordinary fish, pointing out that spring comes to the sea just as it does to fields, woods and hedgerows on shore, and that it is then that the first herring begin to gather in the North Sea. These immature fish are the ones sold in May on every street corner in Holland: passers by stop and swallow one or two, just as they are, with no more than a seasoning of onion and salt. As the herrings begin to fatten up in June, the kipperers of Craster and the Isle of Man get ready to produce their superlative, and undyed, fish (see p. 343). In September and October the shoals come south, and so do the fleets after them, until the end of the year, when the great season is over. Herring are available all the year round, but the time to eat them at their best is from midsummer to the end of October.

They are simple to prepare (guard the roes carefully). And simple to bone – slit along the belly and clean it out; turn the fish on to a board and press firmly all along the backbone; turn the fish again, and the backbone can be picked off with a quantity of tiny bones as well. The herring need not be beheaded first, though it makes things easier if you do.

Grilled Herring

Like mackerel and sprats, herring are an ideal fish for the grill because they are so rich in oil.

If they are to be served whole, clean them and score them twice diagonally through the skin on each side. This allows the heat to penetrate the thickest part more rapidly, so that the thinner part does not overcook. Brush with melted oil, butter or bacon fat, and

[5] Published by Routledge and Kegan Paul, 1957.

grill under a maximum heat, 4–5 minutes a side, depending on the plumpness of the fish.

If the herrings are boned, they will need a little less cooking time. Brush the cut side with butter and season it. Cook for 5–6 minutes, then turn the herring over and give the skin 2–3 minutes to become crisp and brown.

Serve with *maître d'hôtel butter*, or orange or mustard butter (p. 23), or with a mustard sauce. Purées of gooseberries or sorrel can take the place of a sauce. Flavours should be strong and clear. Remember the verse written by Swift for the Irish women crying herrings in London streets:

Be not sparing,
Leave off swearing,
Buy my Herring
Fresh from *Malahide*,[6]
Better ne'er was try'd.
Come eat 'em with pure fresh Butter and Mustard,
Their Bellies are soft, and white as a Custard.
Come, Sixpence a Dozen to get me some Bread,
Or, like my own Herrings, I soon shall be dead.

___

To Fry Herrings in the Scottish Fashion

This is the best way of cooking herrings. The knobbly oatmeal coating and the flavour of bacon set off the fish in a most subtle way.

6 servings:

6 herrings	freshly ground black pepper
3 oz. coarse oatmeal	chopped parsley, lemon
3–4 oz. bacon dripping	quarters
sea salt	

Clean, bone and dry the herrings. Season them well and press them into the coarse oatmeal so that they are well coated. Fry in the bacon fat until brown and crisp on both sides. Serve sprinkled with parsley, and flanked by lemon wedges.

In *English Recipes*[7], Sheila Hutchins observes that dry mealy

[6] Malahide, famous for oysters, is a mile or two from Dublin.
[7] Methuen, 1967.

potatoes in the Lancashire style are excellent with herrings. One of the two recipes she gives used to be popular in Liverpool and the Wirral. The potatoes are peeled and left to soak for a couple of hours in very salty water (see that they are well covered). They are then put in a pan with fresh cold water to which plenty of salt has been added; some cooks make use of sea water. When the potatoes are nearly cooked, pour in some cold water to stop the boiling. Then drain off the water completely, put the lid on the pan, and cover it with a cloth. Let the potatoes finish cooking over a low heat.

Fried Herrings with Cream and Roe Sauce

6 servings:

6 soft-roed herrings	½ pint thick cream
3 oz. butter	chopped parsley and chives
2 tablespoons oil	salt, pepper, lemon juice
3 shallots, chopped	seasoned flour

Clean herrings, and set aside the roes. Cook shallot in 2 oz. of the butter, until soft and golden; add the roes and mash the whole thing together. After a moment or two's cooking, stir in the cream and herbs. Bring back to the boil, season with salt, pepper and lemon juice.

While the sauce is cooking, flour the herrings and fry them in the remaining butter and oil. Place on a serving dish, and cover with the sauce.

Fried Herrings with Sauce Chausey

When herrings do not have the soft roes required for the recipe above, fry them in butter and serve them with the mustard, cream and herb sauce from the Îles de Chausey (p. 38).

Baked Herring

An excellent way of cooking herrings is to bake them in the oven. Fill them with a little stuffing, not too much or their delicate flavour will be drowned. They can be served with lemon quarters, or with one of the yoghurt sauces given below, which go particularly well with an oily fish like herring. Once the fish is boned (p. 162), it can be either left whole, or divided into two fillets which are spread with stuffing, then rolled up, skin side outside, and secured with a cocktail stick. Oven temperature fairly hot (mark 5–6; 375–400°F.); time 20–30 minutes.

This kind of recipe turns a cheap fish into something special; the boning removes the biggest obstacle to the popularity of the herring, and allows people to enjoy its fine flavour without dismay. In the recipes following, the skill comes in balancing various ingredients to your own taste; in choosing fine-flavoured apples and mildly-pickled beetroot and so on. For this reason the quantities I give are guide-lines. The pleasure of cooking, after all, is in the making of something delicious, not in blindly doing what you are told. Such recipes as these are not great classic dishes, which should I think be treated with a certain reverence, but the relaxation, the *jeu d'esprit* of feeding a family and friends. Quantities are for 6 herrings.

HERRING WITH CUCUMBER

6 servings:

6 herrings	½ teaspoon sage, chopped
stuffing:	1 small onion, finely chopped
5 oz. breadcrumbs	2 oz. butter
3 inch piece of cucumber, peeled and diced	1 egg
1 teaspoon thyme	juice and grated peel of 1 lime
1 tablespoon parsley, chopped	salt, pepper

Mix breadcrumbs, cucumber and herbs in a basin. Cook onion gently in butter until soft. Add to the basin with lime juice and peel. Bind with egg; season to taste. Bake as above, and serve with the following sauce:

sauce:	1 tablespoon parsley
1 carton natural yoghurt	juice of 1 lime or lemon
3–4 tablespoons thick cream	salt, pepper
2-inch piece of cucumber, peeled and diced	

Mix all ingredients together, adding lime juice, salt and pepper to taste.

HERRING WITH APPLE AND BEETROOT

6 servings:

stuffing:

5 oz. breadcrumbs
1 eating apple, peeled, cored, diced
¼ teaspoon cinnamon
1 teaspoon sugar
1 small onion, finely chopped
2 oz. butter
1 egg
salt, pepper
2 tablespoons chopped celery (optional)

Mix breadcrumbs, apple, cinnamon and sugar in a basin. Cook onion (and celery, if used) in butter until onion is soft and add to the basin. Bind with the egg, season with salt and pepper, and add more cinnamon to taste, if required. Bake as above, and serve with sauce:

sauce:

1 pot natural yoghurt
3–4 tablespoons thick cream
2 heaped tablespoons boiled or lightly pickled beetroot, chopped
½ large eating apple, peeled, cored and diced
lemon juice
salt, pepper

Mix all the ingredients together, seasoning with lemon juice, salt and pepper to taste. For this recipe use the mildly pickled, 'Rosebud' cocktail beetroot if possible; but plainly boiled beetroot can be used instead. More seasoning will be required, in particular more lemon juice, and perhaps a hint of sugar. The thing to avoid is beetroot fearsomely drenched in malt vinegar.

HERRING WITH MUSHROOMS

6 servings:

stuffing:

4–6 oz. mushrooms, finely chopped
4 oz. breadcrumbs
1 small clove garlic, finely chopped
1 small onion, finely chopped
2 oz. butter
1 egg
1 tablespoon parsley
good pinch *origano* or marjoram
lemon juice
salt, pepper

Melt the onion and garlic in the butter. When they are soft, add the mushrooms and continue to cook gently for 3 or 4 minutes. Mix with the other ingredients, seasoning to taste. Bake as above.

Note. 1 oz. of grated cheese may also be added, for extra piquancy. The curry-flavoured *béchamel* sauce on p. 28 can be served with this dish. Or no sauce at all; provide some lemon quarters, and buttery new potatoes, instead.

HERRING WITH GOOSEBERRIES. Instead of the mushrooms in the stuffing above, use gooseberries. Serve the fish on its own, or with one of the gooseberry sauces on p. 49 – but keep the quantity small so that the herring flavour isn't dominated by the sharpness of the fruit. A little sugar may be needed for seasoning the stuffing.

HERRING WITH SOFT ROE STUFFING. See the mackerel recipe on p. 170. Serve with lemon quarters and potatoes turned in *maître d'hôtel* butter (p. 22).

Swper Scadan (Welsh Supper Herrings)

A dish of a kind popular over much of northern Europe. This is the Welsh version.

1 lb. herrings, filleted	1 large onion, sliced
mustard, salt, pepper	¼ teaspoonful dried sage
1½ lb. potatoes, peeled, sliced	1 oz. butter
1 large cooking apple, peeled, cored, sliced	

Spread herring fillets with mustard, season with salt and pepper, and roll up. Line a buttered pie-dish with half the potatoes, then half the apple, then half the onion. Put herring rolls on top, then scatter them with the sage, and lay remaining onion, apple and potatoes on top. Pour in boiling water to come half way up the dish. Dot with butter. Add seasoning. Cover with foil and bake in a moderate oven (mark 4; 350°F.) for half an hour. Remove the foil, and turn up the heat to mark 5, 400°F, for another 20–30 minutes.

Soft Herring Roes

The creamy texture of soft roes lends itself to some delicious recipes. Provided, that is, you can find them in good shape. Often they have been flung together and frozen into an enormous damaged heap, so that they're good for nothing but the sieve. Keep these poor creatures for the roe paste below or roe stuffing on p. 171, or to make a creamy sauce for shrimp and prawn boats (p. 164). Unblemished, dignified pairs of roes may be fried in butter and served on fried bread, with lemon quarters, or cooked as follows. The recipes following may also be used for mackerel and other soft roes.

FRITURE DE LAITANCE, SAUCE MOUTARDE

6 servings:

18 pairs of large herring roes (more will be needed if they are small)	pinch salt
	2 tablespoons oil
	6 oz. tepid water or beer
batter:	2 small egg whites
4 oz. flour	mustard sauce, p. 28

Divide and season the herring roes. Set them aside. Make the batter by mixing together flour, salt and oil with the tepid water or beer – aim for a pouring custard consistency. Leave to stand for a while, if this is convenient. Beat the egg whites until stiff and fold into the batter just before it is required. Make the mustard sauce and keep it warm.

Coat the roes in batter and fry golden brown on both sides (or use deep-frying pan). As each batch is cooked – it's important not to overcrowd the pan – keep it warm on crumpled kitchen paper, set on a baking tray in the oven. When all are cooked, serve with the mustard sauce.

This is one of the best dishes in the book. I've adapted it slightly from a recipe in Ali Bab's *Gastronomie Pratique* (1928).

If you cannot find roes in good shape, an enjoyable, if second-best, solution is to make soft roe puffs. Buy half a pound of roes. Chop them into a rough purée and season with salt, pepper and lemon juice. Make up the batter above, but with rather less liquid:

¼ pint will be enough. Mix the soft roes into the batter before folding in the stiffly beaten egg whites. Drop spoonfuls of the mixture into hot, deep oil. Remove when they are crisp and golden brown. Keep warm in the oven until the batter is used up. Serve with mustard sauce, or with lemon quarters.

SOFT ROE PASTE. Like the smoked fish pastes on p. 387, this makes a good first course. Serve with brown bread and butter, or with baked bread.

Fry ¼ lb. of soft roes in a little butter. Season well and sieve or mash to a paste. Mix in 3 oz. of softened, unsalted butter, and 1 tablespoon of double cream. Taste, and add more salt and pepper if necessary, and a little lemon juice to sharpen the flavour. Cayenne pepper can also be used to spice this very smooth and delicate mixture, or a few drops of chili sauce.

Canned herring roes can be used, and will not need cooking, but fresh ones are preferable.

OMELETTE WITH SOFT HERRING ROE. Soft herring roes make a good filling for an omelette. Fry them gently in butter, season with lemon and parsley and use as a filling. Or else cook them gently in butter, chop them and add them to the beaten eggs before making the omelette in the usual way. For a dozen eggs, allow ½ lb. of soft roes.

For a more elaborate dish, turn to the recipe for tunny omelette on p. 205; the famous curé's omelette described by Brillat-Savarin in *Physiologie du Goût*. Herring roes can be used instead of the less easily obtained carp roes.

SOFT ROE STUFFING: see below (large mackerel, baked).

SOFT ROE AND CREAM SAUCE: see page 164.

Salted and Cured Herrings

These are dealt with in the chapter on cured and preserved fish, see pp. 341–57.

Mackerel of various kinds (Maquereau)

Mackerel need something: in fact, two things. First – freshness. Dorothy Hartley remarks in *Food in England* that the fish should be 'so fresh that the light shines from it like a rainbow'. A dull, tired mackerel is not worth the trouble of cooking and eating.

Secondly – they need a sharp or positive flavour to set off the richness of the slightly pink flesh. This has been such a cliché of the kitchen over centuries that in France a gooseberry is distinguished from other currants by being called *groseille à maquereau* (though a French cook nowadays is more likely to use sorrel or mustard, pp. 47 and 28).

These svelte and beautiful fish, which winter in the cold depths of the North Sea, taking no food during their long rest, have various relations in the warmer seas of the world. The king-mackerels (French *thazards*), for instance, include the *Cero* of the Mexican Gulf, and the Monterey Spanish mackerel; also the *Sierra* of the Pacific coast, and species off the coasts of China, Japan and India. In Britain, or on holiday in southern Europe, you may well see the Spanish mackerel which has the usual pattern of dark squiggled markings, but on a smaller, less bold scale. All recipes for mackerel, and many recipes for herring or sardine, are suitable for king-mackerel as well.

As a general rule, go for the smaller fish and grill them. Slash three times diagonally each side of the backbone so that the heat may penetrate more quickly to the thickest part; 4–7 minutes a side should be enough, depending on size. Serve them with one of the gooseberry or sorrel sauces (pp. 49, 47), or with mustard butter (p. 23), or a mustard-flavoured *béchamel* sauce. The ideal is to have a crisp, richly-browned skin.

Large Mackerel, Baked (1)

Baking is the best method for the larger fish. One good way is to split, bone and stuff them like the sardines on p. 176. The following mixture provides an alternative to the Sicilian stuffing given there:

6 servings:

6 large mackerel	heaped tablespoon chopped
soft roes from the fish	fresh herbs: parsley and
2 oz. white breadcrumbs	chives, or tarragon
milk	grated rind of half a lemon
1 medium onion, chopped	1 teaspoon anchovy essence,
2 oz. butter	or 2 anchovy fillets chopped
	salt, pepper, lemon juice

Chop the soft roes. Soak the breadcrumbs in a little milk, then
squeeze out any surplus liquid. Sweat the onion in butter until soft
and golden. Mix in all the other ingredients, seasoning to taste.
Bake in a well-buttered dish in a fairly hot oven (mark 5; 375°F.)
for 20–30 minutes, until done.

Note. The stuffings and sauces for baked herrings, given on pp.
164–7, are also suitable for baked mackerel.

Large Mackerel, Baked (2)

An alternative method is to bake the fish in a piquant sauce like
this one. The first time, while I was making it, the flavour did not
seem very distinguished or particularly appetizing; but when it
came to eating it with mackerel the combination was just right.

6 servings:

6 large mackerel	8 oz. water
1 large onion, chopped	*bouquet garni*
2 tablespoons oil	2 heaped tablespoons French
1 heaped tablespoon flour	mustard
8 oz. dry white wine	sugar, salt, pepper

Season the cleaned mackerel, place them head to tail in a buttered
overproof dish, and set it aside while you make the sauce. Cook the
onion gently in oil until soft, stir in the flour, then the wine and
water. Add the *bouquet garni*. When the sauce is smooth and moderately thick, add the mustard and season to taste. Pour it over the

fish. Set in a fairly hot oven (mark 6; 400°F.) for 20 minutes or a little longer, until the fish is cooked.

Mackerel with Bacon

Cold mackerel can be delicious (see the recipe for pickling it in white wine on p. 355). This time bacon provides the piquancy.

6 servings:

3 large cooked mackerel	butter
6 rashers unsmoked back bacon	6 slices brown bread, buttered mayonnaise

Skin the cold, cooked mackerel and carefully remove the fillets. Cut the bacon into strips and fry lightly in a very little butter. Leave to cool. Put the mackerel fillets on slices of bread, pipe mayonnaise on top, and arrange bacon strips across it.

Horse Mackerel or Scad

Various kinds of Horse mackerel or Scad (French *Chinchards*), including Jack Mackerel, Round Robin, Round Scad and Mackerel Scad, are not of such a high quality – from the cook's point of view – as the true mackerel. The name reflects this, like horse chestnut, which is a coarse object compared with the edible Spanish chestnut. They are on sale sometimes in Britain, though again you are more likely to come across them in southern Europe. Shoals appear quite unpredictably by the coast, huge dark masses of fish with a blueish green glow to their backs but without the elegant markings of the mackerel. Vast quantities are caught and sold in South Africa, where the fish is known as *maasbanker*. Some are dried into *bokkems*, that piquant relish described on p. 334; many are eaten fresh. In honour of that abundance, here is a recipe from *Sea Foods of Southern Africa* by Lydia Morris.[8] It's a thoroughly European dish, a refined version of the *Welsh Swper Scadan* (p. 167), and is suitable also for herring, mackerel, mullet, sardines and pilchards.

[8] Purnell and Sons, Cape Town.

8 servings:

4 large horse mackerel	1 dessertspoon seedless raisins
1 large cooking apple	1 tablespoon finely chopped
1 dessertspoon sugar	suet
1 level dessertspoon fresh	lemon juice, salt, pepper
breadcrumbs	1 tablespoon each butter and
1 small onion, chopped	oil

Ask the fishmonger to remove the heads and to take out the roes without splitting the fish. Wash, and remove bits and pieces from the cavities with a sharp knife. Season inside and out and cut through the skin diagonally three times, on each side of the fish.

Now make the stuffing. Peel and chop the apple. Mix with raisins (which have been soaked for 5 minutes in hot water), suet, crumbs, sugar and lemon juice. Season.

Stuff the fish, and lay them on the chopped onion in a buttered fireproof dish. Melt butter and oil together and brush them over. Set in a fairly hot oven (mark 6; 400°F.) until cooked; about 20–30 minutes. Mrs Morris covers them over with foil, but I think it is best to leave the fish uncovered.

Serve with the following mustard sauce:

1 generous tablespoon butter	1 teaspoon sugar
1 tablespoon flour	pinch cayenne pepper
¼ pint light chicken stock	dash of Worcester sauce
¼ pint milk	salt, pepper, vinegar
1 scant tablespoon French	
mustard	

Melt the butter, stir in the flour. Cook for two minutes, then pour in the stock and milk. When the sauce has a good consistency, add the rest of the ingredients; add vinegar last of all, and only if necessary to sharpen the taste a little more.

Fresh Sardines and Pilchards (Sardines, pilchards)

It irritates me to see fresh sardines on sale occasionally in Soho, presented as an exotic fish (at an exotic price) for the travelled housewife, when they are really no more than junior pilchards. It also irritates me to see pilchards in tomato sauce, can upon can of this rather coarse confection at the grocer's, and never a fresh pilchard at the fishmonger's.

But then I live in Wiltshire. Fresh sardines at a sensible price belong to holidays in France and Italy, to small parties in summer moonlight when they are grilled out of doors over a wood fire and eaten with bread and butter and a squeeze of lemon juice, and several glasses of white wine. Pilchards are a Cornish speciality, swimming to their northern limit in great shoals (the younger sardines wisely choose to remain off Brittany and the west coast of France). 'The least fish in bigness, greatest for gain, and most in number is the pilchard,' says Richard Carew[9] in his *Survey of Cornwall*. The picturesque fishery of Elizabethan times that he described continued unchanged until the beginning of this century. It was quite as exciting as the Mediterranean fishing of sardines and anchovies, which takes place more romantically – for the spectator at least – in darkness, with the aid of flaring lamps which attract the fish.

When the shoals were expected, 'between harvest and Allhallowtide', boats with seine nets would 'lie hovering upon the coast'. The masters turned their eyes towards a man stationed on the cliffs, sometimes in a special tower or towered house like the one at Newquay. This was the Huer. It was his job to direct the boats when he saw the dark red shadow approaching, by making a hue and cry with a loud voice, 'whistling through his fingers, and wheazing certain diversified and significant signs with a bush which he holdeth in his hand. At his appointment they cast out their net, draw it to either hand as the shoal lieth or fareth, beat with their oars to keep in the fish, and at last either close and tuck it up in the sea, or draw the same on land with more certain profit, if the ground be not rough of rocks.' There would be several waves of boats, each with their seine nets drawn round as much of the shoal as possible. On shore the country people waited with their horses and baskets; so did the merchants who would 'greedily and speedily' seize the major part of the catch.

The merchants were concerned with a large export trade. Their fish would be salted and pressed and barrelled for France; or salted and smoked for hotter countries like Italy and Spain. The local people would pickle fish for their own use. Or they might bake

[9] Richard Carew was appointed High Sheriff of Cornwall in 1586.

them in a marinade of spiced vinegar like the soused herring on
p. 354. For more immediate use, some of them were split and hung
up in the open air to dry for a couple of days like the wind-drieds,
and rizzard haddock of Scotland, p. 333. With a nice skill in judging
weather and humidity, the fish would be taken down 'in the very
nick of time' and put in pairs, skin sides outside, on a gridiron over
the fire, to roast or 'scrowl'. The insides of the fish were first well
peppered.

Fresh pilchards straight from the boats – in recent times at any
rate, if not in Carew's day – were used to make:

Stargazey Pie

This is a plate pie containing whole pilchards, arranged so that
their heads emerge from the crust as if they are gazing heavenwards.
Sometimes the heads pop out in a bevy from a central hole, and the
tails decorate the rim of the pie. More usually, and more conveniently, the heads are on the outside as if the fish were lying under a
round blanket on a round bed. This second style allows for the
decent concealment of the tails, and of the varying sizes.

To make a good effect, buy at least 8 pilchards – or medium-
sized herrings, or large sardines if the fishmonger has them. Make
some shortcrust pastry with 12 oz. flour, 6 oz butter and lard
mixed, 1 egg and a little water. Roll out half the pastry to cover a
greased pie plate.

Gut and bone the fish, leaving their heads on. Season each one
lavishly inside with salt and pepper, then *either* with finely chopped
onion and green herbs, *or* with French mustard. Fold them into
shape again and arrange on the pastry so that the heads lie evenly
round the rim. If you like, put pieces of fat bacon between the fish,
and crumbled hard-boiled egg. Roll out the rest of the pastry and
cut a round blanket to cover the fish, all but their heads. Press down
firmly between each fish. Brush with beaten egg (or saffron milk, if
you want to follow the Cornish style). Bake for 30 minutes in a
fairly hot oven (mark 6; 400°F.), then for about 15 minutes at
moderate (mark 4; 350°F.).

There were all kinds of variations on the basic recipe. Sometimes
the under-crust of pastry was omitted, and the fish were laid on a
bed of breadcrumbs, chopped onion and herbs, the plate being well

buttered first. Sometimes cider, or a custard of egg and cream, was poured over the fish to make a moister pie.

The main puzzle of the recipe is the fish heads. They are, after all, uneatable. In *Food in England*, Dorothy Hartley says that 'When eatable pastry was used it was wasteful to cover the uneatable fish-head – yet, if the fish-head was cut off, the rich oil in it was lost. Therefore, it was better to cook the fish whole, so that this oil could drain back into the meat (as marrow out of the bones internally bastes a roasting joint). So the cooks covered the body of the fish – but left the head sticking out.' She also remarks that stargazeys were sold by the yard at markets: the stuffed whole fish would be laid on a strip of pastry, then covered with another, which would be well pressed down between the fish. After baking, it would be quite easy to cut individual portions without making a crumbly wasteful mess.

Sarde a Beccafico (Stuffed Sardines)

A most savoury and appetizing dish from Palermo in Sicily. Its sweet-sour mixture of ingredients – pine kernels, sultanas, anchovies and lemon juice – echoes ancient and modern dishes from the Arab world. This isn't surprising as Sicily belonged to the Saracens from the beginning of the 9th century until the end of the 11th century, when the Normans arrived. Even then Muslim culture wasn't wiped out, but continued to flourish under the benign influence of Roger II, King of Sicily. I like to think of tough Normans encountering the delights of sherbet and of dishes like this one, then taking the recipes back home to their families beyond the Alps. Such mixtures as this are the background to mincemeat and plum porridges, in which dried fruits were mixed sometimes with meat, sometimes with herrings. (One must admit that the hands of northern cooks were cruder and heavier in their enthusiastic galli-maufries.)

Beccafico is the Italian word for a warbler. It refers to the shape of the stuffed sardines, tucked side by side in the baking dish like a row of little birds.

If fresh sardines are unobtainable, you could use herring or, better still, whiting fillets. I also find that the firm sweetness of cod contrasts well with the rich stuffing; lay the slices in a greased baking dish, and pile the stuffing on top – very simple.

The quantities of the various ingredients can be adjusted to taste. The ones below are taken from *Italian Regional Cooking*, by Ada Boni, published by Nelson.

4 servings:

2½ lb. fresh sardines	about 1 teaspoon sugar
salt	6 salted anchovies, boned
olive oil	pepper
5 heaped tablespoons soft white breadcrumbs	3 sprigs parsley, finely chopped
	3 bay leaves
3 oz. sultanas	1 small onion, finely chopped
3 oz. pine kernels	juice of 1–2 lemons or oranges

Cut off the heads of the sardines, clean them and split them open down the belly. Turn them, back up, on a board, and press gently but firmly down the backbone. Turn them again and you will find it easy to remove the backbone. Wash quickly in salted water, and dry.

Heat ½ pint olive oil and sauté 4 tablespoons of the crumbs in it until they're lightly browned. Put the crumbs into a bowl. Add sultanas, pine kernels and sugar. Wash anchovies until they're clear of salt, pound them, and add to the bowl with the parsley and onion. (If you can't buy salted anchovies, use anchovies which have been canned in oil but drain and dry them well first.) Season with plenty of freshly ground black pepper, and mix the ingredients with your hands.

Put some stuffing into each fish cavity and roll the sides together round it. Rub a baking dish with olive oil and arrange the sardines in a single layer in it. Tear the bay leaves into pieces and sprinkle them on top, plus any stuffing left over. Finally sprinkle the remaining breadcrumbs over the whole thing with a little olive oil. Bake in a moderate oven (mark 4; 375°F.) for 30 minutes, until the breadcrumbs are brown and the sardines cooked. Squeeze plenty of lemon or orange juice over the dish and serve immediately.

Whitebait

One of the treats I best remember as a child was being taken by my mother – rather stealthily – to Lyons Corner House, at Piccadilly Circus, for the purpose of eating whitebait, with lemon and brown bread and butter. It was the dish of her nostalgic youth in London. Now she lived in the north, and felt that my education was lacking in this vital experience, and must be remedied. At first I was alarmed at the crisp mound of minuscule bodies, complete with eyes, which were placed in front of me. Then I saw my mother tucking in with an expressive wave of her fork, and had to follow suit. I soon found out how right she had been.

Whitebait used to be part of a privileged education, decidedly a rich man's pleasure. These tiny creatures – literally the small fry of herring and sprats – were caught in the Thames in shoals off Blackwall and Greenwich every year between May and August. They became the main dish at a series of annual dinners held at Dagenham to celebrate the completion of complex engineering work which saved the low land of Essex from flooding. As prime minister, Pitt was invited one year; another year he came with several members of his government. Soon the dinners turned into a regular function at the end of the parliamentary session, and were transferred to Greenwich, where they took place more or less regularly, until 1894. Whitebait parties at Greenwich soon became a fashionable summer ritual.

Nowadays whitebait can be eaten anywhere by anyone. They are sold in deep-frozen packages, and they freeze well, much better than shrimps and prawns. I can thoroughly recommend them.

There is only one way to cook them. After thawing, dip them in milk and shake them in a paper bag with a little flour. Put them into a chip-basket and deep-fry until golden brown and crisp; two or three minutes. Some people use the chip method of double frying, but this is hardly necessary. Serve with lemon quarters and brown bread and butter. For devilled whitebait, sprinkle with cayenne pepper before serving.

They seem to be a peculiarly English delicacy, though in the Mediterranean a similar fry-up of tiny pellucid soles and other tiny fish of the *Gobiidae* family is popular. You may come across it on holiday in Southern France, under the name of *nonnat*.

Sprats (Sprats, esprots)

Although sprats may look – hopefully – like smelts, it is wise to distinguish between the two for culinary reasons. The sprat, being a member of the herring family, is rich in oil and therefore tastes best when grilled. The smelt, being a member of the salmon family, is less rich and is usually fried.

Confusing them is not however a matter for deep anxiety. For one thing, the sprat has a tubbier, more homely appearance. For another, it is by many times the more common of the two fishes. According to official lists, over one million eleven thousand hundredweight of them were landed in 1971. Smelts do not even rate an individual mention.

Sprats should be cleaned through the gills – if you slit them they become raggy as they cook. Grill them for a few moments on each side, 3 minutes a side is the maximum, and serve with lemon quarters, or a piquant French mustard. They can be turned into an *escabèche* like smelts (p. 180), but are better baked in the oven, skinned, and left to marinate in an oil and lemon dressing, with plenty of fresh green herbs and chopped spring onion.

Smoked sprats are a bargain, they should be served as part of a mixed hors d'oeuvre, and are most delicious. So, too, are the tiny sprats or 'brisling' canned by Skippers – again for a mixed hors d'oeuvre rather than the sardines-on-toast treatment.

Smelts, Argentines and Atherines (Éperlans, argentines and atherines or prêtres)

These slim silver fish, all about 7 inches long, look much the same although they are unrelated. The best of them is the smelt. When freshly caught, it is said to smell of cucumbers, but this elegant fragrance has usually departed by the time it is bought. Chefs of the past have loved the smelt, and used it as part of their elaborate garnishes. Nowadays it is a fish for the first course of a meal, like the argentine and atherine.

The classic way of cooking these fish is to string them on skewers, through the eye sockets, and fry them. They are then served with lemon and bread and butter. Sometimes they are brought in on a base of well-buttered spinach.

If you want something a little more unusual, try this *escabeche*:

2 servings:

1–1½ lb. smelts, argentines or atherines	1 medium onion, sliced
	2 cloves garlic, halved
milk	¼ pint wine vinegar
seasoned flour	*bouquet garni*
½ pt olive oil	salt, pepper, cayenne
1 medium carrot, sliced	

Dip the fish in milk, drain, and coat them in flour, shaking off any surplus. Fry not too fast in the oil, until golden brown, then transfer to a serving dish. Refresh the oil with a spoonful or two more, then cook vegetables and garlic until lightly coloured. Add vinegar and bouquet, plus about 2 oz. of water. Simmer until vegetables are cooked. Season and pour, boiling, over fish. Serve chilled.

Skate, Ray or Roker (Raie)

The ribbed wings of skate are sometimes described as 'coarse', which I resent. Those rosy wedges, leaved one over the other on a white tray at the fishmonger's, do not deserve such an adjective. The French have more discrimination and describe the flesh as very fine; delicate.

It can be cooked in several different ways, and is always a success particularly with children. The ribs of flesh part sweetly and easily from the layer of soft, unvicious bone, a relief after the troublesome and spiky nature of herrings. Skate, like dogfish and shark, belongs to the cartilaginous *Selachians*: this makes all the difference to a child dealing with fish. I remember admiring the neat way it was all put together, but had no idea of the kite-shaped beauty of the total creature, with its long tail, until I saw the shimmering skate of James Ensor's painting many years later. As children, our only contact with its reality was the black, four-handled egg sacs that washed up on the beach with the sea-weed; we called them 'witch's purses'.

The pieces of skate one eats are taken from the wings only, though sometimes small nuggets are cut from the tail and sold as 'skate nobs' (in French, *joues de raie*, skate's cheeks). Floured and fried in butter, and served with lemon, they are delicious. Apparently they are popular in the north-west, at Lytham in Lancashire, but I have never seen them in the south of England. They are worth looking out for. Incidentally do not be put off by a slight smell of ammonia, it disappears in cooking.

Fried Skate

If the pieces are small, each whole wing weighing about half a pound, they will be tender enough to be fried in clarified butter, or half butter and half oil. Turn them in seasoned flour first, and give them 4 minutes a side, until the flesh begins to part from the bone easily and loses its transparent look. Serve with a creamy caper sauce, or a shrimp sauce to which capers have been added.

Pieces of skate make good fritters. Cut the wings into manageable strips or wedges. Dip them in batter (p. 19) and deep-fry. Serve with lemon quarters or a piquant mayonnaise.

Large pieces of skate may also be fried, but they should first be cooked briefly in a *court-bouillon* as in the next recipe.

Raie au Beurre Noir

The classic recipe for skate, particularly suitable for larger wings. These are usually sold cut into pieces; choose the thick middle strips, rather than the side wedge pieces. Put them into cold *court-bouillon* (no. 2, p. 17) and bring to the boil. After one strong bubble, lower the heat to keep the liquid below simmering point. In 15 minutes the skate should be cooked (10 minutes will be enough if you wish to fry it as in the recipe above).

For six people, you will need 3 lb. skate, prepared as above. Drain the pieces and put them on a warm serving dish, while you make the *beurre noir*, which is not really black at all – that would be disgusting – but a deep golden brown.

Melt a nice large knob of butter in a frying pan – 3 or 4 oz. for six people – and cook it until it turns this deep golden colour. Pour it over the fish. Swill out the pan with a couple of tablespoons of wine vinegar, bubble it for a few seconds and pour that over the fish, too. Scatter with capers and chopped parsley and serve immediately.

Boiled potatoes, preferably new, go well with this dish. Turn them in parsley butter.

Raie à la Crème

Particularly rich and good.

6 servings:

3 lb. skate	5 oz. heavy double cream
4 oz. unsalted or lightly salted butter	2 egg yolks, beaten
	2–3 tablespoons parsley

Cook the skate in *court-bouillon* (no. 2, p. 17) as in recipe above. Drain, arrange the pieces on a serving dish, and keep warm. Melt the butter in a frying-pan, pour in the cream and stir until well amalgamated and bubbling; a few moments, that's all. Pour on to the beaten yolks, whisking with a fork, then return to the pan and heat without boiling until very thick. Add the parsley. Pour some of the sauce over the fish and serve the rest in a sauceboat.

Croustade de Raie

6 servings:

1 shortcrust pastry case, baked blind	*or* anchovy sauce (p. 29) plus capers
2½ lb. skate	*or* Mornay sauce (p. 26)
either mushroom sauce (p. 29) plus capers	4 tablespoons Gruyère cheese and breadcrumbs mixed (optional)

Cook the skate in *court-bouillon* in the usual way (p. 181). Remove the flesh from the bones and cut into pieces about 1 inch square. Put a layer of sauce into the pastry case, then the fish, then enough sauce to cover well. Reheat in a fairly hot oven (mark 6; 400°F.) for 10 minutes, and finish under the grill. If you like, sprinkle the top with a couple of tablespoons of grated Gruyère cheese, mixed with two tablespoons of breadcrumbs.

Skate Mayonnaise

6 servings:

3 lb. skate
mayonnaise, pp. 50–55
vinaigrette dressing, p. 61

crisp lettuce, such as Webb's Wonderful

Cook the skate in *court-bouillon* in the usual way. When just done, remove and drain well. Put on a plate and pour over it, while it is still warm, a little vinaigrette dressing, made with lemon juice and olive oil.

Choose a lemon mayonnaise, or any other with a sharp seasoning. Put some lettuce leaves on a dish, arrange the skate on top and pour the mayonnaise over. Decorate with capers, olives or anchovies (depending on what kind of mayonnaise you have chosen to make) and chopped parsley. Serve chilled.

Note. It is a refinement to remove the skate from the bones before arranging it on the lettuce, though not strictly necessary.

Dogfishes – Flake, Huss and Rigg (Aiguillats, roussettes)

I cannot be the only person to associate dogfish with the appalling smell of formalin. On dissecting days at school, too often Fridays, the smell became unforgettably united, about halfway up the stairs, with the smell of fish pie. No wonder the fish authorities prefer the names of flake, huss and rigg.

There is good warrant for these names. Frank Buckland visited Folkestone harbour in the last century and saw that most of the fishermen's houses were adorned 'with festoons of fish hung out to dry. There was no head, tail or fins to them . . . the rough skin on their reverse side told me at once that they were a species of dogfish. I asked what they were? "Folkestone beef," was the reply. What sort of fish is this? "That's a Rig;" and this? "That's a Huss;" and this other? "That! A 'bull huss'." ' He went on to say that as soon as the boats arrived, the fish-dealers could be seen cutting off the heads, tails and fins and halving the fish, which were then salted and hung out to dry. When grilled they tasted like veal chops, and were eaten 'by the poorer class, as a relish for breakfast'.

The word dogfish covers a variety of small sharks, as fierce as a pack of wild dogs. They have a keen sense of smell, and hunt mackerel, herring and whiting like a pack of hounds.

All this being said, the name will not do. We are too closely attached to family dogs to eat anything that bears their name. The same with cats. I think that flake, huss and rigg are therefore reasonable. Rock salmon or rock turbot for catfish is a less happy choice of alias. It verges on a con trick, because catfish is not remotely like salmon or turbot at any point; rockfish is a better choice.

Good quality huss is certainly a wiser buy than a piece of tired white fillet of nothing-in-particular. It repays attention. Cut it into 3-inch pieces – the body is long and roughly eel-shaped – and coat them in seasoned flour. Fry gently until a true golden-brown, in butter, or preferably clarified butter. Serve them with natural brown rice, boiled and tender, and with a creamy sauce. The curry sauce on p. 28 is an excellent choice. So is *sauce aurore* (p. 31), or a white wine sauce; seasoning and richness.

Another way is to brown the floured pieces lightly in olive oil flavoured with garlic, and to transfer them to a tomato, *créole* or *américaine* sauce to finish cooking (p. 44 and p. 46).

Very fresh huss can be deep-fried in batter (p. 19) and served hot or cold, with an olive-oil and lemon vinaigrette, or one of the highly flavoured mayonnaises.

Cod and Hake, etc. (Cabillaud, merlu or colin, etc.)

You can do a number of things with fresh cod, it just depends on whether it is worth it. Escoffier once remarked that if cod was a rarer fish – at the moment it represents 45% of the total catch landed in this country every year – we should all be after it. 'It would be held in as high esteem as salmon; for when it is really fresh and of good quality, the delicacy and delicious flavour of its flesh admit of its ranking among the finest of fish.' This may be true, but I notice that he was not inspired to give more than 6 recipes for it.

The truth is that if you can buy very fresh cod, the big white flakes will be sweet and firm, and worth a good sauce such as *hollandaise* or *béarnaise*. I remember as a child, in the north-east before the war, that we regarded cod as something special because it tasted special. It came, I think, from local fishing boats. In general, cod from Icelandic waters, huge cod, frozen cod, amounts to no more than an abundant form of easily digested protein.

It can certainly be improved by sauces and strong additional flavours, applied with discretion. Yet the simple ways on the whole are best. For instance, packaged frozen cod steaks and fillets – often a better buy than the pieces lolloping greyly on the counter – are enjoyable when cooked with mushrooms in butter, or with bacon. One cannot, though, escape the fact that cod owes its popularity to its enormous abundance (and consequent cheapness) in northern waters. Discrimination in buying is even more necessary with cod and its lesser relations than it is with expensive fish. Always ask for inshore cod.

Cod may not be an epicure's delight, but as the fish of human martyrdom, of the tragedy of lost lives, it does have a splendid novel to itself: *Pêcheurs d'Islande*,[10] Pierre Loti turned the sufferings of this dangerous trade into a work of art; a sustained elegy for the tough, inarticulate Bretons, who spent the summer in a frail 'house of planks', rocking on the north sea in the pale void of Arctic summer nights – and for the families who often waited in vain for the returning boats in September. Nowadays the cod fishermen

[10] Translation – Everyman Library.

spend the winters there as well, in vast modern trawlers with wireless, and refrigerated chambers for the catch. But even they are not always a match for the ice of those bitter seasons off Iceland and the North Cape.

And when you come down to the other members of the cod family, you may wonder even more if such suffering is worthwhile. Haddock (*aiglefin*) is best when small, and smoked in the manner of Findon or of Arbroath (p. 363). Hake (*merlu* or *colin*) is somewhat tasteless, so are coley or saithe (*lieu noir*), pollock (*lieu jaune*) and ling (*linque*). They are eatable and good for soups, but they don't have the merits of cod. Monday fish, hardly worth elevating to Friday.

For good eating, one needs the tiny members of the family, whiting (*merlan*), and the foot-long hake which are sold in France as *colinot* but which I have never seen here. When they are fresh and bright-looking the flavour is delicate, the texture sympathetic. When they are tired, the flavour vanishes. Whiting has many recipes of its own (see pp. 118–22), and is worth considerate treatment When the tiny *colinots* are fried in clarified butter and served with lemon quarters, they are delicious.

Returning to cod and its larger kin, treat them with vigour. They make good fritters (dip pieces in milk, in flour, then in batter, and deep-fry until golden), and are worth a home-made mayonnaise embellished with chopped herbs and pickled cucumbers or capers. As you will see from the following recipes, bacon, mushrooms, cheese, curry powder, but particularly bacon, are the kind of embellishments that they require. The recipes are suitable for all the larger white fish, and for Norwegian redfish, sometimes sold under the deceptive name of 'bream' (real bream is something much better, see pp. 141–4). See also the soups on pp. 62–88. In this connection, I should also mention the pout (*tacaud*), a fish with a skin looking rather like brown paper. Apart from soups, it is also simmered in a *court-bouillon* (p. 15) and served hot or cold with an appropriate sauce.

Cod with Mushrooms

6 servings:

6 cod steaks, or pieces of fillet	¾ lb. mushrooms, sliced
seasoned flour	1 clove garlic, crushed
4 oz. clarified butter	salt, pepper, parsley

Turn the fish in seasoned flour. Heat the clarified butter, add the cod, the garlic and the mushroom slices. Fry at a moderate temperature until the cod is golden brown and cooked. Remove it to a serving dish. Taste the mushrooms and pan juices, correct the seasoning and pour over the cod. A little unclarified butter may be added to the mushrooms at this stage; it depends how much juice there is. Sprinkle with parsley and serve.

The important thing is to cook mushrooms and cod together so that the flavours intermingle. A surprisingly good dish.

Curried Cod

6 servings:

2–3 lb. cod fillet	curry sauce, p. 28
seasoned flour	1 large eating apple
2 oz. clarified butter	1 lemon

Cut the fillet into pieces. Turn them in the flour and fry in the butter. Put them on to a serving dish and keep warm. Peel, then grate the apple into the hot curry sauce, and give it a moment or two to soften in the heat. Season with lemon juice, and squeeze the remaining juice over the cod. Pour some of the sauce over the fish and serve the rest in a sauce boat. Boiled rice is the obvious accompaniment to this dish, even if it does belong to the European rather than the Indian tradition of cookery.

Cod with Mustard

Mustard goes well with cod; even better with coley, ling, pollock *et al.* It can be served in several ways.

The fish can be brushed with clarified butter and grilled, then served with pats of mustard butter (p. 23) or with a bowl of whipped cream flavoured with mustard of the French or German variety.

With fried fish, or with fish baked in a little white wine on a bed of shallots, a mustard-flavoured *béchamel* or *velouté* (pp. 25, 32) is the answer. The liquor from the baked fish should be added to the sauce. Some boiled potatoes are a good addition.

Cod-in-the-Hole

A recipe from the Shetland Islands; a family version of cod fritters.

6 servings:

6 cod steaks	salt, pepper
4 oz. flour	2 oz. lard
1 large egg	lemon quarters
½ pint milk	

Cut the cod steaks into 1-inch pieces and season them well. Make the Yorkshire pudding batter with flour, egg and milk in the usual way. Heat the lard in a baking tin about 11″ × 7″ × 1″ deep, and pour in a thin layer of batter. Bake in a hot oven (mark 7; 425°F.) for 5 minutes. Then arrange the cod pieces on top and pour on the rest of the batter. Cook for 50 minutes, or a little longer, until the pudding is brown and crisp and well-risen. Serve with lemon quarters.

Gratin of Cod

Another good family dish, filling, and full of flavour. It is really a variation of *Jansson's Temptation* (p. 377).

6 servings:

6 cod steaks	bay leaf
18 thin slices bacon	bunch of parsley
1½ lb. potatoes, peeled	bunch of chives
4 large onions	6 oz. cream
4 oz. butter	salt, pepper

Season the cod. Cut the rind from the bacon and divide each rasher into three or four pieces. Slice the potatoes very thinly on a mandoline or on the wide cucumber blade of the grater. Slice the onions as thinly as possible, too. Grease a large gratin dish with half the butter.

Arrange the ingredients in layers, seasoning as you go, in the following order: half the potato, bay leaf, half the onion, half the parsley and chives, half the bacon, all the cod, the rest of the parsley and chives, the rest of the bacon, onion and potatoes. Dot the rest of the butter over the top, pour on the cream and put into a fairly hot oven (mark 6; 400°F.) and leave for 45 minutes. When the dish begins to bubble at the sides, and has really begun to cook, the heat may be lowered to moderate to fairly hot (mark 4–5; 350–375°F.). The secret of success is to cut the potatoes and onions wafer thin so that they are properly cooked, without the cod being over-cooked. Anchovies could be substituted for bacon.

Cod Chowder: p. 76.

Cod in other Fish Soups: pp. 62–88.

Cod en Brochette. See pp. 130, 210, 302.

Cod Steaks au Fromage. See p. 116.

Cod Steaks au Poivre. See p. 111.

Catfish, Wolf-fish, or Rock Turbot (Poisson-loup, loup de mer)

This fierce creature, with its blunted head like a fold-eared cat, makes good eating. The long single-boned body provides firm flesh which, like tunny and anglerfish, can be treated like veal. The first time we bought it – in France – we were advised to pierce it with slivers of garlic, and either bake it in tomato sauce (see anglerfish *à l'américaine*, p. 130), or fry it in clarified butter. It benefits from a little sharpness, such as vinegar or lemon, in the final seasoning. Try it cooked *au poivre*, p. 111.

Owing to its fierce aspect, catfish is sold without the head and skin. In Britain the pinkish white fillets appear under the name of rock turbot – or rock salmon, which is more usually applied to dogfish. I dislike such names: they make comparisons which lead inevitably to the lesser fish's disadvantage. The French call it sea wolf. Are we too squeamish for this – or for the straightforward catfish or wolf-fish?

Catfish with Fennel and Beurre Noisette

6 servings:

2–3 lb. tailpiece or fillet	4 oz. butter
seasoned flour	2 oz. clarified butter
3 large heads Florentine fennel, sliced	3 cloves garlic
2 large onions, chopped	wine vinegar, salt, pepper, parsley

Cook the fennel in boiling, salted water for 5 minutes. Drain. Melt 2 oz butter; stew the onion and fennel in it for about 20 minutes, until cooked but not brown. Season. Cut the garlic into slivers and push into incisions made in the fish with a sharp pointed knife. Turn the fish in seasoned flour, and fry gently in the clarified butter. Put the vegetables on a dish, with the catfish on top. Clean the fish pan and melt the last 2 oz. butter in it. When golden brown, pour it over the fish. Swill out the pan with a good dash of vinegar and pour on top of the butter. Sprinkle with chopped parsley and serve.

Conger Eel (Congre)

When it's my turn for the ferry boat across the Styx, one of the people I hope to encounter in Hades is Nereus of Chios, a Greek chef who worked in Sybaris. He was famous for his preparation of conger eel, and I should like to know how he did it. I suspect he followed the cookery tradition of classical times and drowned the fish in seasonings and strong sauces. Now conger eel, being firm and insistent in flavour, might survive this treatment well – better, at any rate, than delicate fish like sole or turbot. The sauce for roast conger eel given some two thousand years ago by Apicius (who got his recipes mainly from Greek cooks working in Italy) included pepper, lovage, grilled cumin, origano, dried onion, yolks of hard-boiled eggs, wine, honeyed wine, vinegar and garum – which was a fermented fish sauce (see p. 369) with a good deal more kick than anchovy essence.

I do not suggest that you follow Apicius to the letter, but remember that a little conger eel goes a long way and can stand up to a collection of other flavours. For this reason it's an excellent fish for soup, as you will see if you try the Breton recipe on p. 82, or the *Matelote Normande* on p. 65. The conger makes a good basis of fish flavour.

Do not be fooled by writers who instruct you to cook conger eel like the silver eel from the Sargasso sea, *Anguilla anguilla*, one of the finest fish you can eat. General shape apart, they have nothing in common and your expectations will be disappointed. I suspect that this instruction is merely handed down from cookery book to cookery book, without anyone trying it out. I have, several times, and it was a disastrous waste. The only possible eel recipe would be the red wine and prunes *matelote* (p. 270) where, Apicius-style, the almost unpleasant flavour of conger in the piece is well subdued by stronger presences.

As a subsistence fish, it has its own little history. In Cornwall, until the end of the last century, 'conger-doust' was exported in quantity to Catholic countries, largely, I gather, for soup-making on fast days. This was conger, split, and dried without salting; a kind of stock-fish. In Normandy, fishermen do the same thing, but season the boned conger with salt and pepper before drying it in the sun. It's eaten for breakfast with bread and butter, and milky coffee, just as the Scots used to eat wind-dried whiting and haddock (p. 333). Conger eel is also cooked, with onions and herbs, in vinegar, and stored as a preserve, like soused herring (p. 354). Pieces are removed from time to time and served at the beginning of a meal with oil and herbs, and bread and butter.

Always buy a thick piece of conger eel from the head end. The bones seem to multiply alarmingly towards the tail.

Sand-eel (Équilles or lançons)

Sand-eels, or sand-lances, look like miniature eels, long and silvery – but this is where the resemblance stops. The flavour is pleasant rather than distinguished. The flesh is firm and sweet, without the rich delicacy of eel.

They seem to be more popular in France than here: we often see them at our weekly market in the Bas-Vendômois, fresh and shining, 150 miles from the sea, displayed in a giant handful amongst the cheaper fish. They are best floured and salted, then fried in clarified butter or olive oil. Serve with lemon quarters, bread, butter and white wine. One or two other small fish may be added to make a mixed fry.

In the last century sand-eels provided a lively holiday occupation at the seaside. 'When it is discovered that a shoal of sand-eels have hidden themselves in the sand, sea-side visitors should sally out, armed with spades, shovels, rakes and forks, and dig them out. When extricated from the sand-beds, the fish leap about with singular agility, and afford much sport.'[11]

[11] Frank Buckland: *History of British Fishes*, 1880.

Squid (Calmars, calamars or encornets)

Although octopus (see p. 199) and cuttlefish and squid are much eaten in southern Europe, the cephalopod most usually encountered at the fishmonger's shop is the squid. It's tender and delicious and easy to cook. Some squid are tiny, the body part about 3 inches long: they're the ones for quick frying. Others are most substantial, the body part over 6 inches long: they're the ones for stuffing and stewing and gentle frying. Whatever the size, they'll have two triangular finny flaps, attached to the body. Unless the fishmonger has removed it, there will also be a fine purplish red veil of delicate transparency: this, alas, has to be removed as its appearance is spoiled by cooking, through it is not inedible. Tentacles tassel out from the head, ten of them, if you care to count. All in all a strange and beautiful creature.

Or don't you agree? Perhaps the appearance is a little daunting to the cook the first time she encounters squid. Even more daunting is the sight of a frozen block of 28 or even 60 lb. of squid, looking like a compressed Last Judgement. Some fishmongers have to buy them this way. Theyr'e tender and good, but not so good as fresh ones, which may look inky and muddled by comparison.

The first encounter with a squid can be memorable and messy. Mine happened years ago, when squid was still an exotic, something one ate in Greek Cypriot restaurants in London. Yet we saw this creature on top of a pile of crabs on the quay at Seahouses in Northumberland. It looked improbable. Surely it should have come out of the Mediterranean, not the bitter North Sea.

We took it back to the cottage in Craster where we were staying. We looked at it. Tentacles, bag of a body – where did one start? How could so rubbery an object be transformed into our favourite *kalamarakia* stew? We rang the restaurant where we had often eaten it. Through the crackling of a bad line, we heard the manager Epaminondas, a patient man, give the simple instructions of the first recipe. We followed them and the flavour was fine, just right, but that squid must have been the old man of the Farne Islands. It could have done with a high proportion of the 99 obligatory octopus bashings.[12]

[12] Octopus is said to be beaten 99 times before it is tender enough to eat.

This is unfair to the squid which do in fact flourish sweetly and tenderly in our waters (and turn up on fish slabs in Soho). I don't understand why they aren't a regular part of our diet. But they may become so. Squid are seen more and more, thanks to foreigners who have made their homes here, and thanks to our new passion for holidays in the sun. Should you go camping, or rent a house in France, Italy or Spain, buy squid in the markets there, not so much because they're still on the scarce side in England compared with cod, but because tomatoes for the sauce will be so much better-flavoured than ours, and wine and olive oil so much cheaper than we can buy at home for the rest of the year.

Squid Stewed with Tomato and Wine

See that the squid are much of a size, so that they will all be cooked at the same time. In a stew of this kind, and for *calamares en su tinta* below, I find that 2 lb. of squid is enough for six people with good appetites, because in both cases the sauce is filling.

6 servings:

2 lb. squid	1 glass of wine; red, dry
1 large onion, chopped	white, or vermouth
1 clove garlic, crushed	sugar, salt, black pepper
olive oil	Spanish paprika (optional)
1 lb. tomatoes, or a 14 oz. tin	chopped parsley
1 tablespoon tomato concentrate	

First prepare the squid. You'll see why it's called calamar in many countries (from *calamus*, the Latin for reed, and so a pen – something to write with). When the head part is pulled gently but firmly away from the bag, inside the bag you'll find a nib-like piece of hard transparency called, in English, the 'pen'. Throw it away. Remove the purplish-red veil of skin from the body, wash it well inside and out and cut it into rings; the two flaplike fins are edible, so include them too. Now chop the tentacles from the head, and cut them into ¾ inch pieces. Put them with the rings. Look carefully at the soft part still attached to the head – you will see a longish narrow ink sac, the dark colour showing through the white enclosing skin; remove it and put it into a bowl. Head and soft entrails should be discarded. This sounds lengthy, but in reality it's quickly done.

Cover the bottom of a large saucepan or frying pan with a thin layer of oil. When it's hot, fry the squid pieces, together with onion and garlic, until they're lightly browned. It's a good idea to dry the squid first with a kitchen cloth, to cut down the spitting of the oil.

Add tomatoes (either skinned and quartered, or with their juice if they're canned), tomato concentrate, and wine. Season lightly. Crush the ink sacs, diluting them with a spoonful or two of water, and strain into the pan.

Simmer uncovered for 15–30 minutes, until the squid is cooked, then remove as many of the pieces as you conveniently can to a warm serving dish.

Now for the sauce. If it's watery and abundant, boil it down. If the consistency seems right, correct the seasoning with salt, black and paprika peppers, and with sugar (which helps the tomato flavour). Add a little more tomato concentrate, if you like. When the taste is rich and appetizing, pour the sauce over the squid; sprinkle with chopped parsley and serve very hot. Provide plenty of good crusty bread to eat with the dish.

This is a recipe for variation. Add a little water and plenty of seasoning for a thick fish soup. Or else divide the mixture between small pots, tuck in triangles of fried bread, and serve as the first course for a special meal: in this case, the sauce should be rich and in small quantity (any left over can be the start of next day's fish soup, or else the sauce for boiled rice or egg noodles).

Calamares en su Tinta

Squid cooked in their own ink, Spanish style. With all the *calamus* names of the Mediterranean (an exception being one French name *encornet*, a reference to the cornet shape of the body) it's surprising that the old English name of 'sea clerk' didn't stick (no one knows the origin of the word squid). After all, with ink as well as pen, one would have expected it.

This nomenclature is man-centred, decidedly. The ink is not intended for the use of clerks, nor is it for providing artists with sepia. (Though it does; the sacs are dried, pulverized and cleaned, to be made into the pigment familiar to every small owner of a water-colour box.) Its purpose is to protect the squid from aggressors. When the creature feels threatened, it puffs out the ink to darken the water, a liquid smoke screen, while it hurriedly retreats. So you can see why the apparently small amount of ink is so concentrated, enough to colour a quantity of sauce in the most intense way.

6 servings:

4 large squid, about 2 lb.	1 glass white wine
4 oz. of chopped onion	salt, freshly ground pepper,
1 large clove garlic, finely	and nutmeg
chopped	level tablespoon flour
handful of parsley, chopped	lemon juice
olive oil	

Prepare the squid in the usual way (p. 194), being particularly careful to remove the ink sacs to a large basin without bursting them. Cut the body into rings and the tentacles into pieces. Put a thin film of olive oil into a heavy frying pan or saucepan. When it smokes, fry the squid, onion and garlic fairly fast for 5 minutes. Add wine, plus enough water to cover the fish, parsley, and a seasoning of salt, pepper and nutmeg (the nutmeg is important – it shouldn't be overdone, of course, but the flavour must be there). Cover and simmer for 10–15 minutes.

Meanwhile crush the ink sacs with three tablespoons water, using a wooden spoon. Mix in the flour to make a smooth paste. Pour into the squid stew, through a sieve, rubbing through as much of the inky mixture as possible. Simmer for a further 5–10 minutes, until the squid is cooked. Serve very hot with boiled rice. Don't forget to correct the seasoning of the sauce at the last moment, adding a little lemon juice if you like.

Stuffed Squid

I like squid cooked in a variety of different ways, but this is my favourite. It's not worth trying, however, unless you can choose squid with bodies at least 6 inches long, preferably 8. Smaller ones are too fragile and burst easily, which spoils the point of the dish.

6 servings:

6 squid	2 oz. smoked bacon, chopped,
stuffing:	or 6 anchovy fillets
4 tablespoons olive oil	2 oz. chopped parsley
3 medium onions, chopped	salt, freshly ground black
3 cloves garlic, chopped	pepper
3 oz. white breadcrumbs	*sauce:*
a little milk or white wine	*either* tomato sauce, p. 194
	or ink sauce, p. 195

Clean the squid in the usual way, making sure that the inside of the body bag is well cleaned. Leave it whole; chop the tentacles into ¼–½ inch pieces.

To make the stuffing, fry onion, garlic, bacon if used, and tentacles in the oil for 5 minutes until lightly coloured. Meanwhile add a couple of tablespoons of milk or wine to the breadcrumbs and squeeze them well – they should be moist, not wet; any surplus liquid should be drained off. Put the crumbs into a basin, add the fried ingredients, anchovies if used, and the parsley. Season well.

Fill each squid about ⅔ full (allowing room for the stuffing to swell without bursting the bag). Sew up the openings with needle and thread. Lay them in a pan in a single layer and pour either the tomato or the ink sauce over them; the sauces can be made quite quickly, since there are no squid pieces to be cooked. Cover the pan (or ovenproof serving dish), and simmer for 30–40 minutes on top of the stove; or cook in a moderate to fairly hot oven (mark 4–5; 350–375°F.) if this is more convenient. Very large squid should be given an hour. You will find that they plump up into appetizing white cushions.

If you don't want to bother about making a sauce, stuffed squid can be stewed gently in olive oil. There should be about ¼ inch of it in the pan, when the squid are in position. Turn them over at half time, and remember to keep the pan covered so that they stew rather than fry. Sprinkle with parsley before serving.

Here is another stuffing, using rice:

2 onions, chopped	1 heaped tablespoon pine
4 tablespoons olive oil	kernels
2 tablespoons parsley	3 oz. rice
1 tablespoon chopped fresh	salt, pepper
dill weed	
(½ teaspoon if dried)	

Fry the onions with the chopped tentacles for 5 minutes in the oil. Add parsley, dillweed and rice, stir them about for a few moments, then cover with water: season, and simmer until rice is done, adding more water when required.

This is a Greek recipe – the first stuffing is French, and excellent for fish of all kinds.

Fried Squid

Tiny squid, once cleaned, can be fried in hot oil without further chopping. As they get larger, it's wise to try this French method of cooking them, which combines frying and stewing.

6 servings:

3 lb. moderate sized squid	2 oz. (large handful) parsley
4 tablespoons olive oil	salt, freshly ground black
4 large cloves garlic	pepper

Clean squid in the usual way; cut the body into ¼-inch thick rings, and the tentacles into ½-inch pieces.

Put the squid into a large heavy frying pan with the oil – both cold. Turn the heat full on. Fry for 8–10 minutes, stirring the pieces about to brown them lightly (if the pan gets too hot, turn the heat down). Season, and cover the pan. Lower the heat to simmering point, and leave the squid until they're cooked – up to 20 minutes, but keep testing. Meanwhile chop garlic and parsley together; add this mixture to the squid when they're almost done. Then turn the heat up again, cook uncovered for 3 minutes, and serve very hot on a hot serving dish.

Fried squid rings are also good when cold, either on their own, or as part of an hors d'oeuvre. Drain them well and serve with a bowl of mayonnaise, well seasoned with herbs, garlic and a little chopped onion. Omit the chopped garlic and parsley in the recipe above.

Squid can also be used in rice dishes of the paella or risotto type (p. 328).

Octopus (Poulpe, pieuvre)

Octopus is easily recognized by its collapsed, blueish-grey appearance and by the myriad crowding of bosses on the eight tentacles (*okto* and *pous* being Greek for eight and foot). By the time it gets to the fishmonger's, the baggy head has been removed. Presumably the preliminary bashing has also been completed, as the octopus we buy here is a most tender creature. (Mediterranean fishermen insist that it requires to be beaten 99 times against the rocks before it is fit for the pot.)

Some say that octopus tastes like lobster. This is not really fair. I have tried it with lobster as an economy measure, a tactful augmentation: this was quite successful, but no one was deceived. On the other hand lobster recipes are more successful for octopus than squid ones (*Newberg, américaine*, p. 280, or cold, with mayonnaise).

Before one embarks on any recipe, the octopus requires preliminary cooking. Put it into a glass oven dish with plenty of room to spare, and cover it. Do not add water or seasonings. Leave in a cool oven (mark 2; 300°F.) for one to two hours. It will exude a dark red liquid in surprising quantity. When it can be pierced with a pointed knife, rinse the octopus under the cold tap and discard the liquid. Now the fine skin and knobby bosses can be rubbed off easily. You will be left with a pinkish white star of tentacles which you then plunge into a pan of boiling water, flavoured with salt, garlic, bay leaf and an onion. In about 10 minutes, a fork will go into it like butter and the fish is ready to be served with the appropriate sauce. Treat it like boiled lobster, i.e. it should merely be reheated in a sauce (see the recipe for squid with tomato and wine on p. 194). In the eastern Mediterranean, pieces of cold cooked octopus are served as part of the *mezze*, the collection of delicious bits and pieces served with drinks, in particular with ouzo, the anise-tasting aperitif of Greece.

It makes a delicious cold dish with avocado pear slices and an avocado mayonnaise. Use it too as part of the *croûte aux fruits de mer* on p. 330. Octopus is a most delicate and pleasing dish, which costs little. Quantities depend on the size of the octopus, but bear in mind that it is going to lose a great deal of liquid and will shrink in the process. I allow one octopus for each person, when they are about 12 inches to the end of the tentacles. If there is too much, it makes a welcome reappearance next day.

The Great Fish

Most of the recipes in this section are interchangeable between the fish: they are also suitable for sturgeon.

Tunny or Tuna (Thon, germon, bonite)

My earliest sight of tunny was at Scarborough before the war, when tunny-fishing first became a fashionable sport there. I remember dark perfect shapes hanging against the usual grey summer sky. Their tails brushed the ground almost, but tall men had to put their heads back to look up at them. In 1933 a record-breaking tunny was landed there, weighting 851 lb. These fish were *Thunnus thynnus* I suppose, the bluefin tunny or *thon rouge*, caught on the way north to recuperate in the rich seas after spawning, and all of 7 feet long.

The second time I saw tunny, many years later, was in Spain on the Basque coast. This time it was a smaller species, *Thunnus alalunga*, which the French call *germon* and the Americans albacore, the prized white tunny, the only one allowed to be sold as *white* meat tunny in the U.S.A. Fat fisherwomen were pulling these tight-skinned shapes over the quays of the small port of Llanes. Natural slime and blood greased the way so that they survived the brutal handling unblemished. We did not eat tunny for dinner that evening.

Next day we were glad to blot out that over-truthful image with a visit to the cave of Pindal where a palaeolithic tunny swims gracefully on the wall. One has to step up on to a stone to make out the engraved lines. And all the time the smell of sea and wild flowers hangs about the cave. I suppose that women have been lugging these meaty, full-skinned fish over the ground hereabouts for 25,000 years and longer. Palaeolithic tunny must have been rather an indigestible chew, without the peppers and potatoes and tomatoes that now seem such an essential part of tunny cooked in the Basque style.

There are a number of other species of fish which come under the general heading of tunny, but this need cause no anxiety to the cook. They are all solid fish, which need to be thought of as meat when you are cooking them. Fresh tunny does not often come our way in England, but it is as well to know that the best part comes from the belly. Look out for the word *ventresca* on canned tunny from Italy; this is the first quality. French canners are not so anatomically inclined, but they do can tunny *au naturel*, as well as in oil like everyone else. This drier tunny is excellent for salads where a good deal of oil is being used in the dressing or mayonnaise. But whatever kind you buy, canned tunny is a useful fish to have in the store cupboard. It is most versatile; and filling, without being too strong in flavour – an excellent ingredient for a large mixed salad on a hot day.

Fresh tunny, as I have said, has to be treated respectfully. It needs to be sealed in butter or oil before being stewed in a sauce. Be very sure of its quality, before serving it plainly grilled or fried. It is wise to choose recipes such as the one for monkfish *à l'américaine* (p. 130), or the recipe which follows, if you have not cooked tunny before. Or else follow the recipe for *turbot au poivre* on p. 111 – quite one of the best for tunny fish too, so long as it is not overdone. With this kind of method, you can always remove the fish from the pot when it seems cooked, so control is never lost and there is time for remedial action.

Basque Tunny and Potato Stew

This is a recipe with many variations; sometimes there are no tomatoes, sometimes there are not so many onions, and so on. The basic ingredients are tunny, garlic, olive oil and potatoes.

6 servings:

1½ lb. tunny	1 lb. tomatoes, peeled and
2 large onions, sliced	chopped
4 cloves garlic, chopped	4 sweet red peppers, de-seeded
4 oz. olive oil	and sliced
6 or more potatoes, peeled	salt, pepper
	6 slices bread

Cut the tunny into pieces about 1 × 2 inches. Cook the onion and garlic in the oil until lightly coloured. Add the potatoes, tomatoes and peppers, and cook them for about 5 minutes. Put in the tunny, making sure it is well embedded in the tomato stew. Place in a very hot oven (mark 8; 450°F.) for 30–45 minutes, or simmer on top of the stove. In either case, keep a watch to see that the tunny does not overcook. The bread can be crumbled or cut into squares and added at the end of the cooking time or the slices can be toasted in the oven and put on top of the stew before serving.

Crostini di Tonno Fresco

A recipe for fresh, good quality tunny fish. Be sure to place the sage leaves next to it on the skewers for the full benefit of the flavour.

6 servings:

1¼ lb. tunny	olive oil
bread	salt, pepper
small sage leaves	lemon juice

Cut the tunny into regular slices about the thickness of a finger, and divide the slices into squares. Cut an equal number of squares of bread, without crusts, of a similar size. Wash plenty of sage leaves.

Thread the tunny and bread on to six skewers, with sage leaves on either side of each piece of tunny. Half-leaves of bay can be substituted for some of the sage leaves.

Brush the skewers with olive oil, and season them. Grill at a very moderate temperature for about half an hour, brushing tunny and bread with oil whenever they begin to look in the least dry.

Squeeze lemon juice over them and serve.

Fricandeau de Thon

A *fricandeau* is usually a piece of veal, which is larded and then braised (or roasted). The name is also used for larded pieces of firm fish such as sturgeon, tunny and porbeagle, which are cooked in precisely the same way.

6 servings:

3 lb. steak of tunny	*bouquet garni*
6 anchovy fillets ⎫ *for*	seasoned flour
hard back pork fat ⎭ *larding*	about ½ pint fish or chicken
2 oz. butter	stock
6–8 oz. belly of pork, diced	¼ pint dry white wine
2 large carrots, chopped	20 small pickling onions
2 large onions, chopped	1 tablespoon sugar
1 clove garlic, chopped	salt, pepper

Lard the tunny with strips of anchovy and pork fat, as if it were a piece of meat, and season it. Melt half the butter, and cook the pork belly gently until the fat runs, and it begins to colour lightly. Add the vegetables and garlic. When lightly browned, transfer to a casserole, and tuck in the bouquet. Turn the tunny in seasoned flour and brown in the remaining fat. Place it on top of the vegetables. Pour in half the stock, then the wine. Add more stock if necessary just to cover the fish. Simmer on top of the stove or in the oven until the tunny is cooked – about ¾–1 hour. Meanwhile put the pickling onions into a pan, cover with water, add the sugar and the remaining butter. Boil hard until the liquid is reduced to a syrupy brown caramel, and the onions cooked.

Put the tunny on to a warm serving dish, surround with the glazed onions and keep warm. Skim any fat from the tunny cooking liquid, then sieve it, reheat and correct seasoning. Pour over the fish and onions, serving any left over in a separate sauce boat.

Note: You can use this recipe for veal, or for any other firm-textured fish.

The Curé's Omelette

In the *Physiologie du Goût*, Brillat-Savarin tells the story of how Madame B, a society beauty who occupied herself with good works, called on a curé one evening in the poor part of Paris. He was dining at an unfashionably early hour, and welcomed her to join him. Poor and unfashionable he may have been, but he ate well (and copiously). After he had finished a salmon trout, the housekeeper brought in a tunny and carp roe omelette which smelled and tasted so good that Madame B could talk of nothing else at the dinner she went on to.

I thought the story much exaggerated – until I tried the omelette. Admittedly herring roes had to stand in for carp, and canned tunny for fresh, but the result was still superb.

4 servings:

8 oz. soft roes	8 eggs, beaten
3 oz. butter	salt, pepper
1 small shallot, finely chopped	*maître d'hôtel* butter, p. 22
3 oz. fresh or canned tunny, chopped	

Pour boiling water over the roes and leave for a few seconds to become slightly firm. Drain and chop roughly. Melt 2 oz. butter in a pan, and cook the shallot gently until soft. Add the tunny and stir for a few seconds, then add the soft roes. After a moment or two remove the pan from the heat: the roes must stay creamy. Season and cool. Stir into the seasoned eggs. Using the final 1 oz. of butter make the omelette in the usual way – or make 4 smaller omelettes. Don't overcook; omelettes should be just liquid in the centre. Spread the *maître d'hôtel* butter on a warm dish and place the omelette(s) on top. Serve immediately. The heat of the omelette should melt the butter into a sauce.

Tunny Mayonnaise with Veal. See p. 52.

Crêpes de Thon. See p. 227.

Swordfish (Espadon)

Swordfish are found all over the world, but usually in warmer waters than ours. Americans are not short of swordfish, neither are Spaniards, Italians, Greeks and other dwellers to the east. Occasionally they swim to our shores, but normally prefer the Mediterranean, which is where you should look out for them on menus and market stalls.

In October of 1970, there was excitement on the Atlantic coast of France, because the fishermen of La Rochelle had encountered a huge shoal of swordfish. The catch weighed twenty tons, and was uncommon enough to justify two or three paragraphs in the French papers. The trawlers concerned, the *Vieux marin* and the *Claude Jean Robert* from the Île d'Yeu, usually bring in no more than 2 or 3 tons of fish. I asked our weekly fishmonger at Montoire market about it. She explained that the firm-fleshed *espadon* was a great treat – the shoal would bring much profitable joy to the fishmongers and merchants of La Rochelle. She obviously envied them. So did I, as swordfish was something I had never cooked.

There was no mention in the paper of any damage caused by this tonnage of swift and powerful fish. I had hoped for some modern record echoing the old reports that a swordfish strikes with the 'accumulated force of fifteen double-headed hammers', and can pierce through 20 inches of timber, even oak.

Like other meaty, rich-flaked fish, swordfish is sold in steaks and cooked like tunny, porbeagle, or sunfish. When marinated in oil and lemon juice, seasoned with bay leaves and slices of onion, it can be grilled *en brochette* (p. 210) very successfully. Sealed by browning in butter or oil, then stewed gently in tomatoes or the marinade juices, it benefits from piquant additions like capers, olives or anchovies. In areas where it is caught in quantity, as in Sicily, it has recipes of its own like the swordfish pie described in *Mediterranean Seafood*, by Alan Davidson (Penguin). This is really a three-layer pastry sandwich, filled with a two-layer mixture of chopped swordfish, onions, tomato and courgettes, spiced with olives and capers; the pastry is sweetened quite forcefully. Altogether a dish which takes one back to the Arab occupation of the island, like the *becca-fico* sardines on p. 176.

Grilled Swordfish Steaks

A good way with swordfish (and with any of the other rather meaty fish such as tunny, sturgeon or porbeagle) is to brush the steaks first with melted butter. and then to grill them on both sides *until half-cooked*. Meanwhile make a sauce of the *béchamel* type, with a piquant seasoning – like the one for lobster thermidor (p. 282) or *sauce andalouse* (p. 33). Finish cooking the fish in this sauce, either in the oven, or on top of the stove.

Braciole di Pescespada

Stuffed swordfish in the Sicilian style, from Ada Boni's *Italian Regional Cooking* (Nelson, 1969). Again a good recipe for other meaty fish.

6 servings:

6 thin slices swordfish	2 tablespoons breadcrumbs
½ lb. swordfish trimmings, chopped	salt, pepper
	6 slices Mozzarella cheese
1 small onion, finely chopped	3 sprigs basil, finely chopped
½ pint olive oil	pinch finely chopped thyme
2 tablespoons brandy	1–2 lemons

Rinse and wipe the slices of swordfish, and lay them on the table. To make the stuffing, fry the chopped swordfish and onion in the oil; as they brown, pour in the brandy; when it has evaporated, stir in breadcrumbs and salt and pepper. Spread stuffing on each slice of swordfish, cover with Mozzarella slices, and sprinkle with herbs and pepper. Roll up and tie with thread.

Grill (preferably over charcoal) for 15 minutes, at a moderate heat. Serve with lemon quarters. Or serve with Salmoriglio sauce: beat ½ pint olive oil in a warm basin with 2 oz. hot water, juice of 2 lemons, 1 tablespoon finely chopped parsley, and 2 teaspoons oregano. Season with salt, heat over simmering water and pour over the fish.

Two Sharks – Porbeagle and Tope (Taupe and milandre)

To see a shark brought low on a marble slab is disturbing; as if the wildness of the sea can no longer be relied on, when such creatures are harvested, or caught like cattle. Scientists, too, have taken away our fantasies. They assure us that sharks, requiem sharks in particular, do not all deserve their tolling name of doom. They do not hover behind ships waiting for a careless lurch overboard. We shall never see a shark swimming off with a dinner-jacketed arm protruding from its aweful jaws, like the mousetail from a cat's. One writer ominously remarks that they are 'not averse to dead meat'. Another says that it is the ship's garbage they are after. They are no more than a scavenging nuisance. Think of it – the man-eating shark a nuisance and no more. They spoil fishing nets and gnaw pointlessly at the profitable shoals of herring; they gobble the bait from the lines. Not much Melville[1] here.

As far as the cook is concerned there are no horrors either; shark is delicious and easy to prepare. The two kinds I have come across in the last few years make me think that many other kinds must be worth trying. Admittedly neither was in the first rank of fish – sole, lobster, turbot, salmon, eel and so on – but both were above the ordinary humdrum level. As well as good flavour and texture, they have the advantages of no bones, beyond a central spine and its few attachments, and of cheapness. This latter must be a reflection of conservative taste and poor cooking ability, because sharks are a rare fish by comparison with the daily fare of saithe, ling, etc.

We first saw the immense porbeagle, or a part of it, at the Wednesday market in Montoire. Its matt velour-like skin stood out among the scaly fish and white fillets around it. The fishmonger's wife explained that it's called *taupe* in France on account of this mole-coloured skin (which makes an excellent shagreen). Then she

[1] Herman Melville, author of the famous novel *Moby Dick or The White Whale* (1851).

turned the piece towards us so that we could see the pale pink, lightly fibred flesh. 'It's just like veal,' she said. 'We sometimes call it *veau de mer*.' She took her great knife across the piece, then cut a section the right size for our small family of three. 'Treat it like veal,' she called after us. We found that she was right; the flavour is so delicate, and the texture so substantial, that I think few people would realize they weren't eating meat. The points to watch are dryness and overcooking. Try larding it with pork or bacon fat, and with a few strips of anchovy. Turn it in flour or egg and breadcrumbs and fry gently in clarified butter. Serve with lemon quarters or a purée of sorrel softened with cream. Tomato sauce and *créole* sauce go well with it; so do the butter sauces like *hollandaise* and *béarnaise*, and the mild *béchamel* sauces or a *velouté* sharpened with white wine (p. 35). It can be poached in a *court-bouillon* and eaten cold with mayonnaise. Tunny, opah and swordfish recipes are all suitable for porbeagle.

Tope is quite another matter both in size and in flesh. We saw a couple recently in Oxford, about 5 feet long, and slender compared to the tight swelling girth of the porbeagle. Tope are much whippier, more like a dogfish in shape. These two creatures were dark on the back, too, but with a brownish tinge, fading to a strange old-rose colour on their bellies which reminded me of some curtains my grandmother had in the Thirties, when old-rose was a favourite colour for furnishing. The flesh, though, was translucent and white, like cod. It clustered in tight sections around the central bone. And how cheap it was – less than a quarter of the price of cod. I've heard it said that the tope is, or rather was, called Sweet William, a sarcastic acknowledgement of its slightly ammoniac smell. But this is so faint, and passes so completely with cooking, that I incline to the opinion that the name is a recognition of the sweet firmness of the flesh, which is striking. For this reason it's ideal for chowders (but include a few mussels or other shellfish to emphasize the fish flavour) or for a patient stew which may have to wait about. We tried tope fritters and found them delicious. Tope *à la meunière* (p. 98) with Mornay sauce (p. 26) was also a success. My only regret was that we never thought to ask for the fins, we were so taken aback at seeing the shark there at all. In Ceylon and the Philippines they're treated with hot wood ash and powdered salt, then dried to a brittle blue-grey crispness in smoke or sun. At last they go to Chinese cooks to be made into soup, a valued ingredient on account of their fine-tasting gelatine. It was a shame not to have thought of asking for the fins, but we consoled ourselves with this most excellent of recipes for tope cooked on skewers:

Tope en Brochette

The diameter of the steaks we bought was about 5 or 6 inches. I found that five of them gave plenty of fish for six people. We also used:

6 servings:

¼ lb. green streaky bacon ⎱ cut into 1-inch squares	½ lb. mushrooms, halved
¼ lb. smoked streaky bacon ⎰	6 large bay leaves
	salt, pepper
	melted butter for basting

Remove the skin from the steaks and cut each one into six chunks. Discard the bone. Arrange the chunks in six lines and fit the rest of the ingredients equitably in between, including the bay leaves which should be cut into four pieces each. Now it's an easy matter to thread the skewers. Brush with melted butter and grill at a moderate heat for 10–15 minutes, turning two or three times, until the fish is opaque to the centre. Serve with buttered rice.

Instead of melted butter, the skewered fish can be basted with a barbecue sauce:

1 medium onion, chopped	1 tablespoon Worcester sauce
leaves from two or three stalks of celery, chopped	1½ tablespoons brown sugar
bacon fat, or a small piece of fatty salt pork	8 oz. tomato ketchup
1½ tablespoons wine vinegar	1 tablespoon French mustard
2 oz. lemon juice	salt, pepper

Melt the bacon fat, or dry out the fatty salt pork, and fry the onions and celery leaves gently until they begin to turn yellow. Add the remaining ingredients and simmer for 10 minutes. Taste and adjust the seasoning to your liking. Serve some of the sauce with the brochettes and rice. Any left over can be kept in a tightly corked bottle, in the refrigerator, for several weeks. It can be used with meat, too.

Tope or Milandre à l'Antillaise. See p. 143.

Opah, Moonfish or Sunfish (Lamprir)

A large fish, of curves and perfect beauty of colour. The aspect of its round eyes and rounded head is mild, almost dolphin-like. The huge, plump body, a taut oval up to 6 feet long, is softly spotted with white. The main blue-grey and green of its skin reflects an iridescence of rose, purple and gold. The fins are a brilliant red. The sickle tail has reminded people of the moon's shape; the ribs of its fins have seemed like the scarlet rays of the sun. Earlier, scientists gave it the magnificent rank of *Zeus luna*. Nowadays it is more correctly classified as *Lampris regius*, which could be translated as 'creature of kingly radiance'.

The opah likes the warm waters of the world (*opah* from W. African *uba*), but in summer it's sometimes caught in the North Atlantic. I saw one at Swindon, in the warm autumn season of 1971. It had been taken on October 29th, off the North Cape of Iceland, by the trawler *Lucida* – appropriate name – and was in perfect condition over a week later. I was given two steaks cut from the centre of this 9-stone majesty; each one weighed over 5 lb. Round the central bone, the flesh fell into closely curved sections the colour of salmon. The flavour and richness, too, were salmon-like (the practical Norwegians eschew poetic names and call it, simply, the 'large salmon', *laksestørje*). The taste was less fishy than salmon; the texture more meaty yet not so dry as similarly meaty fish like tunny or porbeagle. Ask your fishmonger about opah (or Jerusalem haddock, or sunfish, or moonfish; or mariposa, or kingfish if he happens to be American). He might have the chance of some one day. Then you will be able to try one of the best fish it's possible to eat.

Sunfish Stroganoff

Chilled sunfish, cut into *escalopes*, can be dipped in egg and bread-crumbs, and fried in butter just like veal. Here's another meat recipe which suits it well.

6 servings:

¾ lb. onions	1 level tablespoon French
¾ lb. mushrooms	mustard
corn oil	½ pint sour cream
1¼ lb. piece of sunfish	salt, pepper, sugar
	chopped parsley

Slice mushrooms and onions thinly. Put a thin layer of oil into a large frying pan and cook them gently until they're soft. Season, and drain off any surplus liquid – which can be used up in soup or other sauces.

Meanwhile put the steak of fish flat on a chopping board and cut it down into thin leaves. Divide them again into pieces about one inch long and ¼ inch wide. Season and set aside until the mushrooms and onions are cooked. This can all be done in advance of the meal: the final stage, the cooking of the fish, must be done at the last minute.

Heat some more oil in another frying pan until it's really hot. Put in the fish, and turn it over for a few seconds only, until it looks an opaque pinkish-white. With a perforated spoon add it to the mushrooms pan. Then stir in the mustard and the cream. Let it bubble for a second or two, correct the seasoning with salt, pepper and a little sugar, sprinkle with chopped parsley, and serve straight-away. Matchstick potatoes go well with sunfish Stroganoff – or some other crispness such as thin toast or fried bread.

Note: it is particularly important not to overcook the fish.

Sunfish in Cream

A beautiful recipe of great simplicity. Baked in cream the sunfish becomes soft and unctuous, delicately flavoured with the aromatic seasonings.

6 servings:

1½–2 lb. piece of sunfish	½–¾ pint thin or whipping
small onions	cream
pieces of carrot	2 oz. butter
bay leaf, parsley, thyme	2 large egg yolks
	salt, pepper, nutmeg

Choose a pot into which the sunfish fits closely. Pack the gaps with onions and pieces of carrot. Lay a large bay leaf on top of the fish, tuck a couple of sprigs each of parsley and thyme down the side. Season well with salt, freshly ground black pepper, and nutmeg. Pour in enough cream to cover the fish by ⅛ inch (the better your packing, the less cream will be required). Dab the butter on top. Cover with kitchen foil or the lid of the pot and bake in a fairly hot oven (mark 5–6; 375°–400°F). Test after 25 minutes. The centre should have lost its transparent look entirely – on the other hand you don't want to overcook fish, particularly solid-fleshed creatures like sunfish, tunny, sturgeon and so on.

When it's just cooked, transfer the fish with its bay leaf to a serving plate, and keep warm while you finish the sauce. Strain the cooking liquid into a small pan. Beat the egg yolks in a basin, add a little of the cooking liquid, then pour the lot into the pan again. Set over a low heat, and stir until the consistency is that of smooth, thick cream. *Don't let it boil* or the eggs will curdle. Correct the seasoning and pour over the fish. Serve with a few small boiled potatoes, or brown bread of not too strong a flavour.

Poached Sunfish

Although sunfish can be poached in a *court-bouillon* of the usual kind (p. 15), I think it's better to use a veal or chicken stock, sharpened with a spoonful or two of lemon juice or wine vinegar. Plenty of flavour without heaviness is the secret.

Put the piece of fish flat into a pan and cover it generously with the stock. Bring slowly to the boil. (A good way is to set the pan on a cold electric ring, then switch the heat to 3 or 4.) After three or four strong, convulsive bubblings, put the lid on and remove the pan from the stove to the larder to cool down. By this time the fish will be perfectly cooked. Serve it with the kinds of salad appropriate to salmon – cucumber in cream (p. 231), hard-boiled egg, slices of tomato and so on. Plus a large bowl of mayonnaise. Or you could flavour the cooking stock with tarragon, and serve with tarragon-flavoured whipped cream sharpened with lemon juice. A small amount of orange and tomato salad, plus an orange-flavoured mayonnaise, is also very good with sunfish.

Should you want to eat the sunfish hot, leave it to simmer gently until the centre loses all transparency. This takes about 10 minutes, but the time will vary according to the thickness of the fish, and how slowly it came to the boil. Serve with new potatoes turned in parsley butter. Sauces to choose are *hollandaise* or Maltese (p. 41), *sauce aurore* (p. 31), or any of the cream and butter sauces on pp. 37–9. Again, tarragon is a good flavouring.

Scalloped Sunfish

Firm fish can be reheated successfully, provided this is done not too long after the original cooking. One way is to make a creamy sauce and add the fish to it at the last moment like the turbot recipe on p. 112. Another is to construct a piquant gratin with a *béchamel*-based sauce. The second method is best if you have only a small amount of fish to go round. By using scallop shells or individual pots you can produce an excellent first course for a dinner party without the idea of left-overs crossing anyone's mind.

The thing is to flavour the sauce in an appetizingly positive way. Choose an anchovy or Mornay sauce, for instance, rather than a plain *béchamel*, and spice it with French mustard. *Sauce aurore* and white wine sauces (p. 35) can be enriched with grated Parmesan and Gruyère cheese.

Put a layer of your chosen sauce into the pots, arrange the cold flaked fish on top, then add some more sauce. Fry 2 oz. of breadcrumbs in 1½ oz. butter until they're golden brown; stir in another ounce of breadcrumbs and a good tablespoon of grated cheese. Again Parmesan and Gruyère, mixed, are the best to use; failing that choose a dry piece of ripe Cheddar. Put the pots of fish and sauce into a fairly hot to hot oven (mark 6–7; 400°–425°F.) until they are bubbling. Remove from the oven and divide the crumb mixture between them. Put under the grill for 5 minutes or so, being careful not to burn the topping.

Serve with fingers of toast, or thin slices of bread which have been baked in the oven.

Note: if scallop shells are used, the reheating can be done entirely under the grill on account of the shallowness of fish and sauce. When the mixture's really hot, add the crumbs and finish as above.

Sunfish à la Créole

Fish stews need quite a different technique from meat stews. Meat, shin of beef say, or neck of lamb, goes into the oven with the sauce ingredients; they all cook together for several hours. Now with fish the method must be quite different because even the most solid, meaty-looking piece of tunny needs a comparatively short cooking time. It's one of the advantages of buying fish. So get the sauce right first, see that it's properly reduced and correctly seasoned. Then add the fish, which may or may not need to be lightly browned first. This is the method of matelotes, chowders, cacciucco, and of *sunfish à la créole:*

créole sauce, p. 46	butter
1½ lb. piece of sunfish	salt, pepper

Make the sauce and adjust the seasoning (this can be done well in advance – the day before if you like). A good half an hour before the meal, brown the sunfish steak lightly in butter and lower it into the pan of simmering sauce. Allow half an hour's cooking time, but test after 20 minutes to see if the fish is ready.

Note: if you don't care for the flavour of peppers, use the tomato marinara sauce on p. 45.

Sunfish Pickled in the Danish Style

See the recipe for pickled salmon on p. 352. For this, a fillet piece cut from near the tail is better than a steak, on account of the slicing. The steak falls into its individual flakes under the knife, whereas one can cut along a fillet.

Fish Caught in Fresh Water

Salmon (Saumon)

The salmon, luckily, is a northern fish. This means that we do not
always have to eat it out of tins – which can change its nature
completely, from the noble to mere pink protein – or out of the deep-
freeze, which makes it flavourless and dry. Salmon is, to man at
least, the king of the fish. Much of its life history is unknown and
mysterious. Its taste is so fastidious that it can only survive in pure
waters (the appearance or disappearance of salmon is a barometer
of a river's pollution).

The salmon is one of those anadromous fish, like eel and shad,
which spend most of their lives in sea water, yet return to the rivers,
mainly to the rivers of their birth, to spawn. And to be caught. The
tiny salmon is called a fingerling, then a parr until it leaves the river
at anything from one to three years old. After that the salmon are
known as smolt. From this point they disappear completely until
their return, either a year later as grilse, or up to three years later as
large and handsome salmon weighing up to 30 and more pounds.
The grilse are often of a size to be confused with salmon trout and
large brown trout; not that this need bother the cook, as similar
recipes are suitable for all three.

The difference in size, and development, and age of the returning
fish has puzzled the scientists. Obviously some salmon go much
farther away into the Atlantic to feed. But why? And where? One
answer to the second question was discovered in the last part of the
1950s. A US nuclear submarine, cruising below the ice between

Greenland and Baffin Island, 'spotted thousands and thousands of fish hanging like silver icicles from the underside of the pack', feeding on the rich plankton. Luckily no one has yet discovered where the grilse feed, which must obviously be much nearer the coasts of Europe. By the time they do, let us hope there is adequate legislation to preserve them from the intensive greedy fishing which has threatened the survival of salmon off the west of Greenland.

But whether grilse, or larger salmon who have made the long journey from the other side of the Atlantic, most of them return to their native rivers. Exactly how is another mystery. They gather in the waters of the estuary, fine fat fish in prime condition, and make their way upstream, sometimes with those immense leaps that have given the salmon the name of *salar*, the leaper, *Salmo salar*. From the moment they enter the sweet water they eat nothing until they return to the sea again. Which means, to the cook, that the sooner they are caught the better. A spent kelt which is managing to get back to the sea – many of them die – is a dish for nobody.

Choosing Salmon

Children are coloured indelibly, it seems, by their mother's expertise – or lack of it – in choosing food. Conversations with butcher, baker, nurseryman, are picked up by a pair of ears at counter level and stored in the infant lumber room. So when I came to buy salmon in my turn, I found myself echoing my mother's words: 'The tailpiece, please.' In restaurants, at weddings and parties, I have often eaten the middle cut with pleasure, but when I have to put my own money down on the fishmonger's counter, it's the moister and better-flavoured tailpiece that I buy. The lower price (bargaining advisable) compensates for the higher proportion of bone to flesh.

As to the frozen Canadian salmon, on sale throughout the year, it cannot be compared in quality with our own. This is because of the handling and freezing. I imagine that if one lived in British Columbia it would be as rich and curdy and delicious as salmon from the Tay or Severn. There are five Pacific species of *Oncorhynchus* salmon, the counterparts of our single species *Salmo salar*. The names are familiar from cans on the grocery shelves – Chinook or King salmon, Coho, Sockeye are the red-fleshed ones; Chum is a paler orange shade; and the Humpback or Pink salmon a light rose colour.

This frozen fish is excellent for some things – for smoking for instance. It is the sensible choice for salmon mousse or the Scandinavian sweet-cured *gravad lax* (p. 352). For such dishes, best Scotch salmon would be a pointless extravagance.

But whatever salmon you buy, the thing is to have as large a surface area of skin as possible. This helps to lubricate and protect the salmon as it cooks. *Salmo salar*, king as he may be, is sometimes dry in his thicker portions. All the cook's art is directed to balancing this tendency with unctuous sauces made of egg yolks, butter, cream or oil. A third texture, that most successful dishes require, is provided by cucumber, new potatoes or the refreshing sharpness of sorrel.

Cooking Salmon

One of my most vivid memories of the Three Choirs Festival at Gloucester is, I am ashamed to say, not the music but the spectacle of a whole boiled salmon consumed at a luncheon party. It came from the Severn or Wye, and tasted marvellous. The cooking of it must have been agony.

Nowadays we can wrap the fish up in foil, without the least worry that it will lose flavour to the water or bouillon. And it cannot become too dry either.

Foil also solves the problem of what so large a fish can be cooked in. Few of us have the space to store an enormous fish kettle, that may only be used once or twice a year. If the fish is too long to go into the oven, cut it in two, or three, pieces; wrap each piece up with appropriate seasonings, and reassemble them, when cooked, on the serving dish. The joins can be masked by discreet decoration. If you do not have a serving dish long enough, invest in a piece of hard wood and oil it nicely. It will come in useful for many other things as well.

This is how you set about preparing the salmon for the oven. Tear off enough foil to enclose it loosely, and an extra piece of foil large enough to fold into two straps. These you lay across the big piece of foil (they're to help with the removal of the salmon when cooked). These straps are only necessary when the fish, or piece of fish, is very large and long.

Brush the foil well with melted butter, if the salmon is to be eaten hot, or with oil if it is to be eaten cold. Season it generously. Lay the fish on the foil, across the straps. Twist the foil edges together to make a tightly closed, but baggy parcel. Cook in one of three ways:

1. Bake in a cool oven (mark 1–2; 275°–300°F.), allowing one hour for a piece, or whole fish, up to 5 lb. and 12 minutes a pound for anything over that. If you have divided the salmon into two pieces, be guided by the weight of each parcel, not by the total weight of the original fish. Leave hot salmon for 10 minutes before serving it, after it is taken out of the oven. If the salmon is to be eaten cold, allow it to cool in the parcel.

2. Put the parcel into a fish kettle – *this is for salmon which is to be eaten cold* – and add cold water to within about 1½ inches of the top. Bring to the boil. Give it four or five convulsive bubblings, then transfer the kettle to the larder to cool down. The fish will be perfectly cooked.

3. Fill a fish kettle half full of water – *this is for hot salmon* – and bring it to the boil. Lower the wrapped salmon into it on the strainer tray. Bring back to the boil, then allow:

up to 5 lb., 5 minutes per lb.

6 to 8 lb., 4 minutes per lb., plus 5 minutes

8 to 10 lb., 50–60 minutes in all.

Bear in mind that the thickness should be more of a guide, when cooking salmon, than the weight alone.

4. For hot salmon, prepare one of the cream and butter sauces on pp. 37–39, or an *hollandaise*. *Sauce chivry*, *sauce nantua*, or sorrel sauce go well with salmon, too. For cold salmon, mayonnaise is the usual choice. As a change, make *beurre Montpellier* on p. 23.

Chaudfroid of Salmon and other Fish

A whole salmon – or sea trout, John Dory, or any other firm fish of good flavour – covered with a jellied mayonnaise and elegantly decorated, makes a beautiful summer dish. The only snag is that it should be made the day it's to be eaten, which can cause problems of organization. For a luncheon party, it is prudent to stick to small items, like salmon or turbot steaks, or fillets of sole. Keep the grand dishes of large fish for an evening meal, so that they have time to cool down after poaching, and you have time for the assembly of the final decoration.

The cooking part is fiddling rather than difficult. The three rules for success are:

the fish must be of good quality, e.g. Scotch salmon, not frozen Canadian

it must be fresh

the jellied mayonnaise must be well-seasoned, of first-class ingredients

If these conditions aren't met, a chaudfroid can be the dreariest of caterer's buffet food, all show and no flavour. My advice is to cut down on the décor, and concentrate on the ingredients. An energetically phrased five minutes with the fishmonger will do far more than an hour devoted to making radish roses. The choice of a light olive oil for the mayonnaise is more important than fussing over a nozzle and forcing bag to produce mayonnaise rosettes.

If this makes you nervous, start with salmon steaks. Allow one for each person, or one for two people, according to their size and the quantity of other food being served at the meal. Put them into cold or tepid *court-bouillon* (No. 1, p. 16). Bring to the boil over a moderate heat, take off the stove, and leave to cool. They will now be cooked. A simpler method is to wrap them in individual pieces of foil (season and brush with corn oil first), and then to cook them in plain water on the same principle.

Discard skin and bone – which will have the effect of dividing each steak into two 'comma' shapes. Place them on a wire rack. Brush with jellied mayonnaise (p. 53), on the point of setting, but still supple, and arrange one or two pieces of decoration neatly on top – sprays of tarragon leaves, hard-boiled egg slices, radish slices, slivers of cucumber peel, capers, and black or stuffed olives. Leave to set in the refrigerator. Take carefully from the wire rack and arrange on a bed of lettuce or suitable salad on a large dish.

With a whole fish, the principle is the same. The problems lie in manipulating such a large creature and peeling off its skin. Unhurried coolness takes care of the first problem: for the other, place the fish on a sheet of damp greaseproof paper on a tray. Using a sharp knife gradually take off the skin, making a neat cut across the tail and round the head. Invert a wire rack on top and turn the whole thing over. Remove the skin on the other side. The next step is to raise the fillets (cut along the central line first) and place them on a dish; snip the backbone at each end with scissors and ease it up. Discard it, and replace the fillets. Mask with mayonnaise, which, mercifully, covers small errors and slips of the knife. Finish as above.

Note: put paper under the rack to catch the mayonnaise drips.

Salmon Steaks

Salmon steaks, up to an inch thick, are best baked in foil too. Wrap them loosely, with seasonings and melted butter, and give them 20 minutes at mark 5, 375°F.

Alternatively, the wrapped steaks can be grilled. Allow 6 minutes a side, then open the foil and give them a moment or two extra, to brown under the heat. Take the opportunity of basting them with butter.

If you are obliged to grill the steaks without foil, put them into a generously buttered pan. Brush the tops with melted clarified butter, and season. Put them under a hot grill for 10–15 minutes until they are cooked. There is no need to turn them. Although salmon grilled in this way can be good, I think it is wiser to stick to the foil method, or a baked salmon recipe, like the one following.

Salmon Steaks in Cream

I owe this deliciously simple recipe to Mrs Charlotte Sawyer, of Woodsville, New Hampshire. It could equally well be used for cod steaks, or slices of angler fish, or porbeagle (Blue Dod, as it's sometimes called in North America); but it's particularly good for the dryness of salmon. The ingredients may sound expensive, but they aren't really as they include the sauce for the fish. Some new potatoes turned in parsley butter are all that's needed to accompany the salmon.

1 salmon steak per person,
   about 1 inch thick
salt, pepper, butter

about ½ pint single or
   whipping cream
bay leaf
lemon quarters

Season the salmon steaks well with salt and freshly ground black pepper. Choose an oven dish into which the steaks will fit closely in one layer, without being jammed tightly together. Butter the dish lavishly, then put in the steaks and enough cream to cover them by about ¼ inch. Tuck in a small bay leaf, and bake in a fairly hot oven (mark 5; 375°F.) for 20–25 minutes, until the steaks are cooked. Baste them once or twice with the cream, adding more if it reduces enough to leave the surface of the salmon much exposed. Serve with lemon quarters, in case people like to sharpen the sauce a little.

Note: I find that half a pint of cream is enough for five or six steaks: but the amount depends entirely on how much space there is between them.

Salmon in Pastry, with Herb Sauce

The Hole in the Wall at Bath is one of the best restaurants in England. Certainly it is our favourite, by a long way. Good food of several traditions; but mainly in that lovely French style which Elizabeth David has shown us, quality without pretension, no gimmicks, freshness above all, and flavour. Here is a dish which appears on the menu when the finest Wye and Severn salmon are available: it is based on a medieval recipe (at that time fish were often seasoned with sweetness and ginger):

6 servings:

2½ lb. salmon
salt, pepper
3 oz. butter
2 knobs ginger in syrup,
   chopped
1 tablespoon currants
shortcrust pastry (made with
   8 oz. flour, 5 oz. butter,
   and 1 egg)
sauce:
2 shallots, chopped

parsley, chervil, tarragon,
   chopped
2 oz. butter
1 teaspoon flour
½ pint cream
salt, pepper
1 teaspoon Dijon mustard
2 egg yolks mixed with 1
   tablespoon cream
lemon juice

Ask the fishmonger to skin and bone the salmon. This will leave you with two thick fillets. Season them with salt and pepper. Mix together the butter, ginger and currants, and use ⅔ of this paste to sandwich the fillets together. Spread the rest on top. Roll out the pastry, turn the salmon over on to it and bring up the edges so that it is completely enclosed. Cut away the surplus pastry, turn the salmon dumpling and put it onto a foil-lined baking sheet, so that the closed pastry edges are underneath. Roll out the surplus pastry, and put a modest decoration on top. Brush the whole thing over with egg yolk and cream, taken from the sauce ingredients. Bake for 30 minutes in a hot oven (mark 7, 425°F.).

To make the sauce, sweat shallots and herbs in butter until soft; stir in the flour, then cream and seasonings, and cook gently for 10 minutes. Finally beat in the egg yolks and thicken without boiling. Add lemon juice to taste.

Transfer salmon to a hot dish, lifting it up by the foil beneath. Ease the foil away, and serve immediately, with the sauce in a separate bowl.

Kulebiaka or Salmon Pie

Fish pie is one of the great dishes of institutional catering. Even in middle age, I find it impossible to forget its gluey texture – and the smell, the revolting smell, which hung, as insistently as the smell of *Phallus impudicus* in an autumn wood, over Friday morning lessons.

So at first I hesitated to try recipes for *kulebiaka* (especially some of the more majestic ones containing *viziga*, which is the dried spinal cord of sturgeons). Then the possibilities of the ingredients conquered prejudice. I found that in this version of the famous Russian fish pie, they blended to a flavour which was both rich and fresh. Like many other Russian specialities, this is a dish of substance. Rice is often used in Russia, but the traditional cereal is *kasha*: buckwheat which is first roasted, then boiled in the manner of rice. *Kasha*, already roasted, can be bought occasionally from health food shops. From a flavour point of view, I prefer natural brown rice to *kasha*, or to polished white rice.

6 servings:

flaky pastry, or brioche dough,
made with 1 lb. flour
1½ lb. filleted salmon, or
turbot, or eel
¼ lb. mushrooms coarsely
chopped
¼ lb. chopped shallot or mild
onion
2 heaped tablespoons chopped
parsley

2 teaspoons dried dillweed (or
2 tablespoons fresh)
¼ lb. butter, unsalted
salt, pepper, nutmeg; juice of a
lemon
3 hard-boiled eggs, sliced
6 oz. rice or *kasha*
egg yolk, or cream, or top of
the milk, for glazing

Make the pastry or dough. While it is chilling, or rising, prepare the
filling. Cut the fish into thin slices, less than ¼ inch thick. Stiffen
them in 3 oz. of the butter – which will take 2 or 3 minutes; the fish
should not be cooked through. Melt half the chopped shallot or
onion in another 2 oz. of butter, without browning them. When
they're soft and golden, put in the mushrooms. Stew them for 5
minutes. Stir in the lemon juice and seasoning to taste.

Fry the rest of the onion gently in about an ounce of butter, until
it's soft. Add the rice, and stir about until every grain is coated with
melted butter. Pour in ¾ pint of water (or chicken stock, if you have
any: but don't use a cube) and leave to cook gently in the usual way.
Add more liquid if necessary, and when the rice is soft, remove
from the heat and flavour with dill, parsley, salt, pepper and
nutmeg.

Take a heavy baking sheet. Roll out half the pastry to an oblong.
Put half the rice on to it, leaving a good margin free. The slices of
fish go on next, then the slices of hard-boiled egg and the mushroom mixture. Last of all the rest of the rice. Roll out the remaining
pastry to a similar sized oblong. Brush the rim of the pastry, round
the filling, with water, or top of the milk, or egg, and lay the second
layer on top. Press down round the rim to seal the pie. Turn over the rim
to double it, and nick the edge all round to make sure of a firm seal.
Decorate the pie with leaves made from pastry or dough trimmings,
and pierce a central hole for the steam to escape. Brush pie and rim
over with beaten egg and cream, or a mixture of both. Bake in a
fairly hot oven (mark 5–6; 375°–400°F.) for an hour. If the pastry
browns quickly, protect it with buttered paper. When the pie is
ready, have the rest of the unsalted butter melted in a little pan.

Pour it through the central hole just before serving: a little more won't come amiss. Serve with a separate jug of melted butter, or, better still, sour cream.

Note: kulebiaka could be made with cooked salmon. In this case omit the quick frying in butter.

Escalope of Cold Salmon Maître Albert

Anjou is a country of just the right *douceur* to have produced that good king, René, Count of Anjou and Provence, King of Sicily. In warlike times, he loved painting and music and tapestries (in particular the Apocalypse tapestries now on display in his castle of Angers), and his two wives adored him. The hotel at Les Rosiers on the Loire is called after his second wife, Jeanne de Laval, and there, in the long quiet dining-room, one may eat the most delicious fish and sea food imaginable. The natural advantages of Loire and Atlantic are submitted to the skill of French cookery in the person of Monsieur Augerau, the proprietor, 'Maître Albert', who invented this summer dish.

6 servings:

2 lb. middle cut of salmon	2 large egg yolks
butter	3 large tablespoons thick
shallots or mild onion	cream
8 oz. mushrooms, chopped	4 oz. unsalted butter
salt, freshly ground black	a large handful of sorrel or
pepper	spinach and lemon juice
1 bottle dry white wine	

Ask the fishmonger to skin and fillet the salmon. Cut it into slices about ¼ inch thick. Butter a large shallow pan and cover the base with a layer of chopped shallots. Put in the slices of salmon, slightly overlapping each other, and scatter the mushrooms on top. Pour on enough white wine to cover. Bring to the boil and simmer for 15 minutes until the salmon is just cooked. Transfer the slices to a serving dish, cover with foil and keep warm. Add the cream to the mixture in which the salmon was cooked. Boil hard, until the liquid is reduced by approximately one third. Strain into a small pan, and whisk the egg yolks into the tepid liquid, which should be kept over a low heat – not enough to cause it to boil. When the sauce is thick, lift the pan from the heat and stir in the butter in little knobs.

Meanwhile in another pan cook the sorrel (or spinach) in 2 tablespoons of butter. It will rapidly turn to a thick purée. Season well with salt and pepper (and with lemon juice if spinach is used). Add the purée to the sauce, pour it over the warm salmon slices and chill as quickly as possible in the refrigerator.

Note: cold fish tastes better when it's eaten the day it's cooked. This is a recipe that could be used for firm white fish of good flavour. And it could be served hot – but cold is better.

Crêpes de Saumon from Mont St Michel

We once saw an amazing spectacle at Mont St Michel. Our September crossing from Southampton had been appalling: a quiet night there seemed a soothing idea. We arrived in moonlight to find the sea swashing against the causeway (which only happens twice a year) and the gate into the town quite cut off. Crowds had come to see the wonderful sight – *La Merveille* surrounded by water, floodlit and triumphant over the black sea. A supple ladder was propped against the town wall and a number of French grannies were bouncing up at speed, encouraged by a high medieval bobbing of heads over battlements, and the bawdy jokes of their grandchildren below. But why did they not wait half an hour for the tide to go down a little? Stupid questions get sharp answers: 'It's dinner time.' Now having been well schooled by native experience, we had not expected to find a meal worth eating at such a popular place, let alone worth climbing a ladder for. All we wanted was peace (which we found, waking at dawn next day to see St Michael shining gold against a pink sky on the highest pinnacle of his church). We never thought of finding food like this; as well as oysters, lobsters and mussels on a bed of ice and seaweed, served with a bowl of real mayonnaise, lamb from the salt grazing marshes, and the famous omelette. In France food is always part of the attraction. One goes out with the expectation of eating better than usual, and of consuming the specialities of the place.

6 servings:

12 *pancakes:*	*filling:*
4 oz. flour	12 oz. cooked salmon
2 large eggs	4 oz. double cream
2 tablespoons oil or melted	salt, pepper, thyme
butter	½ pint Normande sauce, p. 33
good pinch salt	2 oz. butter
generous ¼ pint tepid milk	2 oz. grated cheese, preferably
	Gruyère

Make the pancakes in the usual way. Pound the salmon with the
cream and seasonings (use an electric beater, if you have one) to
make a thick paste. Put a spoonful on each pancake and roll it up;
fit them closely together in a buttered ovenproof dish. Choose a
cream sauce preferably made from fish stock and cream (or use
thick cream on its own) and pour it over the pancakes. Dot with
butter, sprinkle with cheese and put into a hot oven (mark 7;
425°F.) until bubbling and brown.

Note: tinned salmon and *béchamel* sauce can be substituted, for a
homely version of this dish. Or tinned tunny and an anchovy-
flavoured *béchamel.*

Saumon à la Crème

If you ever have some cooked salmon left over, it can make a most
luxurious first course. Buy or bake some small *vol au vent* cases, and
fill them with salmon reheated in Mrs Beeton's cream and butter
sauce (p. 112; *turbot à la crème*).

Although the three following recipes are placed under Salmon, they
can be adapted to other kinds of fish – smoked, canned or fresh,
salt-water fish, fresh-water fish, or shellfish. The one essential
quality in the chosen fish is good flavour. (Efforts would be wasted
making a soufflé of plaice: I'm equally against canned lobster which
is disappointingly tasteless.) Suitable adaptation can be made to the
seasoning ingredients, but basic methods and quantities are the
same whatever the fish. Don't be surprised by the use of cheese – it's
to emphasize the flavour of the fish, to bring it out. Parmesan and

Gruyère mixed are the usual choice, but a good Cheddar does quite well instead.

Quiche de Saumon

6 servings:

½ lb. flaky or shortcrust pastry	1 heaped tablespoon Gruyère
½ lb. cooked, flaked salmon	or 2 tablespoons Cheddar
1 heaped teaspoon dill weed or	2 large eggs, plus 2 egg yolks
chopped green fennel leaves	½ pint cream
1 heaped tablespoon	salt, cayenne and black pepper
Parmesan	

Line a 9 or 10-inch tart tin, with a removable base, with the pastry Bake blind in the oven for 15 minutes – flaky at hot (mark 7; 425°F.),. and shortcrust at fairly hot (mark 6; 400°F.).

Spread salmon evenly over the base. Sprinkle with herbs and cheese. Beat the eggs and cream together, season well and pour over the salmon mixture. Bake in a fairly hot oven (mark 6; 400°F.) for 30–40 minutes, or until the filling is nicely risen and brown. Serve hot, or warm.

Note: Instead of salmon and dill weed or fennel, use the following combinations:

Tunny with capers or anchovies.

Jugged kipper with 1 tablespoon French mustard, and juice of a lemon, squeezed over before serving.

Good white fish with vermouth, Pernod or anisette.

Shellfish with 3 or 4 rashers of chopped, lightly fried bacon. Reduce mussel liquor to concentrated essence, and add to eggs and cream, or to the thick panada of a soufflé; the same treatment for oyster liquor; 4 oz. of whiting fillet should be included with these 2 shellfish or with clams.

Salmon Soufflé

6 servings:

¼ lb. cooked salmon	2 tablespoons grated Gruyère
2 tablespoons cream	salt, and black pepper
4 tablespoons butter	cayenne or paprika
3 tablespoons flour	scant tablespoon tomato
½ pint milk, hot	concentrate (optional)
2 tablespoons grated	4 medium egg yolks
Parmesan	5 medium egg whites

Beat the salmon to a smooth paste with the cream (an electric beater helps). Melt the butter in a heavy pan, stir in the flour and cook gently for 2 or 3 minutes. Incorporate the milk gradually, until the thick sauce or panada comes away from the sides of the pan. Remove from the heat while the salmon mixture is added, and then the seasonings of cheese, salt, and peppers; tomato concentrate, if used, should be added gradually to taste. In the matter of seasonings remember that the addition of egg yolks and whites will soften the flavour.

Return the pan to the stove, and reheat to just below boiling point. Whisk in the egg yolks one by one, with the pan off the fire, and then fold in carefully, with a metal spoon, the stiffly beaten whites. Pour into a lavishly buttered soufflé dish and bake for 30–35 minutes in a fairly hot oven (mark 5; 375°F.). Timing is difficult to state exactly, because it will vary according to the depth of the mixture. Aim to have a soufflé which is creamy inside, brown outside, and nicely risen.

Salmon Mousse

¼ lb. cooked, flaked salmon	1 small tablespoon wine
¼ gill water or beef stock	vinegar or lemon juice
½ oz. gelatine	1 heaped tablespoon
¼ pint whipping cream or	Parmesan or Cheddar
thick cream	cheese, grated
2 egg whites	1 tablespoon brandy, sherry or
seasonings:	vermouth
salt, cayenne pepper	

Put the gelatine and hot water, or stock, into the goblet of a blender, and start it whirling. Add the fish gradually, together with wine vinegar or lemon juice, alcohol and cheese, to make a smooth purée. (If you rely on a *mouli-légume* instead of a blender, melt the gelatine in the hot water, and sieve the salmon into it; then stir in the vinegar etc.) Whip the cream until stiff, and fold in the salmon mixture gently. Put in a cool place until almost set, but just liquid enough to stir. Taste and season again, if you think it necessary.

Beat the egg whites until they stand up in soft peaks, and fold them into the salmon and cream, using a metal spoon. Do this slowly and lightly. Turn into a serving dish (use a small, collared soufflé dish, if you like – don't forget to brush the 'collar' with oil) and leave to set in the refrigerator.

Serve with *cucumber salad:*

1 whole cucumber	salt, pepper,
4 tablespoons thick cream	lemon juice

Slice the cucumber, unpeeled, on the wide cutting edge of a grater, or mandolin. Spread out in a colander, and sprinkle with salt. Leave for at least 2 hours to drain. Rinse well, and dry in a clean cloth. Season the cream with salt, pepper and lemon juice, and *just before the meal* stir in the cucumber slices. Avoid wateriness at all costs.

Salmon Trout, Sea Trout or Sewin (Truite saumonée)

These three and many other names – phinock, gillaroo, Galway or Orkney sea trout, orange fin, black tail or fin, bull trout and seal; and, in America, brown trout – all refer to the same fish. The finest of all the river fish, just as the sole is the supreme fish of the seas. Given the choice between these two, I should be in a quandary, but in the end I would always choose salmon trout because it is a rarer experience. How lucky people are on the Welsh coast, or the north-east coast, where one can buy it in perfect freshness.

Sea trout may be the official name for *Salmo trutta,* but it is useless to ask for sea trout at the fishmonger's. The usual name is salmon trout, just as the French one is *truite saumonée*. I am sure this name will stick because it so well describes the excellence of the fish, which combines the finest qualities of both salmon and trout, and is better than either. It may be no more than a sea-going variety of our native brown trout, but there is a great difference in flavour. The pink flesh is firm, without the salmon's tendency to dry up in cooking, and the tidy disposal of the flakes most happily resembles the trout's. As it weighs between 1½ and 4 lb. it is the ideal fish for a small dinner party in the spring. Worth saving up for.

Many trout and salmon recipes are suitable for salmon trout, with little adaptation, but the best method of all is to bake it in foil.

Truite Saumonée en Papillote

For four people, buy a 2½–3 lb. salmon trout; a 4 lb. one will be enough for eight.

Cut a piece of foil large enough to fold comfortably round the fish. Brush it with melted butter (or with oil if the fish is being eaten cold). Sprinkle sea salt and freshly ground black pepper on to the butter, and inside the fish. Place the foil on a baking sheet, and the fish on the foil. Pour over 4–6 tablespoons of good dry white wine, or put a lump of butter forked up with herbs into the cavity. Fold the foil round the fish, making a baggy parcel. Twist the edges together into a firm seal. Bake in a moderate oven (mark 4; 350°F.) for 40–50 minutes.

To make a sauce from the juices, turn to p. 47 and follow the recipe for *sauce Bercy*.

Transfer the whole thing to a warm dish (or remove the tray from the foil if you prefer it) and fold the edges of the parcel back neatly to show the fish.

With hot salmon trout, I like to see and to eat the skin, but this is a matter for individual preference. Certainly cold salmon trout, skinned and coated with aspic or chaudfroid (p. 53), looks impressive on a buffet table. But why embellish something so good? How can one improve on it with a triviality of 'flowers' made from hard-boiled eggs, capers, radishes and so on? The salmon trout is a beautiful fish. My own feeling is to leave it alone, and keep sauces, salads or potatoes quite separate.

Sewin in Wales

Mrs Freeman, who ran the Compton House Hotel at Fishguard until a year or two ago, was famous for her food, which included a number of Welsh specialities. She always cooked and served sewin: ' ... in the local way, i.e. simply and gently grilled, with salty butter, and rough brown bread and butter. The rough texture of the local brown bread contrasts marvellously with the smooth delicate texture of the fish. We advise people to put lots of the salty butter on the hot flesh as they work through the fish as this brings out the delicate flavour best of all.'

Sometimes she served a cucumber sauce with it (*béchamel*, flavoured with cucumber purée; peel and steam the cucumber first, before putting it through the *mouli-légumes*), which complements it well. She remarks that rich and highly-flavoured sauces will not do, and that cooking must be simple: 'I once baked a biggish sewin with one or two fresh sage leaves and a thin strip or two of lemon rind along its inside, and it ruined it.'

The Trout (Truite)

The best trout, whatever the size, variety or place may be, is the one you catch yourself and eat within an hour or two. Given these happy circumstances, the style of cooking hardly matters at all – baking in newspaper, frying, grilling, simmering in salted water; whatever you do it will taste perfect. If anyone can suggest a finer food, apart from salmon trout, I should be grateful to know about it.

This is one reason why people pay apparently ridiculous sums for a stretch of trout fishing, and why people since the Middle Ages have been studying the trout's habits with that passionate, contradictory love that hunters seem to devote to their prey.

In their book on trout, in Collins's New Naturalist series, W. E. Frost and M. E. Brown point out that long before Izaak Walton was born, Dame Juliana Berners was discoursing on the joys of trout fishing and the correct comportment of trout fishermen (to be

summed up as 'Don't be greedy'). The two modern authors delight
in the variety of size and colouring in our native brown trout. In
Lough Derg and Lake Windermere the trout are large and silvery
with black spots. In the small brown tarns near Windermere, the
little fish have 'yellow bellies and red spots on their dark sides'.
Some trout have pink flesh like salmon – they are the best of all to
eat – some have white flesh. 'As trout swim and turn gracefully in
their native waters – in rushing becks, placid lakes or yellow bog-
pool – they are, simply, beautiful.'

To come down to the practicalities of trout, I had always thought
that failing river trout, the second-best fish were the ones swimming
about in restaurant-tanks. The clients choose the one they fancy; it
is caught and cooked, and served half an hour later. Country
restaurants in France sometimes have a little pool carved out of the
river bank, where they keep a store of trout in a more natural
milieu. But even these taste insipid.

Far better in flavour – and this surprises me, I admit – are the
deep-frozen trout from Denmark, rainbow trout in plastic bags sold
in grocers' shops all over the country. They survive unadorned
treatment most creditably. Given a little encouragement – mushrooms and pastis, or a fine rich sauce – they become a really good
dish. One thing worth noticing is that they have been frozen so
rapidly after being taken from the water that they still have the
natural moisture on their skins. This turns to a slate-grey bloom, as
it does with fresh trout, when they are cooked *au bleu*.

How would you characterize the flavour of trout? How would you
describe it to someone who had never eaten it? You would say that
the flesh is firm, and sweet, that it parts from the bone with an
ease that contributes so much to the enjoyment of some fish. But
what then? The essence of the matter remains undescribed.

Charles Cotton's Boiled Trout

This recipe is given by Izaak Walton's friend, and co-author, in
The Compleat Angler. It's not so fierce as it sounds – think of
Escoffier's horseradish sauce to be served with trout, on p. 58, and
the Danish way of serving turbot on p. 113.

Clean and slash each fish three times on one side only. Make a
bouillon of strong beer, vinegar and white wine, and when it boils

put in a handful of sliced horseradish, some salt and the rind of a lemon, plus a little bunch of rosemary, thyme and winter savory. Cook the trout in this. For sauce, soften some butter and beat in a ladleful or two of the cooking liquor (a kind of *beurre blanc*). Pour it over the fish, and garnish with grated horseradish, pounded ginger and slices of lemon.

Truite au Bleu

By this method of cooking, the natural slime on the trout's skin is turned to a slatey blue of great softness.

If the trout are still alive, bang their heads smartly against the table and clean them quickly. Whatever you do, don't rinse them. Any blood left in the cavity can be removed by rubbing it with a little salt.

Have ready a pan with 4 pints of boiling water plus 6 tablespoons of wine vinegar. Slip the trout in and simmer for 5–10 minutes according to their size, until cooked. Serve hot with one of the cream and butter sauces on pp. 37–39, or with the walnut and horseradish sauce on p. 58.

If you wish to eat the trout cold, slip them into the boiling water, bring it back to the boil and then remove the pan from the heat and leave to cool. By the time the trout are cold, they will be properly cooked. Serve with mayonnaise, or with a whipped cream sauce like the walnut and horseradish one mentioned above, or with *beurre Montpellier* on p. 23.

Note: if you are only cooking one or two trout, halve the quantity of water and vinegar.

Trout in White Wine Jelly

A good recipe for summer lunch on a hot day. Serve with brown bread and butter, or, if you like, with one of the sauces suitable for cold trout. A lot of decorative salad stuff is not necessary, or advisable, for a dish like this.

6 servings:

6 trout, about 6–8 oz. each	½ bay leaf
¾ pint water	2 sprigs parsley
¼ pint dry white wine	2 sprigs thyme
1 tablespoon wine vinegar	¼ teaspoon salt
1 onion, sliced	6 peppercorns
1 small carrot, sliced	

Simmer all ingredients except the trout in a covered pan for 30 minutes. Leave to cool. This can be done the previous day.

Arrange the trout in an oval pan, side by side. Strain over them the cold *bouillon*, and bring gently to the boil. Simmer for 8 minutes, or until the trout are done (turn them over at half time, if they are not quite covered by the liquid). Remove the fish to a plate. Skin them; raise the fillets, and arrange them in an inch-deep dish. Put skin, bone and heads into the cooking liquid and boil it down to half the quantity as quickly as possible. Taste for seasoning – the flavour should be rather strong. Strain over the trout, and put into the refrigerator to chill for several hours. The liquid will set to a light jelly.

Trout with Mushroom and Wine Sauce

The ideal mushroom for this recipe is the cep, *Boletus edulis*, but as it does not, alas, flourish in every wood, most of us have to fall back on cultivated mushrooms. Even so this is a good dish.

6 servings:

6 trout	6 oz. cultivated mushrooms,
¼ pint dry white wine	sliced or 12 oz. prepared
¼ pint light meat stock	sliced ceps
1 medium onion, chopped	2 tablespoons chopped
2 oz. butter	parsley
1 tablespoon flour	salt, pepper
1½ tablespoons tomato concentrate	

Put the trout into a shallow pan. Pour over wine and stock, and simmer gently until just cooked.

Meanwhile soften the onion in the butter, stir in the flour and moisten with the liquid in which the trout have cooked (keep the trout warm). Add the tomato concentrate gradually, stopping when the flavour is spicy and rich, but not conspicuously of tomato, then put in the mushrooms. Simmer for about 10 minutes. Add parsley and pour over the fish. Glaze under the grill for a few seconds.

Note: you may need to add more stock or wine or both to the sauce – this will depend on how much moisture is given out by the mushrooms.

Truite du Gave

One of the best trout recipes (it comes from the Pyrenees where the fish are taken from the *gaves* or mountain torrents) and a welcome change from trout with almonds, which is becoming too much of a restaurant cliché. Measure out the pastis carefully – a lavish hand can sometimes be the cook's undoing.

For each trout allow:

seasoned flour	½ clove garlic, crushed
1 oz. clarified butter	1 tablespoon *pastis Ricard*
3 oz. sliced mushrooms, or ceps	2 tablespoons thick cream
	salt, pepper

Turn the trout in seasoned flour, shaking off the surplus. Fry it in butter, over a moderate heat, allowing 5 minutes a side. Remove to a serving dish and keep warm. Cook the mushrooms in the pan juices at a slightly higher heat, together with the garlic. Season well. Stir in the pastis; let it bubble hard for a moment or two, then add the cream and stir everything well together until the sauce is amalgamated. Correct seasoning. Pour round the trout and serve at once.

Note: if you want to cook trout with almonds, which is not to be despised, it tastes better when cooked at home, because you can attend properly to the butter, and serve the fish immediately everything is ready. (See p. 99.)

Truite aux Noisettes

Everybody knows about trout with almonds. Here is a finer version, with almonds and hazelnuts, from the *Albert Ier et Milan* at Chamonix.

6 servings:

6 trout	3 oz. fresh butter
4 large eggs	4 oz. hazelnuts
milk	lemon juice
seasoned flour	6 slices lemon
½ lb. ground almonds	chopped parsley
6 oz. clarified butter	

Clean and season the trout. Beat up the eggs in a bowl. Dip the trout first in milk, then in seasoned flour, then in the eggs, and finally roll them in the ground almonds. Shake off any excess, and place them on a sheet of greaseproof paper. Mix the remaining almonds with the remaining beaten egg and put this mixture into the trout cavities.

Brown the trout lightly in the clarified butter, and transfer the pan to a warm oven (mark 3; 325°F.) to finish cooking.

Meanwhile grill the hazelnuts, until their skins can be rubbed off, and chop them. Melt the fresh butter in a small pan and cook the hazelnuts until golden brown. Pour this over the cooked trout, which have been transferred to a serving plate, then sprinkle with lemon juice and seasoning. Decorate quickly with lemon slices and parsley and serve.

Potted Trout, Salmon, Char, Grayling etc.

This makes an excellent hors d'oeuvre. Weigh any cooked, left-over trout etc., and flake it or break it into ½-inch pieces. Melt an equal quantity of lightly salted butter. Mix in the fish, and season to taste with mace, nutmeg and pepper. Put into small pots and chill. When firm and cold, pour clarified butter over each pot to a depth of ½ inch. Store in the refrigerator until required, but keep covered with foil or the clarified butter seal will contract from the pot and cease to do its job. Serve with brown bread and butter, and dry white wine.

Note: do not be tempted to include any of those delicious cooking juices left over with the fish. They will go sour and ruin the whole thing.

Baked, Stuffed Trout

Make a delicate stuffing, such as the soft roe mixture (p. 171), or the cucumber stuffing (p. 165), or the hard-boiled egg stuffing for river fish (p. 252). Even a mixture of breadcrumbs, butter and herbs, moistened with a little cream will do very well.

Fill the cleaned trout, and lay them, head to tail, in a well-buttered baking dish. Pour over some white wine – 5–6 oz. for six trout, if they are closely fitted into the dish. Put a butter paper over them, and bake in a moderate oven (mark 4; 350°F.) for 20–30 minutes. Just before they are taken out of the oven, pour over them 5 oz. thick cream.

Truite à la Meunière

The best way of cooking really fresh trout. Turn to the recipe for *sole à la meunière* on p. 98.

Some trout fishermen declare that the skin of the fish when fried in butter is the best part of all, crisp and succulent. It profits from a fine sanding of freshly-ground black pepper. This adds a marvellous piquancy to the rich skin, without being in the least too much for the lovely flavour of the flesh inside it.

Brithyll a cig Moch

In other words, trout with bacon in the Welsh style.

Take a pie dish or gratin dish, and line it with thin rashers of fat bacon, unsmoked or smoked, according to the flavour you prefer. Clean and season the fish. Arrange them head to tail on the bacon. Sprinkle with chopped parsley, salt and freshly ground black pepper. Fold any long ends of bacon round and over the trout. Bake, covered, for about 20 minutes in a moderate oven (mark 4; 350°F.). The time depends on the size of the fish.

If you are just cooking a couple of fish, it is more sensible to wrap each one in two rashers of bacon. Lining a whole dish would be too much.

Grayling, Char and Whitefish (Ombres, ombles and corégones)

The salmon family includes, as well as trout, sea trout and salmon, the grayling, char and whitefish of the freshwaters of Europe and north America.

Grayling are white-fleshed and firm like trout, falling beautifully from the bone when cooked, but lighter in flavour. Which means they are not so good as trout, but very welcome all the same. When newly caught, they are said to smell of thyme. A few hours later this is not perceptible, any more than the cucumber fragrance of smelts survives their journey to the kitchen. Charles Cotton, in *The Compleat Angler*, remarks that grayling caught in the winter is 'little inferior to the best trout'.

The chars are another firm, white-fleshed fish. Varieties include the Arctic char, once so prolific in Windermere that locally potted char became a famous delicacy in the eighteenth and early nineteenth century. (Occasionally one still finds the shallow dishes they were packed in; white pottery with gaily coloured fish swimming round the outside, and a high price ticket underneath.) Different varieties include the Dolly Varden, and the Lake and Brook trout of north America; also the famous *omble chevalier* of the French and Swiss alps.

Whitefish are not as finely interesting as char or grayling, but they are still very worth while. At Lake Annecy in France they appear as *lavarets* on the menus. In England they are more often called powan, vendace (*corégone blanche*) and pollan (*corégone*) than whitefish, which to the ear can be a confusing if accurate description.

Whitefish (or Grayling) with Morels

The flavour of morels is so exceptional that it is worth buying a small packet of dried ones to make this dish, if you aren't lucky enough to find your own.

6 servings:

2½–3 lb. whitefish fillets	juice of 1 lemon
1 lb. fresh morels, or	salt, pepper, pinch of paprika
1½–2 oz. packet dried morels,	4 oz. thick cream
plus ½ pint *béchamel*, p. 25	seasoned flour
1 shallot, chopped	2 eggs, beaten
6 oz. butter	slices of lemon
4 oz. dry white wine	chopped parsley and chives 21
1 tablespoon *beurre manié*, p. 21	

Season the fish, and leave in a cool place while you prepare the sauce.

Wash the morels carefully and slice them up (or soak the dried ones according to instructions on the packet). Put into a pan with the shallot, a generous oz. of the butter, and the wine. Simmer for 20 minutes. Thicken with the *beurre manié*, and add lemon juice, seasoning, cream, and *béchamel* if used. Keep just under the boil for a few moments. Pour on to a serving dish and keep warm.

Dip the fish into flour, then egg, and fry in 2½ oz. of the butter until golden brown. Place on top of the morel sauce. Cook remaining butter in a small pan until golden brown and pour over the fish. Arrange the lemon slices on top, sprinkle with herbs, and serve.

Note: a recipe suitable for perch and pike, and for sole.

Grilled Grayling with Fennel

Brush scalded grayling with clarified butter, and sand them generously with freshly-ground black pepper. Grill them in the usual way.

Serve them on a bed of Florentine fennel and onion – see recipe on p. 139 for *Baked red mullet with fennel* – cooked in butter. Serve

with pats of tarragon butter and lemon quarters, with a sprinkling
of parsley.

Baked Grayling, Char and Whitefish

Most recipes for cooking these fish come from the mountain districts
of France. They are variations and refinements of the simple
method of baking freshwater fish described on p. 251.

Sometimes the fish are laid on a bed of shallots only, sometimes
the shallots are mixed with ceps or cultivated mushrooms. The
wine-flavoured juices are thickened with cream, or with cream and
egg yolks.

Perch (Perche)

Perch is undoubtedly worth pursuing, a most desirable fish; one
15th-century writer described it as 'daynteous and holsom'. The
snag is that one rarely finds it for sale, even in France. Obviously
perch fishermen, throughout northern America, and across Europe
to China, keep their treasure for themselves. As it has been placed
next to salmon and trout for deliciousness, and sometimes above
trout, one can hardly blame them for their piscatorial greed.

The name goes back to ancient Greece, where the fish was known
as Περχη. A word of the same origin, apparently, as the adjective
meaning dusky, like grapes or olives when they begin to ripen.
Which is a good description of its body colour. The fins and tail are
sometimes the most vivid orange and red, which may account for
the Italian name, *pesce persico*, the fish of ancient Persia.

One point: a perch should be scaled the moment it is caught,
otherwise it is a most tricky job. If this has not been done, the whole
fish should be plunged for a few seconds into boiling, acidulated
water. And then the skin, complete with scales, can be removed.
(Carp with recalcitrant scales can also be given this tomato-skin
treatment.) Scratches from the spines of the fins can be painful, so
cut them off before attending to the scaling and cleaning.

Small perch can simply be fried, or they can be filleted and turned into fritters. Large perch should be stuffed (p. 252) and braised in red or white wine: or they can be treated in the Delmonico style (p. 244). One of the favourite recipes in the past for perch was the Dutch stew, known here as water-souchy (p. 72). Modern recipes include a number of freshwater fish, but the flavour must have been particularly good when perch alone were used. Many of the ways of cooking trout are suitable for perch.

Pesce Persico Alla Salvia

Since the Middle Ages, or I suppose one should say since Roman times, the perch has been appreciated in Italy; a fish 'of great esteem'. Sometimes it's served in the Milanese style (dipped in egg and breadcrumbs, then fried in butter and served with lemon wedges). But this recipe, given in Ada Boni's *Italian Regional Cooking*, is more unusual and quite delicious. The Italians are as fond of sage as we are, and they use it more adroitly, with a greater variety of food.

6 servings:

12 fillets of perch	12 leaves of sage, roughly
seasoned flour	chopped
2 eggs, lightly beaten	*marinade:*
fine, dry breadcrumbs	6–8 tablespoons olive oil
4 oz. butter	juice of 1 lemon
3 tablespoons olive oil	1 green spring onion, chopped
	salt, pepper

Mix ingredients to make the marinade, and steep the fish fillets in it for at least an hour, turning them occasionally. Drain and dry. Dip in flour, egg and breadcrumbs. Fry in 3 oz of the butter, and all the oil, until nicely browned. Remove to a warm serving dish. Add the rest of the butter and the chopped sage to the pan. Bring to the boil, stirring vigorously, pour over the fish, and serve at once.

Note: if you cannot get perch, try this recipe with grayling.

Perch Delmonico

6 servings:

1 2–3 lb. perch	6 hard-boiled eggs
4 pints *court-bouillon*, no. 1, p. 16	2 oz. grated Gruyère cheese
double quantity *velouté* sauce, p. 32, made with *bouillon*, milk and cream (see recipe, below)	2 tablespoons breadcrumbs salt, pepper, paprika

Put cleaned and scaled perch into the cold *court-bouillon*. Bring to the boil and simmer for about 20 minutes until the fish is just cooked. Remove the skin and take off the fillets in smallish pieces. Use some of the *court-bouillon* to make the *velouté* sauce – about 1¼ pints sauce is required.

Remove 12 good slices from the eggs, for garnish, and cut the remains into wedges.

Fold fish and pieces of egg into the sauce. Turn into a lightly greased shallow baking dish. Mix cheese and crumbs and sprinkle over the top. Brown under the grill. Lay the 12 slices of egg down the middle, put a little paprika on top and serve very hot.

Perch with Mushrooms

Follow the recipe above, but serve the fish whole and skinned, with a creamy mushroom sauce (which has been made with some of the *court-bouillon*, reduced by boiling).

Perch Stewed with Prunes

See *matelote of eel*, p. 270.

Fried Perch in the Loir Style

See *river fish and white wine*, p. 250.

Pike, Pickerel and Maskinonge (Brochets)

The long-snouted, tyrannical pike is the hero of one of the best chapters in *The Compleat Angler*. Izaak Walton obviously enjoyed the prolonged game of wits involved in catching it. He also enjoyed eating it. His famous recipe, in which the fish is stuffed with herbs, spices, oysters, anchovies and a pound of butter, and then roasted on the spit, is followed by the comment that this is 'too good a dish for any but anglers, or very honest men'.

Pike fishing is again popular in Britain. I read that many pike are caught in a year, some of them over 40 lb. in weight. Yet one never sees them for sale, as one does in France. I wonder why? Do successful pike-fishermen treasure them for their own secret enjoyment? Or would it be more accurate to assume that hundreds of these fine fish are thrown back into the water every year?

So you must excuse me if all the recipes following come from France, where pike is one of the more highly-regarded – and expensive – of freshwater fish. Do not be chauvinistic in the matter, for all the recipes can be applied with equal felicity to the pike of this country, or to the pickerels and maskinonge of Canada and the United States. Maskinonge, a word which has many forms, is the Ojibwa name for the large pike of North America. French settlers took the name to mean *masque allongé* (which it undeniably is), which didn't help the spelling.

Pike in the Loir Style

6 servings:

1 pike	*bouquet garni*
court-bouillon	2 inch piece of celery
½ bottle white wine, 'Coteaux du Loir' or other dry white wine	salt, 8 peppercorns
	plus
	sorrel pureé, p. 47
equal quantity of water	*beurre blanc*, p. 42
1 carrot, sliced	new potatoes
1 onion, sliced	

Put the *bouillon* ingredients into a pan, and simmer them for half an hour. Wine from the *coteaux du Loir* is not easy to come by. I'm lucky enough to live near Jasnières, by La Chartre-sur-Loir, but if I can't get hold of a bottle (or can't afford it) I use an ordinary dry white wine.

If the pike is alive, stun and clean it without washing or scaling it (the treatment is similar to that of trout *au bleu*). If the pike is dead, it can be cleaned and scaled with the aid of water – but as little as possible.

Put the fish on to the strainer of a fish kettle. Pour the tepid *bouillon* slowly round it, through a sieve. Bring to the boil and simmer until the pike is cooked.

Prepare sorrel and potatoes while the *court-bouillon* is simmering on its own. They won't hurt if they are kept warm while the pike cooks. *Beurre blanc*, apart from the initial reduction, must be prepared at the last minute. So if possible get somebody else to drain and dish up the pike and vegetables, while you concentrate on the sauce.

Note: remember that spinach and lemon juice can be substituted for sorrel. Or else tart gooseberries.

Dos de Brochet au Meursault

The best dish of pike I have ever eaten was at Saulieu in Burgundy. It was brought to the table in neat pieces, dressed with a delicious sauce and surrounded with crescents of fresh-water crayfish in puff pastry, and small *quenelles* of pike, containing truffles. See p. 248.

One cannot hope to emulate Monsieur Minot, who is chef-patron of the *Côte d'or* at Saulieu, but I asked him for the recipe, and assure you that even a simplified version is worth attempting.

A 3-lb. pike is first skinned and filleted, then larded. For six hours the long strips of fish lie in a bath of brandy and old madeira, with a seasoning of salt and pepper. The fish is drained and turned in seasoned flour before being fried gently in butter.

When the fish is cooked – here is one secret – divide the fillets into 2 inch slices and remove the bones which pop up automatically from between the flakes as the knife goes through. Keep the fish warm, while you pour 2 glasses of Meursault into the cooking pan. Reduce it to almost nothing, then quickly stir in plenty of thick cream. Correct the seasoning and boil down to the right consistency.

Up to this point, the recipe is not too difficult for any enthusiastic cook. It tastes very good without the final touches that are only within the resources of a first-class French restaurant. These are the supreme touches. Finish the sauce with some *hollandaise* and some *sauce nantua*; garnish with crayfish tails in puff pastry, and the *quenelles* mentioned above.

Braised Pike

A simpler recipe, which can be adapted to fillets of pike by reducing the cooking time.

6 servings:

2½–3 lb. pike	¾ pint fish or light meat stock
6 shallots, chopped	¾ pint dry white wine
1 onion, chopped	1 tablespoon flour
big bunch parsley, chopped	4 oz. double (heavy) cream
4 oz. butter	salt, pepper
lemon juice	slices of lemon

Clean and scale the pike, discarding the roe along with the rest of the innards – it can upset people's digestion, I am told. Mix the chopped vegetables together with half the parsley. Grease a long ovenproof dish with half the butter, and make a bed of the vegetables in it. On this bed lay the fish. Sprinkle it with lemon juice, salt and pepper, and pour in enough stock and wine to cover it. (The exact amount will depend on the fit of the dish.) Bake in a fairly hot oven (mark 5; 375°F.) for about half an hour, until cooked.

Transfer the fish to a large serving plate to keep warm. Reduce the cooking liquor to half its quantity, then strain into a clean pan. Mash the flour with the remaining butter, and use it to thicken the sauce in the usual way (*beurre manié*, p. 21). Pour in the cream, and reheat. Coat the fish with some of the sauce, sprinkle parsley on top and arrange slices of lemon at suitable points. Serve the rest of the sauce separately.

Note: see the recipe for *Tench baked in the Loir style* on p. 251. A pike should be stuffed with 4 oz. of butter mashed with salt, pepper and parsley.

Stuffed Pike

A milder form of the kind of dish Izaak Walton so enjoyed. It comes from *Clarisse or The Old Cook*, which was written by an anonymous French gourmet, and translated into English by Elise Vallée, in 1926. When larding the fish with strips of bacon fat, allow the ends to stick up so that they can catch the heat.

'Stuff a good pike with a mixture composed of breadcrumbs soaked in milk, butter, parsley, mushrooms already cooked, and, if you like, mashed up fillets of anchovy. Lard your fish and put it in the oven. You will know when it is cooked by the larding being browned, serve it with its own sauce, to which I would beg you to add a little lemon juice and some melted butter.'

Do not omit the anchovies, and be liberal with the butter. Instead of lemon, you could use a mixture of orange and lemon juice. Izaak Walton used oranges, but they must have been Seville or bitter oranges. Nowadays their season is so brief that it does not correspond with the pike's.

For another good sharp stuffing for pike, turn to p. 263, and follow the recipe for *Alose farcie à l'angevine*. Sorrel is undoubtedly very good with pike, either as a stuffing or as an accompanying vegetable.

Quenelles de Brochet

A *quenelle* is a kind of dumpling, an aristocratic dumpling I hurry to say, a light and delicate confection with little resemblance to the doughy bullet of mass catering.

There are two basic kinds, for which recipes follow. I advise you to attempt neither unless your kitchen has electrical machinery such as a liquidizer or moulinette. Pike is the classic fish to use, which is why the recipes are placed at this point in the book, but any good firm fish can be used instead – sole, salmon, turbot, sea-bream, John Dory, whiting or monkfish.

Both kinds of *quenelle* are poached in barely simmering water or fish *fumet*, and served with a fine creamy sauce. The best is *sauce Nantua*, or lobster sauce; but for most of us a *sauce aurore*, a white wine sauce, mushroom sauce or Mornay sauce is more practical.

Quenelles de Mousseline (1)

1 lb. fillets of fish	1 pint double cream
4 large egg whites	salt, pepper, nutmeg

Cut up the fillets and reduce them to a purée, with the egg whites, in a blender. Push the purée through a fine sieve (electrical, again). Whip the cream until it is very thick but not stiff. Fold it into the fish until you have a thick, homogeneous mass. The problem with *quenelles* is to get the fish to absorb the cream; the egg whites help, and if you are attempting the recipe by hand the bowl should stand in a larger bowl with plenty of ice cubes.

Season the mixture, and leave it in the refrigerator to chill for several hours. As the meal approaches, make the sauce and keep it warm: boiled rice is sometimes served as well, so cook that too. Last of all, put a wide flat pan of salted water on to boil. Shape a *quenelle* with 2 warmed tablespoons and slip it into the water, which should barely simmer; the *quenelle* will disintegrate in boiling liquid. Add more *quenelles* until the pan is comfortably full. Remove them with a perforated spoon as they are cooked – 8 to 10 minutes should be right, but taste the first *quenelle* to make sure; the inside should be a little creamy. Keep hot, and serve with the sauce poured over them.

Quenelles (2)

This recipe produces the more solid, cylindrical *quenelles* that are sold in cans and frozen packages in many French grocery shops. You will sometimes see them in high-class food shops in this country. They are not cheaper to make at home, but you will be sure of the ingredients and of a finer flavour.

1 lb. pike or other firm fish fillets	7 oz. unsalted butter
	2 eggs
8 oz. white breadcrumbs	2 egg yolks
4 oz. milk	salt, pepper, nutmeg

Purée the fish in a moulinette, or mince it twice. Mix the bread-crumbs with the milk and squeeze them together in your hand so that the surplus milk runs away and you are left with a thick paste. Cut up and soften the butter. Using the electric beater, mix the bread paste, then the softened butter, into the fish, until the mixture is smooth and firm. Add the eggs and yolks one by one. Mix well, season and chill.

Roll into sausage shapes on a floured board, or put through a forcing bag with a wide, plain nozzle. Most *quenelles* of this type are about ¾ of an inch in diameter, and 4–5 inches long.

Cook them as above, in water if you like, but preferably in a well-flavoured fish *fumet* made from the bones of the fish being used (p. 17). Serve with one of the sauces mentioned already, and with boiled rice if the *quenelles* are to be the main course.

In the past *quenelles* have really been a garnishing element in grand cookery, part of the delicious bits and pieces surrounding a large carp or salmon, or a dish of sole. The wonderful dishes that Carême invented in his kitchens at Brighton, for the Prince Regent, often contained *quenelles*; with a crayfish purée, poached oysters, poached soft roes, slices of truffle and mushroom heads, they were certainly a garnish *à la régence*. Later, less majestic chefs formed the *quenelles* round a couple of poached oysters or a piece of soft roe, and served them on their own with a fine sauce. Thanks to electricity (instead of a collection of kitchen boys) we can now make them at home, store them in the deep freeze (after they have been rolled into shape), and produce them whenever a light but tempting dish is required in the evening.

River Fish and White Wine

Hairdressing in France is so expensive (and prolonged) that I've become ruthless in exacting compensation. My usual hairdresser specializes in mushrooms; he's also a great fisherman. Alas no display of English simplicity has managed to extract a map reference for the morels and ceps he finds by the kilo every year (such inform-ation is part of a family's inheritance, I gather). But with river fish, it's another matter. Between explanations of what's going on at the back of my head, he will deliver himself of heretical culinary opinions.

Take perch, of about 1½ pounds weight. He insists that the best method is to fry them *very slowly* in butter, half an hour on each side – I recommend the use of an asbestos mat and clarified butter. The skin turns thick and crisp, a rich golden brown. 'And inside – *no*, Madame, it does *not* get overcooked – inside the flesh is moist and full of flavour. But of course, you must drink a good white wine with it. Of course. But better still, when you have a bottle of good white wine, is to drink it as an apéritif with little bits of eel – yes, little bits, ooh not much more than a centimetre long. Flour them and shake them and put them in a chip basket. Keep them in deep hot oil until they are a nice brown. You have to try one to see.' The little bits are turned on to a plate and quickly sprinkled with salt. He's right – they go much better with the wine than salted nuts or crisps or even olives.

Tench or other River Fish Baked in the Loir Style

Every cook in the *val du Loir* – and in north and western France, I suspect – uses this recipe for river fish because the ingredients are always in house or garden. The sudden return of a fishing party causes no flurry. By the time a couple of bottles are emptied, the fish is on the table, its freshness in no way masked, but honoured without pretension.

This kind of recipe has felicity and seemliness – like our church at Trôo, whose Norman walls, tower, capitals and keystones, arches and arcades have been cut and dragged out of the cliff which it crowns, and which shelters still a number of its parishioners.

3–8 servings:

1½–4 lb. whole fish, scaled and cleaned	generous ¼ pint dry white wine
shallots or onion	generous ¼ pint thick cream
butter	lemon juice
parsley, salt, pepper	

Butter generously an ovenproof dish which is large enough to hold the fish, without too much room to spare. Put in enough chopped shallots or onions to cover the base. Scatter with parsley, salt and pepper. Lay in the fish, and brush it with melted butter. Bake in a fairly hot oven (mark 6; 400°F.) for 10–15 minutes according to size, then pour in the wine. Baste occasionally with the juices, until the flesh turns opaque. Pour over the cream, and return to the oven for 5 minutes. A squeeze of lemon juice before serving compensates for the blandness of English cream. Serve with plenty of bread or plainly boiled potatoes.

You can omit the bed of onion if you like, and stuff the fish – particularly the larger fish. See the recipe following.

Egg and Mushroom Stuffing for Fish

The simplest stuffing for any fish, whether it comes from sea or river, is made from breadcrumbs mixed with butter, parsley and seasoning. Chopped shallot, bacon and grated cheese may be added for extra flavour. If you are presented with a fine river fish, a bream, tench, barbel, or perch, I suggest you follow another excellent French recipe, and combine hardboiled egg and mushroom in a more elaborate recipe:

6 servings:

2 oz. butter	salt, pepper, nutmeg
1 heaped tablespoon chopped shallot or onion	about 1 tablespoon each, chopped chives and parsley
2–3 oz. roughly chopped mushrooms	1 large hard-boiled egg, chopped
3–4 tablespoons breadcrumbs	thick cream
grated rind of half a lemon	

Melt the butter and fry the shallot or onion gently in it for 5 minutes. Add the mushrooms, raise the heat slightly and cook for 10 minutes. Stir in the breadcrumbs – a little more or less according to the size of the fish – and remove from the heat. Season to taste with salt, freshly ground pepper and freshly grated nutmeg. Stir in lemon rind and herbs, then the hard-boiled egg. Mix in a little cream, so that you have a lightly bound, but not pasty, consistency. Correct the seasoning.

Any stuffing left over can be augmented with some extra onion, plus mushroom if you like, and laid on the well-buttered base of the baking dish. Follow the recipe above, but omit the final addition of cream. A little more white wine may be needed.

Note: this recipe does well for carp, too, though on the whole I think that the following stronger-flavoured Italian mixture is more successful.

Fennel Stuffing for River Fish

Flavourings of the aniseed type go well with fish of all kinds as you'll see if you try the trout recipe on p. 237, or the *mouclade d'Esnandes* (p. 322), or salmon pickled with dill. Here's a mixture, a *battuto*, from Italy which can be used as a bed for baked fish, or as a stuffing, if breadcrumbs and egg are added. It can also be used with salt-water fish, but originally it belonged to the *regina* (carp) of Lake Trasimene.

6 servings:

2–3 slices Italian *prosciutto*, or lean smoked bacon	1 head of fennel
1 large clove garlic	olive oil or butter

Chop *prosciutto*, or ham, with the garlic and fennel. Melt enough oil or butter to cover the base of a frying pan thinly, and stew the chopped mixture in it over a low heat, until the fennel softens. Don't let it brown.

To make a stuffing, add about 2 or 3 oz. of breadcrumbs, and a beaten egg. Season well. (A good stuffing, too, for chicken and turkey.)

In Umbria by Lake Trasimene, the *regina* will be deeply scored, and the slits as well as the cavity filled with the *battuto*. The fish is then speared by a spit, and tied firmly together, for roasting. As it cooks, a little rosemary, oil and lemon are used to baste the fish, plus salt and pepper for seasoning. The *battuto* and method are primarily used for sucking pig, so the recipe is known as '*Regina in porchetta*' – in sucking pig style.

Carp (Carpe)

For centuries carp have been the pet fish of domestic waters. Frank Buckland described them as 'water-sheep – herbivorous – gregarious – of a contented mind'. Still at great houses, like the château of Chantilly in France, they rise in crowds to the surface of moat or lake to be fed (not, I believe, on account of the bell which is rung, but because they see people collecting together and have learnt that this means food). Another of the French châteaux, Chambord, has given its name to a much-truffled preparation of carp in the princely style.

The first carp I encountered came from no such elegant waters, but from the river Loir, in May. The clammy creature was handed to me by a friend, who observed that he had brought his lunch with him. I recognized the handsome large-scaled fish from Chinese plates and paintings; but I had not the least idea of how to cook it. Neither did I know that it should have been soaked in vinegar and water in case it had a muddy flavour.

As it turned out I was lucky. That carp had been kind enough to avoid the murkier depths of the Loir. And the only means I had of cooking it – foil, a double row of bricks with a grill, and charcoal – were just right for its fresh liveliness of flavour. Butter, shallots, parsley, and white wine all went into the package, and we remember its taste many years later.

Our second carp did not turn out so well. It was not *Cyprinus carpio* from the Loir, but a Mirror carp, a variety which has been bred for fish-farming. It looked strange, even amongst the exotic fish of Soho. The skin had a soft, washleather appearance, an opulent nudity, as the huge scales were few and dotted about in irregular rows. That fish must have been a long way from home, because the flavour had faded. In fact carp are good travellers. I should have been more careful to choose a livelier looking specimen. Although one could not expect the wild freshness of river-caught carp, these domestic varieties please the Chinese, and the Germans, and the French, all in their very different ways serious eaters of good things. Obviously carp are not selling in large quantities all over the world just because they are tough survivors and easily fed. (Some of the ponds extend to thousands of acres.)

I have learnt since that the carp is a surprisingly interesting fish for the cook, as I hope you will agree after reading the following recipes. It should be added that, for the eater, the flesh is firm and sweet, the arrangement of bones satisfyingly comprehensible. The soft roe is a great delicacy. If it is not required specifically in the recipe, turn to p. 205 and make the *Curé's Omelette* with it.

Fish-pond carp, sold usually after their third summer, weigh about 2½–3 lb.; though carp can be very much larger than that, up to 50 lb. and more. Soak them in 4 pints (10 cups) of water with 6 tablespoons of vinegar, after cleaning them. Be sure to remove the bitter gall sac at the back of the head. If you wish to remove the scales and they prove difficult, a little boiling water helps.

Carpe à la Juive

A strange thing about carp is the unanimity with which it is treated by cooks right across the world – as if everyone agreed with Kenneth Lo in emphasizing its 'uncomplicated sweet-freshness'. Certainly his braised carp from Peking has something in common with this recipe and with the Polish style carp on p. 258. I do not imagine a traceable connection, because I suspect that the carp recipes still used in Europe are living fossils of the sweet-sour style of medieval cookery. But it is interesting that they should be so appropriate to carp that they have survived in our northern repertoire, when so many other similar medieval fish recipes have not. This Jewish way of cooking carp comes from Lorraine:

6–8 servings

1 or 2 carp, totalling 4–5 lb.	1 tablespoon vinegar
½ pint olive oil	salt, pepper
2 large onions, chopped	*bouquet garni*
4 shallots, chopped	3 oz. raisins
2 tablespoons flour	4 oz. blanched and split
1 tablespoon sugar	almonds
water, or light fish stock	

Clean and scale the fish, which is best left whole. However, if you have a large carp and no fish kettle, it can be cut into thick slices.

In the oil, cook onions and shallots lightly. When they begin to brown and soften, stir in the flour, sugar and 2–3 pints water or stock. Add vinegar, *bouquet*, raisins and almonds. Pour, boiling, over the fish in its pan or kettle. The sauce should just cover the fish; add more water if it doesn't. Simmer until done. Transfer the fish to an oval plate (re-forming the pieces, if it was cut up). Reduce the sauce by boiling until it has a good, fairly strong, flavour. Correct the seasoning if necessary with salt, pepper and sugar. Pour over carp and leave to get cold. The sauce turns to a jelly. Serve chilled.

Carp Stuffed with Chestnuts

A more conventional recipe, from *The Alice B. Toklas Cook Book*, though again there is the sweet note, in this case of chestnuts.

4 servings:

3 lb. carp	2 generous tablespoons butter
¾ pint dry white wine	2-inch thick slice of bread
salt	dry white wine
cracker crumbs	1 tablespoon chopped parsley
2 generous tablespoons	1 teaspoon salt
melted butter	¼ teaspoon each pepper, mace,
stuffing:	powdered bay leaf, thyme
1 medium onion, chopped	12 chestnuts, boiled, peeled
2 chopped shallots	and roughly chopped
1 clove garlic, crushed	1 egg

First make the stuffing. Cook onion, shallot and garlic until soft and golden in the butter. Cut crusts off the bread, dice it and soak in a little dry white wine. Squeeze out the surplus. Mix stuffing ingredients together and put into the cleaned carp. Sew or skewer together. Leave for 2 hours. Bake for 20 minutes in a fairly hot oven (mark 5; 375°F), with the white wine. Sprinkle with cracker crumbs, pour over the melted butter and put back into the oven for another 20 minutes. Serve with noodles.

Christmas Carp

Carp is the Christmas Eve dish of many German families. Sometimes it is cooked with a sweet–sour sauce which includes honeyed spice-cake and beer; sometimes *au bleu* with a horseradish sauce. Each person saves a scale (the usual fish from the fish-farms is the huge-scaled Mirror carp) to bring them luck during the coming year. See recipes below.

Carp au Bleu with Horseradish Sauce

6 servings:

3½–4 lb. carp	2 oz. ground almonds
¼ pint wine or tarragon vinegar	1 teaspoon sugar
court-bouillon, no. 2, p. 17	grated horseradish to taste, or prepared horseradish
½ pint double cream	salt

After cleaning it, tie carp in a circle, nose to tail. (Do not wash or scale.) Put it into a pan. Bring the vinegar to the boil and pour it over the fish. Add the *court-bouillon*, bring to the boil, and simmer until the carp is cooked. Drain and serve with the following sauce:

Bring cream, almonds and sugar to the boil. Stir in grated or prepared horseradish to taste and season with salt. A little lemon juice can also be added.

Meurette de Carpe

4 servings:

1 carp, 2–3½ lb.	3 large cloves garlic
1 bottle red Burgundy	*bouquet garni*
4 oz. mushrooms, sliced	salt, pepper
1 medium onion, chopped	2 oz. butter
3 oz. currants	1 tablespoon flour

Simmer the mushrooms, onion, currants, garlic, *bouquet garni* and wine together for half an hour, uncovered, until the wine has reduced by a good third. Season. Clean the carp and cut it into pieces. Add to the pan, cover, and simmer for another half hour, or until the fish is cooked.

Mash butter and flour together, use it to thicken the sauce (*beurre manié*). Reheat and serve with croûtons of bread fried in butter. Remove the *bouquet garni* before serving, and the head of the carp.

For other stews of freshwater fish, see pp. 79, 259, 270.

Karpfen Polnischer Art (Carp in the Polish Style)

6 servings:

4 lb. soft-roed carp	1 clove, or pinch powdered clove
4 medium onions, sliced	6 peppercorns
3 stalks of celery heart, chopped	3 oz. *pain d'épices* (spice loaf) crumbled
6 oz. butter	about 4 pints beer
bouquet garni	lemon juice, salt, pepper

Soak the carp in vinegared water (see p. 254). Do not scale or rinse it, but take care when cleaning to take out the roe carefully and to remove the bitter sac at the back of the head. Melt onion and celery over a gentle heat in 2 oz. of butter. Put them into a pan, then add the *bouquet*, the cloves and peppercorns, and the *pain d'épices*. The carp goes on top, with its roe alongside. Cover with beer and simmer until cooked, removing the roe when it is done. Lay the cooked carp on a dish, and surround with the roe, which should be sliced. Keep warm. Sieve the sauce into a clean pan, reduce to ¾–1 pint. Season to taste with lemon juice, salt and pepper. Beat in the remaining butter, bit by bit. Pour some over the carp, serve the rest in a sauce boat. Serve with boiled potatoes.

Carpe Farcie

Carp stuffed with sorrel makes a good dish. Turn to the recipe on p. 263 for *Alose farcie*, but once the fish is stuffed, bake it in white wine rather than butter.

Catigot

Catigot or *catigau* is a freshwater fish stew from southern France. Two or more varieties are cooked in white wine, the sauce thickened with egg yolks. Bacon or lard is used instead of olive oil or butter. This recipe is based on one from *La Cuisine Rustique – Languedoc*, by André Bonnaure.

4–6 servings:

1 eel, ¾–1 lb.	4 oz. water
1 carp, 1–1½ lb.	salt, pepper
1 large onion, sliced	3 egg yolks
1 medium carrot, sliced	½ tablespoon wine vinegar
2–3 cloves garlic, crushed	croûtons of bread fried in lard
lard or bacon fat	or cooking oil and rubbed
6 oz. dry white wine	with garlic

Skin and clean the eel. Scale and clean the carp. Cut them into chunks about 1½ inches wide. Cook the onion, carrot and garlic, until lightly coloured, in just enough lard to cover the base of a saucepan. Put the pieces of fish into the pan. Pour in the wine and water. Season, and cook over a good heat for 10 minutes. Meanwhile beat the egg yolks with the vinegar. When the fish is cooked, strain a little of the liquid into the egg yolk mixture, stirring all the time. Return to the pan and keep over a low heat, *without boiling*, until the sauce is thickened. Turn into a serving dish and serve with the *croûtons* tucked around the edge.

Allis Shad, Twaite Shad and American Shad

(Alose, alose finte and alose canadienne)

The shad, of whatever kind, is a fine fat member of the herring family – it is sometimes known as the king of the herrings – which has the unherring-like habit of coming into rivers to spawn. And it is in rivers that it is caught. The allis and twaite shads used to honour the Wye and Severn, but now you have to go to the Loire or Garonne, or even further south, if you want to enjoy one. Going there to eat shad with sorrel sauce, or sorrel stuffing, and *beurre blanc* is one of the springtime rituals of the French who are lucky enough to live near the Loire. And I notice a similar air of celebration about American recipes.

All three kinds of shad have the richness of herring, and a good flavour. Alas, they also have its bones. I pass on two American ways of causing the bones to disintegrate, but feel the price paid – 5 and 6 hours in the oven – is probably too high for any fish.

The great delight of shad is the roe. The soft milt is good, but the hard roe has a moist crunch, a most delightful texture that begins to approach the foothills of caviare. This is because the individual eggs are almost the size of those coloured beads which adorn some dressmaking pins.

How to get rid of Shad Bones

1. THE OLD WAY. Grease the bottom of an oval, lidded, ovenproof pot. Put in the cleaned fish, without its roe, and with slices of unsmoked bacon in the central cavity and on top. Pour in enough water to leave the top part bare. Season. Bring to the simmer, then transfer to a very cool oven (mark $\frac{1}{2}$; 250°F.) and leave for 5 hours.
2. THE MODERN WAY. Clean shad, brush inside and out with seasoned melted butter. Take a large sheet of foil, brush it with cooking oil and put the fish on it. Seal the edges tightly. Place in an oval covered pot and bake in a very cool oven (mark $\frac{1}{2}$; 250°F.) for 6 hours.

Planked Shad with Creamed Roe

From *Fanny Farmer's Boston Cook Book.*

'Clean and split a 3-lb. shad. Put skin side down on buttered plank, sprinkle with salt and pepper, and brush over with melted butter. Bake 25 minutes in hot oven (mark 6; 400°F.) or broil in gas or electric broiler 2 inches from heat. Spread with butter, garnish with parsley and lemon, and serve on the plank.'

If you do not have a hardwood plank, the shad can perfectly well be placed on a buttered baking dish.

1 shad roe	4 oz. thick cream
3 tablespoons butter	2 egg yolks
1 teaspoon finely chopped	salt, pepper, lemon juice
shallot	2 oz. breadcrumbs fried in
1 rounded tablespoon flour	butter

Put the roe into $1\frac{1}{2}$ pints water with 1 tablespoon vinegar or lemon juice and 1 teaspoon salt. Simmer for a few moments until the roe begins to turn white. Remove the membranes and mash the roes. Melt the shallot in the butter until soft, add roe, then flour and cream. Cook gently for 5 minutes. Stir in beaten egg yolks. Season highly.

Take the baked planked shad from the oven, and spread it with the creamed roe. Sprinkle the buttered crumbs evenly over the top and brown in the oven or under the grill.

Baked Stuffed Shad

A French recipe with a delicious whiting stuffing.

6 servings:

3 lb. shad	*sauce:*
stuffing:	2 oz. butter
10 oz. whiting fillet, without	3 tablespoons chopped shallot
bones or skin	7 oz. mushrooms, chopped
1 egg	scant $\frac{1}{2}$ pint dry white wine
3 tablespoons chopped	scant $\frac{1}{2}$ pint *court-bouillon* or
almonds	light stock
5 oz. thick cream	1 tablespoon flour
1 tablespoon each parsley and	$\frac{1}{2}$ pint cream
chives	2 tablespoons chopped chives
salt, pepper	lemon juice, salt, pepper

Clean, scale and rinse the shad. Prepare the stuffing – liquidize the whiting with the egg white, add the cream little by little. Transfer to a bowl and incorporate the egg yolk and chopped almonds. Add herbs, and seasoning, and stuff the shad.

If you do not have a liquidizer, mince or pound the whiting finely, put the bowl into a bowl of ice, and add the egg white, then the almonds and yolk, and finally the cream, very very slowly. (This will take up to 10 minutes.) The ice prevents the mixture from separating, but is not necessary with a liquidizer.

Butter an ovenproof dish with half the butter. Put in the shallot and mushrooms, season with salt, pepper and lemon, place the stuffed fish on top. Pour in wine and *bouillon* or stock. Cover with kitchen foil and bake in a fairly hot oven (mark 6; 400°F.) for 30 minutes.

Meanwhile fork the flour into the remaining butter (*beurre manié*). Transfer the shad when cooked to a serving dish. Pour the cooking liquor etc. into a pan, reduce it by boiling to half quantity, and pour in the cream. Thicken with the *beurre manié* in the usual way. Add chives and seasoning.

Alose à l'Oseille

Shad, as I have said, is a favourite fish of the Loire springtime. Usually it's baked, and served with sorrel purée or sorrel stuffing. At other times it's poached, and served with *beurre blanc*. The second recipe I give combines both these accompanying delights in a dish of ceremony. The two recipes come from *La Vraie Cuisine de l'Anjou et de la Touraine*, by Roger Lallemand:

4 servings:

1–1¾ lb. shad, cleaned and scaled	1 lb. sorrel
4 oz. softened butter	3 oz. thick cream
salt, black pepper	nutmeg

Butter an ovenproof dish generously. Place the shad in it and dab the rest of the butter on top. Season well, and bake in a fairly hot oven (mark 5; 375°F.) until cooked – about 30 minutes. Baste often with butter in the dish. Meanwhile wash the sorrel and cut it into strips with a pair of scissors.

When the shad is ready, pour off the butter and juices into a saucepan. Cover the fish with foil; put it back into the oven – reducing the temperature – to keep warm. Stir the sorrel into the butter and juices, and cook rapidly to a thick purée. (Spinach with lemon, or tart gooseberries, can be substituted: the point is to provide the fish with a sharp but rich sauce.) Stir in the cream. Season with salt, freshly ground black pepper, and nutmeg. Pour on to a long serving dish, and place the shad on top.

Alose Farcie à l'Angevine

4 servings:

1–1¾ lb. shad, cleaned and scaled	½ lb. sorrel
	½ lb. spinach
2 oz. butter	2 full tablespoons thick cream
3 shallots, chopped, or 3 oz. mild onions	2 hard-boiled eggs
	salt, pepper

Melt the shallots or onion in the butter. They should cook until soft, without browning. Stir in the sorrel and spinach, cut into strips. Cook until the purée is thick and all wateriness has disappeared. Season and bind with the cream. Shell the hard-boiled eggs and fork them to crumbliness. Stir into the stuffing. Place in the cavity of the fish, and sew it up well so that none – or very little – can escape. Bake in butter, as in the recipe above.

Serve with *beurre blanc* (p. 42). *Beurre blanc* is also served with shad poached in a white wine *court bouillon*, but I think that this recipe is better, as shad, to me at any rate, needs sharpness.

Note: if you're lucky enough to have a female shad, stir the eggs into the stuffing.

Eel and Elvers (Anguille and civelles)

I love eel. Sometimes I think it's my favourite fish. It's delicate, but rich; it falls neatly from the bone; grilled to golden brown and flecked with dark crustiness from a charcoal fire, it makes the best of all picnic food; stewed in red wine, cushioned with onions and mushrooms, bordered with triangles of fried bread, it's the meal for cold nights in autumn; smoked and cut into elegant fillets, it starts a wedding feast or a Christmas eve dinner with style and confidence. Its skin is so tough that it was used to join the two parts of a flail together (think of the strain on that join as the flails thumped down to winnow the corn at harvest), or to make a whip for a boy's top, or to bind the elastic to his catapult. The eel has picturesque habits, often lurking in old mill leats under willow roots, until it's seduced by a waisted eel-trap set by the sluice gate.

It has mystery, too. Aristotle wondered why no eel was ever found with roe or milt. This question had become a matter for poetry, or poetical prosing, by the time of Izaak Walton – 'others say, that as pearls are made of glutinous dew drops, which are condensed by the sun's heat in those countries, so Eels are bred of a particular dew'. The true poet, though, of this strange creature, was not Izaak Walton, or any other mystified ancient, but a biologist; the great Danish biologist Johannes Schmidt. In 1922, after 25 years of back-tracking eel larvae, he came right over the spawning ground, the correct 'particular dew'.

The first larva was found by chance near the Faroe Islands in 1904; a willow-leaf of transparency, 77 millimetres long and, as it turned out, 3 years old. Other smaller larvae were found in the following years, further away from the coasts of Europe. Schmidt realized that if he could follow this trail of diminishing larvae, he would come to their home. Which he did in 1922 (the First World War had held things up). Right over the spawning ground, at the seaweedy eastern side of the Sargasso Sea, he brought up in his net the tiniest larvae of all – 5 millimetres long. Millions of them radiate out in all directions, but only those caught in the Gulf Stream survive and make the journey to Europe. There, almost in sight of land, the willow-leaf becomes a wriggling, vigorous, wormlike object, the glass-eel or elver, ready to swarm up the rivers of Europe from the Atlantic, the Mediterranean and the Black Sea. (Apparently the slowness of larval growth increased over unimaginable time, as the continents drifted slowly apart: the eels clung tenaciously both to their spawning ground, and to their familiar rivers, however long the journey between them became.)

The elvers now come together in broods. They can be seen stringing along for miles in a yard-wide cordon or eel-fare (from which we have the word elver), pushing upstream at night with a strength incredible to anyone who has bought a pound of elvers, feeble, threadlike things, from Gloucester market. Winds, tides, the hours of daylight, and of darkness which is their travelling time, all affect their speed, but they aren't stopped by obstacles in their way. One French biologist remarked that he'd seen them pass waterfalls, weirs, locks. He'd seen them climb vertical walls, lock walls, even coming out of the water so long as there was a little moisture. The bodies of the casualties stick to the walls to make a sort of ladder for the push of elvers behind. They can wriggle themselves through the narrowest cracks ... 'and so they manage to populate the smallest stretches of water, even those which might seem to have no connection at all with a river'.

It's at night, between ebb and falling tide, that the Severn elver-fisherman sets out. He carries a scoop net, and a bucket for the catch; he has a lamp too, and sticks to support it. The elvers are mainly dispatched to the eel farms of northern Europe, but some are kept for the housewives of the Severn area as a spring delicacy for suppertime. If you live anywhere near Gloucester, it's worth making a visit in March (or April according to the season), to find elvers, to see the elver-fisherman's equipment in the Folk Museum in West-gate Street, and buy an excellent illustrated guide to the Severn Fishery collection, by John Neufville Taylor. At Frampton-on-Severn, there is an annual elver-eating competition: the record – 1 lb. in a minute – is held by the village garage mechanic.

The elvers which survive the journey, and the attentions of fishermen, grow slowly to maturity in the hidden crannies of streams. Young eels are yellowish at first (yellow eels are not worth eating), then after eight years or more their flanks turn to silver and they're ready for the long swim home. In autumn, the ones who can return downstream, avoiding nets stretched across many rivers, and barriers of basketwork and reeds, with more or less success. These silver eels, mature eels, are the best. They're caught in tons at the mouths of some rivers: at Comacchio on the Po, it's been known for 1000 tons to be caught in a single night. A favourite dish there is a simple soup of eel layered with slices of onion, carrot, and celery and seasoned with parsley and lemon rind. The eel is covered with water, and half way through the cooking a spoonful or two of tomato concentrate and wine vinegar are added. (For other eel soups, see p. 71.)

Once in salt water, the silver eel streaks out for the Sargasso sea, thousands of miles away, fathoms down, along dark cold currents, with no light or fishing nets to impede its path. Eel from the Black Sea may take a year, but eel from Western Europe will do it in about six months, ready to spawn in the spring.

Only the European eel, *Anguilla anguilla*, makes so arduous and – to our mind – so moving a journey (other species, *Anguilla rostrata*, or *japonica*, or *australis*, have their spawning grounds comparatively close to the streams of North America, or Japan or Australia). As the salmon knows its way back to the river where it was born, so the eel knows its way back to the Sargasso sea – but how much longer a journey that is. Mature eels are never found returning to Europe, so it seems that once they've spawned they die exhausted by the double effort: 'The Sargasso Sea is at once their grave, and the cradle of their descendants.'[1]

As to the elvers which are sent to eel-farms, they are destined to lead a pampered life, with the result that they'll reach maturity in only two or three years. At Le Croisic in Brittany, old salt-marsh workings have been turned into great basins to accommodate the elvers or *civelles* of the Loire. Their sea-water is regularly changed to avoid pollution, they're anxiously scrutinized for the first hints of disease, and their favourite food is flung to them in abundant quantity. Fish-farming seems to be more satisfactory than intensive meat-farming, because the end-product has a much better flavour. Nobody, I think, could tell the difference between eel-farm eels and the ones we're often given from the Loire. Both are absolutely delicious, the occasion for rejoicing.

What to do with Elvers

Elvers are extremely filling; I think you will find that 1½ lb. is enough for four people with good appetites. When you set out to buy them, take an old, clean pillow-case into which the fishmonger can tip them. At home, add a large handful of kitchen salt to the elvers, and swish the pillowcase about in a big bowl of water. Squeeze firmly to remove as much water as possible. Then add another handful of salt, and repeat the process with more cold water.

[1] L. Bertin.

This may be enough to get rid of the slight sliminess of the elvers, but be prepared to wash them a third time.

1. WHITEBAIT STYLE. Turn the elvers into a plastic or paper bag with some seasoned flour and shake them about so that they are coated with flour. Tip into a chip basket, allowing surplus flour to fall off (into the sink or on to a piece of paper). Fry them in hot deep fat for a few minutes until they're crisp; give them a second frying time at a higher temperature, like chips, if they aren't crisp in a few moments the first time. Serve with lemon quarters, and brown bread and butter.

2. KEYNSHAM STYLE. Keynsham is a small town between Bath and Bristol, which, according to the 1748 edition of Defoe's *Tour through Great Britain*, used to supply both cities with elver cakes. The elvers were well seasoned and baked in shortcrust pastry for about 20 minutes. Modern oven setting would be fairly hot (mark 5; 375°F.).

3. GLOUCESTER STYLE. Fry 8 rashers of very fat bacon until crisp. Take the rashers from the pan, and fry 1 lb. elvers in the bacon fat. When they turn white – after a few seconds – stir in a couple of beaten, seasoned eggs, to make a kind of omelette. Eat with the bacon. Don't overcook the elvers; the omelette should just be set, not at all leathery.

4. LOIRE STYLE. Put the elvers into a saucepan and cover them with cold water. Add some salt and a bayleaf. Bring the water to boiling point and simmer for 5 minutes. Line a colander with muslin and pour the eels into it – leave them to cool.

When you want to eat the elvers, melt 3 ounces of butter in a large frying pan with a crushed clove of garlic. Allow the garlic to cook slowly in the melted butter for a few seconds, then add the elvers. Turn them about over a gentle heat for seven minutes or so. Sprinkle them generously with chopped parsley and serve straightaway with bread and butter and dry white wine.

How to prepare Eels

Eel should be bought alive. Insist on this. Then ask the fishmonger to kill and skin it for you. He should have no hesitation, considering the price you are about to pay.

On the other hand, it's as well to know what to do in case an angling husband or neighbour presents you with an eel in a bucket of water. If you're really squeamish, ask someone to hold it down while you kill it with one blow at the back of the head with a cleaver, and chop the rest rapidly into chunks without skinning them. I don't like doing this; it makes me understand why people about to be beheaded were often anxious about the axeman's aim.

A better system is to kill the eel by piercing through the back of the head, through the spinal marrow, with a strong skewer; it's fair to ask the angler to do this. Now suspend the eel from a strong hook, using a slip loop of rope. Make a circular cut with a Stanley knife just below the rope, right through the skin. Sprinkle the cut with salt, and with the assistance of pliers, ease the skin away from the body for about quarter or half an inch, enough to provide a grip. Now pull the skin down the body as if you were removing a tight glove, pliers in one hand and a piece of thin cloth in the other. This can be tricky. I must admit that I've sometimes swung round an eel as if it were a rope-swing on a streetlamp. But once you get going, it's easy. Untie the eel, cut off and discard the head, chop the rest into appropriately sized pieces, and wash and clean them. A warning – pieces of eel may continue to jerk about in a disconcerting way. Leave them for a while in a covered pot.

Grilled Eel

Unlike many French rivers, the Loir has never been canalized into straight, poplar-lined elegance. It runs into a medieval diversity of side streams and leats, which once turned the wheels of a hundred and more mills from Proust's Illiers down to Angers. A paradise for eels. And for eel fishermen – after a successful inspection of their nets they return to house or *cave* for wine. Most of the catch goes into a tank for the time being, but one or two are strung up and skinned. A bundle of vine prunings is reduced to embers, and pieces of eel are rubbed with coarse grey sea salt, placed on an iron rack and grilled gently to golden brown.

It's true that vine embers give a delicious flavour, but even at home with only gas or electricity, grilled eel is a good dish.

6 servings:

2–3 eels, skinned	salt, black pepper
wine vinegar	bay leaves
lemon juice	breadcrumbs
olive oil	lemon quarters

Cut the eel into 1½- to 2-inch pieces. Put them in a flat dish, season well and sprinkle with wine vinegar, lemon juice and olive oil – enough to coat the pieces lightly. Leave for 2 hours.

Thread the eel pieces on to skewers, alternating them with bay leaves. Grill at a moderate heat until the flesh separates from the bone without too much trouble (test a thin piece). As they cook, brush them from time to time with such marinade as remains in the dish. When they're done, brush them over again, this time with fresh olive oil, and sprinkle them liberally with breadcrumbs. Return to the grill for a few minutes, until the crumbs are appetizingly browned. Serve with lemon quarters.

Note: eel can be grilled without bay leaves, and then served with snail butter (p. 23) or *sauce tartare*.

Italian Grilled and Baked Eel

Grilled eel is very popular in Italy: bay leaves, again, are used, sometimes a little rosemary. In the north a dish of *mostarda di Cremona* will go with it; this is a mixture of many fruits pickled in a mustard and garlic-flavoured syrup, an exquisite chutney of some antiquity. Montaigne sampled it twice in 1581, near Cremona, on his way back to France. Very good, he said, but omitted to mention what he ate it with. It's usually a relish for meat, poultry and game, but if you can get a jar from an Italian grocery do try it with eel. A mustard sauce could be substituted, but would not have the same enchantment and deliciousness.

The recipe for grilling eel can easily be adapted to the oven. Some friends of ours, who spend the summer at Lake Bracciano to the north of Rome, are able to buy the most enormous fat eels. They cut them into chunks about two inches long, and arrange them on a grid in a roasting pan. They're brushed with olive oil, seasoned and topped with a bay leaf for each chunk. The pan goes into a fairly hot oven (mark 5; 375°F.) until the eel is cooked. It's essential to place the eel on a grid or rack of some kind, so that the fat can drain away. Serve with lemon quarters, or with the *mostarda di frutta* from Cremona.

Matelote of Eel

When eel is prepared, not at the wine *cave* but at home, or in the kitchens of an inn such as the Hôtel de France at La Chartre-sur-Loir, the style will be richer, more elaborate. It's stewed in the red wine of the district, often with mushrooms from the old quarry caves that warren the low cliffs of the Loir. At Vouvray, on the great Loire, white wine's the natural choice. So it is at Saumur, and in Anjou where the dish is often called *bouilleture de Loire*. There, too, prunes are used to set off the delicate flavour of eel. They were once produced in Touraine, at Huismes in particular, but now come from Agen far to the south – even (in small type, at the bottom corner of the packet) from California. It's surprising how well prunes go with river fish such as perch and lampreys; they're browned in butter, sprinkled with flour and left to stew or bake for half an hour in wine, with soaked prunes. Eel, though, seems to demand a little more grandeur.

6–8 servings:

3–4 lb. eel, skinned and cut up	salt, freshly ground black
3–4 tablespoons *marc* or	pepper.
brandy	*either* 1 bottle white wine plus
4 tablespoons oil	1 large egg yolk and 3 oz.
bouquet garni	thick cream,
6 oz. chopped shallot or onion	*or* 1 bottle red wine plus 1½
white of 1 leek, chopped	tablespoons flour and 2
(optional)	tablespoons butter
2 cloves of garlic, crushed	
(optional)	

Also choose an appropriate garnish:

Loir   20–30 small glazed onions
20–30 small button mushrooms, cooked in butter

triangles of bread fried in butter
chopped parsley

Anjou   as above, plus 25 large prunes
quarters of hard-boiled egg (optional)

Vouvray 20–30 small glazed onions
strips of streaky green bacon, browned in butter
20–30 small button mushrooms, cooked in butter
25 large prunes (optional)

Turn the pieces of eel in the brandy and oil, season well and leave for several hours or overnight. At the same time, put the prunes to soak in half the bottle of wine – that is, if you're including prunes.

A good hour before the meal, simmer the rest of the wine with onion, leek and *bouquet garni* for half an hour. Arrange the eel and prunes, with any liquor from them, in a large pan, and strain the seasoned wine over them. The eel and prunes should be just covered. Stew gently for 20–30 minutes until the eel is cooked. Meanwhile prepare the garnish.

To thicken the sauce: *either* mash butter and flour together, dividing the mixture into small lumps, then add them to the red wine stew gradually, stirring all the time so that the sauce thickens smoothly; *or* beat the egg yolk and cream, whisk in a little of the simmering white wine stew, and return to the cooking pot, which should be kept below the boil so that the sauce thickens without curdling.

Correct the seasoning, pour into a serving dish and arrange the garnish on top. With triangles of bread, dip one corner into the sauce, then into chopped parsley, and tuck the opposite corner into the stew.

Note: A quick version of this dish. Brown the eel pieces in oil with mushrooms, onions, and strips of bacon if used. Flame with warmed *marc* or brandy. Add seasoned wine, and soaked prunes if you like, then simmer for half an hour. Thicken as above. (Triangles of bread have to be cooked separately, of course; so do hard-boiled eggs.) This is good, though less rich in flavour than when onions and mushrooms are cooked separately. If you really cannot bear the thought of prunes, substitute seedless raisins, soaked 10 mins in boiling water, and drained.

Anguilles au Vert

I know it's not the usual thing to serve vegetables with fish. Imagine a sole assisted by cabbage! But an exception must be made for spinach and sorrel. They are so good with fish that it's difficult not to believe that they were created for this role in life. The intensity of the one, and the gay sharpness of the other, enhance the altogether different flavour of fish; and then, their substance falls into a pomade-like sauce when it encounters butter or cream, and a gentle heat. Everyone can buy spinach, but sorrel is not so easy. If you don't grow it in your garden – or a 17th floor window box – already, put sorrel seed at the top of the shopping list. A cook without sorrel is a deprived creature, a subject for lamentation. With variations of green herbs – or rather additions – this dish is popular all over France and Belgium.

6 servings:

2 lb. skinned eel	6 sage leaves, chopped
4 oz. butter, preferably clarified	6–7 tarragon leaves, chopped
	12 oz. dry white wine
3 handfuls (about 4 oz.) of sorrel	2 large egg yolks
	lemon juice, salt, pepper
3 handfuls (about 4 oz.) of spinach	6 slices fried bread, if dish is to be eaten hot
1 handful of parsley, chopped	

Cut the eels up in such a way that the pieces will divide nicely between the 6 slices of bread: if they're to be served cold, this doesn't matter so much. Fry the eel pieces gently in the butter until they begin to brown, then add the sorrel and spinach which will rapidly reduce to a purée. Pour in the wine and add the chopped herbs; simmer for 15 minutes or until the eel is cooked. Beat the egg yolks, stir a little of the hot sauce into them and add to the frying pan (make sure the heat is low, or the eggs will curdle). Turn with a spoon until the sauce is thick – it mustn't boil. Put the eel pieces on the hot croûtons and cover them with the sauce. If it is to be served cold, arrange the eel on serving dish and pour the sauce over it. Chill.

An Eel Pie worthy of Eel-Pie Island

From the 17th century until recently, people went to enjoy themselves at Twickenham Eyot in the Thames – in other words Eel-Pie
Island. Boating parties, anglers, picnickers, gathered on its leafy
acres, and bought eel pies from the inn. How sad that the famous
inn should have ended up as a hippy battleground. Here's a recipe
from *The Cook's Oracle* by Dr William Kitchiner. It was published
in 1843, at a time when Eel-Pie Island was at the height of its
prosperity, and soon after the inn had been enlarged to include a
splendid assembly room.

'Skin clean and bone two Thames eels. Cut them in pieces and
chop two small shallots. Pass the shallots in butter for five minutes,
and then add to them a small faggot of parsley chopped, with nutmeg, pepper, salt and two glasses of sherry. In the midst of this
deposit the eels, add enough water to cover them and set them on
the fire to boil. When boiling-point is reached, take out the pieces of
eel and arrange them in a pie-dish. In the meantime add to the sauce
two ounces of butter kneaded with two ounces of flour, and let them
incorporate by stirring over the fire. Finish the sauce with the juice
of a whole lemon, and pour it over the pieces of eel in the pie-dish.
Some slices of hard boiled egg may be cunningly arranged on the
top, and in it *amung* the lower strata. Roof the whole with puff
pastry; bake it for an hour. And lo! A pie worthy of Eel-Pie Island.
It is a great question debated for ages on Richmond Hill whether
this pie is best hot or cold. It is perfect either way.'

Note: use dry or medium-dry sherry – or white wine if you prefer
it. Put into a hot oven (mark 8: 450°F.), and after about 20 minutes
– by which time the pastry should be well risen – lower the heat to
moderate (mark 4; 350°F.). No need to bone the eel.

Eel Pie from Touraine

I expect that most of the eel pies, once sold at fairs and markets all
over Britain, were much closer to this simple French recipe than to
Dr Kitchiner's splendid dish.

6 servings:

2 lb. eel, skinned	salt, pepper
puff pastry made with ¾ lb. flour	thyme, a bay leaf, chopped parsley and chives
4 oz. butter	small glass of *marc* or brandy
1 small beaten egg	

Cut the eel into approximately 3-inch pieces. Put them into a dish with salt, pepper, herbs and *marc* or brandy, and leave overnight, covered, or for several hours.

Roll out the pastry, and cut six circles. Divide the eel pieces between the six, and arrange them on one half of each circle. Brush the edge with beaten egg and fold the other half of the pastry over the eel. Pinch the pastry edges together firmly, and make a small hole in the top of each turnover for the steam to escape. Brush over with beaten egg. Put into a hot oven (mark 8; 450°F.), and when the pastry has risen and looks brown lower the heat to moderate (mark 4; 350°F.). Protect the turnovers with a butter paper if necessary. Cooking time – about 20 minutes at the top heat, then another half hour to make sure the eel is cooked.

Note: this is the kind of recipe that can be altered to your pleasure. Some chopped onion, mushroom and garlic, sweated gently in butter, can be added to the eel pieces; and some chopped hard-boiled egg, with a fillet of anchovy.

Shellfish and Crustaceans

Lobsters and Crawfish (Homards and langoustes)

A 14th century German painter, Master Bertram, who lived at Hamburg and who should therefore have known better, included a ready-boiled lobster in his painting of God creating the animals. The sturgeon and other creatures look perfectly alive and clear-eyed – but there is the lobster at the bottom of the painting flat on the ground and ready for the table.

I suppose that most of us do think of lobsters as red. (Red-coated soldiers used to be known as lobsters, though the term really started as a name for cuirassiers with shiny breastplates like the lobster's carapace.) In fact they are a dark blueish colour, which is more suitable for the rocky parts of the sea they choose to live in. It is in this state that you should buy lobster, if you want to taste it at its best. The trouble is that it usually means ordering in advance from the fishmonger. It is less trouble all round to buy one ready-boiled, and if the fishmonger has a good turnover and if you are a regular customer, you will probably not regret it. I have the feeling, though, that as lobster is one of the best things to eat in the world, and as it is one of the most expensive, too, it should only be eaten at its best and in the peak of condition. Otherwise disappointment and financial loss are too disillusioning. This means that one should, ideally, find a seaside town where lobsters are caught, and make an expedition, an occasion if you like, which will become part of one's family ritual. Luxuries should be enjoyed with a little ceremony:

deep-frozen lobster is a kind of denial, a bringing-down of excellence.

The season for fresh lobsters is from April or May to October, although many fishermen store them in tanks and caves until the prices rise in the winter. I began to understand why they are so rare and expensive after reading *Lobsters, Crabs and Crawfish* by R. C. O'Farrell. Although they are known as the Common Lobster, they are not nearly as common as one might wish. He describes from his own experience the contest between the fishermen's skill in baiting and placing lobster pots, and the animal's lack of interest in food – except when it has shed its shell and is therefore soft and unmarketable.

This (un)Common European lobster, and the North American lobster, are northern creatures. They like cool water and are not to be found south of the Bay of Biscay or of the coast of Maine. The crawfish or spiny or rock lobster, the lobster without the huge front claws, can live anywhere as far as temperature is concerned. This is the *langouste* and *aragosta* of Mediterranean restaurants. And it is as well to be aware of the difference, if you use Italian, Greek or Provençal cookery books, because you may be left wondering what to do with the claws of a common lobster and the fairly large supply of delicious meat in them. The answer is to remove the meat and use it to make up the tail meat, which is less copious in the lobster. I'm talking, of course, about recipes of the Thermidor type, where meat and sauce are served up in the shell.

Crawfish and lobster recipes are interchangeable, and crawfish tails in frozen packages can be bought in many towns these days. The flavour cannot be compared in quality with the lobster's, partly because it is not so good to start with, but also because of the freezing. I have eaten 'Caribbean crawfish with mayonnaise' – a standard item on one cross-Channel ferry – which was tasteless to the point of nullity; an iced chewy fibre I would not have recognized had I eaten it blindfolded. Crawfish are caught around Great Britain, too, and I imagine one would be luckier with these.

Like most expensive foods, the lobster and crawfish are simple to cook. If they are ready boiled, you have to remove the shell and serve them with mayonnaise – or split them in half, crack the claws of the lobster, and serve them as they are. The meat can also be removed and reheated in one of the delicious lobster sauces – Newburg, Américaine, Mornay and so on. The creamy part in the head of the lobster, and the coral, if there is any, should be beaten into hot or cold sauces; the tail meat is usually cut across into slices; the claw meat diced.

How to Boil a Lobster

The best lobsters weigh between 1½ and 2 lb. Larger than this they become cheaper per pound, and are not so good. I once bought a 3–4 lb. lobster, costing as much, and it was very poor. Best to buy two or three smaller lobsters, for four or six people. Mrs O'Farrell's advice is to grip the creature across the carapace, which should 'be firm and unyielding, and if there is any inward movement of the fingers it should be discarded, as this indicates a recent shell-change and resulting loss of meat. A hen lobster has a wider body and smaller claws than the cock, but there is no difference at all from the culinary point of view.'

The ideal cooking liquid is its natural element, seawater, plus enough salt to make an egg float in it. Be guided by this when using tapwater – 6 oz. salt to 3 pts water is about right. Put the lobster into the cold water, and bring it up to simmering point: weight the lid to stop the lobster jumping out. This method is recommended by the RSPCA as being painless – the lobster gets dopier as the temperature rises, and expires quietly at 80°F. When simmering point is reached, allow 15 minutes for the first pound, and 10 minutes for each pound after that. Remove the lobster, put it on a dish and allow it to cool in the larder.

Restaurants usually stick to the old method of plunging the lobster into boiling salted water. And many people insist that the flavour of lobster cooked this way is better. Michael Field has this to say in *All Manner of Food:* 'Lobsters are at their best only if they breathe their last either in the dish in which they are cooked or moments before they are added to it. . . Scientists long ago demonstrated that crustaceans have nervous systems of such simplicity that they scarcely feel pain as we do.'

So you must make your choice.

How to cut up Live Lobster

This is essential if you are using live lobster for a fine dish of *Homard à l'américaine*, or *Lobster Newburg*, as it saves you the prolonged business of boiling and cooling. It will also taste better.

The thing is to kill the lobster instantly. To do this, place a cleaver across the join between carapace and tail and hammer it down with one hard blow. Cut off the claws, and crack them. Cut the tail across into slices, following the joints. Split the head lengthwise and discard the sac of grit and the black intestinal canal and gills. Put coral and lobster liquor and the creamy part, which is the liver or tomally, into a separate bowl for the final stages of the sauce.

Lobster Mayonnaise

Here is the traditional way. Extract the soft parts etc. from the carapace, taking care not to damage the feelers; rub it over with a little oil or a butter paper to give it a gloss, and stand it upright at the back of the serving dish, with some crisp small lettuce leaves. Split the tail lengthwise, *not* across in rings, and arrange the pieces in front of the head. Crack the claws carefully so as not to spoil their appearance and put them at either side. The rest of the garnish can be as opulent (oysters, other shellfish) or as simple (hard-boiled egg, tomatoes, olives, anchovies, capers) as you like. The mayonnaise is served separately.

You can, if you like, dice up the lobster meat and fold it into the mayonnaise along with some of the extra ingredients mentioned above. I think this is a pity, unless you are lucky enough to eat lobster very often. Being a luxury for most people, it should surely be served with a little formality. This can be achieved without the realism of the carapace: just split the tail lengthwise, extract the claw meat in one piece and arrange them, with neat rows of cucumber and egg, or what you like, in a formal manner.

The mayonnaise can be varied with herbs, or with cognac and orange juice (see p. 50), or with a little *pastis*. Alexandre Dumas gives a most delicious dressing, which many people like better than mayonnaise, in his *Grand Dictionnaire de Cuisine*. (It can go with other shellfish, too, such as crab or prawns.) Mix together:

6 servings:

5 tablespoons olive oil
1 tablespoon Dijon mustard
a handful of parsley, tarragon, and chives, chopped
1 heaped tablespoon finely chopped shallot or onion

12 drops soya sauce
freshly ground white pepper
small glass of *anisette*, or *pastis* or *Pernod*

Fold the diced lobster into the dressing.

Hot Lobster Dishes

Most hot lobster dishes can be reduced to two basic methods. Once they are firmly in one's mind, a number of personal variations can be introduced.

The first method is to serve the lobster in a rich sauce, with rice. The second is to mix it with a small amount of sauce and some piquant flavourings, and then to grill it in the half-shell. This is a particularly appetizing way of cooking lobster; the only snag is that half a lobster is essential for each person, whereas 2 lobsters can be quite enough for six people when prepared by the first method.

Lobster with Sauce

6 servings:

2 lobsters, live or ready boiled
cooking base:
4 oz. butter
1 large onion, chopped
1 clove garlic, chopped
alcohol:
1 glass brandy, gin, whisky
¼ pint wine or fortified wine

liquid:
½ pint cream, preferably thick
thickening:
2–3 egg yolks
seasoning:
salt, pepper, cayenne, herbs

Cut up live lobsters as indicated on p. 278. Melt the butter, cook the onion and garlic until soft. Add the lobster pieces, raise the heat and turn until they are red. Flame with the brandy, gin or whisky. Remove the lobster to a dish and keep it warm. Pour the wine into the pan, and reduce to a syrupy essence. Stir in the cream; reduce slightly. Mix the egg yolks with the lobster coral, the creamy part and any liquor. Stir in a spoonful of sauce, then add to the pan and thicken without boiling in the usual way. Add seasoning to taste.

With a ready-boiled lobster, remove the meat and dice it. Add to the softened onion and garlic, reheat, and push to the side of the pan while the sauce is completed. If there is any risk of it overcooking, transfer to a covered dish, and keep warm in the oven, or over a pan of boiling water.

LOBSTER NEWBURG. No onion or garlic. *Alcohol:* brandy and Madeira or brown sherry. *Final seasoning:* salt, pepper and 2 oz. of butter cut into bits and whisked into the sauce without further cooking. Otherwise, as above.

A recipe invented by the French chef at Delmonico's in New York, at the end of the last century.

LOBSTER À L'AMÉRICAINE. Cook the onion and garlic in olive oil. *Alcohol:* brandy and dry white wine. *Liquid:* a good half-pint of tomato purée, made from fresh tomatoes cooked down in a tablespoon or two of olive oil, and seasoned with sugar and tomato concentrate. *Thickening:* omit egg yolks; use a little *beurre manié* (p. 21), only if absolutely necessary – lobster coral etc. should be mashed with 2 oz. butter or the *beurre manié*, and added to the sauce at the end. *Herbs:* should include parsley and tarragon.

The name is sometimes given as *Armoricaine*, but a look at the ingredients shows that the dish is unlikely to have originated in Brittany, particularly as early as the 19th century when that area was depressed waste, and its inhabitants struggling to keep alive. Provence is the most likely source of the recipe, which was improved in Paris restaurants, in particular at the Restaurant Bonnefoy by Constance Guillot. The name *à l'américaine* seems to have been given to the dish by Pierre Fraisse of the Restaurant Noel Peters: he came originally from the port of Sète in the south of France, and had worked for a time in the United States.

LOBSTER À LA CRÈME. Omit onions, garlic and brandy; use white wine as the alcohol. The rest unchanged.

LOBSTER À L'AURORE. As basic recipe above, but with white wine as the only alcohol, plus a spoonful of wine vinegar. To the cream, add ¼ pint concentrated tomato purée, well seasoned. To make the purée, use fresh tomatoes, see *lobster à l'américaine* above.

LOBSTER À L'ANISE. As in the basic recipe above, but add ½ lb. sliced mushrooms when cooking onion and garlic. *Alcohol:* 2 tablespoons *pastis* or *Pernod. Herbs:* can include some chopped tarragon. Good, and unusual.

Grilled Lobster

3 lobsters, ready boiled, or 3 crawfish	*piquancy:* mustard, or chopped anchovies, or grated cheese (mixed Gruyère/Parmesan)
cooking base:	
2 oz. butter	
1 onion, chopped	*seasoning:*
alcohol:	salt, pepper, Cayenne
1 glass dry white wine, or dry sherry	*gratin:*
liquid:	breadcrumbs
béchamel, or *Mornay,* or *Normande* sauce etc., pp. 24–34	grated Gruyère
	melted butter

Remove and crack the lobster claws; take out the meat and dice it. Split the lobsters or crawfish in half lengthwise, remove the tail meat and coral and soft parts, chop them and add to the claw meat. Discard the rest, scraping the shells as cleanly as possible.

Cook the onion in butter until soft. Add the alcohol, and reduce to 1½ tablespoons. Stir in the liquid and add mustard, anchovies, or cheese to taste. Season. Put some of this sauce in the base of each shell, then the meat, then some more sauce. Mix the crumbs and cheese and sprinkle them on top; pour a little melted butter over them. Arrange on a baking sheet, and set under the grill until hot and bubbling, and lightly browned.

To steady the half-lobsters or crawfish, put two bands of crushed kitchen foil for the ends to rest on.

LOBSTER THERMIDOR. As grilled lobster above, using *béchamel* or *Mornay* sauce; and cheese and French mustard as the piquancy.

CURRIED LOBSTER. Add two teaspoonfuls of curry powder, with the *béchamel* sauce. No other flavouring, apart from the Gruyère and breadcrumbs for the topping.

LOBSTER WITH OYSTERS (OR CLAMS OR MUSSELS). As grilled lobster above. *Liquid* should be *béchamel*. *Piquancy*, anchovies. Arrange a line of shelled oysters (or clams or mussels) along each half-shell before sprinkling on crumbs etc. Serve with lemon quarters.

Lobster Alla Marinara

A simpler, Italian version of *lobster à l'américaine*. The seasoning of the marinara sauce can be varied – it can be made hot with cayenne, or sharpened by the addition of a tablespoon of vinegar and a teaspoon or two of French mustard. Half a pint of the sauce can be softened by the addition of ¼ pint of boiling cream – with Marsala as a final flavouring. Warning: be sure to get the sauce right, i.e. right to your taste, before adding the lobster, and remember that mustard loses its virtue if it's cooked – always add it as a last seasoning.

4 servings:

1 large or 2 small lobsters, live	salt, pepper
olive oil	*marinara* sauce, p. 45
1 medium onion, quartered	walnut-sized lump of butter
8–10 oz. mussel or clam liquor	*to serve:*
	egg noodles, boiled

Prepare the ingredients for the marinara sauce, and set it to cook. (Unless you have some already prepared.) Cut the lobster in pieces as for *lobster à l'americaine*. Heat up a large heavy frying pan, covered with a thin layer of olive oil. Turn the lobster pieces in the hot oil until they turn red (about 10 minutes). Add the mussel or clam juice – from a previous day's cooking, or from bottle or can –

and the onion. Season with salt and pepper if necessary. After another 10–15 minutes, remove the onion, and turn the lobster and juices into the pan of hot, sieved marinara sauce. Stir in the butter and serve immediately.

Note: if boiled lobster has to be used, simmer the mussel or clam liquor with the onion for 15 minutes. Add to the hot marinara sauce with the sliced lobster, and heat through. Add butter last of all.

Lobster in Gin

Under French influence, one tends to think that brandy is the only spirit worth using in cookery (or, occasionally, Calvados if the recipe is in the Normandy style). In fact whisky or gin does very well instead, gin in particular adding a delicious and subtle flavour to shellfish.

Buy and cut up 2 small live or 1 large lobster. Turn to page 304 and follow the recipe for scallops in gin, omitting the seasoned flour. The lobster meat can be removed from the shells while the sauce is reducing.

Tourte Béarnaise with Lobster. See p. 132.

Norway Lobsters or Dublin Bay Prawns or Scampi (Langoustines)

The first time I ate an unknown shellfish – unknown, that is, to me and to most English people then – called '*scampi*', I thought I had discovered the secret of an earthly paradise. It was in Venice, at the very beginning of the fifties. Twenty years later, a hundred, two hundred pub lunches later, I am not so sure. How can this plateful of desiccated catering clichés, surrounded by chips, and mocked by a sprig of parsley, have anything to do with those Adriatic *scampi*? Or with those miniature lobsters, the *langoustines* of French restaurants?

And yet the *Multilingual Dictionary of Fish and Fish Products*, compiled by a galaxy of marine experts, backed by the Fisheries Division of the O.E.C.D., insists that they are all the same; whatever you call them, whatever you do to them, they are *Nephrops norvegicus* of the same family as the lobster. One cannot argue with authority of this kind.

You will be lucky if you can find *scampi* still in their shells, and if you do, they will have already been boiled to a coral pink more beautiful than the lobster's lustier tone. If you have a stalwart determination, you can try asking local fishmongers for them. But you will most likely be met with the kind of stare that indicates you are a fool. By *your* age, you should have learnt that *scampi* are born shell-less, and frozen, in a straitjacket of batter, with a plastic sachet of *sauce tartare* as afterbirth.

Should you be successful, serve them on their own or as part of a mixed array of shellfish (oysters, mussels, clams, crab, all on a bed of ice with a little sea-weed to show off their beauty). This allows people the pleasure of shelling them (only the tails are eaten). A big bowl of lemon-flavoured mayonnaise should be on the table as well – never use malt vinegar for fish, least of all for shellfish. You can tartarize it or not as you please.

Alternatively the shelled tails can be reheated in a Newburg sauce, like the boiled lobster on p. 280, or in a creamy curry sauce (p. 28); or in a whisky and cream sauce – many of them do, after all, come from Scotland, or rather from Scottish waters by way of Scottish fishing boats.

Langoustines à l'Écossaise

If the *langoustines* are in their shells, you will need about 3 lb. If, moreover, they are alive, you should plunge them into boiling, salted water, and cook them for 10–15 minutes once the water has come back to the boil. Shell them when cool, and set the tails aside.

If the *langoustines* are already shelled, 1½ lb. should be enough. You will also need:

6 servings:

2 oz. butter
4 tablespoons whisky
sauce:
3 large onions, chopped
1 large clove garlic, chopped
2 tablespoons oil
1 tablespoon butter

1 tablespoon flour
¼ pint dry white wine
¼ pint fish *fumet* or light meat
  stock
¼ pint double cream
salt, pepper

First make the sauce by cooking the onion and garlic gently in the oil and butter, until soft but not brown. Stir in the flour, then moisten with wine, *fumet* or stock and cream. Simmer for 15 to 20 minutes, longer if you like. Season.

Reheat the langoustine tails in the 2 oz. butter. Warm the whisky, set it alight and pour it over them, turning them about in the flames until they die down. Pour on the sauce. Bring to the boil. Pour into the centre of a ring of boiled rice and serve immediately.

Note: the flour may be omitted, but flame the onions with 3 or 4 tablespoons of whisky instead, before adding the various liquid ingredients. Reduce by boiling until the sauce is of good consistency and taste.

Gratin de Langoustines

From the excellent *Hotel de France* at Montmorillon, in Vienne, comes this simple dish of *langoustine* tails, mushrooms and cream.

8 servings:

2½ lb. shelled *langoustine* tails
2–3 oz. butter
10 oz. mushrooms, sliced
1¼ pints double cream
salt, freshly ground black
  pepper

grated nutmeg
pinch cayenne
2 oz. grated Gruyère
extra butter

Cook the mushrooms in the butter. When they are nearly done, add the tails. Butter a gratin dish and put the mushrooms and cooked *langoustines* into it. Heat the cream and season with salt, pepper and spices to taste. Pour over the fish. Sprinkle with the Gruyère and a little more nutmeg. Place under the grill to brown slightly, for 5 to 6 minutes.

Freshwater Crayfish (Écrevisses)

Pollution has not helped the freshwater crayfish, which likes very clear, oxygenated streams. These miniature lobsters have been favourite eating for a long time. Hannah Glasse gives recipes for crayfish soup, one demanding fifty, and the other two hundred: 'save out about 20, then pick the rest from the shells'. But there are less extravagant and more delectable ways of cooking them, for those who are lucky enough to live in chalk and limestone parts of the country where they can indulge in crayfishing parties at night. (The best bait is not-too-fresh meat; a sheep's head is the thing, or some bits of meat concealed in the centre of a faggot of sticks: the crayfish cling to the head, or crawl right into the sticks, and can then be drawn out of the water in quantity – this is the theory.)

The most famous of all crayfish recipes is, I suppose, *sauce Nantua*, p. 27. But a simpler crayfish sauce is also excellent with chicken, as you will see if you try the following recipe. If you begin to approach Hannah Glasse's abundance, you could enjoy *écrevisses à la nage* on p. 287.

Chicken with Crayfish

A beautiful recipe from *Le Lièvre Amoureux*, at Saint Lattier in the Isère.

6 servings:

1 chicken, cut into joints	1 glass cognac
4 tablespoons butter	2 tablespoons flour
8 oz. dry white wine	4 oz. chicken stock
2 large tomatoes, peeled, chopped	4 oz. dry white wine
salt, pepper	pinch saffron
crayfish:	*to finish:*
2 lb. crayfish	1 3-oz glass Madeira
4 tablespoons butter	3 tablespoons thick cream
1 tablespoon chopped shallot	1 tablespoon fresh chervil,
1 clove garlic, crushed	chopped

Fry the chicken in the butter until lightly browned. Season, and add a third of the wine. Cover and leave to simmer, adding the rest of the wine at intervals. About 10 minutes before the chicken is cooked, put the tomatoes into the pan and finish the cooking.

To cook the crayfish, fry them in their quota of butter until they turn red. Add the shallot and garlic, stirring them into the pan. Pour on the cognac and set it alight. Sprinkle on the flour, let it brown a little and moisten with the chicken stock and dry white wine. Add the saffron and seasoning, and leave to simmer for 3 minutes. Pour in the chicken and its cooking liquor. Cover and leave for another 3 minutes. Stir in finally the Madeira and cream.

Put the chicken pieces on a warm serving dish with the crayfish, keeping a few of these to garnish the top. Pour the sauce over, without sieving it, and sprinkle with chervil.

Écrevisses à la Nage

A favourite French way of serving these rare and delicious creatures. Allow a minimum of six per person: nine or twelve will be more gratefully received.

36 or more crayfish	a few grains of aniseed
white wine *court-bouillon*,	some cayenne pepper
No. 5, p. 17	half a stick of celery

Boil the *court-bouillon*, with the extra aromatics, until reduced by half.

Meanwhile wash the live crayfish in plenty of water, drain them well. Remove the intestine if you can, by pulling out the middle tail fin. Tip them into the fast-boiling liquid and simmer for 12 minutes, with the lid on the pan.

Put the unshelled crayfish into a bowl (they are often piled up in an elegant arrangement) and strain the *bouillon* over them.

Shrimps and Prawns (Crevettes grises, and crevettes roses or bouquets roses)

I agree with something I read recently about prawns and shrimps –
the prawn was described as a 'tasty morsel', but the writer[1] went
on to say that it was 'less of a palate-tickler than a freshly-cooked
brown shrimp', preferably eaten out of a paper bag while walking
along the promenade at Morecambe. (He also said – again I agree –
that both are ruined by deep-freezing.) Certainly Lancashire
shrimps are excellent, particularly when they come potted in mace-
flavoured butter, one of our true regional delicacies. Further down
the coast from Morecambe, Lytham is also proud of its shrimps –
fresh Lytham shrimps. They are caught by the local fishermen, or
rather netted from small boats, and handed over to their wives,
mothers, daughters, aunts, sisters and grandmothers for boiling
and picking. This used to be done at home in the family kitchen, but
now there is a centre where everything is done – still by the wives etc.
– including potting and freezing.

The odd thing is that these delicate creatures feed on the rubbish
of the sea and shore. This tends to be glossed over in modern books
on the subject, by the use of genteel latinate words – 'organic
remains' – and scientific phrases. For realism one has to go to the
Victorians who took a very concrete look at the animal life they were
describing – 'If a dead small bird or frog be placed where ants can
have access to it, those insects will speedily reduce the body to a
closely cleared skeleton. The shrimp family, acting in hosts, as
speedily remove all traces of fish or flesh from the bones of any dead
animal exposed to their ravages. They are, in short, the principal
scavengers of the ocean; and, notwithstanding their office, they are
highly prized as nutritious and delicious food.'

Precisely. One has only to think of the hygienic insipidity of a
battery hen's food, and the manure heap picked over by a farmyard
hen, to see that fine flavour is not always produced in the way we
might prefer.

The word prawn does cover an enormous variety of shellfish

[1] R. C. O'Farrell, *Lobsters, Crabs and Crawfish*, 1966. The Fisherman's
Library.

these days. The large pink prawn we are used to, *Leander* or *Palaemon serratus*, the one the French call *bouquet rose*, is now jostled by deep-frozen prawns from many other parts of the world including the striped tiger prawn from Asia. The situation is further confused by our habit of calling the Norway *lobster* a Dublin Bay *prawn*. And in America many of the creatures we label prawns are called shrimps.

This need not worry the cook, apart from plain curiosity. Try all these exotic shrimps or prawns, and you will probably agree that none of them can beat the shrimps or prawns from our own seas. There is no comparison between freshly-caught, freshly-boiled shellfish and the deep-frozen kind – and the smaller the shellfish the more this seems to apply. As to cooking, tiny shrimps and prawns are suitable for potting (below), for eating out of a paper bag, for making sauces (pp. 24, 31, 109). More can be done with the larger ones without spoiling their immediacy of flavour – all large prawns can be used in the same kinds of recipe, so don't let distant origin and strange appearance put you off.

I have assumed that the prawns and shrimps you buy have been boiled already by the fishmonger. But if you are handed a bucket of live ones, this is what you do:

a) Bring a big pan of seawater to the boil, plus salt. Or a pan of tap-water, plus enough salt to make a strong enough brine for an egg to float in (p. 295). Put in the shrimps or prawns. By the time the water comes back to the boil the shrimps will probably be done (i.e. the tiny shrimps, not American large shrimps). Prawns and larger American shrimps will take 5 to 6 minutes further boiling. Be guided by the change of colour and keep trying them. Under-boiled ones are mushy. Overboiled ones are hard.

b) In *The Home Book of Greek Cookery* (Faber), Joyce M. Stubbs says that prawns lose far less flavour if they are put without water in a tightly covered pan and set over a high heat to cook in their own juice (the mussel system). Shake the pan occasionally, for about 10 minutes. Cool a little before shelling.

To Shell Shrimps and Prawns

'Take hold of the creature by the head and tail and straighten it out. Then press head and tail towards each other in a straight line, and afterwards pull them apart. The entire coat of mail will come away in your right hand, merely leaving the edible portion to be tweaked from the head.'

(*Pottery*, by A. Potter, Wine and Food Society, 1946)

Potted Shrimps

'Melt 3 or 4 oz. butter in a saucepan, and into it cast a pint of picked shrimps (the pink ones are the nicest), a blade of mace powdered, cayenne and, if liked, some grated nutmeg. Heat them up slowly, but do not let them boil. Pour them into little pots, and when they are cold, cover with melted (clarified) butter. One experiment will tell you just how much pepper and spice to use.'

(*Pottery*, by A. Potter, Wine and Food Society, 1946)

Prawn Paste

I first came across this recipe in Elizabeth David's booklet, *Dried Herbs, Aromatics and Condiments*, and have used it many times. If you're in a hurry, put all the ingredients into a liquidizer and blend at top speed; it may be necessary to add a little more olive oil. The combination of prawn and basil is delightful.

3–4 servings:

½ lb. cooked, peeled prawns
4–6 teaspoons olive oil
dried basil, cayenne pepper

juice of 1 lime or half a lemon
saltspoon crushed coriander or cumin seed (optional)

'Mash or pound the prawns to a paste. Very gradually add the olive oil. Season with cayenne pepper and about half a teaspoonful of dried basil warmed in the oven and finely crumbled. Add the strained juice of half a lemon or of a whole fresh lime (when available the lime is much the better choice). When the mixture is smooth, and is seasoned to your satisfaction – salt may or may not be necessary, that depends how much has already been cooked with the prawns – pack it into a little jar or terrine. Cover and store in the refrigerator. Serve chilled, with hot thin toast. Do not attempt to store for more than a couple of days.'

If using freshly boiled prawns in the shell, allow approximately $1\frac{1}{2}$ pints gross measure. The shells and heads will make the basis of a good shellfish soup (see p. 68).

Prawns with Rice, and Prawns in Pastry Cases

Prawns are so full of flavour that they are the ideal fish for serving in rich sauce with boiled and buttered rice. This is usually pressed into a ring mould, before being turned on to a serving dish; the prawns in their sauce are poured into the centre. If for rice you substitute deep-fried *caissettes* – 2-inch thick, crustless slices of bread, hollowed out in the middle – you have an even better method of making a few prawns go a long way. If you are pampered by the proximity of a first-class pastrycook, you can buy *brioches* and use them to hold the prawns and sauce (scrape out the soft dough inside first, having removed the little topknot). A solution which is open to everyone is to buy or make puff pastry or short-crust pastry cases. The three mixtures following are offered as suggestions – they can easily be varied to suit your resources and tastes:

Curried Prawns

6 servings:

$1\frac{1}{2}$ lb. prawns	1 rounded tablespoon flour
1 large onion, chopped	$\frac{1}{2}$ pint fish stock
2 oz. butter	$\frac{1}{4}$ pint thick cream
1 heaped teaspoon curry powder	salt, pepper

Shell the prawns (use the shells in making stock). Melt the onion in butter till soft. Stir in the curry and flour and moisten with the strained stock and the cream. Reduce to a thick sauce and season to taste. Reheat the prawns in the sauce for a few seconds, just before serving.

Prawns in Tomato and Vermouth

4 servings:

1½ lb. prawns	1 teaspoon sugar
1 small onion, chopped	2–3 oz. vermouth
2 cloves garlic, chopped	2–3 oz. thick cream
2 oz. butter	good pinch of cinnamon
8 oz. peeled, chopped tomato	salt, pepper
1 sprig rosemary or sweet basil	

'Shell the prawns. With a tiny teaspoon, scrape the soft part from the heads and set it aside. Melt the onion and garlic, till soft, in the butter. Add scrapings from the prawns, tomato, rosemary or basil, and cinnamon. Season with salt, pepper and sugar (eventually, with northern tomatoes, you may find it necessary to add more sugar and plenty more pepper). Simmer, uncovered, for half an hour. Sieve into a clean pan. Pour in the vermouth and the cream and stir the sauce together. Reheat the prawns in it at the last moment.'

(*Home Book of Greek Cookery*, by Joyce M. Stubbs, Faber)

Prawns and Mussels in a Cream Sauce

6 servings:

4 pints mussels	1½ oz. butter
1 onion, chopped	1 oz. flour
½ pint dry white wine	2 shallots, chopped
bouquet garni	3–4 oz. thick cream
¾ lb. prawns	salt, pepper, parsley

Put the onion, wine and *bouquet* into a pan, and bring to the boil. Add the mussels and leave them to open in the usual way. Discard the shells. Strain the liquor. Cook the shallots gently in butter until soft. Stir in the flour, moisten with mussel liquor and cream, and reduce to a good thick consistency. Season to taste. Meanwhile shell the prawns. Reheat the prawns and mussels for a few seconds in the sauce just before serving.

Prawn and Jerusalem Artichoke Salad

As a combination of delicious flavours, artichoke and shellfish would be hard to fault. The subtle, earthy-grey sweetness brings out the lighter sweetness of prawns; or of scallops, as in the soup recipe on p. 70. Incidentally in spite of the name – a corruption of *girasole*, the Italian for sunflower, which belongs to the same genus – Jerusalem artichokes came originally from North America, at the very beginning of the 17th century. The French name of *topinambours* owes nothing to botany. In 1613 some members of the Brazilian tribe of Tupinambas were brought to France, and their name was borrowed for the vegetable which had also just arrived from the New World. Perhaps one knobbly eccentricity seemed to look a little like the other – at least to Parisians, who took a fancy to both.

6 servings:

2 lb. Jerusalem artichokes	vinaigrette dressing made
¾–1 lb. prawns in their shells[2]	with good olive oil
	chopped parsley

Scrub the artichokes and peel them. (Keep the rather lumpy waste for soup stock, if you have a frugal mind.) Cook them in boiling salted water until the centres are just done; test like potatoes.

Meanwhile mix the vinaigrette in a large pudding basin, seasoning it with a little sugar, salt and pepper, and a nice dollop of French or German mustard. Use a good *olive* oil because the flavour goes so much better with both artichokes and prawns than the nothingness of corn oil. Put the cooked artichokes, while still warm, into the vinaigrette, dividing them into pieces. When cool, arrange on a shallow dish – without any surplus dressing – and sprinkle with

[2] Ready-shelled prawns have no taste to speak of, or so I find. It gets frozen out of them.

plenty of parsley. Arrange the shelled prawns on top, keeping one or
two in their armour as garnish. Serve well chilled.

Fonds d'Artichauts aux Crevettes

A summer version of the recipe above, when Jerusalem artichokes
are out of season. Do not be tempted to use canned artichokes: they
have no flavour.

Mix together:

6 servings:

½ lb. shelled prawns	lemon-flavoured mayonnaise,
1 teaspoon chopped tarragon	p. 50
or pastis or Pernod to taste	6 cooked artichoke bottoms,
3 shallots, chopped	diced

Put small crisp lettuce leaves into 6 large glasses. Arrange the salad
on top. Serve chilled.

Crabs (Crabes, tourteaux, araignées de mer, étrilles)

Before the war, I remember that one of the few attractive things
about our depressed town was the regular arrival of fisherwomen
from Cullercoats, further up the coast, in Northumberland. They
came with baskets of crabs and other fish balanced on their heads.
They swung down the hill by our house in long striped skirts. Their
weatherbeaten faces were shaded – incongruously it seemed to me –
by the prettiest of lilac-sprigged sunbonnets. They were tough, un-
smiling, magnificent if you like, and their fish was fresh, their crabs
the best in the world. On rare days when we went to Seahouses or
St Mary's lighthouse, we would stop by the row of little houses at
Cullercoats and choose a crab to take home, weighing them thought-
fully in our hands to see if they felt heavy for their size. No crabs
were ever so good.

Of course you will not agree with me (particularly if you live in
Maryland, where crabs have restaurants to themselves). I am not
sure if I agree with myself either, having tasted now the sweet spider

crabs from the Atlantic coast of France; but those Cullercoat crabs set up a standard of deliciousness in my memory, however embroidered by time, which I cannot escape from. The point is that in this country at least, crab is a great luxury that very many people can afford, without feeling guilty. Lobsters have soared, scallops have joined them, oysters are not yet the poor man's food, as they once were and as they may be again. Prawns and scampi, toughened by freezing, are a disappointment. But fresh crabs, like fresh mussels, are an unalloyed pleasure.

Unless your fishmonger is beyond reproach, the crab you boil yourself is far superior to the ready-to-eat kind. Be wary about ready-to-eat crab meat too. Sometimes it is mixed with foreign substances to pad it out. This may be approved by health inspectors, but does absolutely nothing for the true crab. Crab is a rich filling substance – it should not be weighed down by stodgy and concealed matter. I have always found canned crab and lobster tasteless, though at the price I have not felt tempted to try many brands.

There is no way out of it. Boiling and excavating your own crab is best. It is also a pleasure. Particularly if you can find someone to read to you, as you jab away.

The point of success lies in salting the water adequately. Even seawater needs extra strength. An egg should float in the brine – use about 6 oz. salt to $3\frac{1}{2}$–4 pints of water. Put the crab in, fasten on the lid, and bring to the boil. Or rather to the simmer. Give it 15 minutes for the first pound; 10 minutes for the second, third and so on. Remove from the pan to cool.

When the crab is cold, lay it on its back. Twist off the legs and claws. Push back and remove the pointed flap, and take out the central body part – a large mass of thin bone, crab meat and 'dead men's fingers'. Remove the small mouth part, too, by pressing down on it: it will snap away.

Have two basins ready. Scoop out all the soft yellowish-brown meat from the shell – the best part – and put it in one basin. Add any yellowish meat still adhering to the central body. Crack the large claws and remove the sweet pinkish-white meat and put it into the second basin. The quick part of the work is now over. Settle down with a larding needle, a small mallet and a teaspoon, and poke out all the residue of delicious white fibres from the central body, and the meat from the legs. Be careful not to add tiny pieces of thin shell to the basin. A good $1\frac{1}{2}$–2 lb. crab can yield 12 oz. of edible deliciousness if you are prepared to be a little patient. Enough for three people, or more if you are going to add sauces, salad ingredients and so on.

The large shell can be turned into a container for the crab. You will notice a beautifully curved line on the undershell. Give a few hard taps on the inner side of it, by the gaping hole, and the rough pieces will fall away along the line. Scrub the shell out, brush it lightly with oil if you want to give it a gloss.

Crab Mayonnaise and Crab Louis

A good way of serving crab is to make a large salad, centred on it. There is nothing original in the idea. To the usual ingredients, add slices of avocado pear (brushed with lemon juice to stop them blackening). This goes well with crab and mayonnaise. Hard-boil some eggs, cream the yolks with crab meat and a little mayonnaise, and fill the whites with this mixture. Try differently flavoured mayonnaise sauces. Or build up an elaborate mixture of crab and other seafood in a large vol-au-vent case (see p. 330). Crab tastes surprisingly good when mixed with grapefruit (skinned and de-pipped segments, diced) in a mayonnaise – add some brandy if you like, and a few blanched, split almonds. Crab dressed with Dumas' *anise* sauce on p. 278 makes a lighter dish than crab with mayonnaise – a little cooked rice can be added.

Here is an American mayonnaise, or rather one version of it. The main point is the chili sauce. Sometimes finely chopped green pepper is included.

Crab Louis

Mix together the following ingredients:

6 servings:

mayonnaise, made with 2 egg yolks, ¼ pint oil, and the usual flavourings
4 oz. double cream, whipped
2 oz. chili sauce
2 tablespoons grated onion
2 tablespoons chopped parsley
dash of cayenne or Tabasco
1 teaspoon green pepper (optional)
extra lime or lemon juice

Arrange the crab meat on lettuce, cover with the dressing and add the usual hard-boiled eggs, tomatoes and so on.

Crab with Béchamel and Cream Sauces

Many lobster recipes can be adapted to crab – scalloped crab thermidor, for instance, is particularly good, so is curried crab. On the whole, I think the *béchamel* mixtures like these go better with crab than the cream and egg yolk sauces of the Newburg type. Here, though, is a recipe from Brittany which combines both types of sauce:

Crab in the Style of Bréhat

To get to the Île de Bréhat, one has to take the ferry not far from Paimpol at Arcouest, in Pierre Loti[3] country. His *pêcheurs d'Islande* would be startled at the elegant dishes one can now eat in the poor villages they knew.

6 servings:

2 crabs 2 lb. each, or 1½ lb. crab meat	2 oz. thick cream
	béchamel sauce, p. 25
4 oz. button mushrooms, sliced	1 tablespoon Dijon mustard
	2 oz. grated Gruyère cheese
2 tablespoons butter	salt, pepper
¼ pint port	

Boil and remove the crab meat from claws and shells. Prepare the two main-shells as above, or butter six scallop shells or small fire-proof pots. Cook the mushrooms in the butter over a good heat, when they are beginning to dry out add the port. Season and boil down to a spoonful or two of liquid. Stir in the cream. Divide this mixture between the shells, or pots. Put the crab meat on top. Heat the *béchamel,* add mustard and seasoning and pour over the crab. Sprinkle with cheese and brown in a very hot oven (mark 8; 450°F.) or under the grill. Serve immediately, bubbling hot.

[3] The French author of the famous novel *Les Pêcheurs d'Islande,* Ed.

Potted Crab

One of the best ways of eating crab, very rich and delicious, taken from Elizabeth David's *English Potted Meats and Fish Pastes*. The system of potting crab is rather different from the general potted fish recipe on p. 238. It can also be used for lobster.

Take all the meat from a 2 lb. crab, keeping the creamy part separate from the white. Season both with freshly ground black pepper, mace or nutmeg, lemon juice and cayenne. Salt will probably be necessary if the crab was bought ready-boiled – taste the mixture and see. Pack the meat in alternate layers (creamy and white) in small fireproof pots or soufflé dishes. Pour in melted butter to cover the crab – allow at least 8 oz. butter to 12 oz. crab-meat.

Put the pots into a baking tin of water. Cook uncovered on the bottom shelf of a cool oven (mark 2; 300°F.) for 25 to 30 minutes. Leave to cool, before sealing with clarified butter. Serve well chilled, with thin toast or baked bread. Mrs David suggests a lettuce salad afterwards, or freshly cooked green beans or purple-sprouting broccoli, eaten when barely cold with an oil and lemon dressing – a delicious lunch.

Étrilles or Fiddler Crabs, and Sauce à l'Américaine

These small 2-inch to 5-inch creatures are common enough round our south and west coasts, but I have never seen them for sale or on hotel menus. In France they often form part of an hors d'oeuvre, or huge dish of sea food, and are obviously regarded as a delicacy. There is little meat to them, and one sucks the juice from the claws – it is said to have a particularly fine flavour, but I cannot say this has been my experience. No doubt I have been unlucky, because the French are not foolish in matters of this kind.

My own feeling is that if you pick up a bucketful of small crabs on holiday, the best thing is to turn them into soup (see p. 68). Or they can be turned into *sauce américaine* to eat with grander shell-fish.

6 servings:

2 lb. crabs	¼ pint olive oil
1 large onion, chopped	2 oz. cognac
1 carrot, sliced	8 oz. dry white wine
1 stalk celery, chopped	4 large tomatoes (1½ lb.
3 cloves garlic, crushed	approx.), peeled, chopped
bouquet garni, including	salt, pepper, cayenne
tarragon if possible	*beurre manié*, p. 21

Wash the crabs. Cook the vegetables in oil until lighly coloured. Add the crabs. When they are red, flame with cognac. Add wine, tomatoes, *bouquet* and seasoning. Cook for ¾ hour, breaking up the crabs roughly about half way through. Sieve, and reduce the sauce to a good flavour and consistency, adding tomato concentrate or sugar if necessary. Thicken with *beurre manié*.

Soft-Shell Crabs

A speciality of Venice, and of the southern coast of North America. They are not a separate species, but crabs which are 'moulting' – i.e. they have shed their shells, and the new one is still fragile. This sudden loss of weight means that they rise to the surface and can easily be caught. The Venetian *molecchie*, a May delicacy, are tiny, about 1–2 inches across. They are washed, then soaked for a while in beaten egg (which they largely absorb). Just before the meal, they are drained, shaken in flour and deep-fried. One eats the whole thing, shell, claws, the lot, and it tastes like a crisp delicious biscuit.

In America the crabs are larger – two or three are a reasonable portion – but they are treated in much the same way. Sometimes they are grilled and brushed with melted butter. Tartare sauce or a similarly flavoured mayonnaise is served with them. Here is a more elaborate recipe from *New Orleans Cuisine*, by Mary Land:

Crabs Seasoned in Rum

'Select six soft shell crabs – female are best. Rinse live crabs gently in lemon water. Place in a crock with enough Myers rum (three-fourths), milk (one-fourth), whole cinnamon and nutmeg to cover. Let crabs stay in liquid two or three hours. If they show evidence of dying remove at once. Clean crabs by removing "dead man" and feelers. Rinse gently in cold water. Place crabs back in milk-rum liquid for half hour. Dry gently and dip in egg batter, then in rolled Corn Flakes. Sauté about ten minutes in sweet butter.'

Scallops and Queens (Coquilles St. Jacques and vanneaux)

Scallops have never been cheap like mussels, but lately they have become most expensive. Almost in the lobster class. Admittedly they are one of the finest in flavour of the shellfish, but the increase seems surprising. Scallops are dredged up all the year round nowadays, because deep-freezing plants have done away with the hazards of summer heat. Many new scallop beds have been discovered. If, like me, you were brought up on the slogan that mechanization and increased efficiency were going to make everything gloriously cheap, you will feel the same sensation of impotent rage when you are faced with a few scallops at the fishmongers and find that they are beyond possibility. The trouble is that our abundance is tempting to other countries who lack the same advantages, or who have foolishly wasted them. To eat Isle of Man scallops you have to be on an expense account visit to Paris or New York.

One would feel less outrage, I suspect, if the scallop hadn't become so companionable a part of our European civilization. One looks up at an 18th century doorway and sees the shell porch or fanlight; sees a child baptized with water from a shell scoop, takes tea from a caddy with a silver scallop shell caddy spoon; the beauty of the shape is never exhausted. It may surprise one in opening the doors of an old corner cupboard; it brings delight, it is never taken for granted. It belongs to great painting. It belongs to the poor, who went on pilgrimages to Spain to the church of St James at Compostela wearing the *coquille St Jacques* on their broad-brimmed hats. In our cave village in France, a room in one house in the cliff has an alcove with a scallop shell carved into the rock as ceiling. Nothing grand. It is said that the room was a chapel for the pilgrims who crossed the Loir to worship at the church of St Jacques on the other side of the river, as they journeyed to Spain.

And I suppose that with the deep-freezing of scallop meat in packages, we shall eventually lose even the shell and have to look at petrol pumps to remind ourselves.

If you ever see tiny scallops about 2½ inches across, you may find that they are cheaper. These are the 'queens' – *Chlamys opercularis* – a different species altogether, not just undersized scallops. You can spot the difference at a glance, because both shells are slightly curved. These *vanneux*, as the French call them, are a favourite item on the menu of the best fish restaurant at Cherbourg, the *Café de Paris*, on the quay near the swivel bridge. They are scrubbed and placed under a very hot grill until they open. Three minutes more on each side and they are brought piping hot to the table, to be eaten with butter and plenty of bread to mop up all the juices. There's no better dish. The allowance at Cherbourg is about 20 per person, but you could get away with a dozen.

Scallops à la Newburg

The famous Delmonico recipe for cooking lobster is as easily adapted to scallops as it is to other sweet, firm fish such as monkfish. The minimum allowance for each person is 3 large scallops, better still 4 or 5. Separate the corals and set them aside; slice the white part across into two discs, discarding the black part and the gristly greyish-white piece of skin around the white central cushion. Other ingredients required are:

6 servings:

4 oz. dry white wine	4 oz. Madeira or brown
4 oz. water	sherry
bouquet garni	5–6 oz. double cream
3 oz. butter	salt, pepper
2 oz. brandy	2 egg yolks *plus* 1 tablespoon
	single cream

Simmer wine, water and *bouquet* together for about 5 minutes. Add the white part of the scallops. Remove and drain after 4 minutes, when they should be just cooked, or very nearly. Melt the butter in a wide pan, and turn the scallops in it for 2 minutes. Warm the brandy, set it alight and pour over the scallops, turning them in the flames. Add the Madeira or sherry, and the coral part of the scallops, and leave for a few moments. Pour on the cream, push the scallops to one side so that they don't overcook, and reduce the sauce a little. Beat yolks and the tablespoon of cream, and use to thicken the sauce in the usual way (p. 33). Season. Serve very hot with a dish of plainly boiled rice.

Scallops en Brochette

6 servings:

18–24 scallops	8 oz. butter
9–12 thin slices smoked bacon	large onion, finely chopped
6 oz. muscadet	3 tablespoons wine vinegar
large bunch parsley, chopped	lemon juice, salt, pepper
3 cloves garlic, chopped	

Poach the scallops cut in two, with the corals, in the white wine for 4 minutes. Mix parsley and garlic on a plate, and roll the scallop pieces in them, before stringing on to 6 skewers, alternated with pieces of bacon. Melt an ounce of the butter and brush it over the *brochettes*. Grill them gently for 10 minutes, turning them from time to time. Keep warm while you make the sauce, which is a kind of *beurre blanc* (p. 42). Put the onion and vinegar into a small pan with 3 or 4 tablespoons of the wine in which the scallops were poached. Reduce at a moderate heat so that the onion cooks and the liquid evaporates to 1½ tablespoons. Remove from the heat, and when just tepid beat in the rest of the butter, bit by bit, to make a thick cream. Stir in any remaining parsley and garlic, plus chopped chervil if you happen to grow it. Correct the seasoning and sharpen with a little lemon juice. Put the sauce into a bowl and serve with the *brochettes*.

Note: monkfish, tope, cod and other firm fish make quite good, and cheaper, substitutes for scallops. Mussels cooked in this way are delicious – use the wine to open them; after that they only need to be very lightly grilled.

Curried Scallops

For the Madeira and brandy in the Newburg recipe, substitute the white wine cooking stock, reduced by boiling. When the scallops are put into the butter, add ½–1 teaspoon of curry powder. A most delicious recipe.

Coquilles Farcies Grillées

A small dish of scallops, an excellent way to start a meal.

6 servings:

12 scallops	2 shallots, or 2 tablespoons
fish stock	chopped onion
6 slices white bread	3–4 oz. butter
milk	*biscottes* crumbs, or toasted
2 tablespoons chopped parsley	breadcrumbs
1 tablespoon chopped chives	

Poach the scallops for a few moments in simmering fish stock until they are just firm enough to chop roughly. Set the coral part aside. Cut the crusts off the bread and add a little milk to make a thick paste. Cook the shallot or onion in 2 oz of butter until soft – do not let them colour. Mix scallops, bread, shallot or onion (with their buttery juices), and herbs. Spread this mixture in 6 shells, after seasoning it. Place the corals in the centre of each one. Cover with *biscottes* crumbs or toasted breadcrumbs, dot with the rest of the butter, and brown under the grill or in a hot oven. A little garlic, cooked with the shallot, will make this dish even more savoury.

Coquilles St Jacques à la Provençale

As this recipe is often given in cookery books, here is a quick summary of it with one important improvement – the separate cooking of the breadcrumbs.

Fry the white part of scallops with garlic and sliced mushrooms –

½ lb. to 20 scallops – adding coral at the end of the cooking time. At the same time fry about 2 oz. of breadcrumbs in butter in another pan, with 2 tablespoons of olive oil as well. Mix in plenty of chopped parsley. Drain scallops and mushrooms, mix with the breadcrumbs and serve quickly with lemon quarters.

Coquilles Saint-Jacques Flambées 'Gordon'

Searching after fish in Normandy and its purlieus last year, we seemed rather to find Joan of Arc instead. At Le Crotoy, near its famous seafood restaurant (*moules à ma façon*, gurnards *provençales*), we saw a tablet in the ruined castle wall to sour our sleep. Here the French had handed Joan of Arc over to the English, and from here on 8 December she had walked across the mouth of the Somme towards her trial and death at Rouen. We looked beyond the exquisite iron cross on the sea wall, over the wide estuary, grey now at low tide, and felt the cold sucking of her feet in the mud and seaweed, as the party forded the crossing to St Valéry. The Somme is a bitter enough river in spring and autumn; but in December?

Then in Rouen, pursuing the best source of local food, being told again and again 'La Couronne', by a policeman, a hotel-keeper and an anglophile bookshop-owner, we passed another tablet – 'Ah Rouen, Rouen, I had never thought you would be my tomb' – and we felt the prickings of historic conscience. But the head waiter, the liveliest of his breed, came and placed before us some of the most delicious scallops we'd ever eaten. We began to feel at peace in that wooden medieval room. 'Gin's the secret', said the headwaiter as he glided by.

2–3 servings:

10–12 scallops	4 oz. double cream
seasoned flour	chopped parsley
4 tablespoons butter	salt, pepper, lemon juice
1 tablespoon oil	puff pastry (optional, see
½ gill Gordon's gin	recipe)

Roll out thinly a very small amount of puff pastry, just enough to line 2 deep scallop shells, which should first be greased. Press the pastry down well, and bake blind in a very hot oven (mark 8; 450°F.)

until golden brown. If you have no scallop shells, 4 inch patty pans can be used instead. If you have no puff pastry to hand, use the scallop shells themselves as containers, or small soufflé dishes.

Slice the scallops across into two discs each. Turn them in seasoned flour. Cook them in butter and oil, turning them once. Meanwhile heat the cream and reduce it slightly. When the scallops are done, warm the gin, set it alight and pour it over the scallops in their pan. Add salt, pepper and the boiling cream; cook for a few seconds and add a little lemon juice to taste.

Place the scallops in their shells or pots, pour the sauce over them, and sprinkle with chopped parsley. Serve very hot.

Note: lobster can be cooked in this way, too. See page 283.

Hannah Glasse's Stewed Scallops

A slightly adapted version of a recipe from *The Art of Cooking*, published in 1747. Over 200 years later, it's still a good way of cooking scallops. The seasoning of Seville orange juice is unusual and piquant.

8–10 servings:

¼ pint dry white wine	18 scallops
¼ pint water	1 tablespoon butter
1 scant tablespoon white wine vinegar	1 tablespoon flour
½ teaspoon mace	juice of a Seville orange
2 cloves	salt and pepper

Put wine, water, vinegar, mace and cloves into a pan. Bring them to the boil, and simmer covered for 5 or 10 minutes. Add salt and pepper to taste, and judge whether or not the spices should be increased. Meanwhile slice the scallops in half across, then slide them into the wine etc., and cook gently for 4–5 minutes. They should not be overcooked.

Pour off the liquor and measure it: if there's more than ½ pint, boil it down. Mash butter and flour together, then add to the simmering liquid in smallish pieces, stirring them in. This will thicken the sauce. Finally season with Seville orange juice, and more salt and pepper if required. Pour over the scallops and serve at once.

Note: for a Seville orange and cream sauce, see p. 121. This recipe would be suitable for scallops, but I think stewing makes the best of their flavour.

Oysters (Huîtres)

That oysters were once a common food, even the food of the poor, is obvious to anyone who has ever had a garden. Time and again shells are turned up in the soil, even in places far inland. Archaeologists come across enormous middens of oyster shells all round the coasts of Europe, going back to neolithic times, when man became a food gatherer searching the edges of the sea. An interesting thing is that while most people enjoyed this natural abundance, others realized as long as two thousand years ago that by judicious oyster-farming the quality could be improved and the quantity assured.

On the whole however the main problem in the past was how to convey oysters inland. Sir Hugh Plat in his *Delightes for Ladies*, which was published in 1602 – one of the earliest cookery books in England – instructs his readers on how to preserve oysters 'for six moneths sweete and good, and in their naturall taste'. His method was to open the oysters, mix their liquor with white wine vinegar, and to barrel them up again covered with this pickle. An excellent way to convey oysters 'unto drie townes, or to carry them in long voyages'. One can judge that oysters, from the Middle Ages to the early nineteenth century, were a great bargain, because of the quantities in which they were sold. Not dozens, but bushels, small barrels (standard items in the Pepys household when they were entertaining a friend or two to dinner), and hundreds. By the time of Dickens, oysters were synonymous with poverty. Like rabbits to the countryman up to the introduction of myxomatosis, they were an almost free and abundant source of protein.

It was the same all over Europe, and in America, until the enormous quantities required by the new populations of the industrial age entailed a ruthless, conscienceless dragging of natural oyster beds. It is pathetic to read now of the stream of legislation that tried to conserve the oyster beds; each new regulation seems like an admission of failure. The rescue of the oyster was in the end achieved by a few men who tried to understand its bizarre sexuality and breeding pattern. This was essential before any successful method of farming them could be devised. The greatest of these people was the French scientist, Coste, not so much perhaps for what he actually achieved, but for his serious study of the problem and the ideas on which, later, more fruitful work was based. The moving thing is that Coste had a vision of feeding the new, huge population of Europe with cheap, *good* food, with lobsters, trout, salmon, and of course oysters. Although this hasn't yet come about within a century of his death in 1873, it seems less of a vision and more practicable than it did fifty years ago. Nowadays many laboratories are involved in improving the production of oysters, which is a subtle business, in no way to be compared with the coarse and tasteless stuffing of chickens into cages, or of calves into the tight confines of a steamy shed.

In about 10 years we may have caught up with France, where oysters can be bought even from market stalls, and at street corners, at a range of prices. Sometimes in the autumn my neighbour, who is a gardener, and general caretaker of a *maison bourgeois* nearby, asks me to bring home four dozen oysters on a Wednesday evening from market. Total cost, £1. His family of four sits down to enjoy them with a bottle of his own new wine. One day I remarked that in England I should only get a dozen oysters, or even more likely ten, for the same money. He was appalled. 'But, Madame, how does the working man pay for his oysters?' This encounter took place, I should add, about 100 miles or more inland. Friends camping on one of the islands off the Atlantic coast below Brittany have told me that the camp store's most conspicuous item was a huge barrel of oysters. Customers brought their buckets along at midday to be filled up. And when the young assistant felt she needed a little something to keep her going, she didn't pop a sweet into her mouth. She swallowed a couple of oysters instead.

Of course these oysters are of the cheaper Portuguese variety, the deep knobbly *Crassostrea angulata*. The other, finer oyster, *Ostrea edulis*, which is flattish and round, bears a price which indicates its higher quality of flavour and more intricate life history. It seems strange that merely by changes of breeding and locality, these two kinds of oyster should provide us with such different subtleties as the Belon and Whitstable or Colchester oyster, the green Marennes, the Blue Point of Eastern America, and the Arcachon and Helford oysters. It seems likely that the largest and least subtle of the *Crassostrea* genus will become the cheap oyster of the future, *Crassostrea gigas*, a giant as its name suggests, at any rate by comparison with our natives, or with the delectable Olympia oyster of Western America. While being grateful for the abundance of any oyster, I hope that it will not crowd out the exquisite products of Brittany and the coast of the Bay of Biscay.

If your enjoyment of oysters is on a spiritual rather than a material level by force of economic necessity, I suggest you console yourself with a copy of *The Oysters of Loqmariaquer* by Eleanor Clark, a classic of perception, of information and of the feeling of place. Nobody who enjoys food should fail to read it. Before she leads you into the history and culture of the oyster, Eleanor Clark tries to define the flavour – which is the whole point. 'Music or the color of the sea are easier to describe than the taste of one of these Armoricaines, which has been lifted, turned, rebedded, taught to close its mouth while traveling, culled, sorted, kept a while in a rest home or "basin" between each change of domicile, raked, protected from its enemies and shifting sands etc. for four or five years before it gets into your mouth.' She remarks that it has no relation to American restaurant oysters, or to canned and frozen ones … 'It is briny first of all, and not in the sense of brine in a barrel, for the preservation of something; there is a shock of freshness to it. Intimations of the ages of man, some piercing intuition of the sea and all its weeds and breezes shiver you a split second from that little stimulus on the palate. You are eating the sea, only the sensation of a gulp of sea water has been wafted out of it by some sorcery …'

Oysters au Naturel

The best way with fine oysters is to eat them raw. But first you have to open them (don't ask the fishmonger to do this for you, or the precious liquor will be lost on the way home). You may never break the records of a professional oyster opener – one *maître écailler* reckoned he had opened 200 dozen oysters a day for 43 years – but it is easy to acquire the skill necessary for the few dozen you are likely to buy. The main thing is to wrap your left hand in a clean tea towel, before picking up the oyster so that it lies in the palm of your hand. The flat side should be on top. Slip a short, wide-bladed kitchen knife under the hinge and push it into the oyster. Press the middle fingers of your left hand on the shell, and with the right hand jerk the knife up slightly. The two shells will soon be forced apart, and you can finish freeing the oyster from its base. At first this is a messy, sodden business, and I find it essential to revive myself with the first two oysters (in France our fishmonger always slips in three or four extra, which I regard as the cook's perquisite). Soon, though, you will complete the operation swiftly and neatly, and be able to lay the deeper shell on the dish with oyster and liquor complete.

Proper oyster dishes are not essential. Cracked ice, discreetly ornamented with a little seaweed, makes an excellent bed on which the shells can be steadied. If you want to cook the oysters, put them on a bed of coarse sea salt, pressing them down, or on a flat disc of bread with holes cut into it in which the shells can rest. I prefer the latter system, as any juices which spill over in preparation and cooking will be soaked up in a most edible way, and will not be wasted. Portuguese oysters, available all the year, are the best for cooking.

All you need now is brown bread, or rye bread and butter, some lemon juice, cayenne pepper or wine vinegar with a little chopped shallot in it, and a bottle of dry white wine. 'Chablis was and remains the accepted wine to go with oysters', said Edmund Penning-Rowsell in an article in *Country Life* a year or two ago, 'although to my mind these are too strong for the delicate, very dry wines of Chablis. Muscadet from near the mouth of the Loire is probably a better and less expensive choice, and if the seawater flavour gets into the wine, no great harm is done to that lesser, often rather acid, Breton favourite.' There are many people, and not just Irishmen, who say that Guinness is even better with oysters.

If a dozen oysters for each person is out of the question, you can serve eight or even six. But when you are down to this kind of quantity, a large dish of mixed sea food on ice is a more attractive way of presenting oysters. On our way to Touraine we sometimes stop the night at Mont St Michel, where this kind of hors d'oeuvre forms a regular part of the menu. The arrangement is simple but effective. Dark seaweed trails over a bed of ice, and contrasts with a large red crab, the orange of mussels in their black and pearly shells, with the shrimps and winkles and the restrained transparency of the few oysters. Sometimes there are a few raw *palourdes* (carpet shells) as well, or *praires* which are the local clams. Lemon quarters and a generous bowl of lemon-flavoured mayonnaise are part of the dish, together with a battery of pins and implements to assist you to your pleasure.

Huîtres Farcies Grillées

This is my favourite way of cooking oysters (it also happens to be my favourite way of cooking mussels – and clams). No other recipe can equal it for piquancy and delight. Garlic butter goes beautifully with oysters, the top layer of crumbs and grated cheese gives the dish a crisp edge. Put plenty of good bread on the table, so that all the juices can be mopped up and enjoyed.

6 servings:

4–6 dozen oysters	3 crushed *biscottes*,
snail butter, p. 23, barely salted	or 3 tablespoons toasted breadcrumbs
4 tablespoons grated Gruyère cheese	

Open the oysters. Pour off the liquid, which is not required for this recipe (drink it, or keep it for sauce or soup). Place each oyster in its deep shell and cover with snail butter. Arrange the shells on oyster plates, or on plate-sized discs (or oblongs) or bread, with holes cut in them with a small scone cutter. Mix the *biscottes*, or breadcrumbs, with the cheese, and sprinkle over the oysters. Place in a moderate to fairly hot oven (mark 4–5; 350°–375°F.) for about 10 minutes, until the oysters are bubbling and the tops lightly browned. The smell is wonderful.

Note: The method is the same for mussels and clams, except that they are opened in a different way, in a saucepan over a good heat (see p. 321 and p. 315).

Oysters Rockefeller

A famous dish said to have been invented at Antoine's, the famous New Orlean's restaurant, at the end of the last century. Some inspired customer is said to have remarked that the oysters stuffed in this particular way were 'as rich as Rockefeller'.

4–6 servings:

4 dozen oysters, opened	3 tablespoons chopped spring onion
4 oz. butter	
8 slices crisply cooked bacon, crushed	6 tablespoons dry bread crumbs
2 handfuls of spinach, finely chopped	½ teaspoon salt
	Tabasco, or pepper and paprika
3 tablespoons chopped parsley	1 teaspoon *Pernod* or *pastis Ricard*
3 tablespoons chopped celery leaves	

For this dish the oysters are usually arranged, on a bed of coarse salt, in 4 or 6 shallow pans according to whether you are serving 4 or 6 people.

Melt the butter. Add the bacon crumbs and spinach, and the rest of the ingredients. Cook for 5 or 10 minutes over a low heat, stirring the mixture until you have a lightly cooked stuffing. Taste and adjust the seasonings. Divide between the oysters. Grill or place in a hot oven until the oysters are bubbling and lightly browned, as in the recipe above. Serve in the pans of salt. Put a few drops of Pernod on each oyster, just before serving, with an eye-dropper. (This is a recommendation I read recently.)

Angels on Horseback

A delicious savoury or first course, consisting of oysters wrapped in thin pieces of bacon, strung on wooden skewers and grilled for a few minutes until the bacon is just cooked. Served on toast.

Huîtres au Champagne

One of the most delicious cooked oyster dishes I've ever eaten was
served at the Hôtel de la Côte d'Or in Saulieu, about 45 miles west
of Dijon, and once a famous posting-stage on the main road from
the Mediterranean to Paris. There you may eat some of the best
food in France cooked by the *chef-patron*, Monsieur François Minot.
For this dish he uses large round Belon oysters that come in 5 and
10 kilo hampers, bedded in seaweed. At Saulieu the following
quantities are served to four people: I think, though, that it would
do for six – or even eight – without anyone feeling ill-used. Provide
plenty of bread for mopping up the sauce.

6–8 servings:

48 round flat oysters	8 oz. unsalted butter
½ bottle champagne	½ pint thick cream, whipped
1 oz. chopped shallot	salt, pepper
4 large egg yolks	

Open the oysters; put with their liquid into a pan, and arrange the
48 deeper shells on baking trays. Boil wine and shallot until there's
barely a tablespoon of liquid left. Cool to tepid, beat in the yolks,
then return the pan to a low heat and add butter bit by bit to make
a sauce *hollandaise*. When very thick, fold in the whipped cream and
season. Put oysters over the fire for a few seconds until they turn
opaque and stiffen slightly. Return them to their shells. Cover with
the sauce. Brown under the grill.

Note: keep the oyster liquor for next day's fish soup. Twenty-
four large scallops and dry white wine can be used instead of oysters
and champagne. Slice each scallop across into two, and poach for a
couple of minutes in the wine before reducing it with the shallot.

Oysters and Sausages

The problem with this dish is not so much affording the oysters, as
finding really good chipolata sausages. If you cannot rely on the

sausages, pass on to the next recipe – or just eat your oysters with lemon and a thankful heart.

'Fry some chipolata sausages. Serve them very hot on a dish and on a second dish a dozen oysters.

'Alternate the sensations. Burn your mouth with a crackling sausage. Soothe your burns with a cool oyster. Continue until all the sausages and oysters have disappeared.

'White wine, of course.'[4]

Olympia Oyster Stew

This simple, lovely recipe of James Beard's shows that America has not been entirely vanquished by the giant oyster, as Eleanor Clark feared it might be, in *The Oysters of Loqmariaquer*.

'It seems to me that the milk we had with cream at the top was richer and more satisfying for cooking than much we have now. I know that if I do an oyster stew today, I use light cream or half-and-half[5] plus heavy cream. So I advise you to do the same with this delectable stew. Naturally if you don't live where the delicious little Olympia oysters are available [all English oysters are suitable] use others or use clams or even scallops.

'For each person heat 1 cup half-and-half and heavy cream mixed according to your taste. Add the oyster liquor and for each person use about ½ cup or a few more oysters.[6] It is plainly and simply a matter of your own taste. Heat the milk and oyster liquor and put a good dollop of butter in the dishes in which your stew is to be served. Add to the stew a dash of Tabasco, salt to taste, and lastly the oysters. Let them cook just long enough to give them a chance to heat through and curl slightly at the edges. Serve the stew very hot with paprika and plenty of buttered toast.

'The utter simplicity of these flavours makes it a classic dish.'

[4] *La Cuisine en Dix Minutes ou l'Adaptation au Rythme Moderne*, by Edouard de Pomiane, translated by Peggie Benton, 2nd edition, 1956.
[5] Half-and-half milk and single cream.
[6] i.e. shelled oysters including the juice.

Clams (Praires)

Everybody knows that clams are American. It's true that in Scotland scallops are often known as clams, and that we use the phrase 'as tight as a clam' about secretive people, but clams really belong to our rosier knowledge of American life. There's clam chowder for a start (not in fact a Red Indian dish, but an adaptation of the name and recipe of a French fish stew, see p. 77). We have probably heard rather enviously of New England clambakes, those summer feasts on the beach when the shellfish are steamed on a bed of seaweed over red hot stones, along with lobster, chicken, sausages and a variety of vegetables. If we remember pioneering tales, we can probably recollect that wampum, the Red Indian money, consisted of strings and belts of clam shells (hence the second word of the specific name, *Venus mercenaria*).

There are two things, though, that are not generally known, although they are much nearer home. First, the bubbling dishes of *praires farcies grillées*, served in Norman and Breton restaurants (p. 310), are clams, real American clams, of the kind known as quahaug, quahog or hard clams. Efforts were first made to introduce them into France in the second half of the 19th century. Now they are acclimatized all down the Atlantic coast of France. As one sops up the last garlicky juices, one does not spend much time regretting the American clams that are *not* acclimatized in Europe – the cherry stone, little neck and butter clams which are eaten raw like oysters; the long razor clams which come to the table fried as well as in chowders; the soft clams which rejoice in the local names of gaper, maninose, nannynose, old maid and strand-gaper. I am sure that none of them can equal the *praires farcies* – or at least surpass them.

The second thing not generally known is that clams can be bought in London. Go to Billingsgate between six in the morning and midday, and ask for the shop of the Seasalter and Ham Oyster Company, whose headquarters are in Whistable in Kent. There you can buy 100 large clams for £3.50 or thereabouts. People outside London can write to the company for information on postal supplies. There was a story going about that a skin diver, a few years ago, came across a colony of clams near the outfall of the

Marchwood refinery in Southampton water. They were romantically assumed to be the survivors of clams flung out of American
ships by American chefs, who had been over-careful in discarding
opened shellfish, to protect the stomachs of their transatlantic
passengers. In fact it is more likely that this large colony was a
survivor of one of the many English attempts in the 19th century to
introduce clam beds here, as the French were doing across the
Channel. It was known after the war that there were clams in
Southampton Water. The hard winter of 1963 killed many of them;
the colony near the warm outfall of the power station was enabled to
survive the unusually low temperatures (clams do not need warm
water normally).

Clams are among the easiest shellfish to grow commercially. It's
true that they take four years, almost as long as an oyster; but they
are more good-tempered, less of a risk. As demand increases, so will
production. At the moment between 10 and 20 tons are harvested
each year, and you can reckon 10,000 clams to the ton, more or less.
It does seem ridiculous to go to France to eat them, let alone
America, when we could be enjoying them at Southend or Torquay
or in our own kitchens. Like many other shellfish, clams are best in
the summer months. We tend to be superstitious about eating them
when the month lacks an R (as we once were about eating pork). It
seems that this is a groundless form of masochistic self-denial.
Apparently only the native oyster, not the Portuguese but *Ostrea
edulis*, should be avoided in July and August, because, as one
authority put it, the shells are 'full of gritty little babies'.

Having found your clams, how are you going to open them? If
they are fresh and alive, use the oyster method. A few moments in
warm water makes it much easier to push a knife through the
hinges.

Some cookery books suggest using the mussel method (a large
pan, covered, over a moderate heat), or, for the large ones, the
scallop method (a few moments in a fairly hot oven, mark 6; 400°F.,
until they begin to open).

Clams which have been deep-frozen are the easiest of all. Put
them in warm water to thaw, until the shells just begin to gape.
Finish the job off with a knife, oyster fashion. Keep deep-frozen
clams for cooking.

Once the black-tipped siphon has been removed, all of the clam
meat can be eaten. The coral foot and pinkish-white muscles are

firmer than the central body part: for some recipes, it is a good idea to chop these parts, while leaving the soft part whole. Most oyster, mussel and scallop recipes can be adapted to clams – the best recipe of all, often encountered in France, is the one for *huîtres farcies grillées* (p. 310). *Oysters Rockefeller* is also particularly suitable. Everybody knows about clam chowder: there are many recipes for it, with small variations and additional ingredients, according to the resources of different places down the east coast of America. A basic recipe for it is given on p. 77.

Clams au Naturel

Fresh clams can be eaten raw on the half-shell, like oysters. Lemon juice and cayenne pepper can be served with them, plus the usual wholemeal or rye bread and butter, and a white wine such as Muscadet, from the mouth of the Loire.

In *The Boston School Cookbook*, Fanny Farmer recommends that clams should be served with individual dishes of melted butter, sharpened with a little vinegar or lemon juice; the clam liquor should be strained, and served in glasses, for drinking at the same time.

Certainly clam liquor should be cherished, like oyster and mussel liquor.

Clams Farcies

As well as the two grilled and stuffed oyster recipes, try this delicious mixture. Bacon and mushrooms are good with most of the small shellfish.

6 servings:

48 clams	breadcrumbs (see recipe)
4 oz. mushrooms	salt, pepper
4 slices bacon, crisply cooked	butter
1 tablespoon chopped parsley	

Like oyster shells, clam shells need to be settled firmly on a supporting base if they are not to wobble about during cooking. Tin pans with a thick layer of sea salt are one solution: the clams can be pressed down into the salt. I prefer large 'platters' of bread, in which holes have been made with a small scone cutter; the shells rest in the holes, and any juice which bubbles over is sopped up – to your ultimate benefit – by the bread. Having settled this point, open the clams, and pour off their liquor into a jug.

To make the stuffing, chop the mushrooms finely and crumble the bacon. Mix them together with the parsley and strained clam liquor. Stir in enough breadcrumbs to make a normal stuffing consistency – spreadable, but not sloppy. Season to taste. Divide this mixture between the shells, to cover the clams. Dot with butter and bake in a moderate oven (mark 4; 350°F.) until nicely browned and bubbling. About 12 minutes.

Clams Mornay

A good recipe, too, for scallops – eighteen should be enough for six.

6 servings:

48 clams	3 tablespoons breadcrumbs
6 oz. dry white wine	butter
4–6 oz. grated Gruyère cheese	Mornay sauce, p. 26

Open, remove and drain the clams. Keep the liquor. Fry the clams for 2 minutes only in just enough butter to cover the base of the pan. Pour in wine and simmer for 4 or 5 minutes – don't overcook. Drain the clams carefully and set aside; reduce the cooking liquor, plus the reserved clam liquor, until you have a strongly concentrated essence. Add this gradually to the Mornay sauce, stopping before it becomes too salty.

Put some of the sauce into the shells, lay the clams on top and then cover with some more sauce. Mix the grated Gruyère and breadcrumbs, and sprinkle over the top. Brown lightly in the oven, or under the grill – the latter is simpler, and more easily controlled. Serve immediately.

Note: you will need a prepared base for the clam shells, see above. Alternatively, you can discard the shells, and divide sauce and clams, on the same principle, between six little pots.

Clam Fritters

Although soft shell clams are recommended for this recipe from *The American Heritage Cookbook* (Penguin), hard clams can be used instead. So can mussels.

By my estimate, 6 or 7 lb. of clams in the shell should produce the required amount, or 8 lb. of mussels.

6 servings:

¾ Imperial pint drained clams
2 eggs, separated
2¾ oz. white breadcrumbs, toasted
1 teaspoon salt
½ teaspoon pepper

½ dessertspoon chopped parsley
½ dessertspoon chopped chives
generous 2 oz. milk
butter or vegetable oil

Chop the drained clams finely. Beat the egg yolks, then the clams, breadcrumbs, seasoning and herbs. Add enough milk to make a heavy batter. Beat the egg white stiffly. Fold them into the mixture just before you intend to cook it. Heat butter or oil in a frying pan. Drop spoonfuls of the mixture into it and cook in the usual way.

Although the recipe doesn't say so, lemon quarters are a good garnish: their juice cuts the richness of the fritters.

Spaghetti Alle Vongole

Small clams in a tomato sauce are often served with spaghetti in central and southern Italy. In the north, in Venice, they would be added to a *risotto* (see p. 328), with a lump of butter rather than tomato sauce.

6 servings:

1 lb. spaghetti
6 lb. clams, washed
3 tablespoons olive oil
1 large onion, chopped

3 cloves garlic, chopped
14 oz. can tomatoes
2 oz. chopped parsley (large bunch)

Cook the spaghetti in plenty of boiling salted water in the usual way, until it is cooked but not slimily soft. Drain and keep warm until the sauce is finished.

Start the sauce as soon as the spaghetti goes into the pan. Open the clams in a large pan over a moderate heat, discard the shells and strain off the liquid from the fish. Brown the onion and garlic lightly in the oil. Add the tomatoes and some of the clam liquor. Boil down to a rich sauce. Add clams, which will be adequately cooked, just to re-heat them. Remove sauce from the stove, stir in the parsley and pour over the spaghetti, mixing it well.

Note: mussels can be used instead of clams.

Carpet-shells (Palourdes or clovisses)

Although two kinds of carpet-shell, the Cross-cut (*Tapes decussata*) and Pullet (*Tapes pullastra*), are common in Great Britain, I have never seen them on sale in a fishmonger's or on the menu of a restaurant. To eat them you will have to go to Brittany, where *palourdes farcies grillées* has made the name of several restaurants, or to Paris – or you will have to go and dig them up yourself. Equip the family with rakes and spoons – this is the advice given by one French writer – and find a large extent of muddy, gravelly shore. Consult *Collins' Guide to the Sea Shore* for a description and illustration.

Open them like oysters or clams. The best recipe, in Breton style, is on p. 310, under *huîtres farcies grillées*.

Mussels (Moules)

I think it is sad that mussels are generally regarded, both here and in America, as the poor man's shellfish. One above winkles, whelks and cockles perhaps, but none the less inferior. Certainly they lack the piquancy of clams, or the exquisite distinction of oysters, but

they have a voluptuous sweetness of their own to add to the repertoire of shellfish recipes.

Perhaps under the influence of holidays in France, this attitude is
changing. Snootiness about mussels cannot long survive experience
of the lovely mussel stews of the Atlantic coast from Boulogne down
to the Gironde, *moules marinière*, *moules à la bordelaise*, *mouclade
d'Esnandes*, or *d'Aunis*. Those tiny French mussels are the sweetest
of all; the mussels grown on stakes in the *bouchots*, or mussel-farms,
around La Rochelle and more particularly in the Anse de l'Aiguillon.
To see a huge steaming tureen of these navy blue miniatures borne
towards one after a tiring day is the most reviving experience I
know.

On the other hand, for the cook at home, there is much to be said
for the opulent monster mussels that the British Isles produce.
Their size makes them easy to pick over and prepare. They are the
most suitable for dishes of stuffed mussels (made according to the
oyster and clam recipes on pp. 310 and 316) and for mussel salads.

A way of using mussels which is often forgotten in England is to
make them a garnish to other fish. Their delicious liquor goes into
the sauce, while the brilliant orange meat, arranged round the dish,
enlivens the rather plain appearance of sole, turbot, whiting and so
on. In this way they can turn a Friday dish of cod into something
worth sharing with friends. Turn to the sauces on pp. 26 and 102–5
to see how this kind of dish is built up.

There is a word of warning. Don't let enthusiasm drive out
common sense. Mussels are abundant round Britain. No need to set
up mussel-farms here, with line after line of wooden stakes to entice
them to our shores; in fact they need to be weeded out and trans-
planted, so that they can grow to their full size. This makes them a
tempting prospect if you are on holiday at the seaside. Unfortunately
sewage is as abundant as mussels, at least in many places, which
means that they can be quite unfit, even dangerous, to eat. Mussels
on sale at the fishmongers have spent a suitable period in sterilized
seawater cleansing tanks. This makes them safe. Cases of poisoning
from mussels occur so rarely that they make the headlines when
they do – which has the sad result of putting people off this most
abundant form of delicious and cheap protein. I read the other day
that an acre of good mussels will in a year produce 10,000 lb. of
mussel meat – far more protein at far less cost than the year's beef
from an acre of rich pasture.

Like all other live shellfish, mussels should be eaten the day they are bought. This is only sensible, because you have no way of knowing how long they have been around. Scrape them free of barnacles and so on under a running tap, and give them a good scrub. Pull away the beard-like threads, which are known as the *byssus*. The mussel clings on to stones by means of the *byssus*, which will not surprise you as you give a good tug with the knife to get it away – its appearance gives you no impression of its toughness. Discard any mussels which are cracked, or which remain obstinately open when tapped. Set a large pan over the heat; you can if you like add a little water or wine, flavoured with shallots and herbs, but this is not necessary – sometimes, though, it is an essential part of the recipe when a sauce is involved. Put the mussels in the pan, and shake it gently – with the lid on – for about 5 minutes until the mussels at the bottom begin to open. Remove them with a pair of kitchen tongs to a colander set over a bowl. With a large quantity of mussels you may have to do several batches. Do not overfill the pan, as it will be difficult to see when the lower mussels begin to open. Shellfish should never be overcooked. Save all the juice you can, and strain out the sand which always seems to be there however carefully you cleaned the mussels. Throw away any mussels that refuse to open.

Note: 1 lb. of mussels is about the same as 1 pint. They provide you with about 3 oz. mussel meat, sometimes 4 oz.

Moules Marinière

The simplest and most famous of the mussel stews, the basis from which many variations have been built up.

6 servings:

6 lb. mussels	½ pint dry white wine
2 large onions, chopped	2 oz. butter
3 shallots, chopped	salt, freshly ground black
2 cloves garlic, chopped	pepper
1 tablespoon chopped parsley	extra parsley

Clean the mussels. Put onion, shallot, garlic, parsley and wine into a huge pan. Simmer for 5 or 6 minutes. Add the mussels, put on the lid and leave to steam open. Remove them to a colander to drain, and discard the empty shell of each mussel if they are large ones (small ones would take too long). Transfer them to a large bowl or tureen. Strain the mussel liquor carefully into a saucepan; set over a low heat. Whisk in the butter, taste and correct the seasoning. Pour over the mussels, sprinkle with extra parsley and serve immediately, with plenty of bread, butter and white wine.

VARIATION. A richer version may be made by stirring a few spoonfuls of hollandaise into the strained mussel liquor, instead of the butter. Don't boil.

VARIATION. Melt the 2 oz. of butter (see ingredients) in a frying pan. When it begins to turn golden brown, stir in ½ pint thick cream, 3 large cloves garlic, finely chopped, and some chopped parsley. When the sauce thickens, season it, and pour it over the mussels. Keep the mussels' cooking liquor for next day's soup or sauce.

Mouclade d'Esnandes

Esnandes in the Anse de l'Aiguillon is famous for its extensive mussel farms, with their stretches of poles set far out into the bay. It is also famous for the legendary tale of their origin, first recorded I believe by the French biologist Armande de Quatrefages in the middle of the last century. In 1253 an Irishman by the name of Walton was shipwrecked off the coast and kept himself alive by netting birds on the shore. In time he noticed that colonies of mussels were clinging to the poles he had set up to support his nets, and he worked out a method of turning the poles into mussel-beds and fish-traps, with wicker-work palisades. He is also credited with the invention of the *accons*, or flat-bottomed boats which the fishermen still propel by one leg instead of a punt pole, as they skim over the shallow water to collect the mussels.

A nice tale. But I do resent the way such stories are often presented as fact, without substantiation, if they are about food or cookery. Nobody would accept them as history or archaeology, once they were out of the nursery. Don't, however, let my sour reflections spoil your enjoyment of the *mouclade d'Esnandes*, which at least is fact of a most delectable kind.

6 servings:

4 lb. mussels	¼ pint milk
8 oz. dry white wine	1 tablespoon *pastis Ricard*, or
6 oz. finely chopped shallot	1 star anise
3 cloves garlic, finely chopped	2 egg yolks
2 oz. butter	3 tablespoons thick cream
1 tablespoon flour	salt, pepper

Open the cleaned mussels in the wine. Discard one half-shell from each if they are large. Strain and save the liquor. Melt the shallot and garlic in the butter, stir in the flour, and add mussel liquor and milk to make a smooth sauce. Add *pastis* or star anise. Reduce by boiling. Beat egg yolks and cream, and use to thicken the sauce in the usual way (p. 32) without allowing it to boil again. Correct the seasoning. Pour over the mussels and serve.

La Mousclade d'Aunis

The Aunis is the area around La Rochelle. This recipe is similar to the *mouclade d'Esnandes* except that 2 bottles of wine are used to open the mussels, and the sauce is started with only a ¼ pint of milk. For the *anise* flavouring substitute a good pinch of curry powder and of cayenne pepper. Serve with a final sprinkling of parsley.

Pancakes with Mussels or Clams

Shellfish of all kinds make a delectable filling for pancakes. Even cheap mussels give a splendid and piquant result, and provide, too, the liquid for the sauce.

6 servings:

12 pancakes, p. 227	1 good tablespoon flour
4 pints mussels or clams	¼ pint dry white wine
2 oz. butter	salt, pepper, parsley
1 large onion, chopped	3 oz. thick cream (optional)
1 shallot, chopped	

Put the scrubbed mussels into a heavy pan and open them over heat in the usual way. Remove from their shells, and strain the liquor carefully. Chop the mussels or clams roughly.

Meanwhile cook the onion and shallot in 2 oz. butter until tender, without browning them. Sprinkle with the flour and stir in the white wine, then the mussel liquor. Simmer until very thick and well-flavoured. Season with salt, pepper and parsley. Reheat the mussels in the sauce for a few seconds and fill the pancakes. Or else layer pancakes and sauce in a stack. Pour boiling cream over the top and serve immediately (or cream may be added to the sauce before reheating mussels).

Salade à la Boulonnaise

Channel ports of the French coast are no more to travellers these days than a minor episode of impatience on long summer journeys. As one drives away thankfully, it's startling to think that our great-grandparents might wait nine days in such places for a wind, up to six weeks, if they could afford it, for a calm. They might even choose to live there for business, for economy on small pensions – and for escape. Some of them are buried under hideous tombstones in the cemetery on the steep Lille road out of Boulogne, which looks across the sea to England: 'beloved wife of . . .', 'leader of the Methodist community of this town'. If you then go, as we once did, from the cemetery to the garish duty-free booths near the Gare Maritime, it's hard to think that Boulogne has its virtues. There's the blue lung-raking air of course; but also the mild *harengs saurs* which are cured here, and simple fresh food *à la Boulonnaise*, with mussels. The best of these Boulogne dishes, and to my mind one of the best of all salads, is this combination of sweet plump mussels and waxy potato, dressed with vinaigrette and parsley.

6 servings:

5–6 lb. mussels	plenty of black pepper
2 lb. waxy potatoes	about 8 tablespoons well-
5 tablespoons white wine	seasoned vinaigrette, p. 61
6 chopped shallots	extra chopped parsley for
good sprig of thyme	garnishing
6 good sprigs of parsley	

Wash, then boil the potatoes in their skins. When cooked, peel and slice them. Meanwhile put wine, shallots, thyme, parsley, pepper and scrubbed mussels in a large pan. Set over a high heat, removing the mussels as they open. Discard the shells, put the mussels in a dish to cool, and strain the cooking liquor over the potatoes. The potatoes are bound to cool down as you peel and slice them, so reboil the mussel liquor before pouring it over them.

Drain the potato slices when cold, mix them with the cold mussels, and pour on enough vinaigrette to moisten the salad. Arrange in a shallow dish, sprinkle chopped parsley on top, and serve well chilled. Put a covering of foil over the dish while it's in the refrigerator.

Note: don't waste any mussel liquor left over. Use it up in fish soup or a sauce requiring fish *fumet.* The salad can alternatively be dressed with mayonnaise, but I think that a well-flavoured vinaigrette is better.

Mussels à la Maltaise

A delicious salad, again from France. Open the mussels in the usual way over a high heat and remove them from their shells as they open; keep the liquid for another dish. Arrange them on lettuce leaves, and cover them with the Maltese mayonnaise on p. 52: i.e. mayonnaise flavoured with orange juice, to which you have added a teaspoonful of brandy.

Mussels in the Turkish Style

Open the mussels over a high heat in the usual way. Make the tarator sauce on p. 59, substituting mussel liquor for olive oil, and adding some chopped fresh mint or parsley. Fry the mussels (discarding the shells first) very briefly in some butter, and serve with the sauce. Be careful not to overcook the mussels.

Sea Urchins (Oursins)

'Sea-urchins (there are several edible varieties) are a menace to bathers on the shore of the Mediterranean, for they cluster by the hundred in shallow waters, hidden in the rocks, and anyone who has ever trodden on a sea-urchin with a bare foot knows how painful and tedious a business it is to remove their sharp little spines from the skin. They are, however, delicious to eat for those who like food redolent of the sea, iodine, and salt. They are served cut in half, and the coral flesh so exposed is scooped out with a piece of bread; they are at their best eaten within sight and sound of the sea, preferably after a long swim, and washed down with plenty of some cold local white wine. . . . Sea-urchins are wrested from their lairs in the rocks with wooden pincers, or can be picked up by hand provided you wear gloves.'

(*Italian Food*, Elizabeth David Penguin)

The voice of experience is worth listening to. If, the first time, you eat sea-urchins which are not perfectly fresh, you may well wonder why anyone bothers with them.

Abalone and Ormer and Sea Ear (Ormeau or oreille de mer)

It is easy to collect shells, whether from the beach or the junk shop, without ever realizing that each once had an occupant; in the case of the beautiful ormer or ear shell, with its nacreous lining of green, purple and silver lights, an occupant of a most desirable kind. In California they come in enormous sizes, and the edible white muscle is sold in large slices, already beaten (if they aren't beaten they are quite exceedingly tough). In Brittany, they are smaller but may still need beating. As far as the British Isles are concerned, you are un- likely to find them north of the Channel Islands.

There are two main ways of cooking them. The American system is to marinate the slices in oil and white wine, flavoured with chopped herbs and shallot. After a while they are removed and dried, and cooked in butter very briefly like a steak. They are also chopped up and used in chowders and soups.

The Breton and Channel Island system is to turn them into a stew. *Guernsey Gache,* a miscellany of 19th century Guernsey dishes published by the Toucan Press, says that to dress ormers they should first be put into a cloth and beaten, before being stewed with onions and gravy for 5 or 6 hours. This sounds rather a brown kind of Victorian dish. I think the following Breton recipe is more likely to suit their flavour:

Ormeaux au Muscadet

6 servings:

2 lb. shelled ormers	*bouquet garni*
8 oz. unsalted butter	plenty of parsley
1 large onion, chopped	salt, pepper
3 cloves	generous ¾ pint muscadet
1 clove garlic, chopped	*beurre manié*, p. 21

Having beaten the ormers energetically with a mallet, arrange them in layers in a flame-proof casserole, dotting each layer with butter, seasoning, chopped garlic, onion and parsley. Add the cloves, *bouquet* and wine. Bring to the boil and simmer steadily for 30–45 minutes until the ormers are tender. Strain off the liquid; stir in the *beurre manié* in little pieces until the sauce thickens – keep it over a low heat so that it does not boil. Pour over the ormers, sprinkle on a little more parsley, and serve.

Some Mixed Shellfish Recipes

Insalata di Frutti di Mare

A lovely Italian salad of shellfish and squid, which is an unusually good mixture. If you cannot get clams, use cockles or oysters or scallops.

6 servings:

1½ lb. clams	or mayonnaise made with
3 lb. mussels	olive oil and lemon juice,
1½ lb. tender young squid	p. 50
olive oil	plenty of chopped parsley
1½ lb. shrimps, prawns, or	crisp lettuce leaves
scampi	salt, pepper
vinaigrette made with olive	
oil, lemon juice and some	
French mustard	

Scrub and open the clams and mussels in the usual way. Discard the shells. Strain and keep the liquor for another dish. Clean the squid and cut the body into rings, and roughly chop the tentacles. Fry them quickly in olive oil, adding seasoning as they cook. Drain and cool. Boil the shrimps, prawns or *scampi* if they are raw; shell most of them, leaving a few for decoration.

Put some lettuce leaves in a salad bowl, a glass bowl is most effective, and arrange the shellfish among them. Pour over some vinaigrette (not enough to set the salad afloat) or mayonnaise, and sprinkle on the parsley. Chill for 3 hours.

Insalata di Funghi e Frutti di Mare

In her *Italian Food* (Penguin), Elizabeth David describes a deliciously simple salad of mushrooms and shellfish. Marinate ½ lb. thinly sliced mushrooms in oil, pepper, lemon juice and garlic, for 2 hours. Season with salt. Add *scampi* or *gamberoni*, the huge prawns from Genoa, and tiny squid, sliced and cooked as above. Stewed scallops and 2 oz. of cooked shelled prawns (shrimps) can be used instead, but it is possible nowadays to find squid. Mix with the mushrooms before serving, and sprinkle with parsley.

Shellfish Risotto

One of the pleasures of eating is good rice. By this I mean Italian rice, or French rice from the Camargue, huge oblong grains which cook to a juicy risotto without losing their individual form. I cannot conceal my preference for this European rice; or my affection for the man-made landscape of the Po, where oriental paddy fields separate one Renaissance or Mannerist city from the next. To the rice add shellfish, as they do in Venice – clams, mussels, oysters, lobster or crawfish, cockles, prawns and shrimps of all kinds – and you have one of those perfect unions which stimulate high respect for the civilization where it came about.

risotto:	*or* 6 pints mussels
2 oz. butter	*or* 6 pints clams
medium onion, chopped	*or* 6 pints cockles
1 lb. rice	*or* ¾ lb. shelled prawns or
8 oz. dry white wine	shrimps
2 pints water	*or* 30 scampi
½ pt concentrated fish stock	3 oz. butter
or mussel liquor	1 clove garlic
salt, pepper	parsley
shellfish:	*plus:*
1 small lobster, shelled and	2 oz. butter
cut up	2 oz. grated Parmesan cheese
or 1 crawfish, shelled and cut up	

Use suitable shells from the fish for making a fish stock, plus the usual trimmings (p. 17); or keep the liquor from opening mussels etc. (p. 321), and use as well as, or instead of, fish stock.

To make the risotto, cook the onion in the butter until soft and golden (don't brown it). Stir in the rice and when it looks transparent, pour in the wine. This will soon be absorbed, so add half a pint of the hot water, and as it disappears, another half pint. Use the fish stock next, and the rest of the water if required. The rice will take 20–30 minutes to cook. It should be tender but not mushy to the tongue, and juicy – juicier, for instance than curry or pilaff rice – but not wet.

When the rice is done, quickly reheat the cooked or opened shellfish in their butter, with the finely chopped clove of garlic. A matter of seconds only, or the fish will toughen. Stir into the *risotto* with the parsley and the final 2 oz. of butter. Turn onto a serving dish and sprinkle with the Parmesan.

Note: 1 lb. of tender young squid, cut in rings and fried in olive oil until cooked, can also be added to a *risotto*. So can pieces of eel fried in olive oil. Chopped anchovies are sometimes used, with a little more garlic, and plenty of parsley. The only rule is that the fish must be piquant in flavour, and firm.

Croûte aux Fruits de Mer

The success of this dish depends on the quality of the seafood, its freshness and sweetness, and on your skill in seasoning. It's a matter of attractive assembly and taste, rather than of any cooking skill. If lobsters are impossibly expensive locally, use chopped mussels or lightly simmered scallops instead. Or even some fine, cooked white fish such as sole, John Dory, turbot, or anglerfish. The thing to avoid is canned lobster and crab, they are too tasteless for this French recipe – and for any other, I think.

6 servings:

1 *vol au vent* case, about 8 inches across

crab salad:	*lobster salad:*
1 large crab, boiled	1 boiled lobster, 2 lb. in
4 finely chopped shallots	weight
small bunch parsley, chopped	Avocado mayonnaise, no. 2,
small bunch chives, chopped	p. 54
5 tablespoons oil	*garnish:*
1 tablespoon wine vinegar	1 avocado pear, peeled, stoned
juice of 1 lemon	and sliced
1 avocado pear	tail meat from lobster above
salt, pepper, cayenne pepper	6–8 oz. unpeeled prawns

If you make the *vol au vent* case at home, you will need 1 lb. total weight puff pastry. Bake in a very hot oven (mark 8; 450°F.) until risen and brown. Leave to cool.

Remove the meat from the crab and mix it with the other crab salad ingredients, and the avocado pear, peeled, stoned and diced.

For the lobster salad, remove the claw meat and meat from the head, and mix it with avocado mayonnaise. Slice the tail meat neatly across and set it aside for the garnish.

Put a layer of lobster salad in the pastry case, then all the crab salad, then another layer of lobster salad. Arrange a circle of avocado slices on top as garnish, with tail meat in the centre. Stand prawns, head up, around the outside of the pastry case. *Serve immediately*.

Shellfish à l'Indienne

6 servings:

shellfish:
3 dozen oysters
or 3 dozen large mussels
or 3 dozen large clams
or 2 dozen scallops, with ¼ pint dry white wine
sauce:
2 oz. butter
1 large onion, finely chopped

1 small clove garlic, chopped
2 teaspoons curry powder
1 tablespoon flour
½ pint cream
½ large eating apple, peeled, cored and sliced
lemon juice
salt
plus:
plainly boiled rice

Open the first three shellfish in the usual way. Reserve the liquor, and chop the fish roughly into large pieces. If using scallops, slice them across, having removed coral and hard part; simmer them for 2 minutes in the wine and drain; the liquor is for the sauce.

Cook the onion and garlic in butter until soft and golden. Stir in the curry powder, then the flour. Moisten with the liquor from the shellfish, then add the cream, and the apple. Simmer until the sauce is reduced to a good consistency, fairly thick without being a paste. Correct the seasoning with lemon juice and salt. Stir in the shellfish to reheat only, not to cook further. Serve in the middle of a ring of rice.

Note: shrimps and prawns could be used instead of the shellfish above; simmer their shells in dry white wine, to extract the flavour.

Cured and Preserved Fish

Wind-dried or wind-blown fish, including Salt Cod

A favourite book of mine is *The Herring and Its Fishery*, by W. C. Hodgson (Routledge, 1957). It's written with a vivid eye, with an immediacy that makes me feel that his experiences have been mine as well. The nuggets of information, recipes, strange facts, become part of the reader's existence. Try his way of making wind dried herrings, still apparently a favourite in East Anglia. 'It is most successful in the winter months, and a frosty night in November is admirably suitable. Take half a dozen fresh herrings and sprinkle them with salt, then leave them in a dish overnight. Then thread them on to a stick passed through the gills and mouths of the herrings, and hang them out in the open air where the wind can get at them. In cold weather time does not matter very much, and they can be eaten any time after they have hung for a day or two. They should be opened and cleaned, and the backbone should be removed before frying.'

We can choose the night, the month, the fish. We can avoid humidity, that enemy of drying food. We can eat wind-drieds as a delicious variation to our everyday diet. This and other curing methods, though, belong to early communities of the prehistoric Atlantic coast. They depended on them to survive the winter. They had to dry fish precisely as and where it was caught; mainly I suppose in the early summer, when salmon and sturgeon leapt up the rivers in a profusion we now find unimaginable. Even allowing for the different climate, I imagine that this was as much a period of changing humidity as it is today, so it became necessary to help the drying along artificially by fire. Wind-blown salmon, smoked salmon – what a feast.

Before you start sighing for the simple luxuries of the past, meditate upon this sentence from an early 19th century cookery book. Here's historical reality for you: 'Be careful to brush away immediately any coal or cinders that may fall out, or the appearance will be destroyed.' And not only the appearance, I would have thought.

Fish was dried on a large scale until recently in Scotland, and it still is in communities which are cut off from regular supplies in the winter; in Shetland today, washing-lines of split and salted piltock (saithe) are pegged out in the summer winds, until they are stiff and hard enough to be put by in boxes. A good description of the traditional method was given by Marian McNeill in *The Scots Kitchen* (Blackie). Whiting were the favourite fish, and they were not always cured for long keeping. They might just be dipped in salt, and hung up overnight in a thoroughly draughty passage. At break-fast next day they would be eaten grilled or boiled, with butter; barley bannocks, wheat scones and tea were put on the table as well. Alexis Soyer, the great French chef of the Reform Club in the mid-nineteenth century, thought they made a fine and delicate breakfast dish. This was not the opinion of Dr Johnson. Boswell once 'insisted on *scottifying* his palate' with just a taste of one of these dried whiting which were habitually on sale in London. He let a 'bit of one of them lie in his mouth. He did not like it.' It surprises me that Dr Johnson should have found it so strange, because in her 1758 appendix to *The Art of Cookery*, Hannah Glasse gives instructions for curing mackerel in the sun after salting them for 12 hours: 'lay them to dry on inclining Stones facing the Sun; never leaving them out when the Sun is off, nor lay them out before the Sun has dispersed the Dews, and the Stones you lay them on be dry and warm. A Week's Time of fine Weather perfectly cures them. . .' Admittedly Hannah Glasse came from the north of England, but nothing indicates that her instructions would seem extraordinary to her middle-class readers elsewhere. Unlike Mr Hodgson's East Anglian wind-dried herrings, which were gutted and boned after drying, these fish were first opened down the back – like kippers – and gutted. Another favourite was rizzared haddock, which often appeared on breakfast tables too. (Rizzared means dried or parched, optimistically in the sun, though no doubt a dry wind often had to do instead.) Like Mr Hodgson, Hannah Glasse fried her cured fish. She remarks that they could also be grilled before, or on, a very clear fire, so long as they were basted 'with Oil and a Feather; Sauce will be very little wanting, as they will be very moist and mellow, if good in Kind; otherwise you may use melted Butter and crimped Parsley.'

In some ways I regret that refrigeration has driven out many old curing methods. After all, a frozen herring is essentially similar to a fresh herring, whereas a kipper or a buckling or a bloater or a wind-dried is not. The old methods increased variety; freezing adds nothing – the only certainty is that it diminishes flavour. Its advantages are all in the matter of distribution. I do not belittle this. In the old days, many people starved to death. Now they don't, if they live in a refrigerated society, where food can be kept over the winter, and sent to where it is needed. I just hope that we shall have the sense to hang on to old methods as well. That even if curing is now a luxury finish, people will not let it go because they like the taste. Irish and Scottish smoked salmon, Finnan haddock, and Arbroath smokies will perhaps be treasured as local specialities, regional quaintnesses for the discriminating tourist. Who will remember that they were once a commonplace over a continent?

In the West Cape Province of South Africa, a number of small fish are caught and salted for 24 hours, then dried – in the sun for one day, and in the cool of shadowy verandahs for three to eight days. They are known collectively as *bokkems*. Individually they may be mullet (*haarder*), horse mackerel (*maasbanker*), bass (*steenbrass*) and shad (*elf*). Cure and names came with settlers from the Netherlands. *Bokkems* can be chewed as a relish, without cooking, and are said to taste like biltong. Or they can be lightly grilled and eaten with a pat of butter – and a glass of white wine.

The stronger cure means that they last longer than the wind-blown whiting and herring of Scotland and East Anglia. In this they are more like the two obvious survivors of an antique Scandinavian method: salt fish and stock-fish. These still come from Norway; and from Iceland, where you could once see green field after green field white with fish, laid to dry on stone walls and stones. Nowadays they are usually hung up on racks in huge open sheds.

Salt fish, which includes cod, hake, coalfish, and large haddock, is highly salted before drying, as its name suggests. The main market is the Mediterranean, and it's to the Mediterranean one must look for interesting ways of serving it. I have never read anything less appetizing than Scandinavian ways of cooking it – for instance, boiled with egg sauce. The recipes reflect the late popularity of tomatoes in the north, the sad lack of wine and olive oil. Perhaps this is why some people declare that salt fish is not worth eating, now that we have the benefits of frozen cod and fish fingers the year round. I have heard it suggested that salt fish is a poverty food for people who know, and can afford, no better. Try the recipes on pp. 335–40 and see what you think.

Stockfish is made from the same cod, hake and so on, but it is dried in wind and sun without salting. This is the board-like fish which hangs in close high rows, fringing shops in Ghana and other parts of Africa, its main market. You will not find it easy to obtain here. Salt fish, though, has now become familiar at the fishmongers, largely I am sure on account of foreign immigrants who have been responsible for so many embellishments to our diet since the war.

This is drying on the grand scale. For home trials I would recommend Mr Hodgson's November herrings on p. 332, or Miss McNeill's whiting. Fishermen might try experimenting with grayling or eel (salmon and trout should be kept for smoking). Pike is said to be excellent when dried: Izaak Walton thought it very good. So, it seems, did those prehistoric Danes who left behind them at Scaerdborg a pile of pike head bones. The body part must have been dried, then carried off to winter settlements.

Ailloli Garni with Salt Cod

The most spectacular dish of summer holidays in Provence is *ailloli garni*. At its most flamboyant, it's a Matisse-coloured salad of salt cod and other fish, vegetables fresh and dried, raw and cooked, hardboiled eggs, snails occasionally, and lemon quarters. With it comes a huge bowl of mayonnaise, a special garlic mayonnaise. The flavour has nothing to do with rubbing a clove of garlic discreetly round a salad bowl. It comes from clove after clove after clove. So important is this sauce that the dish carries its name of *ailloli – ail* being French for garlic – with all the rest reduced to the status of a garnish, lordly abundance being just an excuse as it were for eating the sauce.

Although mayonnaise has a way of dominating nomenclature – *mayonnaise de saumon, mayonnaise de homard* – I think no other name touches the grandeur of *ailloli garni*.

The sauce (on p. 56), is the last thing to be made. First you must assemble the other ingredients. A nice piece of salt cod is the first requirement. Soak it for at least 24 hours, changing the water, then drain it and put it into a large pan. Cover with cold water, and add *bouquet garni* and a little salt. Bring slowly to the boil and simmer for about 20 minutes (or less) until the fish flakes away from skin and bone. Don't overcook. Put on a perforated dish to cool. Remove the skin, and put on a large serving dish. Surround it with as great a variety of vegetables as you can assemble. Crispness is required (raw Florentine fennel, cauliflower, radishes, peppers and celery); so, with that sauce, is mild solidity (potatoes, haricot beans). Decorate finally with lemon quarters, egg quarters, and unshelled prawns.

Salt Cod Fritters

The kite-shaped boards of salt cod, hanging from the fishmonger's hooks, look far too unyielding and dry for batter treatment. In fact they make delicious fritters. The important thing for success is to give the fish its full 48 hours soaking time. It's also worth buying two pieces of cod. Cut off the thinner looking extremities and keep them until the following week for a *brandade*, and just soak the plump middle section.

6 servings:

batter with beaten egg white, p. 19
salt cod, soaked and simmered, see above
oil for deep frying
serve with:
lemon quarters (*alla Milanese*)
or skorthalia and beetroot salad, p. 58

or tomato and pepper salad
or a mayonnaise sauce, such as *ailloli, sauce tartare,* anchovy mayonnaise
or tomato sauce, with 1 tablespoon capers, 2 oz. black olives, and 4 oz. shelled walnuts, added at the end

Cut the cod roughly into 2-inch pieces. Remove bones and skin and pat dry. Make the batter. Heat up the oil for cooking and see that the sauce, or whatever you are serving with the fritters, is ready. If lemon quarters are the only accompaniment, the fritters are best fried in olive oil (shallow frying makes this an economic proposition, but the fritters will be less beautiful in shape): otherwise corn oil will do.

Dip the pieces of cod into the batter and fry only a few of them at a time. When they are cooked and golden, put them to drain on a baking tray covered with crumpled kitchen paper. Keep warm in the oven while the other fritters are being cooked. Serve as quickly as possible.

Brandade de Morue

Brandade has had its devotees ever since Grimod de la Reynière 'discovered' it in Languedoc and wrote down the recipe at the end of the 18th century. He concealed the name of the place where he first ate this cream of salt cod, which has led to much pleasurable but fruitless speculation. (Like *lobster à l'américaine* – or *armoricaine*.) Was the place Béziers, an ancient cathedral town between Sète and Narbonne? Or was it Nîmes, where one cooked food shop at least sends *brandade* to customers all over France? To add to the mystery, an almost identical dish, *baccalà mantecato*, is a great speciality of Venice and the Veneto.

Brandade is a fascinating dish to make. Poor-looking greyish-white boards of dried cod are transformed into richness by the gentle attentions of olive oil and cream. Less gentle are the attentions of the cook, who must keep up a steady crushing of the ingredients, combined with a shaking of the pot (the name is said – by Grimod de la Reynière – to come from *brandir*, an old verb meaning to stir, shake and crush with energy, for a long time: one may wonder on what other occasion it might have been employed). Such a slow transformation of substances may sound tiresome in a busy life, but it has its own relaxed pleasure, and a delicious result. A consolation – fruit is the only possible follow-up. The modern recipe has changed little. I use cream, you may prefer to use rich milk and some butter instead.

6 servings:

1½–2 lb. piece dried cod	salt, pepper, nutmeg
¾–1 pint olive oil	lemon juice
½ pint single cream, or ½ pint milk and 2 oz. butter	1 tablespoon chopped parsley
large clove of garlic, crushed	16 triangles of bread, fried in olive oil

Soak the cod and cook it in the usual way (p. 336). Remove and discard all bony parts, but keep the skin. This is often discarded, but as Ali-Bab remarks in his *Gastronomie Pratique*, it helps the flavour and the consistency of the *brandade*, being gelatinous.

Put the pieces of cod, and skin, if used, into a stoneware or enamelled iron casserole, over a low, steady heat (with an asbestos mat underneath, if gas is used). Have the oil and garlic together in a small pan, keeping warm. The same goes for the cream or milk and butter. Pour a little oil on to the cod, and crush the two together with a wooden spoon, moving the pan about. Then add some cream, or milk and butter. Continue in this way until oil and cream are finished. You should now have a coherent creamy mass, very white if you've omitted the skin, white flecked with grey if you haven't, which needs seasoning with salt, pepper, nutmeg and lemon.

The thing to avoid is overheating, which could cause the *brandade* to separate. Should this happen, take the unorthodox step of putting the mixture into a bowl and beating it vigorously and, if possible, electrically.

Serve either in the cooking dish (though this will probably be too large), or on a plainly coloured earthenware dish. Dip one corner of each triangle of fried bread first in the *brandade*, and then into the parsley, before tucking the croûton into the edge of the *brandade* as a garnish.

Any left over can be reheated another day, and served in tiny pastry cases. Or it can be made into little cakes – bind it with one or two eggs – dipped in egg and breadcrumbs, and fried.

New England Salt Cod Dinner

This kind of homely food only tastes good if it is well cooked. The cod should be flakey and succulent, the vegetables nicely seasoned, the bacon or salt pork crisp: and the sauce, above all, must be made with loving care and without meanness. The New England habit of using salt pork with cod is a good one (see *Cod Chowder* on p. 76).

6 servings:

6 oz. salt pork or streaky green bacon, diced	6 boiled onions
1½ lb. salt cod, soaked and simmered	12 small beetroot, boiled parsley sauce made with cream, p. 27
6 potatoes boiled in their skins	

Arrange the cod, cut into pieces for serving, in the centre of a large dish. Pour over the parsley sauce and arrange the vegetables round the edge. Keep warm in the oven, while you fry the bacon or salt pork pieces in their own fat until crisp and brown. Scatter them on top of the fish.

Salt Cod and Tomato Stews

Salt cod and tomato stews, or rather stew-soups, are made all over the Adriatic, Aegean and Mediterranean coasts and inland as well. Delicious they are too, piquant and soothing at the end of the day. As salt cod keeps so well, one variation or another can always be made from store cupboard ingredients.

6 servings:

marinara sauce, p. 45	*or* ¼ pint olive oil plus ½ pint milk plus ¼ pint (full ½ cup) water
piece of salt cod, well soaked	
1 lb. potatoes	
3 inch piece of celery	*or* 1 pint light stock: fish, veal or chicken
bouquet garni	
1 pint liquid:	triangles of bread fried in olive oil
¼ pint dry white wine plus ¾ pint water	

Cut the soaked cod into pieces roughly 2 inches long: remove the bones, but not the skin. Make the *marinara* sauce, simmer it for 15–20 minutes according to the recipe, then add the cod. Put the potatoes, celery and herbs on top. Pour in the liquid chosen, and simmer uncovered until cod and potatoes are done. Don't season until the dish is cooked (as soaked cod is still fairly salty) apart from the normal seasoning of the *marinara* sauce at the beginning.

As salt cod and its skin are more gelatinous than fresh cod, the stew has a smooth coherent texture; but the recipe could be made from fresh cod. In this case, don't add the cod until the potatoes are almost cooked: it will need no more than about 5 minutes. Serve, in either case, with triangles of fried bread.

Note: if unexpected visitors arrive, add more liquid. And if you never buy potatoes (or prefer a less filling dish), substitute 3 oz. of tapioca or rice. When using stock as the liquid, a final glass of dry vermouth or very dry sherry makes a good last seasoning.

Tourte des Terre-Neuvas

A Normandy recipe – remember that fishermen from that coast and from Brittany, as well as from the Basque country and Portugal, have been catching cod off Newfoundland since the very end of the 15th century, though it is now thought that fishermen from Bristol were the first in those waters, in the 1480s, before Columbus 'discovered' America. The cod was gutted and salted on board, then it would be landed and strung up on wooden flakes (frames) to dry before it was brought back to protein-hungry Europe. This long history explains why the best salt-cod dishes come from France, Spain and Portugal: these countries rather than Britain were the ones to develop the great salt-cod trade of the 16th century.

6 servings:

1 lb. puff pastry	3 shallots, chopped
1 lb. dried salt cod	plenty of chopped parsley
¾ lb. potatoes boiled in their skins	4 oz. butter
	salt, pepper
1 large onion, chopped	8 oz. thick cream

Soak the cod for 48 hours, put it into cold water and bring slowly to the boil. As the water begins to bubble at the edge, remove from the heat. Leave until skin and bone can easily be removed from the flakes of fish. Peel the boiled potatoes and slice into rounds. Cook the onion and shallot gently in half the butter.

Using just over half the pastry, line a tart tin with a removable base and a 9-inch or 10-inch diameter. Put in the flaked cod, the potatoes, and the onion mixture. Sprinkle with parsley, season well and dot with the remaining butter. Brush the pastry rim with water, and lay on top a lid made from the rest of the pastry. Cut a circle, about 1½ inches across, from the centre of the lid – put it to cook beside the pie on a baking tray. Cook in a very hot oven (mark 7–8; 425°–450°F.), until the pastry is high and golden – about half an hour. Remove from the tin, if possible, to a hot serving dish. Pour in the cream, put the circle of pastry in place in the centre and serve immediately. It should be very hot.

Salted, smoked and pickled fish

Pickled Herring

If wind-drieds were suited to early nomadic life, salted fish indicates a settled pattern of existence; a pattern of hamlets, of fishing, and fishing communities where people were skilled enough to catch quantities of fish at a time. And had storage space, and adequate containers for salting down the catch to last the winter. It also indicates the developed working of salt mines and salt pans, which took place from the 7th century BC onwards. I suppose a tub of salted fish is as much a symbol of civilization as a gold torque.

The interesting thing is that herrings, destined to become the basic fish of medieval Europe, do not seem to have been caught by prehistoric fishermen, Professor Clark[1] suggests that too much labour would have been involved in making the necessary drift nets: the needs of small communities of farmer-fishermen would not have justified it. The first herring fisheries must have started obscurely in the Dark Ages. By the Norman Conquest, in Great Britain at least, they were flourishing.

Barrels of salt herring must have been excessively cumbersome to move about. Obviously, drying them by smoking would solve the problem of getting them inland, to people who for health – and for religious reasons – needed a particularly cheap and abundant form

[1] J. G. D. Clark, *Prehistoric Europe*, Methuen, 1952.

of protein. Gradually a most efficient technique was evolved. Salted herring were smoked, then left to drip for 2 days, before being smoked and smoked again. They hung over slow fires – like row upon row of washing in Venetian alleys – suspended from rods in great smoke houses. The resulting dryish red object, the 'red herring', was then able to stand up to changes of humidity and temperature without going bad: and it was tough enough to survive the rough jolting of ancient transport.

The red herring even had its poet, Thomas Nashe, Shakespeare's contemporary. According to him: 'The poorer sort make it three parts of their sustenance; with it, for his dinner, the patchedest *Leather pilche laborattro* may dine like a Spanish Duke . . . it sets a-work thousands, who live all the rest of the year gaily well by what in some few weeks they scratch up then.' – i.e. in the herring season. 'Carpenters, shipwrights, makers of lines, ropes and cables, dressers of hemp, spinners of thread, and net weavers it gives their handfuls to, set up so many salt houses to make salt, and salt upon salt; keeps in earnings the cooper, brewer, the baker, and numbers of other people to gill, wash and pack it, and carry it and recarry it.'[2] He might as well have been writing about the herring trade of Germany and Holland – Amsterdam is said to be built on herring bones.

With the development of refrigeration in the 19th century, the red herring disappeared in favour of less harshly cured fish. Henry Sutton of Great Yarmouth still make them, but almost entirely for export to hot countries (although a few delicatessens in this country do stock them for their West Indian customers). They are still required where domestic refrigerators are few. There is even a 'black herring' imported by Africa and the West Indies: it will, it seems, stand up to any climate, indefinitely, without cold storage. When I heard that Rhodesian farmers buy them to supplement the porridgey diet of their black workers, I felt that herrings were still too close reminders of slavery to be comfortable. (Southern American and West Indian plantations once provided a huge market for our hard-cured herrings.)

Cookery books of the past instruct you to soak red herrings in small beer or milk – often poured over them boiling. Hannah Glasse[3] says that 2 hours should be long enough, which makes me

[2] Nashe's *Lentern Stuffe*, in praise of red herring; 1599.
[3] Hannah Glasse, *The Art of Cookery*, 6th edition, 1758.

think that our ancestors had a far greater taste for smokey saltness than we have. The herrings were then grilled, or toasted on forks in front of the fire. Butter was used to baste them, or olive oil, which 'supples, and supplies the fish with a kind of artificial Juices'. Egg sauce, scrambled or buttered eggs, or potatoes mashed and well buttered, mollified the sharp piquant flavour. Cut into strips they could be used like anchovies (p. 368).

By comparison, the bloater is a decadent upstart with a pedigree going back a mere three or four centuries. Its lighter cure reflects pleasure, the realization by many ordinary people that eating could be a source of delight as well as survival. The bloater being un-gutted, like the red herring, keeps a certain gaminess of flavour, but it has been 'roused' in salt for one night only, before being smoked a mere twelve hours. Obviously it cannot be kept without refrigeration, which means that until recently it was a speciality of East Anglia. However, as refrigeration is no improver of flavour, it is still true that you need to go to Yarmouth, or that part of the coast, to eat bloaters at their best (i.e. no more than 36 hours after the cure is finished). This plumped creature – hence the name bloater or bloat herring, *bouffis* to the French – is really a mild yet piquant delicacy. Which is what Clara Peggotty, in *David Copperfield*, meant when she said she was 'proud to call herself a Yarmouth bloater'. This particular kind of curing has also been developed in Europe, in Holland in particular, and in France, where the *harengs saurs* from Boulogne are finer even than a Yarmouth bloater.

We usually grill bloaters in England, and serve them with butter. Or we turn them into bloater paste (p. 387). Like salted herring, kippers, etc., they can be used for the hot dishes on p. 350. Do not be dogmatic about cooking them, because they taste delicious raw in salads of various kinds. I find that a filleted bloater (pour boiling water over first, leave for 1 minute, like a tomato, before skinning), mixed with 2 filleted kippers, makes an excellent substitute for the far more expensive *matjes* herring of the delicatessen counter.

The mildest of all cured herrings is the kipper. As you would expect, it's the latest comer. John Woodger of Seahouses, in Northumberland, decided in the 1840's to adapt the salmon-kippering process to herrings. He split the fish down the back and gutted it, soaked it briefly in brine – half an hour or more depending on the fatness of the fish – then hung it up on hooks fixed to long rods or 'tenters' to be smoked over slow oak fires for 6 to 18 hours.

His methods are still followed by the small family firm of Robson at Craster down the coast from Seahouses, by a firm or two on Loch Fyne, and by all kipperers on the Isle of Man.

Larger concerns cheat time and loss of weight, and make up for the skill of individual judgement, by dyeing the kippers to various shades of mahogany. The browner a kipper is, the more pains you should take to avoid it. This is not crankiness on my part. Try a silvery brown kipper from one of the places I've mentioned, or from the Hamburg fish shop in Brewer Street in Soho; at the same time try one of those sunburnt objects from a deep-frozen package, and you will see what I mean. (Canned kippers I find disgusting: they do not come into it at all.) The practice of dyeing was introduced during the first World War, when it was excusable to pass off inferior kippers because people were hungry. The dye disguised the fact that the kipper hadn't been smoked for long enough: which meant that it had lost less weight, so it took fewer kippers to fill the boxes. Good kippers are sorted out after the curing is over: dyeing disguises the poor ones, and so lessens the need for skilled sorters who know what a kipper should be.

In *The Herring and its Fishery*, W. C. Hodgson remarks: '. . . in fairness to many respectable curing firms, it is true to say that, *provided the fish are properly smoked*, a little added colour will do no harm, but at the same time it is difficult to see why if colour was unnecessary in the "old days" it should be necessary now. However one looks at the problem, there is always the chance that the colour will be used to speed up the processing of the herring.'

Kippers may be grilled, skin side to the heat, baked in foil, fried, or jugged – i.e. put into a large pot, with a kettleful of boiling water, and left for 10 minutes. I like them best raw, arranged in strips round the edge of some well-buttered rye bread, with an egg yolk in the middle as sauce. Or I like them, raw again, in the herring salad recipes on p. 347. They make an excellent *quiche* (p. 229), or soufflé (p. 230), and are an obvious candidate for the fish paste recipe on p. 387.

Two hints from Mr Hodgson:
'Put a pair of kippers together, flesh to flesh, in the frying-pan with a small piece of butter between them. Fry very slowly, turning them over from time to time, but always keeping them together like a sandwich. In this way the oil runs continually from one kipper to the other and the result is excellent. Incidentally mustard is good with

kippers, and mustard sauce is correct with most kinds of cooked fresh herrings.' (See p. 28.)

'Many people object to eating kippers because they have difficulty with the bones ... Eating a kipper is quite simple if it is laid correctly on the plate to start with, that is, with the skin uppermost ... With the head towards you, lift up the skin from half of the kipper by running the point of the knife along the edge and fold the skin back. This exposes the flesh *on top of the bones*, and it is quite easy to remove it in fillets, leaving the bones untouched. When this side has been eaten, turn the kipper round on the plate so that the tail is towards you and repeat the process on the other side.' This works.

Since the war, we have all become familiar with two kinds of cured herring originally imported from abroad. First the *matjes* or *maatjes* fillets on sale in many supermarkets and Continental stores. These come from young fat virgin herrings (which is the meaning of the word *matjes*) and have been cured in salt, sugar and a little saltpetre. They have a richer flavour than ordinary salted herrings, but after soaking can be used in exactly the same ways. The other kind, *bückling*, are a different matter altogether, because they have been partially 'cooked' by hot-smoking. (The other smoked herrings are cold-smoked at temperatures not higher than 90°F., which flavours the fish without cooking it.) They are ungutted, so have the slightly gamey flavour of a bloater but in a milder form. Eat them, like smoked trout, with bread and butter and lemon, or with horse-radish cream. If you must have them hot, reheat them as briefly as possible under the grill or in the oven. The appetizing gold colour comes from their final exposure to really dense smoke. This is the luxury fish of the herring trade.

Herring preserved in vinegar and wine, soused herrings, and roll-mops, are given on p. 356. The French *maquereau au vin blanc* are on p. 355, the Southern American *ceviche*, fish cured solely by marinating overnight in lemon juice, on p. 150, and *escabeche*, another Spanish form of marinated fish popular in England in the past, on p. 353.

How to Salt Herrings at Home

When I first started housekeeping and was full of the enthusiasm of novelty, I came across a Danish book mainly concerned with pickling herrings. One recipe gave a splendid mixture for spiced salt, including sandalwood and Spanish hops. Chips of sandalwood I managed to find (and have some still in a jar in my spice cupboard – occasionally I unscrew the lid and the lovely smell brings back a pungent memory of the enormous enterprise we undertook). Spanish hops remained elusive, so we did without them. Macfisheries were surprised to receive an order for 100 fine fat herrings, but sent a patient young man out to our village with the load. He came in and out of the house with endless white trays of herrings. He talked to us gingerly and placatingly, as if he were not quite sure of our sanity.

Down those herrings went, into a stoneware crock, and they were excellent. At that time there were only two of us; they seemed to last for ever. But I would advise putting down 50 herrings if you have a family, particularly if you live near a herring port and can buy them really fresh. The thing is to get them when they are at their fattest and most plentiful (and therefore cheapest).

Gut and scale them, but leave the heads. Put into vinegar overnight, and drain well. For 50 herrings mix:

1 lb. sea salt	½ oz. allspice, slightly crushed
½ lb. sugar	1 handful small bay leaves
½ oz. black peppercorns crushed	

and – if you have any sandalwood chips – half an ounce of them. Put a layer of this mixture in the bottom of a stoneware crock (earthenware is too porous), then a layer of herrings belly upwards. Repeat, ending with a layer of salt. Put a piece of foil on top, with a weight to keep the fish submerged in the brine – which soon forms as the juices of the herring mix with the salt. The important thing is to keep the herrings submerged to avoid contact with the air. Store the crock in a cool place.

Before use the herrings will need soaking. The length of time will depend on how long they've been in salt. Milk and water, half and half, is the usual liquid, but water alone can be used. They can be boned before or after soaking, whichever is most convenient. It follows that if they're boned first, and reduced to elegant fillets, they will need less soaking time than if they are left whole – and less soaking liquid.

The herrings are usually marinated in all kinds of delicious mixtures, before being served on their own or in a salad, *without any cooking whatsoever*. They *can* be cooked – see recipes on p. 350 – but usually they form part of a cold platter or *smörgasbord* table.

Note: herrings can be quick-salted by soaking 6 or 8 of them, after boning, in a solution of 1 pint water to 2 oz sea salt. Leave for 3 hours, then drain well. The flavour is not so rich and spicy, but they will pass.

Salted Herring Salads

Having made or bought your salted herrings, they will provide you with a number of hot dishes (see recipes on p. 350), and, even better, with a variety of salads and hors d'oeuvre which can be varied to suit your own tastes.

I. DANISH PICKLED HERRING. In Denmark salted herrings are given a richer flavour by being soaked in a sweet-sour marinade. First of all, though, the herrings must be soaked until they are mild in flavour:

6 servings:

8 oz. granulated sugar	1 teaspoon pickling spice,
¼ pint wine or cider vinegar	including a chili
6–8 peppercorns	2 or 3 large onions and a few
	bay leaves

Put 4 to 6 salt herring fillets to soak in milk and water. Simmer together the first four marinade ingredients for 3 minutes. Leave to cool. When the saltiness of the herrings is reduced to a palatable level, drain and arrange them in a plastic box or glass jar, with slices of onion and bay leaves in between. Pour over the marinade and leave for at least 5 days in the refrigerator.

The fillets can then be cut up into pieces, to be eaten with bread and butter, as they are. Serve the pieces in a dish, garnished with a few slices of the onion, a bay leaf or two and the chili. They are an essential part of the cold table in Denmark, and on a smaller scale can be included in a mixed hors d'oeuvre.

2. SOUR CREAM SALAD. To 8 oz. soured cream, add 2–3 tablespoons chopped spring onions (the green part) or chives, and 2 oz mild sliced onion. Season with lemon juice and Worcester sauce, plus mustard, sugar, cayenne and freshly ground black pepper. Mix in the herring fillets, cut into pieces, and leave to chill overnight. Sprinkle with fresh, chopped dillweed.

3. HORSERADISH CREAM SALAD. Flavour 8 oz. cream, half thin half thick, with horseradish to taste: the quantity required will depend on whether you are using the freshly grated root from the garden, or one of many brands of prepared horseradish – start with a very little and you can't go wrong. Season with salt and sugar (bear in mind the flavour of the herring fillets) and lemon juice. Mix in the pieces of herring fillet and leave overnight in the refrigerator. Garnish with parsley.

4. MUSTARD SALAD. Make a strong mustard-flavoured mayonnaise (p. 52). Fold in 4 oz. whipped cream. Pour over pieces of soaked, salted herring fillets. Garnish with dillweed. Serve very cold.

5. TOMATO SALAD. To half a pint of the *marinara* sauce on p. 45, add brown sugar, French mustard and vinegar, and some chopped onion. The mixture should be piquant. Spice with Tabasco, *or* with cinnamon. Pour over the soaked salt herring, garnish with onion rings, and chill well.

6. BOULONNAISE SALAD. Soak and cut up the salt herring fillets; put them in the centre of a serving dish. Beat 4 oz. olive oil into 1 large tablespoon of French mustard, as if you were making a mayonnaise. Pour this over the herrings and top with raw onion rings. Round them put a circle of diced, boiled beetroot (about 1 lb.) dressed in a sauce of 4 oz. of thick or soured cream, flavoured with chopped shallot, chives and lemon juice. Fork 4 hardboiled eggs to crumbs and put in a ring between herring and beetroot. Chill well.

7. LIVONIAN SALAD. Dice ¾ lb. potatoes, boiled in their skins and then peeled, 2–3 large Cox's orange pippins, half a head of Floren-

tine fennel *or* 2–3 stalks of celery. Put into a bowl with vinaigrette dressing, chopped parsley, chervil and chives. Soak and drain four salt herring fillets, cut them into dice and fold them in last of all. Serve well chilled.

Beetroot can be added, so can a chopped dill-pickled gherkin or cucumber. Tomatoes and lemon quarters, too. Thick or soured cream can take the place of vinaigrette sauce, appropriately seasoned.

8. DANISH SALAD. (From *The Great Scandinavian Cook Book.*[4]) Make a sauce by the *béchamel* method from 2 tablespoons each butter and flour, moistened with ¼ pint each cream and water. Season with 1 tablespoon vinegar, 1 teaspoon made mustard, salt, and sugar. Leave to cool. Cut into small dice 2 salted herring fillets which have been soaked, 3 boiled potatoes, 1–2 pickled beetroots, 1 salted gherkin, *or* cucumber, 1–2 apples and 7 tablespoons boiled or roasted meat. Mix carefully with the sauce. Correct seasoning. Garnish with egg and lettuce and serve well chilled.

9. SALTED HERRINGS IN WINE AND CREAM. Cook sliced onion and bay leaf in 3 oz dry white wine for 15 minutes. When cold, stir in 4 oz. thick cream. Season with cayenne, dillweed and salt. Mix in pieces of soaked, salt herring. Leave in refrigerator for 2 days before serving.

10. SALTED HERRINGS IN OLIVE OIL. My favourite recipe for *harengs saurs* and kippers (neither should need soaking). Put fillets into a jar with enough fruity olive oil to cover. Leave in refrigerator until required. Serve with potato salad, dressed with olive oil vinaigrette and chives.

11. POLISH CHRISTMAS EVE HERRINGS. If the herrings are very salty, soak them. If you are using the packets of mild *harengs saurs*, or kipper fillets, there is no need to do this. Put them on individual plates, and cover them with double cream well seasoned with chopped onion and lemon juice. Serve with glasses of chilled vodka.

This is the best and simplest way I know of eating *harengs saurs*.

[4] Allen & Unwin Ltd. Ed. Ellison.

IMPORTANT. These salads can be made with most pickled herrings, whether or not they have been soaked in the sweet-sour marinade. If you are using soaked salt herring or soaked *harengs saurs*, if you are using kipper or buckling fillets which do not need soaking because of the light cure, the dressings may be improved with a little sugar.

After filleting oily fish, wash hands and utensils first in cold water. Surprisingly, this gets rid of the smell: with warm or hot water, it lingers disconcertingly.

Hot Dishes made from Salted and Smoked Herring

Soak *harengs saurs* and bloaters: buckling and kipper may be used straight away.

1. HARENGS SAURS À LA BRUXELLOISE. A dish of Carême's. Take half a dozen fish, preferably with soft roes. Remove the fillets, discarding skin and bones. Mash up a generous 4 oz. unsalted butter with plenty of chopped parsley, some chives, lemon juice and a little crushed garlic. Put two ounces of chopped onion into boiling water and cook them for 2 or 3 minutes. Drain, rinse with cold water and add to the butter. Chop 4 oz mushrooms. Spread the bottom of an ovenproof dish with most of the butter mixture. Place the mushrooms on top, then the herring fillets, with the soft roes between and bits of the remaining butter. Cover with breadcrumbs, dot with more butter, and put into a hot oven (mark 7; 425°F.) for 20 minutes.

Carême remarks that this dish was always a great success in Lent. People grew very tired of eating fish and were glad to have something particularly good to tempt their bored appetites.

2. HERRING WITH POTATOES AND EGGS. In hot dishes as in cold, potatoes and eggs are the most popular modifiers of salted herring. So it is not surprising that variations of the same recipe are found all over northern Europe. In Scotland, salted herring were laid on top of potatoes, which were then boiled in the usual way and eaten with butter. Scandinavia has a more refined version – potatoes are set to boil, the fish is put on to a buttered plate, which fits nicely on top, covered with foil and left to steam. The dish is finally garnished with chopped hard-boiled egg and dill, chives or parsley.

3. HERRING WITH CREAM. Another modifier is cream. Here are several Scandinavian versions of this idea. They are best made in a small quantity and served as a first course, provided the rest of the meal isn't too heavy. Cook them in small individual ramekins or 3-inch to 4-inch soufflé dishes.

Butter the dishes well. Put in a layer of pieces of buckling or kipper fillet, or very well soaked *harengs saurs* or bloaters.

Cover with a layer of chopped leek and about 2 oz of cream. Dot with butter. Bake in a hot oven (mark 7; 425°F.) for 15–20 minutes.

Or sprinkle with a teaspoon of dillweed, and then pour in the cream. Dot with butter. Bake in the same way. This is the version I like best: it really is delicious.

Or cover with a nice layer of potato cut into small matchstick strips. Pour over the cream. Dot with butter. Bake in a hot oven (mark 7; 425°F.) for about 30 minutes, until the potatoes are cooked and slightly browned.

Serve with rye bread and butter, or toast.

4. HARENGS SAURS À L'IRLANDAISE. A recipe from an American friend which is unusual and magnificent. Soak the fish if necessary and fillet them, or use kippers. Spread them out in a large dish and cover with Irish whiskey. Set it alight. When the alcohol has burnt away the fish are ready to eat.

5. SMOKED HERRING AND EGG SAUCE. Follow the recipe for smoked finnan haddock and egg sauce on p. 363. 10 minutes cooking time should be enough for the fish.

Home-Pickled Herring, Salmon, Mackerel or Trout

The high pleasure of holidays in Denmark – Tollund man, amber and archaeology apart – is working one's way through the pickled fish. In hotels or friends' houses, one never seems to eat the same kind twice. And I suppose this to be the case in Sweden and Norway as well.

An English schoolfriend, now married to a Dane in Kolding, first introduced me to this recipe – and to the sweet-pickled herrings on p. 347. Both are common Scandinavian dishes, and I cannot think why they are not common here as well.

Pickled salmon is much cheaper than smoked salmon. Everyone enjoys the unfamiliar flavour. Pickled herrings are almost as good, and make a wonderful standby in the refrigerator. Don't be put off, though, by the unfamiliarity of dillweed. Dill is easy to grow for the future, and for the present freeze-dried leaves of dill – known as dillweed as opposed to dillseed – can be bought in small jars from good grocers and delicatessen stores. In desperation, one could substitute fennel leaves, or chopped fresh tarragon, but dillweed is what gives the unmistakeably right note.

Incidentally this is an excellent recipe for frozen Canadian salmon (keep the finest Scotch for the recipes on pp. 220–31). Buy a tailpiece – bargaining is advisable – and ask the fishmonger to remove the bone, so that you have two kite-shaped pieces. With smaller fish, slit them along the belly and remove the innards; and the head, if you like. Press them, cut side down, firmly on to a board and press steadily along the back. Turn the fish over and you will be able to pick out the backbone quite easily, with the small bones which adhere to it.

The pickle recipe is enough for a 1½–2 lb. piece of salmon, or for two, even three pairs of small fish.

Mix together in a bowl:

1 heaped tablespoon sea salt	1 teaspoon crushed black or
1 rounded tablespoon sugar	white peppercorns
	1 tablespoon brandy (optional)

Have a quantity of dillweed to hand, a good tablespoon should be enough.

Put some of the mixture, and some dillweed, into a dish. Put in the first piece of salmon, or the first whole fish, skinside down. Spread some more of the pickle on the cut side, with some more dillweed. Put in the second piece of salmon, or the second whole fish, cut side down. (Repeat this with the rest of the small fish.) Finally put the last of the pickle and dillweed on top, then some kitchen foil, and a couple of tins to press the fish together so that it is permeated by the pickle and dillweed; in fact, I use a Roman brick which we picked up in France, at the fortress of Jublains, because it is a good shape for the fish.

Leave for at least 12 hours, and not more than 5 days. To serve, slice off the flesh – well drained – in thinnish slivers and arrange on plates or on buttered rye bread: the sweet/sour mustard and dill mayonnaise on p. 52 is usually served with this dish (the egg yolk can be omitted). The pickled fish can also be heated in a little butter, and served with baked potatoes and the mustard and dill sauce.

Escabeche

Escabeche has a fine sound, almost a flourish to its tail. By origin Spanish, it comes from the West Indies, where they use it to describe a particular method of pickling fish. In England it turns up, briskly abbreviated to caveach, in the middle of the 18th century. Mrs Elizabeth Raffald gives two recipes in *The Experienced English Housekeeper* (1769). Hannah Glasse in *The Art of Cookery* (1747) gives the following recipe:

'To pickle Mackrel, call'd, Caveach

'Cut your Mackrel into round Pieces, and divide one into five or six Pieces: To six large Mackrel you may take one Ounce of beaten Pepper, three large Nutmegs, a little Mace, and a Handful of Salt. Mix your Salt and beaten Spice together, then make two or three Holes in each Piece, and thrust the Seasoning into the Holes with your Finger, rub the Piece all over with the Seasoning, fry them brown in Oil, and let them stand till they are cold; then put them into Vinegar, and cover them with Oil. They will keep well covered a great While, and are delicious.'

I can imagine that this rich southern confection must have made a pleasant interruption in our ancient Friday diets of salt-and-vinegar-soused herring. The interesting thing is that the 18th century English recipes are unchanged in modern books of Central and Latin American cooking: the fish is first fried, then submerged in oil, vinegar and aromatics such as onion, peppers, oranges, spices – whatever the particular district may have to offer.

Any fish can be used – sole, mackerel, whole fish, filleted fish, chunks of fish, even frozen haddock fillet. For this particular recipe, which is a preserve for entertainment rather than serious storage, I should choose the finest, freshest white fish you can afford.

4 servings:

1¼ lb. fish
salt, pepper, olive oil
marinade:
6 oz. each lemon juice,
    orange juice, olive oil
1 ripe avocado, peeled and
    sliced
1 large orange, sliced

1 small pepper, seeded and
    diced
half an onion, sliced
Angostura bitters or dry
    Vermouth
garnish:
1 avocado pear, peeled and
    sliced
half an onion, sliced

Season the fish. Leave for half an hour, then cook in olive oil until golden brown on both sides. Do not overcook. Put into a dish.

Heat all marinade ingredients, except bitters or Vermouth, and let them boil together for a couple of moments. Pour them over the fish. Add Vermouth to taste, or bitters, and a little salt, though this will most likely not be necessary. Cover when cold, and leave in the refrigerator overnight. Add extra slices of avocado pear and onion just before serving.

Apart from the juices, which take the place of vinegar, and the olive oil, the quantities of the other flavouring ingredients are variable. The important thing is that the fish should be covered; and that you should find the balance of flavours agreeable to *your* taste. A beautiful dish – particularly if you use a pink Spanish onion, to contrast with the orange, deep green and soft pistachio green of the other ingredients. The juice will become slightly jellied. A most refreshing dish.

Soused Herring and Bratheringe, and Soused Mackerel

The German method of preparing soused herring, or *bratheringe*, is a form of *escabeche*, because the fish are fried before being soaked in a vinegar marinade. The second method, more familiar in this country, bakes the fish in vinegar without frying it first.

6 servings:

(1) 6 herrings, preferably
     soft-roed
   seasoned flour
   oil, preferably olive oil
   marinade:
   8 oz. vinegar

4 oz. water
2 oz. olive oil
1 teaspoon each peppercorns,
   mustardseed
3 bay leaves
1 medium onion, sliced

Remove the heads and tails from the herrings and bone and clean them, setting the roes aside. Flour lightly, then brown them in olive oil. Cool, and arrange in a dish. Fry the roes in some fresh oil and put them on the herrings. Bring the marinade ingredients to the boil, cool, then pour over the fish and roes. Cover and leave in the refrigerator for at least 24 hours.

6 servings:

(2) 6 herrings or mackerel
   salt, pepper
   ¼ pint each water and
     malt vinegar, or ½ pint
     dry cider

1 tablespoon pickling spice,
   including a chili
3 bay leaves
1 medium onion, sliced

Behead, bone and clean the fish. Season them and roll up, skin side either all inwards or all outwards. Arrange closely together in an ovenproof dish. Add the rest of the ingredients. Cover with foil and bake in a cool oven (mark 1; 300°F.) for about 1½ hours. Serve cold. Use the roes for another dish (see p. 205).

Note: soused herrings can be turned into large mixed salads, by following salt herring dishes on pp. 347–50.

Mackerel (or Herring) au Vin Blanc

A delicious hors d'oeuvre, which can be prepared up to 8 days in advance, and kept in the refrigerator. Serve with unsalted butter and wholemeal bread.

6 servings:

White wine *court-bouillon*,
   No. 5, p. 17
4 fat mackerel or herrings

1 teaspoon pickling spices,
   including a red chili

Clean the fish and put them into a pan. Strain over them the *court-bouillon*, which should be cold and reduced by half. Add the pickling spices. Bring slowly to the boil, let it bubble two or three times, remove from the heat and allow to cool.

Remove skin and bone from the fish, so that you have nice looking pieces. Place them in a dish with the red chili, some slices of carrot and perhaps a fresh bay leaf. Taste the white wine liquid. It should be strongly flavoured, so may benefit by further reduction. When cool strain over the fish. Cover with foil and leave until required. Should you be keeping the fish for several days, it ought to be well covered with the *bouillon* while it waits. Pour off a little before serving so that the dish does not look sloppy.

Note. This is the French method of sousing herring and mackerel. The flavour is finer, because white wine is used instead of vinegar: a good dry cider can be used instead, as in the recipe for soused herring on p. 354.

Bismarck and Rollmop Herrings

Like the *ceviche* on p. 150, Bismarck and rollmop herrings are not cooked by heat, but by an acid liquid – this time vinegar, which is better suited than citrus juice to an oily fish like herring.

Bismarck herrings are boned fillets, soaked in spiced vinegar, seasoned with slices of onion, cayenne pepper and salt. Rollmops are the whole boned herring, curled up round pieces of onion, pickled cucumber and peppercorns: they are packed into jars and covered with spiced vinegar, bay leaves and mustard seeds, more onion and cucumber being added to improve the flavour.

Here are two recipes for home-made rollmops – one using fresh herrings, the other salt or *matjes* fillets.

6 servings:

(1) 6 herrings
1 pint water
2 oz. salt
marinade:
1 pint white wine or cider vinegar
3 bay leaves

peppercorns
1 tablespoon pickling spices, including chili
1 large onion, sliced
2–3 sweet-sour pickled cucumbers or gherkins

Cut the head and tail from the herrings, bone and clean them. Mix the salt with the water and leave the fish in this brine for 2–3 hours. Meanwhile make the marinade: bring the vinegar and pickling spices to the boil slowly, with peppercorns and bay leaves. Leave to cool. Drain and dry the soaked herrings. Wrap each one round a piece of onion and a piece of cucumber. Arrange the rolled herring side by side in a refrigerator box or glass or pottery jar. Pour the vinegar over them. Tuck any pieces of onion and cucumber left over between the herrings. Leave for at least four days before eating. Drain, and add fresh onion slices and parsley. A little soured cream can be poured over them as well. Serve with rye bread, or pumpernickel, and butter.

6 servings:

(2) 12 salted or *matjes* fillets	3 cloves
marinade:	1 teaspoon whole black
½ pint water	peppercorns, crushed
½ pint wine or cider	3 bay leaves
vinegar	German mustard
½ teaspoon each slightly	1 large onion, sliced
crushed allspice and	2–3 dill-pickled cucumber
juniper berries	

Soak the fillets for at least 12 hours, changing the water twice.

Make the marinade by bringing the water and vinegar slowly to the boil with the spices and bay leaves. Cool. Drain and dry the fillets; spread each one with a little mustard, then roll up round pieces of onion and cucumber. Finish as above.

Other Smoked Fish (Poissons fumés)

Many more fish than you would imagine are smoked in different parts of the world. The curing started as a preservative measure in prehistoric times, when it was no doubt a harsh supplement to salting, but a useful one in damp climates where it was difficult to air-dry food without its spoiling. Nowadays smoking is more of a cosmetic process than a necessity. It is still done because it adds a most delicious flavour if applied briefly, after a brief salting. The fish can then be stored in cold cabinets, so there is no longer any need to salt and smoke it to a hard invulnerability. I suspect that the smoked salmon, eel, trout that we eat today are better than they have ever been. Another good thing, there are many small firms smoking fish. All their products taste a little different and it's well worth trying out as many as you can, to see which firm's cures you prefer.

It is often stated as a general principle that fish exposed to hot smoke needs no further cooking (buckling, eel, trout) while fish exposed to cool smoke does (kipper, Finnan haddock). This is not always helpful. Some cool-smoked fish are at their best when eaten as they are; smoked salmon is the obvious example, but try a good Craster or Isle of Man kipper this way too – with bread and butter, and a dressing of lemon juice or raw egg yolk. Contrariwise hot-smoked fish can be grilled *lightly*. For instance eel, sprats and trout – with Arbroath smokies as the obvious example. I emphasize the word lightly; the point is only to reheat the fish, not to cook it any further. Butter helps to prevent dryness. Eel can be grilled with its skin on (no butter required for this rich creature), but the skin should be removed before serving. The same with smoked sprats. Smokies and bloaters should be brushed with melted butter and warmed through: they can then be split open, and a pat of butter put into the centre, before they are returned to the grill for a few seconds longer. Serve them unskinned.

If you are an angler, you may want to smoke some of your catch. There is a small smoking box on the market (trade name of Abu). It gives a pronounced flavour, which I personally find too strong, though with experience one might learn to counteract this. Certainly I know anglers who find it satisfactory.

The traditional means of home-smoking is to use an inverted barrel. Mrs Beeton suggests an '. . . old hogshead, stop up all the crevices, and fix a place to put a cross-stick near the bottom, to have the articles to be smoked on. Next, in the side, cut a hole near the top, to introduce an iron pan filled with sawdust and small pieces of green wood. Having turned the tub upside down, hang the articles upon the cross-stock, introduce the iron pan in the opening and place a piece of red-hot iron[5] in the pan, cover it with sawdust, and

---

[5] Or some red-hot charcoal.

all will be complete.' You will rapidly discover from experience how many hours different fish require. And remember that they must first be salted in a strong enough solution of water and salt to keep an egg floating: soak the fish in this from 30 minutes upwards according to size. Alternatively, the fish can be dry-salted with say 1 lb. of coarse sea salt to 3 oz. brown sugar and ½ oz. of saltpetre. Rub this mixture in, and turn the fish over in it from time to time, for an hour or two. Rinse and then smoke. Remember that dry-salting takes longer to penetrate than brine.

If you are ever in the happy position of catching enough salmon to spare some for smoking, I suggest you turn to William Heptinstall's *Hors d'oeuvre and Cold Table*, first published in 1959 by Faber & Faber. Sections 50 to 52 deal with smoking fish, salmon in particular, and tell you how to construct a more efficient smokehouse than Mrs Beeton's hogshead. Mr Heptinstall served his own smoked salmon at his hotel in the Highlands for many years: he really understands the process.

Smoked salmon is sold all over the country now, even in deep-frozen packets. It is better to buy it freshly sliced from a good supplier, and best of all to buy a side from one of the many curers in Scotland and Ireland. Look out for their advertisements in the papers, you will sometimes find quite a bargain. It is surprising how widely the cures differ, so if you find one you like particularly, stick to it. To slice a side of salmon, start cutting from the tail end towards the head in thin slices, parallel to the board on which you have placed the salmon. Put a tack or two at each end to hold it steady.

Smoked Salmon

First-quality smoked salmon should be left alone: eat it with brown bread and butter, and lemon juice if you like, and be thankful. Sometimes, though, one can buy most advantageously the odd bits and pieces and chunks left from slicing a whole side. These can be turned into luxurious dishes. They are the obvious thing to use for the smoked fish paste on p. 387. They can be used to give extra flavour to a salmon mousse, p. 230, or to a dish of *paupiettes de sole*, p. 95. Pounded up with cream or mayonnaise, seasoned with lemon, they enliven sandwiches, pancakes, baked potatoes, hard-boiled eggs, and salads of cold, poached white fish.

SMOKED SALMON OMELETTE. Beat the whites of 4 eggs until stiff. Fold in the lightly beaten yolks, and about 6 oz. of smoked salmon cut into strips. Cook in the usual way. Makes 2 servings.

SMOKED SALMON QUICHE. Into one large or six small pastry cases, baked blind, put about 4 oz. of cold cooked salmon and 4–6 oz. smoked salmon. Beat up ¼ pint each thin and thick cream with 3 egg yolks and 1 whole egg; season with salt, pepper, and mace and pour over the fish. Bake in a moderate to fairly hot oven (mark 4–5; 350°–375°F.) until cooked; about 30 minutes for the small quiches, 45 minutes for one large one. 6 servings.

SALMON BOATS. For about 18 pastry boats (or tartlets) baked blind, you will need:

6–8 oz. cooked salmon flaked	lemon juice, salt, pepper
4 oz. thick cream	3–4 slices smoked salmon
2–3 oz. softened butter	

Cut the smoked salmon into ovals or circles to form lids for the pastry cases. Put these aside. Blend the trimmings with the cooked salmon, cream and butter. Season and fill the cases. Cover with the smoked salmon lids. Eat straight away.

Because of the native excellence of smoked salmon, it is easy to forget that there are other kinds of smoked fish which are just as good. Sometimes, better, for instance:

Smoked Eel

Certainly my favourite smoked fish. Outside London, though, look carefully at what you are buying. Sometimes the eel has dried up with the fatigue of waiting for the next customer. The ideal is to buy one on holiday in Holland (a better reason for going there than the bulbs). Then you can choose a moderately fat, moist-looking eel of your own. Allow a 3½-inch to 4-inch chunk per person, peel off the skin, remove the fillets from the backbone, and place them side by side on a plate. Because this looks on the mean side (in fact it's not, because eel is a rich, satisfying fish), add some brown bread and butter and slices of lemon. A great delicacy.

Smoked Sturgeon

More difficult to come by, but worth pursuing. About the same price as salmon and eel. Insist on having it thinly sliced. Last year the owner of the Hamburg fish shop in Soho managed to get hold of a sturgeon caught off Scotland. We were lucky enough to visit the shop while there was still some left; we bought thin, thin slices, cut, like smoked salmon, along the side. It was the first time we had eaten it, and we found it unimaginably delicious. So when I saw some, a while later, in a grand provision shop not so far away, I asked for a quarter. And unwisely turned my back while it was being cut. When we ate the thick, dryish slices, cut down the chunk instead of across, we wondered what had happened, it was so dull. Thickness is inimical to smoked sturgeon, as it is to smoked salmon.

Smoked Trout

Another delicate luxury. With small trout, allow one per person. Usually the fish is skinned neatly, with head and tail left in place; I think there is something to be said for leaving the skin in place, too, and allowing people to remove it for themselves: the skin of trout is a pleasing sight. Serve lemon quarters and brown bread and butter, in the usual way, or else small pots of cream flavoured *lightly* with horseradish, lemon juice and sugar. Ninette Lyon in *Fish for all Seasons* remarks: 'The little white morsels found beneath the gill covers in the head are very delicate, so be sure to prise them out before the head is thrown away.'

Smoked Chicken Halibut

A rarity of small smoking establishments, but worth buying if you see it. Remove the skin, then the fillets on each side, and serve in portions, with the usual accompaniments. Excellent with horse-radish cream, as above. It can be used for open sandwiches most successfully, like kipper; put strips of it, like a nest, on a slice of well buttered rye bread, with a yolk of egg carefully placed in the centre, and a lemon quarter to one side. To eat, squeeze the lemon over the whole thing, and fork the yolk and strips together. Don't over-garnish smoked halibut, or the flavour will be drowned.

Smoked Sprats

These rich little creatures are a good cheap buy. As they can be indigestible, I think they are best served as part of a mixed hors d'oeuvre. Skin and fillet them first. A tablespoon of dry white wine poured over them makes a good dressing. They can also be heated quickly under the grill (skin them first and brush with clarified butter); serve with plenty of bread and butter, and lemon quarters.

Smoked Mackerel

Like smoked sprats, these need modifying to be really enjoyable with-out regretful afterthoughts. A good fish for a large cold table of food. Or again in a small quantity in an hors d'oeuvre: white wine makes a dressing which cuts the richness. One firm, which smokes macke-rel, suggests reheating the fillets under mushroom sauce (p. 29) in a hot oven for 10 minutes, garnished with tomato slices. Small quantities can be added to omelettes or scrambled eggs, or used with fresh fish for a kedgeree.

Smoked Haddock

Fine Finnan, or Findon, haddock is a most excellent fish. The cure was originally developed in the village of Findon, to the south of Aberdeen. I hope there is a statue there to the inventor (though I doubt it). You can be sure that you are getting haddock by looking at the skin of the fish: there on either side are the two black finger marks of St Peter – an honour which it shares with the John Dory (p. 122). Notice, too, that the bone is usually to the right hand side of the split fish, the opposite way to the kipper. Recipes on pp. 363-7.

Eyemouth Cured Haddocks and Glasgow Pales

These are even more lightly cured than Finnan haddock – only 20–30 minutes in brine, and a light smoking. They are split open in the same way, and are cooked the same way.

Arbroath Smokies, Aberdeen Smokies, Pinwiddies

The smaller haddock (and sometimes whiting), beheaded and cleaned, but left whole. They are hot-smoked, unlike *Finnans* and *Eyemouths*, and look a much darker brown. In spite of this they are usually eaten hot; brush with butter and place under the grill for a few minutes, or in a hot oven. Put a nice knob of butter in the middle and serve straight away.

Smoked Finnan Haddock with Egg Sauce

It may seem odd to use a French recipe for one of our best known national dishes. I think, though, that the sauce is greatly superior to the careless, pasty egg sauce we so often produce in our kitchens. If you're in too much of a hurry to follow Ali-Bab's careful instructions, don't take refuge in 'white sauce' but turn to Eliza Acton's melted butter recipe on p. 24, and add chopped hard-boiled egg.

Another point for care is the haddock itself. I would suggest that unless you can buy Finnan haddock, the dish is not worth preparing. So much 'smoked fillet' on sale is neither haddock nor smoked: it's been dyed bright yellow, and flavoured artificially to give the illusion of having been exposed to the fire. Apart from the coarse taste, it can give one indigestion and is to be avoided. Finnan haddock are split like kippers to expose the most beautiful flesh, coloured in tones from silvery fawn to rich tan. A great treat.

6 servings:

3 Finnan haddock (approx. 2 lb.)	1 small carrot, chopped
about 1½ pints milk	1 small onion, chopped
sauce:	1 small turnip, chopped
generous 6 oz. butter	*bouquet garni*
3½ oz. double cream	chopped parsley
¼ pint milk, heated	lemon juice
1 oz. flour	nutmeg
2 hard-boiled eggs	salt, freshly ground pepper

Make the sauce first. Melt 1½ oz. of the butter in a heavy saucepan, and cook the vegetables in it until they are lightly coloured but not brown. Stir in the flour, and after 2 minutes add the hot milk gradually. It will make a rather liquid sauce, but don't worry – it should simmer slowly for a long time getting thicker as the moisture evaporates. Put in the *bouquet garni*, and a light seasoning of salt, pepper and nutmeg.

When the sauce has been cooking for 30 minutes, put the haddock into a large flat pan (a roasting tin does very well) and cover with the milk. Bring gently to simmering point, and keep the liquid at this temperature until the haddock is cooked. Approximately 20 minutes altogether, but this naturally depends on how slowly the milk is brought to the boil.

As the haddock finishes cooking, sieve the sauce into a clean pan set over a moderate heat. Beat in the cream and the remaining butter, and correct the seasoning with salt, pepper, nutmeg and a little lemon juice. Crush the hard-boiled eggs with a fork and stir them into the sauce at the very last moment of all, with some chopped parsley.

Put the haddock on to a serving dish, surround with plainly boiled potatoes finished with butter and parsley, and pour a little of the sauce over the fish, serving the rest on a sauceboat.

(From *Gastronomie Pratique*, Ali-Bab.)

Note: don't throw away the haddock-milk, or the sauce vegetables. Simmer them together with the haddock bones, then sieve into a clean pan (the carrot will add an appetizing orange tone), season, and thicken with 2 egg yolks beaten up in ¼ pint of cream. A marvellous soup. Don't let it boil after the yolks and cream have been added.

Omelette Arnold Bennett

The Savoy Hotel in the Strand was the scene of Arnold Bennett's novel, *Imperial Palace* (see also p. 106). He knew it well, and often had late supper there when he was writing as theatre critic. One of his favourite dishes was this omelette, which still appears regularly on the menu.

3–4 servings:

½ lb. cooked, flaked Finnan haddock	salt, pepper
	6 eggs
2 tablespoons grated Parmesan	a little butter
	3 tablespoons double cream

Mix fish and cheese, and season. Beat eggs and cook omelette with a little butter in the usual way. When it is almost ready but still fairly liquid on top, spread the fish mixture over it. Pour on the cream, and place under a hot grill for a few minutes until slightly browned and bubbling. Slide on to a warm serving plate without folding the omelette over.

Caisses à la Florence

Don't be put off by the strange-sounding combination of ingredients on this recipe from *The Gentle Art of Cookery*, by Mrs C. F. Leyel and Miss Olga Hartley. It's particularly delicious if you take trouble to use Finnan haddock, and I would suggest that you set aside 4–8 oz. when preparing the recipe for *Haddock with Egg Sauce* on p. 363.

You will also need a packet of very large prunes (for instance Epicure Giant Prunes, which can be found in health food stores), about 3 tablespoons of double cream, salt, cayenne pepper, and some oblong pieces of bread fried in butter.

Soak and stone the prunes if necessary (some prunes these days are sold free of stones, and plump with juice). Mash the cooked haddock up with the cream to make a smooth paste, flavour with cayenne pepper and with salt if necessary. (If the haddock has not previously been cooked, pour boiling water over it, and leave over a low heat or in a moderate oven (mark 4; 350°F.) for 10 minutes.)

Stuff the prunes – allowing 3 or 4 per person – with the haddock mixture. Arrange them by twos or threes on the fried bread, and heat them through in a moderate oven (mark 4; 350°F.). They don't need to cook, nor do they need to be more than comfortably warm.

Kedgeree

This favourite Victorian breakfast dish was a convenient assemblage of yesterday's cold fish and yesterday's cold boiled rice. Unless the cook had a generous hand with the butter, I feel it was not always an inspiriting start to the day. The dish is based on Indian cookery, but the name is closer to the Hindi name, *khichri*, than to the recipe for it. *Khichri* was – and is – a mixture of rice and lentils with various seasonings; it might be eaten with fish or meat, or it might be eaten on its own. By whose genius the final dish was evolved, I do not know; but one thing is sure, *kedgeree* made with freshly cooked smoked haddock and freshly cooked rice is an excellent dish – not for breakfast perhaps, but for lunch or supper. I've tried a number of different recipes, and always come back to this one of Elizabeth David's from *Spices, Salt and Aromatics in the English Kitchen*. Her quantities are for two or three people.

2–3 servings:

3 smoked haddock fillets	2 tablespoons of sultanas or
2 tablespoons olive oil	currants
1 medium onion, sliced	salt, pepper
4 heaped tablespoons of rice:	2 hard-boiled eggs
Basmati, preferably	parsley, butter
scant teaspoon of curry	lemon quarters and mango
powder	chutney

Pour boiling water over the haddock. Drain after 2 or 3 minutes. Remove the skin and divide into pieces.

Fry the onion in olive oil, in a heavy frying pan or sauté pan, until pale yellow. Stir in the curry powder, then the unwashed rice, then the sultanas. Pour in 1 pint water. Boil steadily but not too fast for

10 minutes. Put in the haddock. Finish cooking – about 10 more minutes – until the rice is tender and the liquid gone. Stir with a fork towards the end, so that the rice doesn't stick to the pan. Taste for seasoning, and add salt if necessary. Turn on to a hot serving dish. Put chopped eggs on top and some parsley, plus a good sized piece of butter. Serve with lemon quarters and chutney.

Note. Bloaters or kippers can be used instead of smoked haddock. Left-over salmon also makes a good kedgeree: of course it doesn't need a preliminary cooking, just add it at the end so that it heats through properly.

Some cooks advocate the addition of cream or an egg yolk. I think this is a good idea when making a kedgeree from leftovers – i.e. when you are reheating the rice and fish in butter without Elizabeth David's loving details. Curry powder is not usually added to this version of the dish, nor are sultanas and currants.

Canned Sardines

Sardines were the first fish to be canned: in 1834, many years before the Canadians started on salmon. They are still, with anchovies, the first in flavour too. This is because methods of canning have produced not just a poor substitute for the real thing (like canned crab and lobster) but a product worth eating in its own right.

From the north to the south of Europe, and to north Africa, one can make a choice between many brands, offering roughly three kinds of sardine.

In Portugal, Spain and North Africa, the fish are large – a little too large, perhaps. They are steamed in oil, and packed in the same oil. The trade to Great Britain is enormous, particularly from Portugal. Marie Elisabeth is the brand to look for, partly on account of the excellent olive oil used, but also because the sardines have been allowed to mature for a year in the can before being sent for sale. This is important. The ideal thing with all sardines is to make a store of them, and turn them regularly every few months, using them in rotation: this gives the olive oil and fish juices a chance to intermingle, to the benefit of the flavour of the sardine.

From France come the finest, most delicate of all sardines. They are mainly a Breton product, the direct descendants of the old salted sardines of pre-canning days. These fish, slightly smaller than Portuguese sardines, have been brined, beheaded and gutted, rinsed in sea water, and dried in currents of warm air. They are then lightly cooked in olive oil, before being packed in fresh olive oil with aromatics. The quality of the French product depends on coolness – on the coolness of the waters from which the fish are caught, on the coolness of the climate of Nantes, Douarnenez and Concarneau where they are processed. For these considerations, one has to pay a little more. A favourite brand is Rodel.

The third category is the brisling, that tiny fish which is really a sprat and not a sardine at all. Smoking is what gives the individual flavour. They are eaten in the same way as sardines, and most people think of them as Skipper's sardines, whatever the law says about nomenclature (they are conscientiously described on the label as Norwegian smoked brisling).

One can do a number of things with sardines, but I cannot recommend any of the made-up recipes. There is always another fish – herring, or the anchovy – which would produce a better result. The thing is to find a good brand of sardines and serve them on their own with proper bread, fine butter and some lemon; or as part of a mixed hors d'oeuvre. In France they sometimes come to table in their can (to show you are being given a decent brand). Once upon a time the French firm of Amieux had specially decorated plates made for them, but you won't find them outside a secondhand shop. The best you can do is to arrange the fish on a round plate like the spokes of a wheel, tails to centre, with some parsley or lemon quarters in the middle. The remainder of the can should be mashed with unsalted butter to make the fish paste on p. 387.

Anchovies

The other day the fishmonger gave me a handful of fresh anchovies, (*Engraulis encrasicholus*, a species related to the herring family). They had come, muddled into a load of sprats, from Brixham – which quite often happens in winter months – and were the same length. The heads have a more pointed appearance: the bodies are slimmer, and rounded. We grilled them and ate them with rye bread and butter, and a seasoning of lemon juice. They were not so fat as sprats, nor so finely flavoured as herrings or the fresh sardines we buy in France.

I suspect that they should be eaten straight from the sea as they are in Italy. On Ischia they are boned and baked in olive oil, flavoured with origano; lemon juice is squeezed over them just before serving. Sometimes they are laid on a bed of breadcrumbs, covered with a 'piecrust' of crumbs and cheese bound together with olive oil, and seasoned with garlic, capers and olives. Rather like some of the baked sardine recipes (see p. 175).

It seems, too, that absolute freshness is necessary for good anchovy preserving, because they quickly disappear after a catch is landed. There are small family businesses in the various ports, each with its own 'secret' variation of the recipe. If you are on holiday in the Mediterranean, it's worth seeking out the local anchovies. One of the best presents I ever had was a large tin of whole, salted anchovies, which my sister brought back from Collioure near Perpignan. The small picturesque port – don't trip over the easels – is mainly devoted to anchovy, sardine and tunny fishing. Similar anchovies in salt may be bought from Italian delicatessen stores sometimes (the best ones come from Gorgona, an island off the Tuscan coast at Leghorn). Before use, they have to be filleted and soaked for several hours, but the flavour is delicious. The oblong tins of anchovies on sale here are more convenient, but tiny; it's pleasing to have a bottomless pit of anchovies in the larder for a change. (Incidentally 'Norwegian anchovies' are really sprats, put down in salt and bay leaves.)

The antiquity of the trade pleases me. It goes back to the ancient Greeks and Romans who relied heavily on a sauce called *garum* or *liquamen* (*garon* is Greek for shrimp, but many other fish were used, including the anchovy). The intestines, liver and blood were pickled in salt, the superb Mediterranean sea salt which still makes a moon landscape of shining white on many parts of the coast. After weeks in the hot sun a dark rich essence was produced and sold in trade-marked bottles. I read recently that a similar product was used in Turkey, for marinating fish, until the last century.

Anyone who has looked at Rosemary Brissenden's *South East Asian Food* (Penguin) will notice the ubiquity of fish sauce in Thai cooking. It seems the precise equivalent of *garum*. So does the Nuoc

Mam of Vietnam. Mrs Brissenden also describes *blachan* or *trasi*, used all over South East Asia, as being 'made from prawns or shrimps, salted, dried, pounded and rotten, then formed into cakes'; as substitute she recommends anchovy or shrimp paste. Right back to 5th century Athens. All these fishy sauces were and are used to enhance meat dishes, rather as the Chinese use soy sauce.

I trust this will encourage you to believe me when I suggest that anchovies and anchovy essence can enrich our own meat cookery. If you have ever eaten pork pies from the Melton Mowbray area, you were not I expect aware that they were probably seasoned with anchovy essence. Try it to flavour a steak and kidney stew or pie. (Substitute it for oysters, which are now too expensive to be used recklessly as a seasoning, as they once were.) If you have no wine, anchovy essence wonderfully improves a shin of beef stew. Anchovy mayonnaise (p. 374) goes well with cold beef and baked potatoes.

With vegetables, less persuasion is needed. Most people know and like cauliflower boiled in the usual way, then dressed with anchovies, melted butter and breadcrumbs (or chicory, or Florentine fennel, or celery). The finest of such dishes comes from Piedmont:

Peperoni Alla Bagna Cauda (peppers with *bagna cauda* sauce)

6 servings:

sauce:
3 cloves of garlic, chopped
3 oz. each butter and olive oil
8 anchovy fillets chopped
white Italian truffle, sliced
   (optional)

thick cream (optional)
salad:
4 large tomatoes, peeled
2 lb. red peppers
6 anchovy fillets
1 large clove garlic, chopped

Grill the peppers until the skin blackens and can be removed. Cut into strips, discarding seeds and stalk. Arrange with the sliced tomatoes on a dish; top with garlic and fillets of anchovy. To make the sauce, cook the garlic gently in butter and oil; beat in the crushed anchovy fillets and simmer for 10 minutes. (Off the heat add truffles, and cream to taste.) Pour hot over the salad, and serve immediately.

Some of the sauce, embellished with some roughly chopped tomato, may be put into peppers which are then baked for 30–40 minutes in a moderate to fairly hot oven (mark 4–5; 350°–375°F.).

Often the sauce is served, fondue-style, in a pot over a table-burner (*bagna cauda* means hot bath). Round it are piles of raw crisp vegetables, which are dipped into it before eating.

This type of dish demands a coarse red wine. *Barbera* is the natural choice in Piedmont.

Two other vegetable dishes from southern Europe, *pizza* and *pissaladière*, demand anchovies as their essential flavouring. I have seen English recipes for *pizza* suggesting the use of kipper fillets instead (the whole thing built up on a scone dough), but this is a typical example of the way we seem doomed to misunderstand and spoil the dishes of other countries by taming them down. Kipper is delicious, but it does not have the much-in-little piquancy of the anchovy, the almost incorporeal sharpness. It's bulky and bland by comparison.

Pizza

The chief difference between Italian – or rather Neapolitan – pizza and *pissaladière* is the use of mozzarella cheese, and either basil or origano. Apart of course from the basis, which is bread dough. If you can't buy or make some bread dough, don't be seduced by the propaganda of the easy-cooks into thinking that a scone dough will do instead. Better to use pastry and make a *pissaladière*.

6 servings:

bread dough, made with approximately 1 lb. flour	½ tin anchovy fillets
filling:	½ lb. sliced mozzarella cheese
generous ½ lb. tomatoes	origano, or basil
sugar, pepper, salt to taste	olive oil

When the dough has doubled in bulk, flatten it down and spread it on an oiled baking tray, in either one or two pieces according to your convenience.

Peel and slice the tomatoes (well-drained canned tomatoes can be used) and lay them over the dough, sprinkling enthusiastically with black pepper, and less enthusiastically with sugar (both help to compensate for the lack of sun: if you're using really first class tomatoes, say on holiday in France, Spain or Italy, omit the sugar and go gently with the pepper). Arrange the mozzarella cheese, chopped anchovy fillets, and origano, or marjoram, over the top. Sprinkle with a little olive oil. Bake in a very hot oven (mark 9; 475°F.) for 30 minutes. Serve immediately, as the whole thing toughens if kept waiting around, snack-bar style.

SICILIANA. Substitute some capers and black olives for the cheese.

ALLE COZZE. Bake the *pizza* without cheese or anchovies. Include some garlic, finely chopped with the tomatoes. Open 2–3 lb. mussels, in a large pan with a little olive oil and parsley, and spread over the cooked *pizza* immediately before serving. Clams (*vongole*) can be used instead.

Pissaladière

If you're a cook living in the Mediterranean area, the sun does half the work for you. Tomatoes and onions have acquired a concentration of sweet richness; olive oil, olives and anchovies flavour them to perfection. This combination is well known to us all in the form of the *pizza* (p. 371), which has sadly become a cliché, now, of snack bars and cookery demonstrations, and as tasteless as you'd expect. For this reason I'm concentrating on *pissaladière*, which is less known. I happen to prefer the filling when set off by pastry rather than by bread dough as in the *pizza*; and it's easier for most housewives to make; unless they bake their own bread, in which case *pizza* can be one of the delicious side-products.

Pissaladière comes from the area of Nice, where they use a conserve of anchovies flavoured with cloves called *pissala*, rather than anchovy fillets. *Pissala* is the modern descendant of those vigorous Roman confections known as *garum* or *liquamen*; they were made of anchovies, or anchovies and various other fish, pickled and fermented in brine, and were used in many dishes, as a kind of antique monosodium glutamate. *Pizza*, which sounds rather the same, means pie, so any connection between the two words is probably coincidental. Both, after all, are made in areas where tomatoes, olive oil, olives and anchovies are to be had in abundance. You don't need to be a diffusionist to arrive at similar dishes.

6 servings:

shortcrust pastry, made with 8 oz. flour, and seasoned with a teaspoon of cinnamon	1 tablespoon tomato concentrate
filling:	2 lumps sugar
6 tablespoons olive oil	*bouquet garni*
2 lb. onions, sliced	4 oz. black olives
3 cloves garlic, crushed	2 tins anchovy fillets, 2 oz. each
14 oz. tin tomatoes	

Line a 10¼-inch to 11-inch flan tin (with a removable base), and bake blind, until the pastry is firm and set, but not brown.

Cook the onions and garlic slowly in the olive oil for an hour, until they're reduced to a soft mass. They must not brown at all (it helps to cover them for the first half hour). In another pan, boil down the tomatoes, sugar, and *bouquet garni*, until the mixture is reduced to about 6 tablespoons of purée. Stir in the concentrate, and remove the *bouquet*. Mix with the onions. Season well, having regard to the saltiness of the anchovies, and spread out evenly over the baked pastry case. Split the anchovy fillets in half lengthwise. Arrange them in a lattice over the filling, then put an olive into each diamond-shaped compartment. Brush over lightly with olive oil. Bake in a fairly hot oven (mark 6; 400°F.) for 20 minutes or so, until the pastry is properly cooked, the filling thoroughly heated, and the olives beginning to wrinkle. Eat hot, cold or warm, with a glass or two of red wine.

It makes marvellous picnic food, particularly if you can manage to bake it just before leaving home. Wrap it loosely in foil, and it should still be warm by early lunch-time. You may find it more convenient to bake small *pissaladières*, as they often do in northern France in the grander *charcuteries*; use patty pans, the ones with almost perpendicular straight sides, and a diameter of 4½ inches. Naturally, more shortcrust pastry will be required; about double the amount.

Haricots à l'Anchoiade

An example of the agreeable southern French habit of eating garlicky mayonnaise sauces with hot food, such as soup, vegetables and fish. *Anchoiade* is often served with boiled salt cod and boiled potatoes. It can also be stirred into fish and tomato soup or fish and saffron soup, instead of a peppery *rouille*. Try it with hard-boiled eggs, instead of the usual mayonnaise. Delicious. Or with baked potatoes and cold beef.

6 servings:

1 lb. haricot beans	1 large egg yolk
1 tin anchovies (9–10 fillets)	¼ pint olive oil
2–3 cloves garlic	chopped parsley

Soak and boil the beans in unsalted water in the usual way. Add salt when the beans are just cooked, and give them another five minutes.

In the meantime pound anchovies, garlic, and egg yolk to a paste. Add the oil (which must be olive oil) gradually, as if you were making a mayonnaise (p. 50). If you use a blender, include some of the egg white when the anchovies, garlic and yolk are being whirled to a paste.

When everyone is ready for the meal, drain the beans and fold in the *anchoiade*. Sprinkle with parsley. *Serve immediately*. The dish can be eaten cold, but the flavours are clearer and lighter when hot.

ANCHOIADE DE CROZE. A splendid elaboration of the simple anchoiade of Provence, which was given – in *Les Plats régionaux de France* – by Count Austin de Croze. In the twenties, he was one of the leaders, with Curnonsky, of the new interest in the food of France outside Paris, and the grand restaurants of the *haute cuisine*.

2 oz. chopped parsley, chives, tarragon	12 anchovies in oil
2 good sprigs green fennel leaves	12 anchovies in brine, washed
2 cloves garlic, chopped	4 or more tablespoons olive oil
1 small onion, chopped	lemon juice
3 dried figs, chopped	1 tablespoon orange-flower water
1 small dried red pepper	12 brioches, bridge rolls or finger rolls
12 blanched almonds	

Mix the first five ingredients. Pound the next four together to a paste. Combine the two mixtures. Add lemon juice to taste, and then the orange-flower water – go slowly because it has a surprisingly dominating flavour. (If you want to do the chopping and pounding in a blender, you will need more olive oil.) Open the brioches, or rolls. Spread the top side with the anchoiade, and brush the bottom side of the cut with olive oil. Close the rolls, and heat for 5–10 minutes at mark 6–7, 400–425°F. Serve surrounded by black olives.

Anchovy Savouries

Nobody, I am sure, needs convincing of the excellence of anchovies when making savouries. Such things, at the end of a copious meal, were much in fashion at the end of the century. Nowadays I think most people serve only a sweet dish, preferably one which has been made well in advance. The trouble with savouries is that they must come straight to the table, without having a chance to lose their piquancy; this means an extra, unseen pair of hands in the kitchen. Such things now are more likely to turn up at the start of a meal; or as a single supper dish. They are far too delicious to lose as people's habits of eating change. Here are three recipes which I am very fond of – first a simple one from *Savouries à la mode*, by Mrs de Salis, which had run into seventeen editions by 1900:

Canapés à la Crème

1 serving:

3–4 anchovy fillets   butter
1 round of bread   1 tablespoon clotted cream

Take the round of bread from a slice half an inch thick, with a large scone cutter. Fry it pale brown in butter (clarified is best). Quickly arrange anchovies on top and place on a very very hot dish. Cover with clotted cream and serve immediately. The contrast between hot crisp bread, sharp anchovy, and cold grainy cream is excellent – whipped cream does not give the same result at all.

Scotch Woodcock

I am not keen on names which give an affected impression of the
reality – rock turbot and rock salmon are two flagrant examples,
however hallowed they may be by antique regional use. Scotch
woodcock is another. In extenuation, I suppose that woodcock has
become as legendary as the phoenix, except to millionaires and
game-keepers: one can hardly be angry at a comparison one is never
likely to be able to make.

This recipe comes from that wonderful book *The Scots Kitchen*,
by F. Marian McNeill. 'Take six small rounds of buttered toast,
spread them with anchovy paste, arrange on a dish and keep hot.
Melt two tablespoons of butter in a saucepan, put in three tablespoons of cream and the raw yolks of three eggs, and stir over
the fire until the mixture is a creamy mass.' (Don't boil, or you will
have scrambled or curdled eggs.) 'Add a little finely chopped
parsley and a dash of cayenne. Heap on the rounds of toast and
serve very hot.' (Anchovy paste can be made by pounding together
anchovies with some unsalted butter – say 2 oz. to the tin.)

Mrs Beeton suggests using ¼ pint cream instead of butter and
cream. In either case, double cream gives the best flavour and
consistency.

Crostini Alla Provatura

An Italian rarebit, improved by anchovies – spectacularly improved.

Provatura was a cheese made from buffalo's milk which has,
according to Elizabeth David's *Italian Food*,[6] almost disappeared
from the market. Certainly Italian shopkeepers in Soho have been
mystified when I've tried to buy it there. Even in Rome, this dish is
now usually made with mozzarella cheese. Other substitutes are bel
paese, Gruyère, and provolone – originally another buffalo milk
cheese, though in fact it is now usually made from cow's milk, like
mozzarella, and is much less tasty in consequence.

The general point of the recipe is to improve cheese-on-toast

[6] Macdonald and Penguin.

with a sauce of anchovies melted in butter. Mrs David's recipe suggests putting slices of cheese – nice thick slices – on rounds of French bread. These are then arranged, slightly overlapping each other, in an ovenproof dish, and put into a fairly hot oven until the bread is crisp and the cheese melted but not runny. For the sauce for 6 to 8 *crostini*, soak 4 or 5 fillets of anchovies in warm water for 10 minutes. Heat them in 2 oz. of butter, having chopped them up first. Pour over the *crostini* and serve immediately.

Ada Boni, this century's Mrs Beeton of Italian cookery, has alternating chunks of cheese and bread on skewers, cooked over a wood fire or in a fairly hot oven (mark 6; 400°F.). The sauce is similar, but the proportion of butter to anchovies is higher.

Incidentally this sauce is excellent with veal or pork tenderloin escalopes, or on vegetables, or slightly dull white fish. Remember that leg of veal to be boiled for *vitello tonnato* is often larded with anchovy fillets. This was common practice in the past, in England, with beef, too.

Jansson's Temptation

The name of this dish is an incitement to culinary myth-making. For instance: 'Eric Janson, the Swedish religious reformer who founded Bishop Hill, Illinois, in 1846, preached rigorous asceticism to his followers, no liquor and a diet that barely sustained life. One day, according to legend, a zealous Jansonist discovered the prophet feasting ...' But as Jansson is a Swedish equivalent of Smith or Jones, why look any further for a meaning than 'Everyone's Temptation?' A gloss which is perfectly convincing when one has tasted this piquant gratin of potatoes, onions, anchovy and cream. Don't use milk instead of cream, as many Swedes do these days, or the beauty of the title will escape you.

6 servings:

3 tins of anchovies	¼ pint single and ¼ pint
2 lb. potatoes	double cream mixed
3 large onions	freshly ground black pepper
	3 oz. butter

Peel and thinly slice the onions. Peel the potatoes and cut them into matchstick strips (a mandolin cutter saves time). Grease a shallow oval gratin dish with a butter paper. Arrange about half the potato strips in an even layer, then make a lattice of the anchovies on top. Cover with the onions and the rest of the potatoes. Season well with pepper only. Pour over the oil from the anchovy tins and half the cream. Dot with the butter and bake in a hot oven (mark 7; 425°F.) for an hour. When the potatoes begin to look appetizingly brown, pour over the rest of the cream. Taste the cooking juices and add salt if necessary. Return to the oven until the potatoes are cooked.

A lunchtime dish, to be followed, prudently, by no more than a salad and some fruit.

Note: the amount of cream can be varied. One recipe calls for a pint of double cream, but this is too much. Half a pint or three-quarters is about right.

The Great Scandinavian Cook Book[7] observes that *matjes* herring fillets or buckling fillets can be used instead of anchovies. So can kipper fillets. But none of them can compare with the sparkling taste of anchovies, which after all are easy enough to buy.

Caviare and other hard Roes

Caviare is a grand and painful subject. It is one of the most delicious, most simple things to eat in the world (and one of the most nutritious, too, but that's an academic point). It is also one of the most expensive. It has an air of mythical luxury – mythical to our modern experience at any rate. The food of Czars, of those incredible tyrants who cherished fine fat fleas and Fabergé knick knacks, while most of their subjects lived in a poverty of indescribable squalor. The mainstay, along with champagne and oysters, of *La Belle Époque*. Odd that the caviare trade should never have been so efficiently organized as now, under the Soviets and their pupils in the business the Iranians.

Another odd thing: caviare isn't a Russian word at all (it's called *ikra* in the USSR). It seems to be a word of Turkish-Italian origin, derived perhaps from the port of Kaffa, on the south-east coast of

[7]Allen & Unwin Ltd., ed. Ellison.

the Crimea, which had been important even in classical times. Under the Genoese, from the mid-13th century, to the mid-15th century when it fell to the Turks, Kaffa was a vast international port, a depot on the trade route to China.

The origins of caviare must be as difficult to trace as the word itself. Aristotle remarked that the sturgeon was prized for its caviare. The Chinese had developed methods of treating and trading in caviare as early as the 10th century A.D. Probably earlier, as they had long used refrigeration to protect delicate foods on journeys across China to the Emperor's court. Edward H. Schafer, Professor of Chinese[8] at Berkeley University, California, sent me this reference from the *T'ai ping huan yü chi*, a 10th century official gazetteer, which says: '. . . at Pa-ling, where the Yangtze river flows out from Lake Tung-t'ing, an area also noted for its tea, the natives catch sturgeon, simmer the roe in an infusion of Gleditschia sinensis seeds (an acacia-like plant, normally used as a black dye), then pickle it in brine . . . extremely delicious!' It sounds like an early form of pasteurization.

I think, though, that one has to look much further back for the origins of caviare. Consider the reality, the basic nature of the product – really no more than the salted hard roe of a sturgeon. Once man came to the skill of being able to trap and catch fish, and to organize a supply of salt, he could not avoid the experience of caviare. Imagine him, squatting over a sturgeon by the mouth of some great grey river on the Baltic or North Sea, slitting up the belly and diving into the incredible mass of eggs – up to 20% of the total weight – with a handful of salt. I'm sure he reflected gratefully that this part at least he could not smoke or dry for winter stores: it must have been a bonus in the hard realities of mesolithic survival. A crude affair by comparison with the finest *malossol* Beluga perhaps but still caviare.

Caviare today is a pampered product compared with those mesolithic feasts. It has to be, because of the problem of conveying a food, which should be eaten immediately, to the far-off societies that can afford it. We've killed our own sturgeon population, and have to look to the Caspian sea, the only place where these vast creatures survive in any quantity. Even there they are in danger

---

[8] Author of *The Golden Peaches of Samarkand*, a study of exotics imported into China in the T'ang dynasty; recommended to anyone who's interested in food, wine, spices etc.

from Russian oil drilling, from hydro-electric stations and from the sinking level of the sea itself. There's also the problem of human greed, politely described as 'over-fishing'. Now, the Caspian sturgeon seek the southern rivers of the sea, the ones flowing down to the Iranian coast, for their spawning. The Persians produce 210 tons of caviare a year, in consequence, which is not so far behind the Russians with 320 tons. They have learned everything they can, from Soviet technicians, about processing caviare, and about farming the fish, and with state control produce caviare of the highest standard. (The Rumanians produce tiny amounts – comparatively speaking – from Black Sea sturgeon; so do the Turks.)

The three main kinds of caviare are called after the species of sturgeon which provide them. The largest-grained and therefore most expensive (the price is based on appearance and not flavour) is taken from the Beluga, *Huso huso*, a giant 12-footer which can live to a 100 years, and which reaches maturity at the same age as a human being. It may – with luck – contain 130 lb. of eggs, from deep grey to a soft moon-white. Next largest are the eggs of the Osetr, *Acipenser gueldenstaedtii*; they are sometimes golden-brown, sometimes greenish, or grey, and are first in flavour with people who know about caviare. The smallest-grained, and therefore the cheapest, comes from the Sevruga, *Acipenser stellatus*: it's the one most widely on sale, and the most reliably steady in flavour.

With these three divisions, caviare is graded. The finest is *malossol*, which means slightly salted. Any of the caviares are best eaten fresh, which is only possible in the largest towns: for the provinces, where trade is not brisk and conditions of storage less ideal, it must be pasteurized. The difference in quality is comparable with the difference between fresh and potted *foie gras* – or between fresh and pasteurized milk and cheese. To me pasteurization spoils the pleasure of eating these foods, because the elusive, vital flavour has been killed.

Caviare is exported fresh in 4 lb. tins, which have been piled up with salted eggs. Sliding lids are placed on top, then gently pressed down at intervals so that all surplus brine is excluded. A rubber band is stretched round to make an air-tight seal. The tins travel in ice in refrigerated containers, to keep the caviare at the correct temperature of 30°F.; one pamphlet observes that it is fatal to put caviare in the deep-freeze: 'it is reduced straightaway to a somewhat expensive soup!' An importer – such as W. G. White Ltd. of

Chapone Place, off Dean Street in Soho – will re-pack it, sending fresh caviare twice a week to London's best hotels and grocers, and putting smaller amounts of pasteurized caviare into little pots, for distribution to delicatessen stores all over the country.

At their offices I was shown the most beautiful of gastronomic spectacles: a tray with three of these tins on it, opened, with a little bowl of Osetr caviare, and a pot of salmon caviare, often known by its Russian name of *keta*. The Beluga in one tin was silky in texture, and lightly delicious. The Sevruga in another tin had a more pronounced and sea-like flavour. The Osetr in the bowl had been pasteurized, so it was difficult to judge if it really was the finest of all: again, the taste was different. The salmon eggs were enormous, and a translucent vermilion. They were certainly the visual stars of the tray by comparison with the Quaker-greys and sombre greens of the caviare, but after the others they tasted bitter. The third tin contained a tacky seaweed-coloured substance, in which the form of the eggs could hardly be seen. This was pressed caviare, made from the damaged eggs of the various species of sturgeon, salted and impacted together. I liked the taste very much, and the slightly toffee-ish substance. Considering that the price is less than half the Sevruga, I recommend it as an ideal candidate for a first sampling of caviare. Everyone needs a celebration occasionally and I think it's worth saving up for caviare: the pressed kind is a possible extravagance for people whose incomes do not quite come up to their appreciation of food. Which, I think, means most of us.

Red caviare is so different. It's delicious enough, like a superior smoked cod's roe, but it's not in the same class as caviare proper. Neither is lumpfish caviare from Iceland or Denmark, which is dyed black like those 10th century roes from the sturgeon of Lake Tung-t'ing (though not with *Gleditschia sinensis* seeds). They're not to be despised, but keep them for lesser occasions.

To serve Caviare

First of all, the amount – allow 1 oz. per person as a decent minimum, 1½ oz. is luxurious. Keep the pot in the refrigerator until required, then place it on a dish and surround with ice. As nothing should impair the delicate flavour of this greatest of all luxuries, avoid wine and vodka. And do not be tempted to mix in some cream cheese to make it go further. All that's required is toast, or water biscuits, or rye bread, or – best of all – the buckwheat *blini* on p. 383.

So much for the finest quality. With lesser grades or pressed caviare, you could add unsalted butter for the toast or rye bread, or melted butter for *blini*. Perhaps some sour cream as well, or lemon juice. Pressed caviare is delicious spread on small split potatoes, baked in their jackets and not larger than duck's eggs (unless you can afford a great deal of caviare).

When it comes to the 'caviare' of other fish, chopped spring onions, hard-boiled eggs, or cream cheese which has not been too processed, can all be added to make a large hors d'oeuvre. And when it's a question of the following recipe for homemade 'caviare', you can experiment as much as you like. Personally I like it quite on its own, too. It's very good, but I won't pretend that it compares with the finest Russian and Iranian product, which has transformed the slightly porridgey quality of hard roe into a most poetic texture.

Caviare Sauce: served with Fine White Fish. See p. 41

Homemade 'Caviare'

My first and best experience of homemade 'caviare' I owe to a fish-monger in Oxford market, who presented me with the unfamiliar grey-crested body of a lump-sucker (otherwise known, being female in this instance, as a hen-paddle). We found that it was stuffed with a vast quantity of eggs, which I didn't count after reading that there might be anything between 80 and 136 thousand of them. It was easy to see how Iceland manages to can and export 32 tons of 'lumpfish caviare' every year. (The rest of the fish was not so good: there's a grey fatty layer between flesh and skin which is difficult to remove, and unpleasant to eat. Apparently the flesh must be smoked; then it tastes all right.)

The strange thing about the eggs is that the male or cock-paddle takes such great care of them, once they've been deposited in rocky crevices above low water-mark, in the spring. As J. R. Norman remarks in *A History of Fishes* (Ernest Benn), there can be few better cases of parental devotion ... 'For weeks and even months he devotes himself to the care of the eggs, fasting rather than leave his post, from time to time pressing his head into the clump of spawn to allow the water to penetrate to the centre, and thus ensuring the proper aeration of the eggs, a process which he further helps by blowing upon them with his mouth and fanning them with his pectoral fins ... While on guard the males have been described as being attacked by rooks and carrion crows, which thrust their sharp beaks through the abdominal walls and feast on the liver of the unfortunate fishes. If removed from the eggs and then released, they will at once rush back to their posts, and after a heavy storm that has swept masses of eggs from their normal positions high up on the beach, as soon as the sea becomes calm again the parents may be seen anxiously searching for their charges.'

Lump-suckers owe this particular name to the powerful suction disc, between the pelvic fins, which enables them to cling tightly to rocks: cock- and hen-paddle refer to the very pronounced crest along its back. Unfortunately you won't find this most interesting creature very often at the fishmonger's. Instead you can use the eggs of the cod, catfish, mullet, salmon, shad, pike, turbot, or whiting – quite a choice.

Remove the membrane from the eggs, and turn them into a basin. Season with salt and freshly ground white pepper, then with a little onion chopped almost to a pulp, some lemon juice, and brandy if you have it to spare. These seasonings should be added to taste.

Serve the eggs with toast and butter, or rye bread. You can give them the full caviare treatment, and make some *blini* from the recipe following. As I have remarked above, hard-boiled eggs, spring onions – both chopped – and some good cream cheese which hasn't been over-processed can all be added if you want to make an hors d'oeuvre.

Russian Buckwheat Pancakes or Blini

In the west, we think of *blini* as the proper accompaniment to caviare, but in Russia they're served with other kinds of preserved fish (and with quite different foods as well – jam, cheese, mushrooms etc.). Although the preparation is lengthy, it's not laborious or painful. The flavour is quite different from our Shrove Tuesday pancakes on account of the yeast – and the buckwheat flour, which can be obtained from good health food stores.

blinis for 6:

6 tablespoons lukewarm water	3 large egg yolks
1 oz. fresh, or ½ oz. dried yeast	good pinch salt
	1 teaspoon sugar
½ lb. plain flour ⎫ or ¾ lb.	¼ lb. melted butter
¼ lb. buckwheat flour ⎬ plain flour	3 scant tablespoons sour cream
¾ pint lukewarm milk ⎭	3 egg whites

Fork yeast and lukewarm water together; leave for 10 minutes, until it froths up. Put the plain flour and half the buckwheat flour into a large warm mixing bowl. Make a well in the middle and pour in the yeast mixture, then ½ pint of the milk. Beat to a smooth batter. Leave for 3 hours, covered, in a warm place – the rack of a solid fuel stove is ideal, but anywhere out of a draught will do. Next stir in the rest of the buckwheat flour, and leave again for two hours. Beat together lightly the egg yolks, sugar, salt, cream and 3 scant tablespoons of the melted butter. Add to the dough, mixing well. Whisk the egg whites stiff, then fold them in carefully. Leave for half an hour.

Have a baking tray, lined with a clean cloth, in a warm oven. Take a large, preferably non-stick, frying pan or griddle, and brush it over with melted butter. Cook the batter in the usual way, allowing a couple of tablespoons or so per pancake, which should be about 3 inches across when done: several can be done at once if the pan is large. When bubbles begin to show through on the upper side, after a couple of minutes or so, brush with butter and turn over. Keep the cooked pancakes warm on the baking tray in the oven, while you cook the rest.

Serve with a big bowl of sour cream, another bowl of melted butter, and dishes of black caviare, or red caviare, or homemade 'caviare'. Smoked salmon, smoked sturgeon, and smoked cod's roe provide excellent alternatives: so do the Danish pickled herrings on p. 351. Sliced kipper, served raw with lemon juice, makes another good filling.

Botargo

Another hard roe luxury. This time provided by the grey mullet, like the true *taramasalata* (p. 386). The roes are salted, dried, pressed into black-skinned, orange-brown firmness, a salami firmness; perfectly adapted, unlike caviare, to the hot climate of the Mediterranean, and the exigencies of transport in all weathers. In Italy *bottarga* or *buttariga* is served in thin slices with bread, and either olive oil or butter; sometimes with fresh figs, like Parma ham. In southern France *poutargue* is a speciality of Martigues: it is eaten in thin strips with a seasoning of pepper, olive oil and lemon juice. Sometimes it is added, anchovy style, to salads of haricot beans or chick peas to give them piquancy. It was once a popular import here, in England. On June 5th, 1661, Pepys remarks in his *Diary* that he and Sir William Penn, father of Pennsylvania Penn, made their way home after a sociable evening with friends. It was so hot that they went out upon the leads in the garden, Sir William in his shirt sleeves. Pepys played his 'flagilette' and the two men stayed there 'talking and singing and drinking of great draughts of Clarret and eating botargo and bread and butter till 12 at night, it being moon-shine'. Next day Pepys had a dreadful headache – but not, I think, from botargo.

It's difficult to find botargo in England nowadays. The best thing is to look out for it if you are visiting Paris, or the Mediterranean countries, and bring it home as a souvenir. Or you can make it. Claudia Roden, who writes about *batarekh* from her Egyptian experience, in *Middle Eastern Food* (Penguin), gives a couple of recipes. One came from Canada, where in Montreal at least one may buy frozen grey mullet roes. In Britain, fresh cod roes have to do instead.

Make sure, before you buy them, that the skins of the roes are perfectly undamaged. Roll them in kitchen or sea salt, and lay them on a wad of absorbent paper. As the paper becomes damp, put a fresh wad down and turn over and salt the roes again. When the paper is at last dry, after several days, hang the roes up in a good draught (steamy kitchens are to be avoided, as always, for drying food). Leave them for 8 days or so, until they're hard and dry. They can now be eaten, or stored in a refrigerator in tightly-sealed polythene bags. Miss Roden remarks that the drying process can be hurried up by putting the roes into a turned-off warm oven from time to time; leave the door open. The danger is that the botargo may over-dry to crumbliness.

A quicker recipe makes use of smoked cod's roe. Put it into the oven, when it's been turned off, from time to time, and hang it up in a dry airy place between whiles. This takes only a few days and little effort.

Taramasalata

The pride of the Abbazia di Loreto, an 18th century monastery of curves and colour at the back of Vesuvius, is the pharmacy. The original 300 majolica jars stand elegantly on the shelves. Even more elegant is the mortar, placed in the centre of one wall. I suppose that mortars were the main piece of equipment in a pharmacy in those days. This one takes the form of a hollowed out Corinthian capital, decorated with gold, and mounted on a waist-high column of pink marble. How much time people had then, how many people were needed about the place, how hard and steadily they worked.

Taramasalata belongs to that pestle and mortar life, which survives, in part at least, in Greece and Turkey still. It's a cream salad, like the *tahina* salads on p. 60. And I'm sure it wouldn't be as popular with us as it is, if electric beaters and liquidizers hadn't come to save work in so many kitchens. And yet, when we first ate *taramasalata* 20 years ago, the head waiter declared that it had been made by hand: 'Downstairs in the kitchen. Here.' I believe him now – I was sceptical at the time – because however I vary proportions and method, I never quite achieve the cool, granular texture of his hand-made *taramasalata*. But it's still delicious and worth making:

6 servings:

4 oz. *tarama* (salted grey mullet roe) or smoked cod roe	1 clove garlic, crushed, or 1 tablespoon chopped onion
$\frac{1}{2}$ inch thick slice of bread	$\frac{1}{2}$–$\frac{3}{4}$ pint olive or corn oil
	juice of 1–2 lemons
	black olives or capers

If you're using a piece of cod's roe, remove the skin first. Soak *tarama* or cod's roe in water for an hour or two to abate the saltiness. Moisten the bread with a little water so that it turns to a thickish paste (cut the crusts off first), then put it into the blender with garlic or onion, and enough oil to keep the mixture moving. Gradually add the *tarama*, or roe, and the oil, alternately to the blender. Should the mixture become unworkably stiff, put in a spoonful or two of water. The amount of oil required depends on your taste and the consistency of the *taramasalata*. Finally season with lemon juice.

If you intend to use an electric beater, it's a good idea to start off with an egg yolk. Beat it with a little lemon juice, then add the bread, garlic or onion, and roe, gradually in small amounts, lubricating the mixture with olive oil or corn oil. This mayonnaise technique ensures that the oil doesn't separate at all from the mixture.

Serve on a dish, well-chilled, and garnished with black olives. Thin toast or bread go with it. *Taramasalata* is also good when served in small pre-cooked pastry boats or tartlets and decorated with capers. Make sure the pastry is thin and crisp, and don't put the *taramasalata* into it more than an hour or two before the meal.

Smoked Fish Paste

Bloater paste makes me think of old-fashioned tea-times, when we made toast in front of the fire and ate it with butter and Gentleman's Relish or some other confection of the kind. Now such things are served as a first course, with thin slices of baked bread or melba toast, something piquant to begin a dinner party. Not too expensive either.

Kipper, Finnan haddock and bloaters need a slight cooking, so pour boiling water over them and leave for 10 minutes before removing skin and bones. Other smoked fish such as buckling, smoked trout, salmon, mackerel, or smoked cod's roe, need no such treatment. Fish tinned in oil – sardines, particularly the small smokey-flavoured *Skippers* brisling, and tunny – should be well drained, before using.

The general principle is to weigh the prepared fish, and pound it with an equal weight of unsalted butter. A blender or moulinette make this task easy, so long as the butter is slightly softened and pasty *but not melted*. Lemon juice is the principal seasoning;

cayenne pepper, in a small quantity, is important to counteract the bland smoothness.

Many recipes substitute whipped cream, or cream cheese, for part of the butter; this makes a light-textured paste, for immediate consumption. The advantage of the butter-only recipe is that the potted paste can be sealed with a layer of clarified butter and stored in the refrigerator; cover with foil to prevent the butter from drying away from the edges of the pot, and spoiling the seal.

Note: when making scrambled eggs, serve them with, or on, toast spread with bloater, kipper or haddock paste.

Comparative Cookery Terms and Measures

It is not simple to convert with absolute accuracy measurements for the kitchen. Generally speaking, absolute accuracy is not required, except when making cakes or pastries. Throughout this book British measurements have been used.

Fortunately for the cook, British and American solid weights are equivalent; but this does not always mean that the British housewife can readily understand American measurements or *vice versa*. In the United States the average housewife has her set of measuring spoons and cups. In Britain this is never so general, although most housewives do have a measuring cup or jug.

Liquid Measures

BRITISH

1 quart	= 2 pints	= 40 fluid oz.
1 pint	= 4 gills	= 20 fl. oz.
½ pint	= 2 gills	
	or one cup	= 10 fl. oz.
¼ pint	= 8 tablespoons	= 5 fl. oz.
	1 tablespoon	= just over ½ fl. oz.
	1 dessertspoon	= ⅓ fl. oz.
	1 teaspoon	= ⅙ fl. oz.

METRIC

1 litre = 10 decilitres (dl) = 100 centilitres (cl) = 1000 millilitres (ml)

Approx. equivalents

BRITISH	METRIC
1 quart	1·1 litre
1 pint	6 dl
½ pint	3 dl
¼ pint (1 gill)	1·5 dl
1 tablespoon	15 ml
1 dessertspoon	10 ml
1 teaspoon	5 ml

METRIC	BRITISH
1 litre	35 fl. oz.
½ litre (5 dl)	18 fl. oz.
¼ litre (2·5 dl)	9 fl. oz.
1 dl	3½ fl. oz.

AMERICAN

1 quart = 2 pints	= 32 fl oz.
1 pint = 2 cups	= 16 fl. oz.
1 cup	= 8 fl. oz.
1 tablespoon =	⅓ fl. oz.
1 teaspoon =	⅙ fl. oz.

Approx. equivalents

BRITISH	AMERICAN
1 quart	2½ pints
1 pint	1¼ pints
½ pint	10 fl. oz. (1¼ cups)
¼ pint (1 gill)	5 fl. oz.
1 tablespoon	1½ tablespoons
1 dessertspoon	1 tablespoon
1 teaspoon	⅓ fl. oz.

AMERICAN	BRITISH
1 quart	½ pint + 3 tbs. (32 fl. oz.)
1 pint	¾ pint + 2 tbs. (16 fl. oz.)
1 cup	½ pint − 2 tbs. (8 fl. oz.)

Solid Measures

BRITISH

16 oz. = 1 lb.

METRIC

1000 grammes = 1 kilogramme

Approx. equivalants

BRITISH	METRIC
1 lb. (16 oz.)	400 grammes
½ lb. (8 oz.)	200 g
¼ lb. (4 oz.)	100 g
1 oz.	25 g

METRIC	BRITISH
1 kilo (1000 g)	2 lb. 3 oz.
½ kilo (500 g)	1 lb. 2 oz.
¼ kilo (250 g)	9 oz.
100 g	3½ oz.

Temperature Equivalents for Oven Thermostat Markings

FAHRENHEIT	GAS MARK	CENTIGRADE
225°F.	¼	110°C.
250°F.	½	130°C.
275°F.	1	140°C.
300°F.	2	150°C.
325°F.	3	170°C.
350°F.	4	180°C.
375°F.	5	190°C.
400°F.	6	200°C.
425°F.	7	220°C.
450°F.	8	230°C.
475°F.	9	240°C.

Glossary of Fish Names

The disadvantage of all fish cookery books is that many more fish have to be left out than can be put in. This glossary is to help anyone who comes across an unfamiliar, or unfamiliarly named fish. Although it is based on the *Multilingual Dictionary of Fish and Fish Products*, compiled by the OECD, it's intended for the cook and not the scientist. As well as an encouragement, it is also a warning to be wary of the many names which include – misleadingly – the words sole, trout, salmon and turbot.

Key:
The usual name of a fish with an entry in the book stands alone, e.g.
   Turbot

An alternative local name is followed by the usual name of the fish in brackets, or the name of the group to which it belongs, or its recommended trade name. Additional names in *italics* will give suitable cooking methods when the book does not give any for the fish itself, e.g.
   Britt (turbot)
   Rock turbot (catfish)
   Rock salmon
      (i dogfish)
      (ii saithe; *cod*)
      (iii catfish)
      (iv US Pacific ocean perch; *sea bass*)
   Owl ray (skate)

Abalone
Abbot
   (i Angel shark, and
   ii monkfish)
Aberdeen smokie
Alaska deep sea crab (crab)

Alaska plaice (plaice)
Alaska pollack (*cod*)
Albacore (tunny)
Alewife (shad)
Allice shad (shad)
Allison's tuna (tunny)

Allis shad
Allmouth (monkfish)
Amberjacks (*mackerel, pompano*)
American butterfish (pomfret; *sea bream*)
American eel (*eel*)
American goosefish (*monkfish*)
American John Dory (John Dory)
American plaice (plaice)
American sand lance (sand lance)
American shad (shad)
American smelt (smelt)
Anchovy
Angelfish
   (i angel shark; *monkfish, shark*)
   (ii monkfish)
   (iii Ray's bream; *sea bream*)
Angel shark (*monkfish, shark*)
Anglerfish (monkfish)
Arbroath smokie
Arctic char
Arctic cod (cod)
Arctic flounder (flounder; *flat-fish recipes*)
Arctic lamprey (*eel*)
Arctic smelt (smelt)
Argentine
Armed gurnard (*gurnard*)
Arrowtooth flounder (flounder; *flat-fish recipes*)
Atherine
Atlantic bonito (tunny)
Atlantic moonfish (*scad, pompano*)
Auchmithie cure (Arbroath smokie)
Axillary bream (*sea bream*)

Bacalao and baccala (salt cod)
Baked herring (soused herring)
Balao (*garfish*)
Ballan wrasse (*soup, gurnard*)
Baltic herring (Swedish cured herring)
Banded guitarfish (skate)

Banded rudderfish (*mackerel, pompano*)
Banjo (skate)
Bar clam (clam)
Barracoutas (*tunny*)
Barracuda (*mackerel, pompano*)
Barred Spanish mackerel (*mackerel*)
Bass (sea bass)
Bastard brill (topknot; *brill*)
Bastard sole (thickback; *sole*)
Bay scallop (scallop)
Beaumaris shark (porbeagle)
Becker (pandora; *sea bream*)
Beleke (Indian cure salmon. US)
Belted bonito (tunny)
Beluga (sturgeon; *tunny*)
Beluga caviare (caviare)
Berghilt, berghylt and bergylt
   (i ballan wrasse; *soup, gurnard*)
   (ii redfish)
Bib (pout; *soup, cod*)
Bigeye tuna (tunny)
Bigscale pomfret (*sea bream*)
Billfish (garfish and saury)
Bismarck herring
Blackback (*flat-fish*)
Black bass (freshwater; *river fish recipes*)
Black caviare (caviare)
Black cod (saithe; *cod*)
Black croaker (croaker)
Black dogfish (dogfish)
Black drum (drum)
Blackfish (carp, pike, shad etc.)
Black fin (sea trout)
Black grouper (*sea bass*)
Black hake (hake)
Black halibut (Greenland or mock halibut; *halibut*)
Black jewfish (sea bass)
Black-mouthed dogfish (dogfish)
Black mullet (grey mullet)
Black pollack (saithe; *cod*)

Black salmon (Chinook salmon)
Black sea bass (sea bass)
Black sea bream (sea bream)
Black skipjack (tunny)
Black snapper (*red snapper*)
Black sole (sole)
Blacktail (sea trout)
Bloater
Blochan (saithe; *cod*)
Bloch's topknot (topknot)
Blonde (skate)
Blueback (Coho salmon, or
    Sockeye salmon)
Blueback herring (shad)
Blue cod (ling, *cod*)
Blue crab (crab)
Blue Dog
    (i porbeagle)
    (ii picked dogfish)
Bluefin tuna (tunny)
Bluefish
Blue halibut (Greenland or mock
    halibut)
Blue ling (ling, *cod*)
Blue mussel (mussel)
Blue pike (pike-perch, *pike*)
Blue point oyster (oyster)
Blue runner (scad, pompano)
Blue sea cat (catfish)
Blue shrimp (shrimp)
Blue skate (skate)
Blue spotted bream (sea bream)
Bluet (skate)
Boddam cure (smoked haddock)
Bogue (sea bream)
Bokkem
Bonito (tunny)
Bordered skate (skate)
Boston bluefish (saithe; *cod*)
Boston mackerel (salted mackerel)
Bottarga and botargo
Bottlenose skate (skate)
Brailles (Dutch cured herring)
Braize (sea bream)

Branco cure (Portuguese salt cod)
Bratbuckling (German cured
    herring)
Bratfischwaren, Bratheringsfilet,
    bratheringshappen, and
    bratheringe (German soused
    herring)
Bratrollmops (German soused
    herring)
Brazilian shrimp (shrimp)
Bream (freshwater; *river fish
    recipes*)
Breet (turbot)
Brett (brill)
Brisling (Scandinavian name for
    sprat)
Brismak (tusk; *cod*)
Brisoletten (German fish cakes)
Brit (brill)
Britt (turbot)
Broad bill (swordfish)
Broad-nosed eel (eel)
Brook char (char)
Brook lamprey (*eel*)
Brook silverside (atherine)
Brook trout (char)
Brown shrimp (shrimp)
Brown tiger prawn (prawn.
    shrimp. US)
Brown trout (sea trout. US)
Browny (topknot)
Buckie (whelk)
Bückling
Bücklingsfilet (fillets of buckling)
Buck mackerel (horse mackerel)
Buffalo cod (lingcod; *cod*)
Bull huss (dogfish)
Bull trout (sea trout)
Burbot (*riverfish, pike, etc.*)
Burton skate (skate)
Butt (turbot)
Butter clam (clam)
Butterfish (pomfret; *sea bream*)
Butterfly skate (skate)

Cabrilla (sea bass)
Calamari (squid)
Calico salmon (Chum salmon)
Calico scallop (scallop)
California corbina (king whiting,
    or in US kingfish; *mackerel,
    pompano, sea bream*)
California halibut (flounder;
    halibut)
Californian bluefin (tunny)
Californian bonito (tunny)
Californian grunion (atherine)
Californian pilchard (pilchard)
Californian scorpionfish (*soups,
    gurnard*)
California round herring (*herring*)
California sole (lemon sole)
California yellowtail (tunny)
Callagh (pollack; *cod*)
Cape Cod scallop (scallop)
Carpet shell
Carp
Carter (megrim)
Catfish
Cavalla (*pompano*)
Caveached fish (escabeche)
Caviare
Cero (kingfish; *mackerel, pompano*)
Chad (sea bream)
Chain dogfish (dogfish)
Chain pickerel (pike)
Channel bass (drum; *sea bass*)
Channel catfish (freshwater catfish;
    river fish)
Chars
Chat haddock (haddock)
Cherrystone (clam)
Chicken halibut
Chilean hake (hake)
Chilean pilchard (pilchard)
Chinook (salmon)
Chub (whitefish)
Chub mackerel (Spanish mackerel)
Chub salmon (Chinook salmon)

Chum (salmon)
Chum salmon
Cigarfish (horse mackerel)
Cisco (whitefish)
Clams
Close fish (Arbroath smokie)
Clovis (carpet shell)
Coal cod (sablefish; *cod*)
Coalfish
    (i saithe)
    (ii sablefish; *cod*)
Cobia (*tunny*)
Cock-paddle (lumpfish)
Cockles (*mussels and clams*)
Cod
Cod cheeks (edible part from head)
Codfish brick (compressed salt cod)
Codling (small cod)
Coho (salmon)
Colchester Pyefleet (oyster)
Coley (saithe; *cod*)
Comber (sea bass)
Common bream (sea bream)
Common dab (dab)
Common grey mullet (grey mullet)
Common mussel (mussel)
Common oyster (UK native oyster,
    and European oyster, *ostrea
    edulis*)
Common pompano (pompano)
Common prawn (prawn, US
    shrimp)
Common scallop (scallop)
Common sea bream (sea bream)
Common shore crab (crab)
Common shrimp (shrimp)
Common sole (sole)
Common squid (squid)
Common tiger prawn (prawn)
Common topknot (topknot)
Common tunny (tunny)
Conger eel
Coquille St Jacques (scallop)
Corb (croaker)

Cork wing (wrasse; *soup*)
Corned alewives (salted shad)
Corniva (drum)
Couch's sea bream (sea bream)
Crabs
Craig fluke (witch)
Crappie (perch)
Crawfish
Crevalle (jack, *mackerel, pompano*)
Crevalle jack (*mackerel, pompano*)
Croakers
Crocus (croaker)
Crooner (grey gurnard)
Crucian carp (carp)
Cuban dogfish (dogfish)
Cuckoo gurnard (red gurnard)
Cuckoo ray (skate)
Cultus cod (lingcod; *cod*)
Curled octopus (octopus)
Cusk (tusk; *cod*)
Cutthroat trout (trout)
Cuttlefish (*squid*)
Cybium (seer; *mackerel, pompano*)
Cyppine (ocean quahaug, *clam*)

Dab
Dab sole (dab)
Darters (perch)
Darts (pompano)
Darwen salmon (dogfish)
Deep sea smelt (argentine)
Deep-water prawn (US pink shrimp)
Deep-water red shrimp (US pink shrimp. UK deep-water prawn)
Devilfish
   (i monkfish)
   (ii octopus)
Diamond (New Zealand sand flounder)
Diamond-scaled mullet (*grey mullet*)
Diamond turbot (*turbot*)
Digby (herring)
Digby chick (red herring, cured at Digby, Nova Scotia)

Dogfish
Dog salmon (Chum salmon)
Dog's teeth (sea bream)
Dollar-fish (butterfish, pomfret; *sea bream*)
Dolly Varden (char)
Dolly Varden trout (char)
Dolphinfish
Dorades (sea bream)
Dorado (dolphinfish)
Dore (*pike, perch*)
Dories, Dory (John Dory)
Double beak (saury pike, *saury*)
Double-lined mackerel (*mackerel*)
Doughboy scallop (scallop)
Dover hake (pollack; *cod*)
Dover sole (sole)
Dried fish (wind drieds)
Dried salted cod (salt cod)
Dried salted fish (*salt cod*)
Drizzle (ling; *cod*)
Drummer (drums)
Drums
Dublin Bay prawns or *scampi*
Dungeness crab (crab)
Dusky sea perch (grouper; *sea bass*)
Dutch cured herrings (*pickled herring, harengs saurs*)
Dwarf goatfish (red mullet)

Ear shell (ormer, abalone)
Eastern crayfish (Australian crawfish; *lobster*)
Eastern king prawn (prawn)
Eastern oyster (blue point oyster)
Edible crab (crab)
Eel
Elver (eel)
English oyster (native oyster)
English sole (lemon sole)
Escallop (scallop)
European eel (eel)
European flounder (flounder)
European lobster (lobster)

European oyster (oyster)
European plaice (plaice)
Eyed sole (sole)
Eyemouth cure (smoked haddock)

Fair-maid (dried pilchard)
Fal (native oyster)
Fall cure (salt cod)
Fall salmon (chum salmon)
False albacore (*tunny*)
Fan shell (scallop)
Fay dog (dogfish)
Fiatolon (pomfret, *sea bream*)
Findon haddock (Finnan haddock)
Finger trout (rainbow trout)
Finnan, Finnan Haddie (Finnan
  haddock)
Fishing frog (monkfish)
Fjord cod (cod)
Flake (dogfish)
Flanie (skate)
Flapper skate (skate)
Flat-fish (sole, turbot, halibut etc.,
  as opposed to round fish)
Flathead skate (skate)
Flat oyster (native oyster)
Flat-tail mullet (*grey mullet*)
Fleckhering (German kipper)
Fleckmakrele (German kippered
  mackerel)
Fletch (fillets of halibut, cut
  longitudinally)
Flitch (fillets of halibut, cut
  longitudinally)
Flounder
Fluke (flounder)
Flying fish
Flying gurnard (gurnard)
Flying squid (squid)
Forkbeard (*cod*)
Forked hake (*cod*)
Fourspot flounder (flounder)
French sole (lascar *sole*)
Freshwater catfish (*river fish*)

Freshwater drum (sheepshead, *sea
  bream*, *river fish*)
Freshwater herring (pollan, i.e.
  whitefish)
Frigate mackerel (tunny)
Frill (scallop)
Frog fish (monkfish)
Fukler's ray (skate)
Fumadoes (Spanish equivalent to
  Cornish dried pilchard)

Gabelrollmops (German rollmops,
  from herring fillets)
Gaffalbitar, gaffelbidder,
  gaffelbitar, gaffelbiter (small
  pieces of cured herring in brine)
Gag (grouper, *sea bass*)
Galway sea trout (sea trout)
Gaper
  (i soft shell clam)
  (ii comber, variety of sea bass)
Gar (garfish)
Garfish
Garpike (garfish)
Garum
Garve (dab)
Garve fluke (dab)
Garvock (sprat)
Gaspé cure (salt cod from Gaspé
  area of Canada)
German caviare (caviare substitute)
Giant sea bass (sea bass)
Giant scallop (scallop)
Giant tiger prawn (prawn)
Gibbers (haddock)
Gila trout (trout)
Gillaroo (sea trout)
Gilt head bream (sea bream)
Ginny (skate)
Gizzard shad (shad)
Glasgow Pale (variety of
  Eyemouth cured haddock)
Glaucus (pompano)
Goatfish (red mullet)

Goby (*whitebait*)
Golden carpet shell (carpet shell)
Golden cure (milder form of red herring)
Golden cutlet and golden fillet (smoked and dyed haddock and whiting)
Golden grey mullet (grey mullet)
Golden mullet (grey mullet)
Golden trout (trout)
Goldline (sea bream)
Goldsinny (wrasse; *soup, gurnard*)
Goosefish (monkfish)
Gorbuscha (humpback salmon)
Gowdy (grey gurnard)
Grainy caviare (normal caviare, as opposed to pressed)
Grass pickerel (pike)
Grass shrimp (shrimp)
Grass whiting (pollack; *cod*)
Gravlax (Scandinavian pickled salmon)
Gray cod (cod)
Grayling
Gray sea trout (weakfish; *mackerel, pompano, sea bream*)
Gray smooth hound (dogfish)
Gray snapper (*red snapper, sea bream* etc.)
Gray sole (witch)
Gray weakfish (weakfish; *mackerel, pompano, sea bream*)
Greater amberjack (*mackerel, pompano*)
Greater forkbeard (*cod*)
Greater sandeel (sandeel)
Greater spotted dogfish (dogfish)
Greater stingfish (greater weever)
Greater weaver or weever
Great lake trout (char)
Great scallop (scallop)
Great silver smelt (argentine)
Great trevally (Australian jacks; *mackerel, pompano*)

Green-backed mullet (*grey mullet*)
Greenbone (garfish)
Green cod
 (i saithe)
 (ii lingcod; *cod*)
Greenfish (pollack, *cod*)
Greenland cod (cod)
Greenland halibut (mock halibut; *halibut*)
Greenland turbot (American flat-fish of flounder family; *halibut, turbot*)
Green moray (*conger eel*)
Green shore crab (crab)
Green sturgeon (*tunny* etc.)
Grey gurnard
Grey mullet
Grey skate (skate)
Grey trout (char)
Grilse (salmon returning to fresh water for first time)
Grooved carpet shell (carpet shell)
Grooved razor (razor-shell; *raw or in soup*)
Groupers
Guitarfish (skate)
Gulf clam (clam)
Gulf flounder (flounder)
Gurnard
Guyniad (powan or whitefish)

Haberdine (large cod, used for salting)
Haddock
Hake
Halfbeaks (*garfish*)
Halibut
Hammerhead shark (shark; *swordfish*)
Hard clams
Hardheads
 (i carp)
 (ii croaker)
 (iii grey gurnard)

Hard roe (female roe of a fish)

Hard salted salmon (US pickled salmon)

Hard smoked fish (e.g. red herring, gold cured herring)

Hardtail (jack; *mackerel, pompano*)

Hareng saur (French salted and smoked herring)

Harvestfish (pomfret, US butterfish; *sea bream*)

Helford (native oyster)

Henfish (lumpfish)

Hen-paddle (lumpfish)

Herling (young sea trout)

Herring

Herring smelt (argentine)

Hickory shad (shad)

Hogchoker (sole)

Hogfish (wrasse; *soup, gurnard*)

Homelyn ray (skate)

Horse mackerel

Horseshoe crab (king crab; *crab*)

Houting (whitefish)

Humantin (dogfish)

Humpback salmon

Humpy shrimp (shrimp)

Huss (dogfish)

Iceland cyprine (ocean quahaug; *clam*)

Iceland scallop (scallop)

Inconnu (*whitefish*)

Indian cure salmon (US brined, smoked)

Indian prawn (prawn)

Indian style salmon (Indian cure salmon)

Inkfish (squid)

Italian sardel (heavily salted and matured anchovy)

Jackfish (pike)

Jack mackerel (horse mackerel)

Jacks (scad, pompano; *mackerel*)

Jack salmon (Coho salmon)

Jago's Goldsinny (wrasse; *soup, gurnard*)

Jerusalem haddock (opah)

Jewfish (grouper; *sea bass*)

Joey (small mackerel)

John Dory

Jonah crab (crab)

Josser (codling)

Jumbo
(i large haddock)
(ii skate)
(iii US shrimps)

Jumbo tiger shrimp (giant tiger prawn)

Jumping mullet (grey mullet)

Kabeljou (drums)

Kaiser-Friedrich hering (canned in mustard sauce)

Kalbfisch (hot-smoked porbeagle, Germany)

Kelp bass (sea bass)

Kelt (salmon after spawning)

Kench cure (salted cod, etc., and salmon)

Keta caviare (salmon caviare)

Keta salmon (Chum salmon)

Kieler sprotten (smoked sprats, from Kiel area, Germany)

King crab (crab)

King croaker (croaker)

Kingfish
(i a species of king mackerel)
(ii opah)
(iii croakers)

King mackerel (kingfish)

Kingmackerel (Spanish mackerel)

King of the breams (pandora; *sea bream*)

King of the herrings (shad)

King salmon (Chinook salmon)

King whitings (groupers and drums; *sea bass*)

Kipper (salted and cold-smoked herring, split from back)

Kippered fish, salmon, sturgeon etc. (US salted and hot smoked)

Kippered salmon (salted and cold-smoked salmon, split from back)

Kipper herring (kipper)

Kite (brill)

Klipfish (split salt cod)

Klondyked herring (fresh ungutted herring, sprinkled with ice and salt to preserve it for brief periods)

Knotted cockle (*raw*, *mussels*)

Knowd (grey gurnard)

Krabbensalat (Germany, cooked shrimps with mayonnaise)

Kräuterhering (salted spiced herring)

Kryddersild (salted spiced herring)

Kuruma Prawn (prawn)

Laberdan (Germany, salt cured cod)

Labrador fish (Labrador cure salt cod)

Lachsbückling (German type harengs saur)

Lachshering (German type harengs saur)

Lake fish (lake herring)

Lake herring (whitefish)

Lake trout (char)

Lake whitefish (whitefish)

Lampern (lamprey)

Lamprey (*eel*)

Lance (sandeel)

Lane snapper (snapper, *red snapper*, *sea bream* etc.)

Langouste (crawfish)

Langoustine (Norway lobster or Dublin Bay Prawn)

Lanthorn gurnard (gurnard)

Large eyed dentex (sea bream)

Larger spotted dogfish (dogfish)

Larger yellow eel (eel)

Large-scaled scorpionfish (French *rascasse*, essential to bouillabaisse; *soups, bake in butter, gurnard*)

Large soles (sole weighing over 1¼ lb. when gutted)

Lascar (sole)

Latchett (yellow gurnard)

Launce (sandeel)

Laverbread (seaweed prepared for table)

Leadenall (frigate mackerel; *tunny*)

Leaping grey mullet (grey mullet)

Leatherjacket (jacks; *mackerel, pompano*)

Lemon dab (lemon sole)

Lemon fish (lemon sole)

Lemon sole

Leopard cod (lingcod; *cod*)

Lesser cuttlefish (*squid*)

Lesser forkbeard (forkbeard; *cod*)

Lesser grey mullet (grey mullet)

Lesser halibut (Greenland or mock halibut; *halibut, cod*)

Lesser ling (blue ling; *cod*)

Lesser sandeel (sandeel)

Lesser silver smelt (argentine)

Lesser spotted dogfish (dogfish)

Lesser weever

Limpet (*raw*)

Lined sole (*sole*) family; *flat-fish recipes*

Ling (*cod*)

Lingcod (*cod*)

Little cuttlefish (*squid*)

Littleneck (quahaug clam)

Littleneck clam (clam)

Little skate (skate)

Little sole (yellow sole or solenette; *fry in butter*)

Little squid (squid)

Little tuna (tunny)

Lobster

Locks (us mild cured sides of king salmon)

London cut cure (split, smoked haddock from Grimsby cured for London market)

Longbill spearfish (*swordfish* etc)

Long clam (soft clam)

Longfin halfbeak (halfbeak; *garfish*)

Long-finned albacore (albacore; *tunny*)

Long-finned bream (pomfret; *sea bream*)

Long-finned grey mullet (grey mullet)

Long-finned gurnard (shining gurnard; *gurnard*)

Long-finned sole (flounder)

Long-finned tuna (albacore; *tunny*)

Long-jaw flounder (flounder)

Long neck (soft clam)

Longnose skate (skate)

Long rough dab (rough dab; *flat-fish*)

Long-tailed tuna (tunny)

Lox (locks: us mild cured sides of king salmon)

Lucky sole (thickback: *sole*)

Lumpfish (lumpsucker)

Lumpsucker

Lute (preparation of stockfish)

Lutefisk (preparation of stockfish)

Lythe (pollack; *cod*)

Maasbanker (horse mackerel)

Mackerel

Mackerel guide (garfish)

Mackerel pike (saury)

Mackerel scad (horse mackerel)

Mackerel tuna (*tunny*)

Maid (twaite shad)

Maiden ray (skate)

Maigre (meagre)

Mailed gurnard (gurnard)

Malossol caviare (best quality, lowest salted caviare)

Mananose (soft clam)

Mangrove snapper (snapper; *red snapper, sea bream* etc.)

Maninose (soft clam)

Margate hake (pollack, *cod*)

Marine catfish (catfish)

Mariposa (opah)

Marling (whiting)

Marlin (*swordfish* etc.)

Maru frigate mackerel (*tunny*)

Mary sole (Lemon sole)

Maskinonge (pike)

Matfull (herring full of milt or roe at least 9¼ ins long)

Matje, Matje cured herring, Matje herring (young fat salted virgin herring)

Matjesfilet, Matjes fillet (young fat salted virgin herring)

Mattie (hard salted herring – *not matje herring*)

Meagre (croaker)

Mediterranean cure (Golden cure, milder form of red herring)

Mediterranean ling (ling; *cod, whiting*)

Megrim

Melker (Dutch cured herring with roe left in)

Menominee (*whitefish*)

Menuke rockfish (Pacific Ocean perch; *sea bass, grey mullet*)

Merluce (hake)

Merry sole (lemon sole)

Mersin (Turkey; salted sturgeon)

Merzea (native oyster)

Mexican bonito (*tunny*)
Migratory trout (sea trout)
Milker herring (Dutch cured
   herring with roe left in)
Milkers (Dutch cured herring with
   roe left in)
Milt (soft roe, particularly from
   herring, mackerel etc.)
Mock halibut (Greenland halibut:
   halibut)
Monk (monkfish)
Monkfish
Monterey Spanish mackerel
   (kingmackerel)
Moonfish
   (i US jacks; *pompano, mackerel*)
   (ii UK opah)
   (iii for tusk; *cod*)
Moray eels (*conger*)
Morays (moray eels; *conger*)
Mort (young sea trout)
Mountain trout (arctic char)
Mud dab (yellowtail flounder;
   flat-fish)
Mud flounder (flounder)
Mud shad (gizzard shad; *shad*)
Muller's topknot (topknot)
Mullets (grey mullet)
Mulloway (drum)
Murry (moray eel; *conger*)
Muskellunge (pike)
Mussels
Mutton snapper (*red snapper, sea
   bream*)

Nannie Nine Eyes (sea lamprey:
   eel)
Nanny nose (soft clam)
Nanny shad (gizzard shad; *shad*)
Nassau grouper (grouper)
Native oyster (oyster grown in
   UK, *Ostrea edulis*)
Navaga (cod)
Needlefish (garfish, and sauries)

Needlenose (saury)
Newcastle kipper (kipper)
Newfoundland turbot (Greenland
   or mock *halibut*)
New Zealand sole (*sole*)
Nonnat (pellucid sole and other
   tiny fish: *whitebait*)
Northern anchovy (anchovy)
Northern bluefin (tunny)
Northern dogfish (dogfish)
Northern harvestfish (pomfret,
   US butterfish; *sea bream*)
Northern kingfish (northern king
   whiting; *groupers, sea bream*)
Northern king whiting (groupers;
   sea bream, sea bass etc.)
Northern lobster (lobster)
Northern pike (pike)
Northern sand lance (sandeel)
Northern squawfish (carp)
Northern wolffish (catfish)
North Pacific anchovy (anchovy)
North Pacific herring (herring)
Norway haddock (red fish; *soup,
   cod*)
Norway lobster (Dublin bay prawn
   or *scampi*)
Norwegian cured herring (hard
   cured summer herring)
Norwegian milkers (milkers)
Norwegian sole (hard cured large
   herring)
Norwegian topknot (topknot)
Nurse (dogfish)
Nursehound (dogfish)

Ocean bonito (*tunny*)
Ocean catfish (catfish)
Ocean perch (redfish; *soup, cod*)
Ocean piper (saury)
Ocean quahaug (clam)
Ocean quahog (clam)
Oceanic two-wing flying fish

Octopus
Offing gurnard (gurnard)
Okow (pike-perch; *pike*)
Old maid (soft clam)
Old wife (sea bream)
Olympia oyster
Opah
Orange fin (sea trout)
Orkney sea trout (sea trout)
Ormer
Osetr (sturgeon)
Osetr caviare
Owl ray (skate)
Oyster cracker (drum, *sea bass, sea bream*)
Oyster

Pacific albacore (tunny)
Pacific barracuda
Pacific black sea bass (*sea bass*)
Pacific bonito (*tunny*)
Pacific cod (cod)
Pacific edible crab (crab)
Pacific hake (hake)
Pacific halibut (halibut)
Pacific jewfish (*sea bass*)
Pacific littleneck (clam)
Pacific long-tailed tuna (tunny)
Pacific mackerel (mackerel)
Pacific moonfish (jacks; *pompano, mackerel*)
Pacific ocean perch (*sea bass, grey mullet*)
Pacific oyster (oyster)
Pacific salmon (5 main species: Chinook, Chum, Coho, Pink or Humpback, Sockeye)
Pacific sand lance (sandeel)
Pacific sardine (*pilchard and sardine*)
Pacific saury (*garfish and saury, gurnard*)
Pacific thread herring (herring)
Pacific tomcod (*cod*)

Paddle-cock (lumpsucker)
Painted crayfish (crawfish; *lobster*)
Painted mackerel (kingmackerel; *mackerel, pompano*)
Painted ray (skate)
Pale cure (lightly cured split haddock, e.g. Finnan haddock, Glasgow pale etc.)
Pale dab (witch)
Pale flounder (witch)
Pales (lightly cured split haddock)
Pale-smoked red (lightly cured red herring, i.e. silver cured)
Palometa (pompano)
Pandora (sea bream)
Pargo Colorado (snapper; *red snapper, sea bream*)
Parr (young salmon before leaving river for sea)
Patudo (tunny)
Peal (sea trout)
Pelamid (tunny)
Pellucid sole (*whitebait*)
Perch
Perch-pike (pike-perch; *pike, shad* etc.)
Permit (pompano)
Periwinkle (whelk; *boil*)
Peter-fish (John Dory)
Peto (*mackerel*)
Petrale sole (*brill, flat-fish recipes*)
Phinock (sea trout)
Picked dogfish (dogfish)
Pickerels (pike, or pike-perch)
Pickled alewife (salted shad)
Pickled herring (salted herring)
Pickled salmon (split and salted salmon)
Pickling (bückling)
Picton herring (Australian sardine)
Piked dogfish (dogfish)
Pike-perch (*pike, shad* etc.)
Pike
Pilchard

Pinfish (sea bream)
Pinger (small haddock)
Ping pong (small haddock)
Pink salmon (one of 5 main Pacific species, sometimes known as Humpback salmon)
Pink shrimp (prawn)
Pintado (kingmackerel; *pompano, mackerel*)
Pinwiddies (Arbroath smokies, cured unsplit haddock)
Piper (gurnard)
Pismo clam (clam)
Pissala (preparation of salted anchovies, made at and around Nice)
Plaice
Plaice-fluke (plaice)
Plain bonito (tunny)
Plain pelamis (tunny)
Pod razor (razor shell; *raw, mussels*)
Polar cod (cod)
Polar plaice (flounder)
Pole-dab (witch)
Pollack (*cod*)
Pollan (whitefish)
Pollock
  (i saithe)
  (ii pollack; *cod*)
Pomfret (*sea bream* etc.)
Pompano
Poor cod (*whiting*)
Porbeagle
Porgies (sea bream)
Portuguese oyster (oyster)
Poulp (octopus)
Pout (*soup, poach in court-bouillon*)
Poutassou (*whiting*)
Pouting (pout)
Powan (whitefish)
Prawn (US shrimp)
Pressed caviare
Pressed pilchards (dry-salted and compressed pilchards)

Prides (young lampreys)
Pumpkin scad (butterfish or promfret)

Quahaug and quahog (clam)
Qualla (Chum salmon)
Queen (queen scallop)
Queenfish (croaker; *sea bass*)
Quenelles
Quinalt (Sockeye salmon)

Rainbow trout (trout)
Rainbow wrasse (wrasse; *soup, fry*)
Rackling (strips of dried, salted halibut)
Ray (skate)
Razor clam (razor shell; *raw, mussels*)
Razor shells
Red algae (seaweed used for laverbread, agar etc.)
Red barsch (redfish, ocean perch: *soup, cod*)
Red bream (used for redfish)
Red caviare (salmon caviare)
Red drum (drum; *sea bass*)
Red emperor (snapper; *red snapper, sea bream* etc.)
Redeye mullet (grey mullet)
Redfish
  (i Norway haddock; *soup, cod*)
  (ii US Pacific Ocean perch; *mackerel, pompano*)
Red goatfish (red mullet)
Red grouper (grouper; *sea bass*)
Red gurnard (gurnard)
Red hake (hake; *cod*)
Red herring (heavily salted and smoked herring)
Red mullet
Red perch (redfish or Norway haddock)

Red salmon (Sockeye salmon)
Red scorpionfish (*soup, bake, gurnard*)
Red sea bream (Japanese *tai*)
Red snapper
Red spring salmon (Chinook salmon)
Red trout (char)
Red wrasse (*soup, bake, gurnard*)
Rex sole (flounder; *flat-fish recipes*)
Rigg (dogfish)
River eel (eel)
River herring (shad)
River lamprey (eel)
River sole (sole)
River trout (sea trout)
Roach (*river fish recipes*)
Rock (striped bass; *sea bass*)
Rock bass (*river fish recipes*)
Rock cockle (clam)
Rock cod (cod)
Rock cook (wrasse; *soup, gurnard*)
Rock crab (crab)
Rockfish
  (i catfish)
  (ii scorpionfish; *soup, gurnard*)
  (iii Pacific ocean perch; *sea bass, mackerel*)
  (iv striped bass; *sea bass*)
Rock gurnard (gurnard)
Rock herring (allis shad)
Rocklings (*whiting*)
Rock lobster (crawfish)
Rock oyster (New Zealand oyster)
Rock salmon
  (i dogfish)
  (ii saithe; *cod*)
  (iii catfish)
  (iv Pacific ocean perch; *sea bass, mackerel*)
Rock sea bass (sea bass)
Rock sole (roughback; *flat-fish recipes*)
Roker (skate)

F.C.–22

Rollmops (rolled herring fillets, pickled in vinegar)
Roncador (croaker; *sea bass, gurnard, cod* etc.)
Rosefish (redfish)
Ross's cuttle (*squid*)
Roughback
  (i American plaice)
  (ii rock sole; *flat-fish*)
Rough dog (dogfish)
Rough hound (dogfish)
Round clam (quahaug clam)
Round-fish (UK fish roughly circular in section, as opposed to flatfish. US ungutted fish)
Round herring (*herring*)
Round robin (horse mackerel)
Round sead (horse mackerel)
Roused fish (fish mixed with dry salt, before curing etc.)
Royal red shrimp (shrimp)
Runner (jacks; *pompano, mackerel*)
Rusty dab (flounder; *flat-fish*)

Sablefish (*cod*)
Sacramento squawfish (*carp*)
Sail fluke (megrim)
Saithe (*cod*)
Salmon
Salmon caviare
Salmon trout (sea trout)
Salt cod
Salt-water bream (sea bream)
Samson fish (jacks; *pompano, mackerel*)
Sand bass (sea bass)
Sand clam (soft clam)
Sand dab
  (i dab)
  (ii American plaice; *flat-fish*)
Sandeel
Sand flounder (New Zealand flounder; *flat-fish*)
Sandgaper (soft clam)

Sand lance (sandeel)
Sand mullet (grey mullet)
Sand perch (sea bass)
Sand pike (*perch, pike, shad*)
Sand scar (catfish)
Sand seatrout (weakfish; *mackerel, pompano, sea bream*)
Sand shrimp (shrimp)
Sand smelt (atherine)
Sand sole (lascar sole; *flat-fish*)
Sand trout (weakfish; *mackerel, pompano, sea bream*)
Sandy dab (yellowtail flounder; *flat-fish*)
Sandy ray (skate)
Sapphirine gurnard (gurnard)
Sardine
Sardinella (*sardine, pilchard*)
Sargo (sea bream)
Sauger (*perch, pike, shad*)
Saury
Saury pike
Scad
   (i UK horse mackerel)
   (ii US jacks, pompano etc.)
Scale-rayed wrasse (*soup, gurnard*)
Scallops
Scampi (Adriatic prawn, or name given to Norway lobster)
Scandinavian anchovy (sprats or small herring, cured like anchovies)
Scandinavian saltfish (salted fish of cod family; *salt cod*)
School mackerel (kingmackerel)
Scollop (scallop)
Scorpionfish (*soup, gurnard*)
Scotch cured herring (mild cured salted herring, unsmoked)
Scotch hake (saithe; *cod*)
Scrod (US medium sized haddock)
Scup (sea bream)
Scurf (sea trout)
Sea arrows (squid)

Sea bass
Sea bream
Sea catfish (catfish)
Sea devil (monkfish)
Sea drum (drum)
Sea ear (ormer)
Sea gar (garfish)
Sea garfish (Australia, halfbeaks; *garfish, gurnard* etc.)
Sea hen (lumpsucker)
Sea herring (US herring)
Sea kingfish (yellowtails or amberjacks; *pompano, mackerel*)
Sea lamprey (lamprey; *eel*)
Sea luce (hake)
Sea needle (garfish)
Sea partridge (sole)
Sea perch (groupers, sea bass)
Sea pike
   (i hake)
   (ii barracuda)
Sea robin (gurnard)
Sea scallop (scallop)
Sea smelt (atherine)
Sea trout (salmon trout)
Sea urchins
Seer (Spanish mackerel)
Seerfish (kingmackerel)
Sevruga (sturgeon)
Sevruga-caviare
Sewin (sea trout)
Shadefish (meagre)
Shad herring (shad)
Shads
Shagreen ray (skate)
Shark
Sharp-nosed eel (eel)
Sharpnose skate (skate)
Sheepshead (salt-water and fresh-water species; *chowder, sea bream* etc.)
Shining gurnard (gurnard)
Ship (sturgeon)
Shortbill spearfish (*swordfish*)

Short-finned sole (flounder; *flat-fish*)
Short-finned tunny (tunny)
Shortnose sturgeon (sturgeon)
Shrimp
Side stripe shrimp (shrimp)
Sidney rock oyster (Australian oyster)
Sierra (kingmackerel)
Sild (Scandinavian name for herring. UK small herring)
Sile (sandeel)
Silver bream (sea bream)
Silver cured herring (milder cure than red herring)
Silver eel (eel)
Silver hake (hake)
Silver mullet (grey mullet)
Silver perch (croaker; and for fresh-water drum or sheeps-head)
Silver pomfret (pomfret; *sea bream* etc.)
Silver salmon (Coho salmon)
Silverside (atherine)
Silver smelt (argentine)
Silver trevally (jacks; *mackerel, pompano*)
Skate
Skider (skate)
Skipjack (tunny)
Skipper (Pacific saury)
Slender tuna (tunny)
Slime sole (flounder; *flat-fish*)
Slimy mackerel (Pacific mackerel)
Slip (small sole)
Slippery sole (flounder; *flat-fish*)
Small-eyed ray (skate)
Small sandeel (sandeel)
Small-scaled scorpionfish (Fr. *rascasse* used in bouillabaisse; *soup*)
Smear dab (lemon sole)
Smelt

Smokie (small unsplit smoked haddock. e.g. Arbroath and Aberdeen smokie)
Smolt (young salmon leaving river for first time)
Smooth dogfish (dogfish)
Smooth flounder (*flat-fish*)
Smooth hounds (dogfish)
Smooth sand lance (sandeel)
Smooth scallop (scallop)
Smoothsides (gurnard)
Snappers (*red snapper, mackerel* etc.)
Snapper haddock (US small haddock)
Snoek (S. African name for barracouta; *tunny*)
Sockeye salmon
Soft (shell) clam
Soft roe (milt, particularly from herring, mackerel)
Soldier
  (i redfish)
  (ii red gurnard)
Sole
Solenette (yellow sole, very small)
Soused herring (rolled herring, baked in vinegar with aromatics)
Soused pilchards (pickled with salt, vinegar and spice)
Southern bluefin (tunny)
Southern flounder (fluke)
Southern harvestfish (pomfret, US butterfish; *sea bream*)
Southern kingfish (southern king whiting)
Southern king whiting (groupers; *sea bass*)
Southport sole (sole)
Southwest Atlantic hake (hake)
Spanish bream (sea bream)
Sparling (smelt)
Spearfish (*swordfish*)

Speckfisch (Germany, hot-smoked pieces of shark)

Speckled seatrout (weakfish; *sea bream, sea bass*)

Speckled trout (char)

Spelding (split whiting, brined and air dried)

Spiced herring (cured in salt with spices)

Spider crab (crab)

Spiegel carp (carp)

Spillanga (Swedish ling stretched on splints and dried)

Spinous spider crab (crab)

Spiny cockle (*raw, mussels, clams*)

Spiny crab (crab)

Spiny dogfish (dogfish)

Spiny lobster (crawfish)

Spinytail skate (skate)

Splittail (*carp, river fish recipes*)

Spot shrimp (shrimp)

Spotted bass (drum)

Spotted cabrilla (grouper)

Spotted ray (skate)

Spotted sea cat (catfish)

Spotted seatrout (weakfish; *mackerel, pompano*, etc.)

Spotted turbot (US flat-fish, not true turbot)

Spotted weakfish (*mackerel, pompano, sea bream* etc.)

Spotted weever (weever)

Sprag (cod between 24 and 30 inches long)

Sprat

Spring dogfish (dogfish)

Spring lobster (crawfish)

Spring salmon (Chinook salmon)

Spurdog (dogfish)

Square (New Zealand sand flounder; *flat-fish*)

Squaretail (char)

Squawfish (*carp, river fish recipes, perch* etc.)

Squeteague (weakfish; *mackerel, pompano, sea bream*)

Squid

Squim (scallop)

Squirrel hake (hake)

Squirt clam (soft clam)

Starry flounder (flounder; *flat-fish*)

Starry ray (skate)

Starry skate (skate)

Steelhead salmon or trout (rainbow trout)

Stellate smooth hound (dogfish)

Sterliad (sturgeon)

Stingfish (greater weever)

Stingrays (skate)

Stockfish (unsalted, dried members of cod family)

Stone bass (wreckfish; *grouper*)

Stone crab (crab)

Stone eel (lamprey; *eel*)

Stone sucker (lamprey; *eel*)

Strandgaper (soft clam)

Streaked gurnard (gurnard)

Streaked weever (weever)

Striped tuna (tunny)

Stripe-bellied bonito (tunny)

Striped anchovy (anchovy)

Striped bass (sea bass)

Striped marlin (*swordfish*)

Striped mullet (red mullet)

Striped wrasse (*soup*)

Stromming (herring caught in Baltic sea)

Stuifin (sprat)

Sturgeon

Sullock (small saithe; *cod*, etc.)

Summer flounder (fluke)

Sundried fish (fish dried in sun and air)

Sunfish
    (i different freshwater species, including black bass; *river fish recipes, particularly frying*)
    (ii also used for opah)

Surf clam (clam)
Surf-fish (perch)
Surf smelt (smelt)
Surmullet (red mullet)
Sweet fluke (lemon sole)
Swimming crab (tiny crab, the
    French *étrille*)
Swinefish (catfish)
Swordfish
Sword razor (razor shell; *raw,
    mussels*)

Tadpole fish (lesser forkbeard;
    whiting)
Tailor (bluefish)
Tarama (fish roe from grey mullet,
    carp etc., used for taramasalata
    in eastern Mediterranean)
Tautog (wrasse: *soup, gurnard*)
Tench
Thickback sole (sole)
Thick-lipped grey mullet (grey
    mullet)
Thin-lipped grey mullet (grey
    mullet)
Thornback ray (skate)
Thorny ray (skate)
Threadfin shad (shad)
Thread herring (*herring*)
Threebeard rockling (*whiting*)
Tidewater silverside (atherine)
Tinker (skate)
Togue (char)
Toheroa (New Zealand edible
    mollusc, sold canned in UK)
Tomcod (species of cod)
Tongue (sole)
Tope
Topknot
Torbay sole (witch)
Torsk
    (i Scandinavian name for cod)
    (ii UK tusk; *cod* etc.)
Touladi (char)

Trade ling (ling, *cod*)
Trevally (jacks; *mackerel, pompano*)
Trifurcated hake (lesser forkbeard;
    whiting)
Tropical two-wing flying fish
    (flying fish)
Trout
True skate (skate)
True sole (sole)
Truff (sea trout)
Tub and tubfish (gurnard)
Tullibee (whitefish)
Tuna (tunny)
Tunny
Turbot
Turrum (jack; *pompano, mackerel*)
Tusk (*cod*)
Twaite shad
Tyee (Chinook salmon)

Undulate ray (skate)

Variegated scallop (scallop)
Variegated sole (thick back sole;
    sole)
Vendace (whitefish)
Ventrèche (Fr.) and ventresca (It.):
    best part of best tunny cut from
    the abdomen; also canned.
Vermilion snapper (*red snapper,
    mackerel* etc.)
Viziga (dried spinal cord of
    sturgeon. USSR)

Wachna cod (cod)
Wahoo (*mackerel*)
Walleye (pike)
Walleyed pike (pike)
Walleye pollack (*cod*)
Warsow grouper (grouper; *sea
    bass*)
Washington clam (clam)
Watson's bonito and Watson's
    leaping bonito (tunny)

Weakfish (*mackerel, pompano*)

Wedge shell (*carpet shell, soup*)

Weever

West coast sole (megrim)

Western crayfish (crawfish. Australia)

Western oyster (oyster)

Whelk (*boil*)

Whiff (megrim)

Whistler (threebeard tockling; *whiting*)

Whitch (witch)

Whitebait

White bass (fresh-water; *river fish recipes*)

White-bellied skate (skate)

White bream (sea bream)

White crappie (sunfish; *river fish recipes*)

White croaker (croaker)

White fish (as distinct from fatty fish like herring; mainly cod, hake etc. with main reserves of fat in the liver)

Whitefish

White fluke (flounder)

White hake (hake)

White marlin (*swordfish*)

White mullet (grey mullet)

White perch (sea bass)

White sea perch (sea bass)

White seatrout (weakfish; *mackerel*; *pompano*)

White shrimp (shrimp)

White skate (skate)

White sole (megrim and witch)

White sturgeon (sturgeon)

White sucker (freshwater; *river recipes, bream*)

White trout (weakfish: *mackerel, pompano*)

White tuna (albacore tunny)

White weakfish (*mackerel, pompano*)

Whiting

Whiting pout (pout; *cod* etc.)

Whitling (sea trout)

Whitstable native oyster (oyster)

Wind dried fish

Winkle (*boil like other small shellfish*)

Winter flounder (lemon sole)

Winter shad (shad)

Winter skate (skate)

Witch

Witch flounder (witch)

Wolf and wolffish (catfish)

Woodcock of the sea (red mullet)

Woof (catfish)

Wrasses (*soup, gurnard*)

Wreck bass and wreckfish (*grouper*)

Yawling (small herring, i.e. sild)

Yellow bass (fresh-water; *river fish recipes* etc.)

Yellow-eye mullet (grey mullet)

Yellowfin croaker (croaker)

Yellowfin grouper (grouper; *sea bass* etc.)

Yellowfin tuna (tunny)

Yellow fish (UK white fish, split, or filleted and cold smoked)

Yellow gurnard (gurnard)

Yellow perch (freshwater perch)

Yellow pike and yellow pickerel (pike)

Yellow sole (solenette, or tiny sole)

Yellowtail (amberjack; *mackerel, pompano*)

Yellowtail flounder (flounder; *flat-fish*)

Yellowtail snapper (*red, snapper, mackerel* etc.)

Zanthe (fresh-water; *riverfish recipes*)

Index

Escabèche:
of smelts, 180
see also Mackerel Caveach

Fennel:
Branches:
Catfish with fennel and *beurre noisette*, 190
Grayling with, 241
Livornian salad, 349
Quiche de saumon, 229
Red mullet baked with, 139
Sea bass *ansiette*, 147
Stuffing for river fish, 253
Seeds, *Surmulets à Niçoise*, 139
Flake *see* Dogfish
Flounder, 91
Fluke, 91
Fluke, Sail, 91
Flying fish, 152–3
Fumet de poisson, 17–19, 26, 47, 107
Aspic jelly, 18

Garfish and Saury, 151–2
Gillaroo *see* Trout, Salmon
Gin:
Coquilles Saint Jacques flambées 'Gordon', 304
Lobster in gin, 283
Gooseberry:
Purée with herring, 163
Sauces, 49–50, 170
with Baked herring, 167
Grapefruit in Crab mayonnaise, 296
Grapes:
Bass or Bream *à la Vendangeuse*, 147
Filets de sole Véronique, 97
Rougets barbets à la Bourguignonne, 140
Sole à la meunière, 100
Grayling, Char and Whitefish, 240–42
Baked, 232
Fried, *Pesce persico alla salvia*, 243
Grilled with fennel, 241
Potted, 238

with morels, 241
Groupers *see* Bass, Sea
Gurnard, 153–6
Moulines farcies à la Fécampoise, 154
with cheese and wine sauce, 155

Haddock:
Rizzared, 333
Smoked, 362–7
Aberdeen and Arbroath Smokies, 363
Eyemouth cured, 363
Finnan:
Caisses à la Florence, 365
Kedgeree, 366
Omelette Arnold Bennett, 365
with egg sauce, 363
Glasgow Pales, 363
Pinwiddies, 363
Hake *see* Cod
Halibut:
Baked:
Flétan au fromage, 116
Flétan de Jonghe Marc, 117
Fried, *au poivre*, 117
Grilled, 116
Halibut, Chicken, 115
Smoked, 361
Hazelnuts:
Truite aux noisettes, 238
see also Ailloli
Hen-paddle *see* Caviare, home-made, 382
Herring, 160–69
Baked, 164
Swper scadan (Welsh supper herring), 167
with apple and beetroot, 166
with cucumber, 165
with gooseberries, 167
with mushrooms, 166
with soft roe stuffing, 167
Fried:
in Scottish fashion, 163
with cream and roe sauce, 164
with *sauce Chausey*, 164